INCENTIVE BARGAINING AND CORPORATE GOVERNANCE

This comparative analysis of business systems examines firms and enterprises across three major economies in the world: the United States, China, and Japan. It asks how the law relates to business practice, economic growth, and social development, and how enterprise law maximizes firm value in these three jurisdictions. The divergent legal, social, and economic approaches toward the market, firms, and business and corporate law in these three major economies justify a scrutiny of enterprise law with the aim of better understanding legal and economic models for social and economic development in a comparative context. This book will be of interest to academics and practitioners in law, business, management, public policy, political science, and economics. It offers a useful framework for legislative policymakers across the world – particularly in developing countries.

ZENICHI SHISHIDO is Professor of Law at Musashino University, Tokyo, Professor Emeritus at Hitotsubashi University, Tokyo, and has been a Visiting Professor at Harvard University, Columbia University, Duke University, and the University of California, Berkeley.

WEI SHEN is KoGuan Distinguished Professor of Law at Shanghai Jiao Tong University KoGuan School of Law, and has been a visiting professor at New York University School of Law, Michigan Law School, University of Pennsylvania Carey Law School, National University of Singapore Faculty of Law, among others.

INCENTIVE BARGAINING AND CORPORATE GOVERNANCE

Comparative Enterprise Law among the US, Japan, and China

ZENICHI SHISHIDO
Musashino University
WEI SHEN
Shanghai Jiao Tong University

CAMBRIDGE
UNIVERSITY PRESS

CAMBRIDGE UNIVERSITY PRESS

Shaftesbury Road, Cambridge CB2 8EA, United Kingdom

One Liberty Plaza, 20th Floor, New York, NY 10006, USA

477 Williamstown Road, Port Melbourne, VIC 3207, Australia

314–321, 3rd Floor, Plot 3, Splendor Forum, Jasola District Centre, New Delhi – 110025, India

103 Penang Road, #05–06/07, Visioncrest Commercial, Singapore 238467

Cambridge University Press is part of Cambridge University Press & Assessment, a department of the University of Cambridge.

We share the University's mission to contribute to society through the pursuit of education, learning and research at the highest international levels of excellence.

www.cambridge.org
Information on this title: www.cambridge.org/9781009152785

DOI: 10.1017/9781009152808

When citing this work, please include a reference to the DOI 10.1017/9781009152808

First published 2026

Cover image: VasjaKoman / DigitalVision Vectors / Getty Images

A catalogue record for this publication is available from the British Library

Library of Congress Cataloging-in-Publication Data
Names: Shishido, Zen'ichi, 1956– author | Shen, Wei, 1972– author
Title: Incentive bargaining and corporate governance : comparative enterprise law among the US, Japan, and China / Zenichi Shishido, Musashino University, Tokyo; Wei Shen, Shanghai Jiao Tong University, China.
Description: Cambridge, United Kingdom ; New York, NY : Cambridge University Press, 2025. | Includes bibliographical references and index.
Identifiers: LCCN 2025025366 (print) | LCCN 2025025367 (ebook) | ISBN 9781009152785 hardback | ISBN 9781009152792 paperback | ISBN 9781009152808 epub
Subjects: LCSH: Corporate governance–Law and legislation–United States | Corporate governance–Law and legislation–Japan | Corporate governance–Law and legislation–China | Venture capital–Law and legislation–United States | Venture capital–Law and legislation–Japan | Venture capital–Law and legislation–China | Stockholders–Legal status, laws, etc.–United States | Stockholders–Legal status, laws, etc.–Japan | Stockholders–Legal status, laws, etc.–China |
LCGFT: Law materials
Classification: LCC K1327 .S55 2025 (print) | LCC K1327 (ebook) |
DDC 346.51/0664–dc23/eng/20250815
LC record available at https://lccn.loc.gov/2025025366
LC ebook record available at https://lccn.loc.gov/2025025367

ISBN 978-1-009-15278-5 Hardback

CONTENTS

FIGURES

PREFACE AND ACKNOWLEDGMENTS

This book attempts to show how three major economies in the world – the United States, Japan, and China – all achieve respectable economic performance using different corporate governance practices and laws. Specifically, it focuses on how "incentive bargaining" among enterprise stakeholders (i.e., human capital providers, monetary capital providers, and the government) affects their respective corporate governance practices and corporate performance.

In 2014, one of the authors of this book published the results of his comparative research of law and business involving the United States and Japan: *Enterprise Law: Contracts, Markets and Laws in the US and Japan* (Zenichi Shishido ed., 2014). This earlier book attempted to tackle two new aspects in the study of comparative corporate law. First, it showed how different laws influence corporate governance practices complementarily with the markets and social norms in each economy. Second, it took various areas of law that affect the incentives of the firm's major players into consideration, as the "enterprise law," and tried to show their complementary effects on corporate governance and corporate practice.

This book takes on two new challenges within the analytical framework of "incentive bargaining," in which the four indispensable capital providers of the firm bargain with each other to offer incentives to other players (positive or negative) to provide their capital to their joint project for maximizing their own payoff.

First, this book adds China as a new jurisdiction for comparative study. Although there are many comparative studies between any two of the three countries on a specific subject of law, there are few such studies that compare all three countries on enterprise law as a whole. This indisputably adds new flavors to many issues.

Second, this book expands the number of players in the game from four market players to five, including the state or government. Although the previous book treated the state as a given infrastructure of the firm's incentive bargaining, as a lawmaker, regulator, referee, and taxing authority, among others, the state and business corporations indeed interact and bargain with each other to pursue their own or joint goals. Also, if we exclude the state from our analysis, comparative law and business studies, including those from China, would be less meaningful.

We believe that this comparative study will raise many issues that should be considered in corporate governance practices and law-making, not only in the three countries examined but also in other countries in the world.

Many people have contributed a lot to this book's publication.

First, we thank Roberta Romano and Robert Bartlett III for introducing us as coauthors in December 2018. Since then, we have discussed the ideas in this book, and it took more than five years for us to accomplish it.

We appreciate the rigorous reviews by the three anonymous referees. In the process of responding to their tough questions and addressing the defects they pointed out, our publication plan has been significantly improved.

We appreciate helpful comments by Ken Ayotte, Douglas Baird, Ken Dau-Schmidt, Mark Gergen, Lin Lin, Curtis Milhaupt, and Frank Partnoy. We also owe a great deal to many scholars and practitioners in various fields for their useful information and suggestions, such as those provided at conferences and workshops.

Yan Zhan, a highly skilled research assistant, contributed to this publication by utilizing his proficiency in three languages. We also appreciate Joe Ng, our patient editor, who has worked with us longer than we initially planned.

Finally, we would like to thank our families for their understanding and invaluable support of our research over the years.

ABBREVIATIONS

ACFTU	All-China Federation of Trade Unions
AMC	Asset Management Corporation
BAPCPA	Bankruptcy Abuse Prevention and Consumer Protection Act
BDC	business development company
CBRC	China Banking Regulatory Commission
CCP	Chinese Communist Party
CEO	chief executive officer
CFIUS	Committee on Foreign Investment in the United States
CHIPS	Creating Helpful Incentives to Produce Semiconductors and Science Act of 2022
CIRC	China Insurance Regulatory Commission
CLO	collateralized loan obligation
COVID-19	coronavirus disease 2019
CPTPP	Comprehensive and Progressive Agreement for Trans-Pacific Partnership
CRO	chief restructuring officers
CSISC	China Securities Investor Services Center
CSRC	China Securities Regulatory Commission
DARPA	Defense Advanced Research Projects Agency
DCF	discounted cash flow
DIP	debtor-in-possession
ERISA	Employee Retirement Income Security Act
ESG	environmental, social, and governance
ESO	employee stock option
ESRI	Economic Structural Reform Institute
FEFTA	Foreign Exchange and Foreign Trade Act of Japan
FERA	Federal Emergency Relief Administration
FIE	foreign invested enterprise
FIRRMA	The Foreign Investment Risk Review Modernization Act
FLSA	Fair Labor Standards Act
FOF	fund of funds
FSA	Financial Services Agency

FTC	Fair Trade Commission
GGF	government guidance fund
GP	general partner
HCP	human capital provider
HSR	Hart-Scott-Rodino Antitrust Improvements Act of 1976
IPO	initial public offering
IRR	internal rate of return
IRS	Internal Revenue Service
J-SOX	Financial Instruments and Exchange Act of Japan
KPI	key performance indicator
LBO	leveraged buyout
LLP	limited liability partnership
LP	limited partner
M&A	mergers and acquisitions
MBO	management buyout
MCP	monetary Capital provider
METI	Ministry of Economic, Trade, and Industry (Japan)
MFW	*Kahn v. M&F Worldwide Corp.*
MIC	manufacturer's investment credit
MITI	Ministry of International Trade and Industry (Japan) (now METI)
MOFCOM	Ministry of Commerce (China)
MOJ	Ministry of Justice (Japan)
NASA	National Aeronautics and Space Administration
National IC Plan	guidelines to promote the national integrated circuit industry
NDRC	National Development and Reform Commission
NEEQ	National Equities Exchange and Quotation System
NIRA	National Industrial Recovery Act
NLRA	National Labor Relations Act
NPC	National People's Congress
NRA	National Recovery Administration
PBR	price-to-book ratio
PE	private equity
PFA	Pension Fund Association (Japan)
POE	privately owned enterprise
PRC	People's Republic of China
R&D	research and development
RMB	¥
ROA	return on assets
ROE	return on equity
RSU	restricted stock unit
SAC	Securities Association of China

SAGE	Semi-Automatic Ground Environment
SAIC	State Administration for Industry and Commerce
SASAC	State-owned Assets Supervision and Administration Commission
SBIR	Small Business Innovation Research
SEC	Securities and Exchange Commission
SETC	State Economic and Trade Commission
SIP	China–Singapore Suzhou Industrial Park
SOE	state-owned enterprise
SOX	Sarbanes–Oxley Act
SPC	Supreme People's Court
SRO	self-regulatory organization
SSE	Shanghai Stock Exchange
STTR	small business technology transfer
SZSE	Shenzhen Stock Exchange
TCFD	Task Force for Climate-related Financial Disclosure
TOB	takeover bid
UD	universal demand
UVTA	Uniform Voidable Transactions Act
VAM	value adjustment mechanism
VC	venture capital

Introduction

This book focuses on a comparative analysis of business systems primarily involving and surrounding the firms/enterprises across three major economies in the world, that is, the United States, Japan, and China. The book will discuss one basic question: how does law matter to business practice, together with the markets and social norms of each jurisdiction?

To answer the question, it is necessary to take into consideration two complementarities. First, the legal system that affects the business practice in a given country consists of a variety of legal subject areas, including corporate law, securities regulation, labor law, bankruptcy law, and tax law, among others ("enterprise law[1]"). These areas of law do not operate in isolation but rather in a complementary manner to affect the business practices in a country. Second, the law operates in conjunction with economic markets, legal infrastructure (such as courts and alternative dispute settlement mechanisms), and social norms.[2]

With this in mind, the book's framework is as follows: the firm acts as a forum for incentive bargaining among four major participants: management and employees as human capital providers, creditors, and shareholders as monetary capital providers. Each participant will bargain with each of the others to maximize their own payoff based on exogenous factors: the situation of various markets (products, labor, intellectual property rights, and capital), social norms (e.g., shareholder value maximization model and stakeholder model), and enterprise law.[3]

[1] Enterprise law is the several different areas of law that affect the incentives of the indispensable capital providers of the firm as a complementary set. *See* Chapter 1, n.1 and its accompanying text.

[2] *See* Zenichi Shishido, *The Incentive Bargaining of the Firm and Enterprise Law: A Nexus of Contracts, Markets, and Laws*, *in* Enterprise Law: Contracts, Markets, and Laws in the US and Japan 1 (Zenichi Shishido ed., 2014).

[3] *See* Chapter 1, n.2 and its accompanying text; *see* Shishido, *supra* note 2, at 2–3.

This book will include the state or government[4] as the fifth player of this game in the sense that the government provides indispensable resources (physical, social, and legal infrastructures) to the firm, shares the pie via tax revenue, and bargains with the other four players.[5] The government is, however, a unique player, compared with the other four players, because of its unique channels of bargaining and its macro-level incentives. Therefore, this book will view the firm as a forum for incentive bargaining among the four players and consider that the government participates at the micro level (or at the individual company level) in incentive bargaining from outside the forum. The government needs to provide the optimal infrastructure for incentive bargaining among the four players of a firm to maximize the firm value, as a result, it could maximize economic value at the macro level.

This book will make a comparative study of enterprise law: how the complementary effects of various laws, markets, and norms affect the incentives of each participant and how this affects the accepted business practices in a country, and in turn, the broader business system, in a comparative context involving the United States, Japan, and China.

The underlying logic of selecting these three jurisdictions not only rests on the fact that these three countries are three major economies in the world, but also on the fact that they have widley divergent legal/social systems hosting, supporting, and regulating firms. These three countries achieve a certain economic success by doing totally different ways. It is interesting to see how they make it.

There are several unique characteristics of this book. First, it will provide a game theoretical view of the firm, different from the conventional nexus of contracts view of the firm. Second, it will provide a concept of enterprise law that grasps a variety of rules and laws that affect incentive bargaining among major participants of the firm, as a complementary setting. Third, it will trace the life cycle of a listed firm, from start-up to distressed firm. Fourth, it will introduce studies of listed family firms in the world and try to show their implications for the corporate governance of listed companies in general. Fifth, it will pay attention to the role of the state or government in corporate governance (visible hand vs. invisible hand), particularly in Asia. And finally, it will raise the question of how to make good enterprise law and will refer to problems of legislative policy (or industrial policy, where relevant).

4 *See* Chapter 2, n.1 and its accompanying text.

5 *See* Shishido, *supra* note 2, at 40–45.

Chapter 1 provides the analytical framework of this book. One of the key concepts of this book is "incentive bargaining." We view the firm as an ongoing joint project, which requires both monetary and human capital. There are two main groups of indispensable capital providers to the joint project: (1) management and employees as the human capital providers; and (2) shareholders and creditors as the monetary capital providers. These two groups need to motivate other capital providers to provide their capital to maximize their own payoff. The bargaining among the indispensable capital providers that motivates each player to provide its capital to the joint project will be called "incentive bargaining."[6]

To motivate other players to provide their capital, it is indispensable to take each player's risk based on the situation of conflicting interests, which distorts the incentive to provide their capital, into consideration. Bargaining over sharing control is useful to decrease the risk. Bargaining over a firm's value added is useful to give a positive incentive to provide their capital.[7] Because the incentive bargaining of the firm is a repeated game, each capital provider needs to care for other capital providers' incentives in the next round to maximize their own long-term payoff.[8] Keeping a good balance between autonomy and monitoring of human capital providers, particularly management, is always a critical issue to corporate governance and corporate performance.[9]

Incentive bargaining among the four players in a stock corporation is made not as a multilateral bargaining but as a complex of three bilateral bargaining processes via management.[10] The way of incentive bargaining, or incentive pattern, in each country, can be categorized into either the balancing image, the monitoring image, or the bargaining image, based on the way of coalition among the four players.[11]

Another key concept of this book is "enterprise law." Enterprise law is an exogenous factor that affects the incentive bargaining of the firm, complemented by markets and social norms.[12] At the same time, enterprise law is not a given condition to the four players, but each player tries to motivate lawmakers to make enterprise law maximize its own payoff.

[6] *See* Chapter 1, nn.1–2 and their accompanying texts; Shishido, *supra* note 2, at 2–4.
[7] *See* Chapter 1, Sections 1.1.3 and 1.1.4; Shishido, *supra* note 2, at 3–4.
[8] *See* Chapter 1, Section 1.5; Shishido, *supra* note 2, at 45–47.
[9] *See* Chapter 1, nn.14–16 and their accompanying texts; Shishido, *supra* note 2, at 4.
[10] *See* Chapter 1, Section 1.2.2; Shishido, *supra* note 2, at 4–5.
[11] *See* Chapter 1, Section 1.4; Shishido, *supra* note 2, at 6–10.
[12] *See supra* note 1.

To stimulate the incentive bargaining among the four players, which will lead to the firm value maximization, taking adequate legislative policy is important.[13]

In the real world, not only the four players but also the state/government participate in the incentive bargaining of the firm by providing legislation, taxation, regulation, enforcement, and industrial policy, and the four players could influence the decision-making of the state. The challenge of taking the state as the fifth player will be discussed in Chapter 2.

Chapter 2, as an extension of Section 1.6 of Chapter 1, provides the image of the incentive bargaining of the firm with the state or government as the fifth player in the three countries.

Section 2.1, as a starting point, compares the industrial policy, which is a typical measure for the state to directly affect the incentives of management, of the three countries. Historically, all three countries have extensively used industry policy to stimulate industries from a macro perspective and motivate the management of individual firms to take risks, typically via tax credits, subsidization, and protectionist policy, at least in some stages and in some industries, although the three governments' approaches to private firms are different; the US government is a regulatory, or market-rational, Japanese government is a developmental, or plan-rational, and Chinese government relies on a more direct approach by using state-owned enterprises (SOEs).[14]

Section 2.2 compares the three different incentive mechanisms of the firm, including the state. The incentive mechanism of US firms can be expressed as a monitoring image incentive pattern, or the principal-agent model.[15] It is shareholder-oriented and market-oriented and uses strong equity incentives. The internal governance is weak, and the external governance is strong.[16] Its growth bias is weak. Since around 2020, ESG and the "purpose" movement caused the shift from extreme shareholder-oriented corporate governance to moderate stakeholder-oriented corporate governance.[17]

[13] *See* Chapter 1, n.23 and its accompanying text.

[14] SOEs are Chinese state-owned enterprises. *See* Chapter 2, n.141 and its accompanying text.

[15] *See* Chapter 2, n.111 and its accompanying text; Shishido, *supra* note 2, at 6–7.

[16] Regarding internal governance and external governance, *see* Chapter 1, n.11; Viral V. Acharya, Stewart C. Myers & Raghuram G. Rajan, *The Internal Governance of Firms*, 66 J. FIN. 689, 705 (2011).

[17] *See* Chapter 2, n.188 and its accompanying text.

The incentive mechanism of Japanese firms can be expressed as a bargaining image incentive pattern, or the company community model.[18] It is stakeholder-oriented and not market-oriented, with a lot of organized markets, and uses weak equity incentives. The internal governance is strong, and the external governance is weak. Its growth bias is strong. The most unique characteristic of Japanese corporate governance is the position of employees. Employees are located in the center of corporate governance, while employees are located in the hierarchical pyramid outside of corporate governance, both in the United States and China. The Japanese government has been trying to change from stakeholder-oriented corporate governance to shareholder-oriented corporate governance since around 2013, and its change is reflected in Figure 2.5, the new Japanese model. However, the company community[19] norm, which used to be the engine of growth, is still robust and turns out to be the anchor resisting change.

The incentive mechanism of Chinese SOEs can be expressed as a party-state model.[20] It is, in two senses, similar to the Japanese company community model, the double appointment of managers at the business corporation and the party-state, or the company community, and a strong growth bias. Different from Japan, however, the internal governance is weak, and the external governance by the party-state as the controlling shareholder is strong. China is politically stakeholder-oriented and economically shareholder-oriented. The incentive mechanism of Chinese privately owned enterprises (POEs) can be expressed as an owner management model. The owner-manager and state and non-state minority shareholders share the strong equity incentive.

The position of the state in the corporate governance of Chinese SOEs is different from that of the United States and Japanese corporations. While the state is located outside of the forum and participates in the micro-level incentive bargaining, basically via management in the US model and the old and new Japanese models, the party-state is at the center of corporate governance in Chinese SOEs.[21] For Chinese POEs,[22]

[18] *See* Chapter 2, n.124 and its accompanying text; Shishido, *supra* note 2, at 9–10.

[19] Regarding company community, *see* Chapter 2, n.124 and its accompanying text; Zenichi Shishido, *Japanese Corporate Governance: The Hidden Problem of the Corporate Law and Their Solutions*, 25 Del. J. Corp. L. 189, 201–205 (2000).

[20] Regarding party-state, *see* Chapter 2, n.142 and its accompanying text.

[21] *See* Chapter 2, nn.143–160 and their accompanying texts.

[22] POEs are Chinese private owned enterprises. *See* Chapter 2, n.176 and its accompanying text.

although the party-state exercises much stronger and more perversive influence than the United States and Japanese states,[23] the state is not at the core of corporate governance, but is located outside of the forum, as in the United States and Japan.

Among the four players, management is the only window or channel for incentive bargaining. The result of the incentive bargaining, filtered by management's own incentive, determines the direction of managing the firm. Chapter 3 categorizes managerial incentives into power-related, reputational, and monetary incentives, and compares the characteristics of managerial incentives in the three countries.

For US management, monetary incentive is the most important among the three categories. US managerial compensation is high and heavily equity-based to align management interests with shareholder interests. Management has a strong incentive to keep stock prices high from all perspectives of the three different types of incentives,[24] that is, for keeping a good reputation in the external manager market, which determines its price tag,[25] and for keeping autonomy from the hostile takeover threat and the monitoring board.[26] Recently, environmental, social, and governance (ESG) activism has been disturbing such a simple US managerial incentive by criticizing its short-termism and requiring balancing different interests of stakeholders.[27]

For Japanese management, the monetary incentive is not the first priority but is subordinated to power-related and reputational incentives. Japanese management is groomed in the company community, and there is no liquid external manager market. Management does not care about its reputation in the external manager market but cares more about its reputation in the company community.[28] Managerial compensation is low, and managers are weakly incentivized.[29] Management tries to keep the company profitable to avoid main bank contingent governance intervention, and is used to not care about stock price and ROE because it was protected from shareholder intervention by cross-shareholding.[30] Now, Japanese management needs to care about shareholder interest

[23] *See* Chapter 2, nn.181–186 and their accompanying texts.
[24] *See* Chapter 3, nn.67–68 and their accompanying texts.
[25] *See* Chapter 3, nn.46–47 and their accompanying texts.
[26] *See* Chapter 3, nn.7–11 and their accompanying texts.
[27] *See* Chapter 3, n.14 and its accompanying text.
[28] *See* Chapter 3, n.53 and its accompanying text.
[29] *See* Chapter 3, nn.58–60 and their accompanying texts.
[30] *See* Chapter 3, nn.16–17 and their accompanying texts.

because of the change of stock ownership structure and corporate governance reform.[31]

In China, managerial incentives are different in SOEs and POEs. For SOE management, monetary compensation is not so important, but political rank is more important, which is accompanied by monetary rewards.[32] To keep political networks, SOE management cares about its reputation in the party-state.[33] For POE management, monetary incentive is important and stock options are widely used.[34] At the same time, the political network is important to POE management and POE management cares about its reputation in the party-state as well so that it can obtain some economic benefits or resources.[35]

Although it is common for almost all major countries to place the board of directors between shareholders and management, both its formal system and role in practice vary among different countries. Chapter 4 will compare the role of independent outside directors in the United States, Japan, and China from the point of view that the board of directors is an intersection of internal governance and external governance.[36]

As a formal organizational structure, the US board is a one-tier board with committees and has wide decision-making power over important business decisions, while managerial decisions can be delegated to management. In practice, the US board is a monitoring board, not only a compliance monitor and conflicts of interest solver, but also an efficiency referee.[37] As a result, the US corporate governance is a board primacy regime. In most boards of listed companies, independent outside directors occupy all seats except a CEO, and their function is a scheme of indirect external governance by shareholders. The role of independent outside directors focused on monitoring management and independence from controlling shareholders is not required.[38]

Because of the existence of unique corporate organs, the company auditor (*kansayaku*) and the board of company auditors, the Japanese board is often misunderstood as a two-tier board. Essentially, it is a one-

[31] *See* Chapter 3, nn.18–20 and their accompanying texts.
[32] *See* Chapter 3, n.67 and its accompanying text.
[33] *See* Chapter 3, n.55 and its accompanying text.
[34] *See* Chapter 3, n.70 and its accompanying text.
[35] *See* Chapter 3, nn.55–57 and their accompanying texts.
[36] *See* Chapter 4, n.1 and its accompanying text.
[37] *See* Chapter 4, nn.4–6 and their accompanying texts.
[38] *See* Chapter 4, n.8 and its accompanying text.

tier board with an audit committee.[39] Besides the traditional board with a company auditor, now two other board systems, one is the US style board with three committees and the other is the board system between the US style board and the traditional board, are available as alternatives.[40] The Japanese board used to consist of all inside directors, and still now boards with a majority of independent outside directors are not common. The major role of independent outside directors is to monitor the "company community" rather than to monitor management, and the independence from the company community has been emphasized by law.[41] The current characteristic of the Japanese board is between managerial board and an advisory board without functioning as an efficiency referee.[42]

The Chinese board system looks like the German type two-tier board with a supervisory board, which includes employee representatives,[43] and a management board.[44] The supervisory board has no power of election and discharge of management board members, although the amendment of the Chinese Company law in 2005 gives the supervisory board the power to "recommend the dismissal of directors or senior managers who act in breach of laws, regulations, articles of associations or shareholders' resolutions."[45] In addition, the supervisory board is granted the power to bring a lawsuit against the director or senior manager for their failure to comply with the fiduciary duty. However, the supervisory board's monitoring function is weak in practice due to the fact that the majority of supervisors are appointed by the controlling shareholder(s). Independent outside directors are required in management boards, and their requirement of independence from major shareholders has been emphasized by law because monitoring majority shareholders is the most important issue in China. Neither supervisors nor independent outside directors, however, substantially monitor majority shareholders to protect minority shareholders.[46] This probably

[39] *See* Chapter 4, n.12 and its accompanying text.
[40] *See* Chapter 4, nn.19–22 and their accompanying texts.
[41] *See* Chapter 4, nn.52–53 and their accompanying texts.
[42] *See* Chapter 4, nn.100–104 and their accompanying texts.
[43] *See* Chapter 4, nn.23–28 and their accompanying texts.
[44] While Chinese Company Law used to only allow a two-tier board system for corporate governance structure, Chinese Company Law of 2023 enables limited liability companies and joint stock limited companies to choose between either a one-tier board and a two-tier board. Chapter 4, n.108 and its accompanying text.
[45] *See* Chapter 4, nn.38–39 and their accompanying texts.
[46] *See* Chapter 4, nn.112–114 and their accompanying texts.

explains why the US type of corporate governance tools do not work in the Chinese context, as the agency problems in these two jurisdictions vary from each other.

As a human capital provider besides management, employees play an important role in corporate governance. Chapter 5 compares laws of employment protection, compensation, and labor unions in the three countries and describes how the different laws affect incentive bargaining of the firm and corporate governance.

Employment protection laws in the United States and Japan are two extremes in the world. The US employment-at-will rule gives employers wide discretion to dismiss employees if there are neither contractual protections nor discriminations.[47] Japanese abusive dismissal rule strictly restricts employers' discretion in dismissing employees even in business downturns.[48] Although the Japanese strict dismissal law restricts management's business judgment in issues related to employees, it gives management wide discretion to balance the interests of stakeholders and the interests of shareholders.[49]

Chinese employment protection law has changed dynamically with the social and economic conditions. Dismissal used to be very difficult because of the requirement for the local government's approval. A large-scale layoff concerns local governments the most due to the societal stability concern. Dismissal rule has been relaxed to attract foreign investments, and the requirement of the government's approval was removed by the Labor Law of 1994, albeit its implicit application in reality. Due to the shift from pursuing faster growth to improving the quality of economic growth in the 2000s, the Labor Contract Law of 2008 tightened the requirements for terminating employees.[50]

Although the laws of employee compensation are not very different among the three countries, the compensation packages vary. Relative to Japanese companies, US companies rely heavily on performance-based pay, which includes generous stock options.[51] Among the compensation packages in Japan, the portion of overtime pay and bonuses is large because they are used as buffers for market changes. After all, it is hard for employers to dismiss regular employees and to decrease the fixed base

[47] *See* Chapter 5, nn.7–11 and their accompanying texts.
[48] *See* Chapter 5, nn.12–16 and their accompanying texts.
[49] *See* Chapter 5, n.27 and its accompanying text.
[50] *See* Chapter 5, nn.43–52 and their accompanying texts.
[51] *See* Chapter 5, nn.64–73 and their accompanying texts.

salary in Japan. Stock options are not widely used.[52] Among the compensation packages in China, the portion of payment for social insurance and welfare benefits is large.[53] Performance-based bonuses play a significant role in POEs in attracting talent. Equity incentive plans have become common and recognized as a measure to improve firm performance and corporate governance.[54]

US labor unions are basically industry unions and adversarial to management,[55] while Japanese labor unions are company unions and rather agreeable to management. Although Japanese labor union law gives labor unions stronger weapons against management than their US counterparts, Japanese unions use their weapons less frequently than US unions. Japanese company unions play an important role as a channel of internal governance.[56] All labor unions in China are government-backed, organized only in individual enterprises, and expected to mitigate labor disputes (which arguably increases social well-being).[57] A labor union is sometimes granted the right to participate in the decision-making process of the employer when the decision will affect the immediate rights and interests of the employees.[58] Labor unions' weapons against management, such as work stoppages and slowdowns, are strictly restricted.[59]

As a monetary capital provider besides creditors, shareholders play a major monitoring role by exercising both voice and exit. Chapter 6 will compare how shareholders in the three countries monitor management by voice from the perspective of the tradeoff between management autonomy and monitoring management.

Japanese and Chinese corporate laws give shareholders wider decision-making power compared to the US corporate law.[60] On the other hand, Japanese and Chinese corporate laws provide ambiguous fiduciary duties of directors, which allows management to balance shareholder and stakeholder interests, while US law imposes on directors a strict fiduciary duty to maximize shareholder interest.[61]

[52] *See* Chapter 5, nn.79–82 and their accompanying texts.
[53] *See* Chapter 5, nn.89–90 and their accompanying texts.
[54] *See* Chapter 5, nn.91–108 and their accompanying texts.
[55] *See* Chapter 5, nn.121–126 and their accompanying texts.
[56] *See* Chapter 5, nn.131–137 and their accompanying texts.
[57] *See* Chapter 5, n.144 and its accompanying text.
[58] *See* Chapter 5, nn.156–158 and their accompanying texts.
[59] *See* Chapter 5, nn.166–168 and their accompanying texts.
[60] *See* Chapter 6, nn.2–5, 12–13, 18–20 and their accompanying texts.
[61] *See* Chapter 6, nn.108, 127–129, 136 and their accompanying texts.

The three countries share similar disclosure regulations both by corporate law and securities regulations, regarding not only accounting information, but also internal control, large-volume shareholding, and proxy solicitation. The three countries also share similar enforcement mechanisms of both public and private enforcement.[62] Enforcement practices are, however, different in the three countries. In the United States, besides public enforcement, private enforcement is sometimes more effective and functional than public enforcement, with its class action mechanism and a much more pro-investor corporate bench in the court system. Both in Japan and China, private enforcement has played a limited role.[63]

In the United States, strong shareholders' right to sue, which is supported by discovery, class action, and attorneys' contingent fee, and safe harbor for directors and officers, which is provided by a clear distinction between the duty of loyalty and duty of care, business judgment rule, and D&O insurance, take a balance of shareholders' monitoring and management's autonomy.[64] In Japan, shareholder derivative action plays an important monitoring role even without a strong attorney's incentive and discovery. The substance of the fiduciary duty of directors and officers, and the business judgment rule, is not as clear as that of their US counterparts.[65] In China, although shareholder suits, both direct and derivative, are codified and expected to play an *ex post* monitoring role, substitute for *ex ante* regulations, they do not yet powerfully function in practice. Chinese corporate law provides both the duty of loyalty and the duty of due diligence, but their substance is ambiguous, and the business judgment rule has not been introduced.[66]

Institutionalization of stock ownership structure strengthened shareholder activism since the 1990s in the United States,[67] and now Japan is catching up.[68] In both countries, hedge fund activism plays a major role in direct shareholder monitoring. In China, shareholder activism is historically nearly absent mainly because most listed companies are controlled by controlling shareholders, particularly the state.[69] Recently,

62 *See* Chapter 6, nn.40–50, 58–68, 72–92 and their accompanying texts.
63 *See* Chapter 6, nn.51–57, 69–71, 93–104 and their accompanying texts.
64 *See* Chapter 6, nn.109–126 and their accompanying texts.
65 *See* Chapter 6, nn.127–132 and their accompanying texts.
66 *See* Chapter 6, nn.136–158 and their accompanying texts.
67 *See* Chapter 6, nn.162–164, and their accompanying texts.
68 *See* Chapter 6, nn.172–174 and their accompanying texts.
69 *See* Chapter 6, nn.176–177 and their accompanying texts.

however, the China Securities Investor Services Center (CSISC) has raised a substantial level of shareholder activism and has become influential in Chinese corporate governance.[70] Occasionally, private equity funds bring some cases to the courts for rights protection.[71]

Chapter 7 will compare how shareholders in the three countries monitor management by exit, that is, the threat of hostile takeover, from the perspective of the tradeoff between management autonomy and monitoring management.

In the United States, substantial numbers of hostile takeovers have occurred since the 1970s, that is, the control market is liquid, but now hedge fund activism plays a more important corporate governance role than hostile takeover.[72] In Japan, hostile takeover attempts have rarely been successfully done since the majority shareholding of listed companies was stabilized by cross-shareholding networks in the 1960s. After 2020, the control market emerged with several successful hostile takeovers by competitors, and at the same time hedge fund activism exploded.[73] In China, hostile takeover is still nearly absent, particularly for SOEs.

Since the inception of the poison pill as a defense against hostile takeovers in the 1980s in the United States, Japan has been catching up with the United States with almost twenty years of time difference. In the 2020s, the divergent paths of the poison pill in the two countries appear to be converging to some degree, being used for both hostile takeover threats and shareholder activism, although there are still many different characteristics and legal rules.[74]

As to the balance between management autonomy and monitoring management, the United States has a relatively buyer-friendly legal system, particularly the weak employment protection law and the neutral tax-free reorganization rule, while no mandatory takeover bid rule and unilateral board discretion to implement poison pill create a balance between monitoring and autonomy at the corporate law level.[75]

Japan has a seller-friendly legal system with a strong employment protection law, a tax-free reorganization rule that discourages changing

[70] *See* Chapter 6, nn.178–185 and their accompanying texts.

[71] *See* Chapter 6, n.186 and its accompanying text.

[72] *See* Chapter 7, nn.6, 13 and their accompanying texts.

[73] *See* Chapter 7, nn.14–24 and their accompanying texts.

[74] *See* Chapter 7, nn.93–106, 107–114 and their accompanying texts.

[75] *See* Chapter 7, nn.134–135 and their accompanying texts.

management and employees, a mandatory takeover bid rule, and weak regulation on board discretion to implement poison pills as long as obtaining shareholders' approval.[76]

China has the UK-type mandatory takeover bid rule and the shareholder primacy corporate law requires shareholder approval to implement poison pill and other defensive measures. Therefore, the black letter law looks to create a UK-type balance between autonomy and monitoring, but the actual implementation of the statutes allows abuses by both buyers and sellers.[77]

Friendly takeovers involve more serious conflicts of interest compared to hostile takeovers.

In the United States, the breach of fiduciary duty claim plays an important role. Target boards will owe the Revlon duty if they commit to a change in corporate control. Even in a conflict of interest case, the business judgment rule has to apply if certain procedures are taken. The fair value in appraisal remedy does not include synergy, and traditionally, the DCF value has been used. Recently, however, Delaware courts tend to use the deal price or the market price.[78]

In Japan, although a recent case made clear that target directors owe a fiduciary duty to pursue the interest of shareholders as a whole, the appraisal remedy is still more important than the fiduciary duty claim. The fair value in appraisal remedy includes synergy and is calculated as the average market price plus the expected premium. A recent case made clear that the deal price (TOB price) is respected if fair procedures are taken, even in a conflict of interest case.[79]

Both Delaware courts and Japanese courts turned out to be less interventionist and respected the deal price if the fair procedure was followed.

Although Chinese law stipulates that directors and management have a fiduciary duty to treat competing bidders equally, "equal treatment" is too ambiguous to prevent the board from abusing discretion. In terms of appraisal remedies, the Chinese courts use market value as the "reasonable price," but a controller can easily manipulate the market value. Minority shareholders are not protected properly.[80]

[76] *See* Chapter 7, nn.136–139 and their accompanying texts.
[77] *See* Chapter 7, nn.141–142 and their accompanying texts.
[78] *See* Chapter 7, nn.144–153 and their accompanying texts.
[79] *See* Chapter 7, nn.154–161 and their accompanying texts.
[80] *See* Chapter 7, nn.162–164 and their accompanying texts.

As a monetary capital provider, creditors play an important role in external governance with shareholders, although they have no legal voting right outside of the bankruptcy process. Chapter 8 will compare the legal institutions and practices regarding the roles of creditors in the three countries, by dividing them into *ex ante* monitoring of solvent firms, renegotiation in financially distressed firms, legal bankruptcy, and debtor directors' fiduciary duty during the zone of insolvency.

As far as *ex ante* monitoring of solvent firms is concerned, in the United States, banks play an active role in the governance of the firm whose business stumbles, by using the loan agreements for the revolving credit facilities. A series of regulations after the financial crisis of 2008 impeded credit supply from the banking sector and raised a wide variety of non-bank lenders to fill the gap, particularly direct lenders, which mostly lend to PE buyout deals and closely monitor their borrowers as banks do.[81]

In Japan, contingent governance by main banks as representatives of monetary capital providers worked well during Japan's rapid economic growth era, but was not able to monitor their client companies' use of free cash flow after the economic growth stopped. Now, the main banks play an insignificant role for top-listed companies, which can raise funds from the capital market easily, but still play an important role for other mediocre companies.[82]

Although China is a bank-centered economy and state banks keep a dominant position, Chinese banks play a less aggressive role in monitoring borrowers, especially when borrowers are SOEs, which can be supported financially by the government with cheap credit. This explains that a high leverage ratio of Chinese banks was not badly hit by the global financial crisis and the COVID-19 pandemic.[83]

Regarding renegotiation in financially distressed firms, in the United States, pre-negotiated or pre-arranged Chapter 11 are widely used because dispersed creditors increase the difficulty of achieving a private solution for financially distressed firms. After the 2008 financial crisis, the foundation of lender control gradually diminished and private equity sponsors turned to be dominant as the owner of large, distressed firms. They often resort to hardball recapitalization, such as the dropdown and the non-pro-rata uptier.[84]

[81] *See* Chapter 8, nn.6–14 and their accompanying texts.
[82] *See* Chapter 8, nn.15–20 and their accompanying texts.
[83] *See* Chapter 8, nn.21–26 and their accompanying texts.
[84] *See* Chapter 8, nn.28–61 and their accompanying texts.

In Japan, when a company becomes financially distressed, its main bank will lead private reorganization and try to obtain compromises from other creditors to avoid legal bankruptcy. Main bank rescue and government subsidization via public credit guarantee for small and medium enterprises create a soft-budget problem.[85]

Huge deficit and inefficiency of SOEs have been a big issue in China, and the banking system is still largely a government-controlled sector. The Chinese government has made a continuous effort to lower the leverage ratio of corporate debt, particularly through the debt-for-equity swap program and mixed share reform, which tended to introduce private capital participation in SOEs but actually failed to attract enough private capital participation.[86]

In terms of legal bankruptcy, easy access to the legal reorganization procedure in the United States encourages the debtor to file early. The bankruptcy court restricts its role as a neutral arbiter. Creditors have a lot of control over bankruptcy outcomes via the creditors' committee. Super-priority DIP financing and Section 363 sales provide liquidity.[87]

Japanese legal bankruptcy laws include severe punishment of management, give bankruptcy judges wider discretion, and restrict party autonomy compared to US Chapter 11. Super-priority DIP loans and Section 363 sales are not available in Japan. Both debtor management and creditors are reluctant to file legal bankruptcy, which leads to delayed filing and a low recovery rate.[88]

China enacted its first bankruptcy code, Enterprise Bankruptcy Law, in 2008, which is modeled on the US bankruptcy law and includes such terms as the absolute priority rule and the creditors' committee. Several important differences, such as unclear eligibility standards and incomplete automatic stay with a fifteen-day time gap between bankruptcy filing and the court's acceptance of the case, discourage bankruptcy filings.[89]

Regarding directors' fiduciary duty during the zone of insolvency, the US case laws have been dramatically changed since 2007. Now, directors owe fiduciary duty only to shareholders and can advance the interest of shareholders at the expense of creditors with the business judgment rule

[85] *See* Chapter 8, nn.62–67 and their accompanying texts.
[86] *See* Chapter 8, nn.68–77 and their accompanying texts.
[87] *See* Chapter 8, nn.82–90 and their accompanying texts.
[88] *See* Chapter 8, nn.91–98 and their accompanying texts.
[89] *See* Chapter 8, nn.99–125 and their accompanying texts.

as long as the company is outside of the formal bankruptcy procedure, even in insolvency.[90]

Many Japanese court cases have imposed civil liability on directors who "gambled" at the expense of creditors by adopting Companies Act Article 429. Japanese law is considered to take the position that directors of companies in the zone of insolvency owe a duty to take creditors' interests into consideration.[91]

In China, even when the company is in the zone of insolvency, directors must act primarily in the interest of shareholders; however, such activities should not harm the national interest, public interest, and legitimate rights and interests of any other person, including creditors. Therefore, directors are, in fact, required to take creditors' interest into consideration in the zone of insolvency.[92]

It is worthwhile to pick up startup companies in this book, which basically focuses on listed companies, not only because it is now widely recognized that disruptive innovation can be made only by startup companies, but also because the incentive bargaining between entrepreneurs as human capital providers and venture capitalists (VCs) as monetary capital providers provides the proto-type incentive bargaining of listed companies. Chapter 9 will compare the two-tier incentive bargaining between monetary capital providers and human capital providers of the VC industry, and the government's role in creating venture ecosystems in the three countries.[93]

As the first-tier incentive bargaining, the structure of venture capital funds in the three countries is now basically the same, albeit with some unique characteristics in each country. They are organized as limited partnerships, which provide investors (limited partners [LPs]) limited liability, venture capitalists (general partners [GPs]) autonomy of management, and both LPs and GPs benefit from pass-through taxation. LPs allow GPs to receive strong equity incentives, called carried interest, in addition to management fees.[94]

Individual venture capitalists in Japanese financial institutions backed by VCs receive no equity incentive, and their LPs are either parent financial institutions or their client companies, which have no incentive

[90] *See* Chapter 8, nn.118–131 and their accompanying texts.
[91] *See* Chapter 8, nn.132–134 and their accompanying texts.
[92] *See* Chapter 8, nn.135–144 and their accompanying texts.
[93] *See* Chapter 9, n.1 and its accompanying text.
[94] *See* Chapter 9, nn.2–4 and their accompanying texts.

to monitor GPs,[95] while LPs of VC funds in the United States are mostly pension funds and university endowments, of which fund managers have a strong incentive to monitor GPs who have strong equity incentive as individuals.[96] Many Chinese LPs are wealthy families and individuals who are more active and eager to participate in management, including investment decisions. Government guidance funds (GGF) have played an important role.[97]

As the second-tier incentive bargaining, entrepreneurs and VCs make incentive bargaining on sharing cash flow and sharing control separately.

In the classic Silicon Valley model, entrepreneurs cede control to VCs in return of gaining sweat equity by using convertible preferred stock. The convertible preferred stock can make it easier to differentiate its issuing price from that of common stock, and give VCs liquidation preference and contractual controlling rights, such as board seats and veto rights. VCs actively monitor entrepreneurs, including replacing them from the CEO position.[98] However, a declining emphasis on active monitoring by VCs can be observed during the last decade. VCs take the strategy to encourage entrepreneurs to take high risks by providing them with safety nets.[99]

In Japan, even after corporate law introduced convertible preferred stock, VCs mostly invested in common stock with contractual arrangements, including the founder's duty to stock buy-back as an enforcement mechanism, mainly because sweat equity was too risky to use under unpredictable tax treatment. After the Japanese Internal Revenue Service (IRS) admitted the price difference between common stock and preferred stock, convertible preferred stock turned to be widely used after around 2020. Although preferred stock is used for giving VCs liquidation preference and giving entrepreneurs sweat equity, its self-enforcing mechanism, such as class voting and veto rights, is not widely used, and founders' stock buy-back duty still remains.[100]

In China, the convertible preferred stock has not been allowed at the corporate law level. Without using the convertible preferred stock, VCs, startup companies, and founder-shareholders agree on major items

[95] *See* Chapter 9, nn.8–11 and their accompanying texts.
[96] *See* Chapter 9, nn.5–6 and their accompanying texts.
[97] *See* Chapter 9, nn.12–25 and their accompanying texts.
[98] *See* Chapter 9, nn.29–41 and their accompanying texts.
[99] *See* Chapter 9, n.42 and its accompanying text.
[100] *See* Chapter 9, nn.43–48 and their accompanying texts.

widely used in the United States and an original contractual agreement, so-called "Value Adjustment Mechanism (VAM)" is invented by the market players as an enforcement mechanism, which is similar to the stock buy-back duty in Japan. Although the Company Law of 2023 explicitly allows the issuance of preferred stock, including class voting and veto rights, whether the convertible stock is permitted or not is still ambiguous.[101]

The availability of exit options for human capital and monetary capital influences the incentive bargaining between entrepreneurs and VCs.

In the United States, a liquid external labor market encourages entrepreneurs to take the risk of starting a business and to cede control to VCs. Liquid M&A market, besides the liquid initial public offering (IPO) market, encourages VCs to take risks to invest in private equities and leave more equity shares to entrepreneurs.[102]

In Japan, although the low listing requirement of the IPO market, which launched in 1999, has contributed a lot to the development of startup companies, many immature IPO cases are recognized as a problem. The illiquid external labor market and the illiquid M&A market make both entrepreneurs and VCs risk-averse and prevent efficient incentive bargaining between them.[103]

In China, since 2004, several IPO markets for startups have launched and provided an exit for monetary capital. Although M&As have been politically regulated, the number of M&A exits in the VC industry has been increasing in recent years. The state started to deregulate M&A activities.[104]

Governments need to play some role in growing venture capital markets in their countries. Silicon Valley is the most successful venture ecosystem in the world and the US federal government has played an important role in stimulating VC industry and nurturing startup companies, via government procurement, subsidies, and providing legal infrastructure. Local governments have also tried to stimulate venture habitats and create venture ecosystems like Silicon Valley.[105]

Although since the 1980s, the Japanese government has tried to stimulate startups and the VC industry through governmental funds,

[101] *See* Chapter 9, nn.57–70 and their accompanying texts.
[102] *See* Chapter 9, nn.74–81 and their accompanying texts.
[103] *See* Chapter 9, nn.82–87 and their accompanying texts.
[104] *See* Chapter 9, nn.88–105 and their accompanying texts.
[105] *See* Chapter 9, nn.109–114 and their accompanying texts.

tax incentives, and the improvement of legal systems, the efforts did not have a significant impact. Japanese startups and the VC industry finally took off in the 2010s, and large companies recognized the importance of startups as their alliance partners. Venture habitat has gradually matured. The growth speed is, however, much slower than in other countries.[106]

Several government-backed VC firms were set up in China to provide financing to high-tech startups, particularly the GGF, both the central and local governments level, plays an important role. Recently, the central government started to position itself as a limited participant by only providing funding, instead of directing the operations of the government-backed funds. Chinese new wave of regional policies aims to create urban high-tech clusters.[107]

The typical listed company in the world does not necessarily have a dispersed ownership and is professionally managed. However, a significant percentage of listed companies are under the influence of founding families by stock ownership and/or family managers, even in developed countries, including the United States. Chapter 10 will compare the characteristics and performance of listed family firms in the three countries and demonstrate their implications for corporate governance in general.

In the United States, when the founders retire, they tend to hire professional managers and sell out their shares. Therefore, the prevalence of family firms in the United States is relatively low compared to other countries. Still, 47 percent of listed companies are family firms.[108] In Japan, around 50 percent of listed companies are family firms, many of which are managed by founders' heirs without substantial family ownership.[109] In China, although family firms are relatively new because Chinese law traditionally prohibited private enterprises, family firms have grown rapidly since the transformation from a planned to a market-oriented economy in 1978. Listed family firms accounted for 64.5 percent of total listed companies in 2018. Most listed family firms in China are controlled through a pyramidal ownership structure.[110]

Generally speaking, founder firms' performance is significantly better than that of non-family firms in most countries, but heir-managing

[106] *See* Chapter 9, nn.115–117 and their accompanying texts.
[107] *See* Chapter 9, nn.118–132 and their accompanying texts.
[108] *See* Chapter 10, nn.12–22 and their accompanying texts.
[109] *See* Chapter 10, nn.23–29 and their accompanying texts.
[110] *See* Chapter 10, nn.30–42 and their accompanying texts.

firms' performance varies in different countries. Although the results of empirical studies in the United States are mixed and contingent on several factors, heir managers perform relatively worse than professional managers.[111] In Japan, heir-managing firms perform better than non-family firms during the low economic growth era on a return on equity (ROA) basis.[112] In China, the performance data for heir-managing family firms are limited because most Chinese listed firms are still managed by the founders.[113]

Prevalent types of listed family firms and their relative performance to non-family firms reflect minority shareholder protection law, the size of manager market, and the corporate governance practice of each country.

Strong minority shareholder protection laws and a large-size manager market in the United States lead founders to transfer their positions to able professional managers and sell their stock without the risk of being squeezed out. Relatively better performance of professional managers over heir managers shows that the separation of ownership and management seems to work in the United States, where the well-developed stock market efficiently monitors management, and equity-based managerial compensation package gives professional managers substantial equity incentive that mitigates shareholder-manager agency problems.[114]

Strong minority protection laws and a small-size professional manager market in Japan lead founders to transfer their positions to their heirs and sell their stock without the risk of being squeezed out. Contrary to the United States, heir managers perform relatively better than salaryman managers. It shows that the separation of ownership and management does not seem to work in Japan. CEO candidates other than heirs are practically limited to salaryman managers in a company community. The company community norm does not allow salaryman managers to obtain substantial equity compensation. Only heir managers can obtain substantial equity incentives in Japanese listed companies.[115]

In the face of weak shareholder protection laws in China, founders usually prefer to appoint family members as CEOs and board members and keep substantial stock ownership to guarantee control, so as to

[111] *See* Chapter 10, nn.45–68 and their accompanying texts.
[112] *See* Chapter 10, nn.69–72 and their accompanying texts.
[113] *See* Chapter 10, nn.73–86 and their accompanying texts.
[114] *See* Chapter 10, nn.90–102 and their accompanying texts.
[115] *See* Chapter 10, nn.103–119 and their accompanying texts.

protect their interests. Small-size manager markets and Confucian norms also let founders transfer their position to their heirs. The impacts of family firms on performance are contingent on several factors, such as the use of control-enhancing mechanisms, whether the family is involved in the management or the board, and the strength of political connections.[116]

Chapter 11 compares incentive bargaining of law-making in the three countries, focusing on corporate law and securities regulations.

Section 11.1 describes major lawmakers and law-making procedures of the three countries by categorizing corporate law and securities regulations into statutory law, case law, and soft law.

The distinct characteristic of US corporate law is the existence of competition among states. Now, the state of Delaware overwhelms and its case law is very influential. Both case law and statutory law of Delaware are made by corporate law specialists who share the interest of keeping Delaware as the most popular forum of incorporation. Securities regulation is a federal law, and the competition between the SEC and the state of Delaware regarding corporate governance regulations has historically been observed.[117]

In Japan, drafters of statutory corporate law and securities regulations are bureaucrats of the Ministry of Justice (MOJ), the Ministry of Economic, Trade, and Industries (METI), and the Financial Service Agency (FSA). The Committee of Legal Reform, which consists of interest groups' representatives and neutral experts, plays an important role. Its decision is made on a consensus basis, and it is hard to deviate from the status quo. A corporate law specialized division of the Tokyo District Court is influential in interpreting statutory corporate law. Soft laws, such as governmental guidelines and best practice codes, are now widely used as measures of policy push reforms initiated by ministries in charge.[118]

In China, although the National People's Congress (NPC) is the highest legislative body, it delegates law-making at several levels to many agencies, including provincial legislative bodies or governments and securities exchanges. Particularly, the State Council has been responsible for many important legislative initiatives in the form of administrative rules, which can be passed faster than formal laws. Although judicial

116 *See* Chapter 10, nn.120–139 and their accompanying texts.
117 *See* Chapter 11, nn.1–17 and their accompanying texts.
118 *See* Chapter 11, nn.18–31 and their accompanying texts.

decisions are not a formal source of law in China, some decisions, particularly judgments or summaries of judgments selected from guiding cases and published by the Supreme People's Court (SPC), do create legal norms and are persuasive or even binding in practice. The Supreme People's Court does have the power to interpret and make rules.[119]

Section 11.2 introduces several examples of incentive bargaining in law-making in the three countries.

The Delaware corporate law is the most influential in the US corporate law, and the Delaware statutory corporate law is made within the Corporation Law Section of the Delaware Bar. The legislation of Section 102(b)(7) after the Van Gorkom decision in 1985 is the most famous case. Although the general perception is that the legislative overturning of judge-made corporate law rarely took place in Delaware except Section 102(b)(7), there is a substantial number of cases. Responding to the lobbying by directors of large corporations, major players of the Corporate Law Section, who share the same interest in keeping Delaware as the dominant franchise of US corporations, have demanded such legislation.[120]

Legislative lobbying also took place at the Federal Congressional level. For example, in 2002, the SEC was forced to abandon the proposal of an SEC rule that bars accountants from acting as consultants as a result of intensive lobbying in Congress by the accounting industry. SOX, which was adopted by Congress just after the Enron and WorldCom fraudulent disclosure scandals, is a good example of salience law and a policy push legislation. At the same time, it is an example of a federal invasion of the state's corporate law area.

In Japan, the incentive bargaining on corporate law-making had taken place almost exclusively in the Committee of Legal Reform, in which each member has a quasi-veto power. After 1997, however, the legislation channel was pluralized, that is, diet member proposal laws were added, and at the same time, corporate law legislation turned out to be a tool for achieving the objectives of economic policy. The pressure of stakeholders' demands strengthened, and as a result, many demand pull legislations were made. J-SOX is an example of salience law and policy push legislation, just like the SOX in the US. Both the existence of scandals and the "globalization" narrative motivated the FSA to enact J-SOX.[121]

[119] *See* Chapter 11, nn.32–85 and their accompanying texts.
[120] *See* Chapter 11, nn.91–120 and their accompanying texts.
[121] *See* Chapter 11, nn.121–139 and their accompanying texts.

Legislation of corporate law in China includes several steps of procedure and inter-agency incentive bargaining. Although the Chinese party-state is powerful, Chinese corporate law is not only a product of bargaining just among government agencies and the judicial courts, but also a product of bargaining among various interest groups. For example, at the 2004 annual meetings of the NPC, although the delegates from coastal wealthy provinces proposed to introduce the common law's veil-piercing doctrine to the new company law, and this proposal gained support from various interest groups, State-owned Assets Supervision and Administration Commission (SASAC), which represents the interest of SOEs, resisted the proposal, and one proposed provision was removed. The courts, on the other hand, practiced the veil-piercing rule well before the formal introduction of the veil-piercing rule into the Corporate Law.[122]

After comparing how different areas of law matter to the incentive bargaining among the major players of the firm, including startups and listed family firms, in the three countries, we can raise several observations on important commonalities and divergences.

The stock majority rule is shared as a premise of incentive bargaining among the three countries. As a result, a change in stock ownership structure affects a lot on corporate governance. The institutionalization effect in the United States and Japan is a good example.

The liquidity of the external labor market and M&A market has a significant impact on incentive bargaining and shapes the corporate governance practice, which is particularly observed in the VC and startup industry.

The government/state plays an important but under-investigated role in stimulating industries in all three countries. Although the ways of state intervention have varied among the three countries, the importance of respecting the incentive of private parties is gradually shared.

As examples of how law matters to the incentive bargaining of the firm, employment law, which reflects markets and social norms of each country, has a significant impact on the incentive bargaining, including the way of coalition among the four participants.

Bankruptcy law is important as it sets the *ex ante* and *ex post* incentive of the major players and affects the economic efficiency of the market and the rights protection of market players.

[122] *See* Chapter 11, nn.140–165 and their accompanying texts.

Sometimes, the existence of a particular legal infrastructure changes the practice by affecting the incentive of the major players. The implementation of convertible preferred stock in Japan and China is a good example.

The positions of the state in Chinese corporate governance and the position of employees in Japanese corporate governance create unique characteristics of both countries. The state is located in the center of corporate governance in Chinese SOEs, while the state is located outside of corporate governance in the United States and Japan. Employees are located in the center of corporate governance in Japan, while employees are located outside of corporate governance in the United States and China. The party-state norm in China and the company community norm in Japan have been engines of economic growth in both countries. In a low-growth era, however, they seem to turn out to be anchors of the status quo and slow down necessary changes.

Enterprise law and corporate governance appear different in three major economies due to the divergence in legal, cultural, and political backgrounds. This shows the complexity of designing and reforming each jurisdiction's own corporate governance regime and the necessity of communicating with each other to appreciate the differences. The end of corporate law has yet to come.

PART I

Theory and Framework

1

The Framework of Analysis

The framework of analysis in this book is to view the firm as an incentive mechanism for its indispensable capital providers and to consider the various areas of law that affect that incentive as a complementary set referred to as "enterprise law."[1]

Section 1.1 articulates the concept of "incentive bargaining" based on a simple example of a partnership between two individuals. Section 1.2 explains the relationship between incentive bargaining and corporate governance, by categorizing corporate governance into "corporate governance in a narrow sense," which is equivalent to "external governance," and "corporate governance in a wide sense," which includes both external governance and "internal governance," in other words, a system for indispensable capital providers of the firm of incentive bargaining. Section 1.2 also raises the issue of tradeoff between internal governance and external governance, and argues that the optimal balance of internal governance and external governance to maximize firm value is idiosyncratic. Section 1.3 describes another main concept of this book, "enterprise law," which is a set of different areas of law that will complementarily affect the incentive bargaining of the firm. Section 1.4 provides three patterns of incentive bargaining practices in different countries. Section 1.5 describes the incentive bargaining of the firm as a repeated game and shows how the game will proceed. Finally, Section 1.6 introduces the state/government's role in the incentive bargaining of the firm and shows the necessity of taking the state as a player in this game.

[1] *See* Zenichi Shishido, *The Incentive Bargain of the Firm and Enterprise Law: A Nexus of Contracts, Markets, and Laws*, *in* Enterprise Law: Contracts, Markets, and Laws in the US and Japan 1 (Zenichi Shishido ed., 2014). (Much of the discussion presented in this chapter is based on ideas discussed in this article.)

1.1 Incentive Bargaining

The firm is an ongoing joint project requiring both monetary and human capital. Each participant in a joint project needs to motivate other participants to provide their capital in order to maximize their own payoff. The bargaining among the indispensable capital providers that motivates each player to provide their capital to the joint project will be called "incentive bargaining" in this book. The result of a successful incentive bargaining is that each capital provider has the optimal incentive to maximize the firm's value added[2] and consequently maximize their own payoff. This section will show how incentive bargaining develops in a simple joint project between two partners.

1.1.1 The Case of a Partnership

Assume a case where two individuals jointly start a restaurant business. Al is a forty-five-year-old individual and has been working as a waiter and a floor manager of several French restaurants for more than twenty years. He would like to start his own restaurant by using his accumulated service expertise and money. Ben is thirty years old and a chef who just came back from France. Al appreciates Ben's talent as a chef and asks him to jointly run a French restaurant with him. Al provides $200,000 and Ben provides $100,000 to open the restaurant.

In this case, the two partners are in a typical give-and-take relationship. Both partners, Al as the general manager and Ben as the chef, will provide their human capital to their joint project. Both roles are indispensable to running a French restaurant, and they highly value their partner's capabilities. They share the same goal of obtaining a Michelin star and value the economic benefit of having such a rating. They understand that the goal can be obtained only when both partners provide their maximum human capital to each other. Even though there is not a small possibility for their joint project to be failed.

[2] The firm's value added equals the firm's revenue minus opportunity costs of monetary and human capital providers, such as the amount of compensation that an employee would have obtained in the external labor market. The discounted present value of the firm's value added is the firm's value. If capital providers other than shareholders obtain the amount of compensation equal to their opportunity costs, the firm's value will be equal the shareholder value. In many cases, however, capital providers other than shareholders also share the firm's value added. *See* ZENICHI SHISHIDO, DOKIZUKE NO SHIKUMI TOSHITENO KIGYO: INSENTHIBU SHISUTEMU NO HOSEIDORON [THE FIRM AS AN INCENTIVE MECHANISM: THE ROLE OF LEGAL INSTITUTIONS] 6, 8 (2006).

1.1.2 Conflicts and Risks

Generally, there are conflicting interests between the capital providers (players) in a joint project, and each player will face certain risks based on such conflicting interests. If the players leave those risks (i.e., both their own risk and other players' risks) unaddressed, the incentive of the players to provide their own capital to the joint project will be distorted. As such, the players will try to incentivize each other by bargaining the share of control, to decrease risk, and the share of value added, to increase incentives.

The basic conflict of this hypothetical joint project is the balance between two payoffs: the payoff as a monetary capital provider and the payoff as a human capital provider. Al provides two-thirds of the monetary capital and Ben provides one-third. If their payoff is shared according to their share of monetary capital, Ben's incentive will be distorted. The reputation and success of a restaurant depend heavily on the restaurant chefs' talent. So, Ben will feel that Al piggybacked his culinary talent once their restaurant business succeeds and makes profit.[3]

Based on such a conflict, Al feels the risk of Ben's exit. Conversely, Ben has a threat of exit against Al. Ben, as the minority partner, feels the risk of being squeezed out and losing autonomy in the kitchen.

If they leave the risks unaddressed, each partner's incentive to provide human capital will be distorted, and their joint project will never succeed.

1.1.3 Bargaining over Sharing the Firm's Value Added

If we hypothesize that Ben's human capital as a chef is more important to the success of their restaurant business than Al's human capital as general manager, Al will be forced to sacrifice his share of the firm's value added to give Ben more incentive to provide human capital. Ben's share of the firm's value added will be increased to the point that the

[3] According to Grossman and Hart, it would be more efficient for Ben, the provider of more important human capital, to wholly own the restaurant and employ Al. *See* Sanford J. Grossman & Oliver D. Hart, *The Cost and Benefit of Ownership: A Theory of Vertical and Lateral Integration*, 94 J. POL. ECON. 691 (1986). However, in cases where both partners' human capital are indispensable, as in this case where not only Ben's incentive but also Al's incentive will directly affect the success of the business, a jointly owned firm is not necessarily inefficient. *See* Eric Maskin & Jean Tirole, *The Remarks in the Property Rights Literature*, 66 REV. ECON. STUD. 139 (1999).

increase in the firm's value added by increasing Ben's incentive and the decrease in Al's share of the firm's value added are balanced. Ben's share of the firm's value added can be increased by either increasing his dividend or increasing his compensation.

1.1.4 *Bargaining over Sharing Control*

In firms where monetary capital providers and human capital providers are separated, the major issue of bargaining over sharing control is how to balance the autonomy of human capital providers and the monitoring power of monetary capital providers. In this joint project, however, human and monetary capital are not separated. Therefore, each partner seeks autonomy when deciding how to use their monetary capital as a human capital provider; each partner also seeks monitoring power regarding the ways of using monetary capital as a monetary capital provider.

The specific items when bargaining to share control are: how to share voting rights, board membership, veto rights, and information rights.

If Al obtains the residual right of control according to his two-thirds equity, Ben will feel at risk of being squeezed out, and he will hesitate to provide human capital. To mitigate this risk, Al could give Ben some veto rights to decrease his risk.

1.1.5 *Bargaining over Exit Rights*

Strong exit rights can decrease the risk of being squeezed out but also make commitment difficult. Generally, stock corporations provide weak exit rights, and partnership provides strong exit rights.

In this joint project, the stock corporation may be a better alternative form because Ben already poses a strong threat of exit of his human capital and can make a commitment to Al by providing $100,000 to the stock corporation. However, if Ben loses his bargaining leverage in the future, for example, if his recipes become obsolete, then the risk of being squeezed out will increase.

1.2 Corporate Governance and Incentive Bargaining

In this section, I will discuss the relationship between incentive bargaining and corporate governance, as well as the role that corporate governance plays in maximizing firm value. The discussion is premised on firms with distinct monetary capital providers and human capital providers.

1.2.1 Corporate Governance in a Narrow Sense: Agency Model

In the traditional corporate governance debate, there are only two players: shareholders as the principal of the firm and management as their agent. The major issue is how shareholders monitor management for maximizing shareholder interest. I will call this concept, which is based on the agency model, "corporate governance in a narrow sense." This term is equivalent to "external governance."[4]

Shareholders can use both stick and carrot to decrease agency costs. Major sticks are hostile takeovers and independent directors to replace managers who are unable to perform effectively. Widely used carrots are equity compensation, such as stock options or restricted stock; these carrots shift the incentive of management toward that of shareholders.

Corporate governance, in a narrow sense, is useful for maximizing shareholder interest by decreasing agency costs. In this scenario, maximizing shareholder interest is the best proxy of maximizing firm value.[5]

1.2.2 Corporate Governance in a Wide Sense: Firm as an Incentive Mechanism

Corporate governance in this book is defined in a wider sense as a system for the indispensable capital providers of the firm to make incentive bargaining.[6]

1.2.2.1 Incentive Bargaining among the Four Players

Firms create value not only by having shareholders and management, but also by having creditors and employees. The firm is an ongoing joint project to which the four players (management and employees as the human capital providers, and shareholders and creditors as the monetary capital providers) provide their own capital to each other. See Figure 1.1.

Because the capital owned by each player is indispensable for the firm, if any one player hesitates to provide their capital, the firm's value added

[4] *See* Viral V. Acharya, Stewart C. Myers & Raghuram G. Rajan, *The Internal Governance of Firms*, 66 J. Fin. 689, 705 (2011).

[5] The firm value is the discounted present value of the firm's value added. *See supra* note 2.

[6] Although Reinier Kraakman, et al., The Anatomy of Corporate Law: A Comparative and Functional Approach (3d ed., 2017) is based on three agency problems, minority shareholders, creditors, and employees are viewed as passive participants, that is, parties to be legally protected. This book frames them as active players in the incentive bargaining system to maximize firm value.

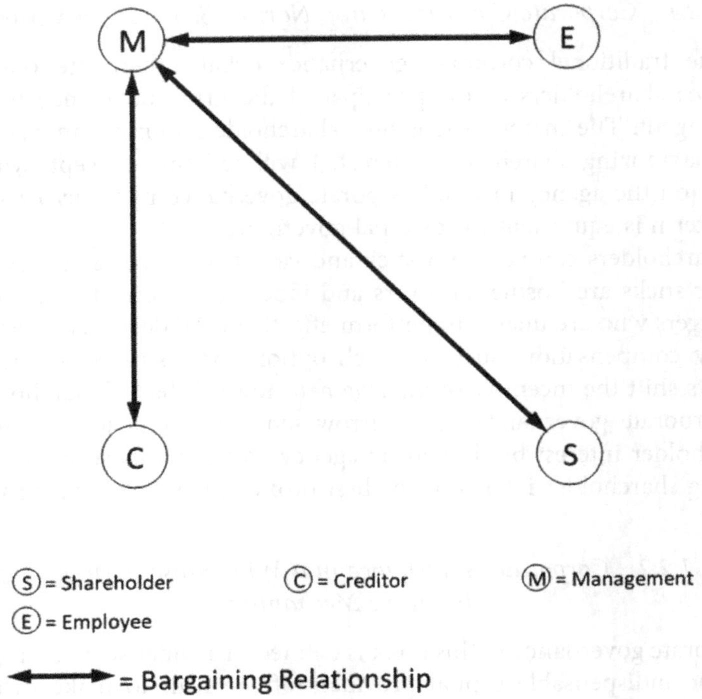

Figure 1.1 Incentive bargaining among the four players: three bilateral bargaining.

cannot be maximized. As a result, the payoff of each player cannot be maximized.[7] Therefore, the four players need to motivate each other to provide their capital to the firm for maximizing their own payoff. The issue of corporate governance in a wide sense is how to make the incentive bargaining efficient to maximize the firm's value added, which would then maximize the firm's value.[8]

Incentive bargaining among the four players in a stock corporation is made not as a multilateral bargaining but as a complex of three bilateral

[7] Although maximizing the firm's value added and sharing it among capital providers are separate issues, if a capital provider dominates, the other capital providers' incentives will be distorted, and they will not provide enough capital in the next round. Because the incentive bargaining of the firm is a repeated game, *see* Section 1.5, each capital provider needs to care for other capital providers' incentive for maximizing their own payoff. *See* Shishido, *supra* note 1, at 3; ZENICHI SHISHIDO, MUNETAKA FUKUDA & MASATO UMETANI, JOINT VENTURE STRATEGIES: DESIGN, BARGAINING, AND THE LAW 1 (2015).

[8] *See supra* note 2.

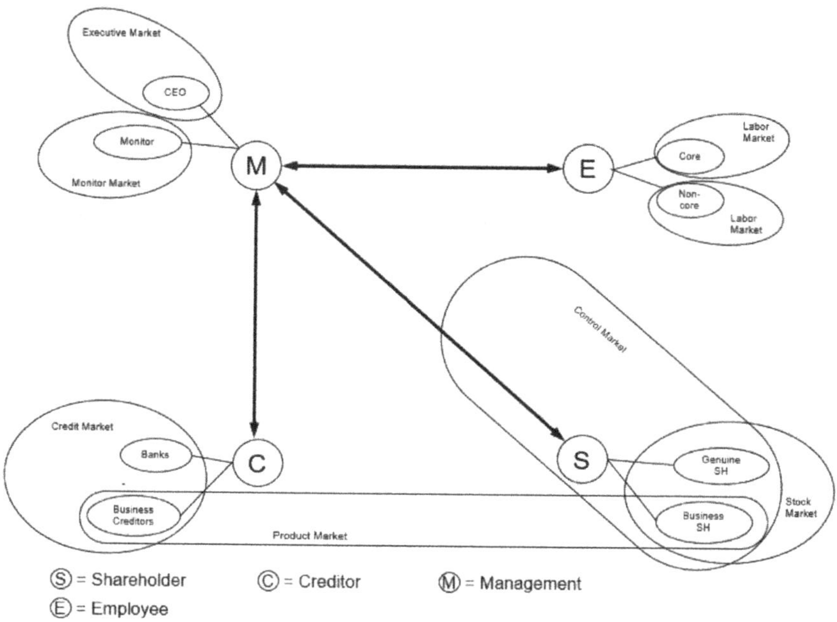

Figure 1.2 Two subcategories of each player and their relevant markets.

bargaining processes via management that function as a single bargaining window. A coalition may be formed between some of the four players which I will discuss in later in this chapter. Therefore, there are three bargaining relationships in the firm: that between employees and management; that between creditors and management; and that between shareholders and management. *See* Figure 1.1.

Although this section has already identified the four indispensable capital providers of a firm, it is necessary to further divide each player into two subcategories to better understand the effects of the relevant market on each player. *See* Figure 1.2.

Management can be divided into executives, such as CEOs, and monitors, like independent directors. CEOs and independent directors constitute the board and make important business judgments together, but the CEO initiates and executes business plans, and the independent directors ratify the plans and review the results of their execution. Because of the different roles of management, the incentives of and markets for CEOs and independent directors are different.

Employees can be divided into core employees and non-core employees. The labor market, which influences employee incentives, can also be divided into the labor market for core employees and that for non-core employees.

Creditors can be divided into secured creditors, such as banks, and unsecured creditors, such as most business creditors and most bondholders. The credit market influences the incentives of both banks and bondholders, while the incentives of the business creditor are mainly influenced by the product market.

Shareholders can be separated into genuine shareholders and business shareholders.[9] The stock market influences the incentives of both genuine shareholders and business shareholders. The incentives of business shareholders are also influenced by the product market. Both types of shareholders create the control market, which influences the incentives of both types of shareholders.

1.2.2.2 Tradeoff between Internal Governance and External Governance

The traditional corporate governance debate ignores an important incentive bargaining process that adds value to a firm: the incentive bargaining between management and core employees, such as middle managers. There are two key aspects that define the incentive bargaining between management and core employees.

One aspect is a bottom-up monitoring of the top manager by core employees. This is the case where core employees may have a longer time horizon when compared to the top manager, who is likely to retire soon. In such cases, the top manager tends to be more focused on short-term goals while core employees are likely to care about the firm's long-term prospects since they have a stake in its future. Here, even this myopic top manager will be implicitly pressured to consider the firm's future to convince core employees that they should follow her leadership.[10]

[9] Genuine shareholders, such as institutional investors, buy and sell stocks, and exercise their voting rights solely in consideration of maximizing their investment return. Business shareholders place a higher priority on their business relationship with the issuing company rather than on maximizing their investment return. Most business shareholders are cross-holding shareholders in Japan. *See* Shishido, *supra* note 1, at 12.

[10] *See* Takaaki Eguchi & Zenichi Shishido, *The Future of Japanese Corporate Governance; Japan's Internal Governance and Development of Japanese-style External Governance through Engagement*, *in* RESEARCH HANDBOOK OF SHAREHOLDER POWER 552, 554 (Jennifer G. Hill & Randall S. Thomas eds., 2015).

This type of core employee bottom-up monitoring is called "internal governance."[11]

Another aspect is that the top manager's commitment to maximize long-term firm value will motivate core employees to providing their human capital to the firm, particularly firm-specific human capital.[12]

Although both internal governance and external governance are indispensable for creating firm value, there is a tradeoff between them.[13] This tradeoff is equivalent to the tradeoff between the autonomy of human capital providers, particularly management, and the monitoring power of monetary capital providers, particularly shareholders.

Too strong monitoring will distort management to make firm-specific investments, such as initiating and executing a long-term project. Firms need to give management a certain autonomy to let them pursue their vision.[14] Contrastingly, too strong monitoring power will also make management risk averse and even give management an incentive to manipulate information.[15] Goshen and Squire argue that not only the agent (management) but also the principal (shareholders) may make mistakes, for example, shareholder may replace management too quickly. They call this potential mistake the principal cost.[16]

To maximize firm value, a firm must decide on the optimal balance of internal governance and external governance, and this decision depends

[11] Internal governance is monitoring management by core employees, while external governance is monitoring management by shareholders. *See* Acharya et al., *supra* note 4, at 690.

[12] How to give human capital providers incentives to make firm-specific investments that contribute to increasing the firm value is a hidden problem of corporate governance. American efforts to give managers and core employees such incentives are various equity compensation packages, such as stock options and restricted stocks. The Japanese answer to this question makes employees quasi-residual claimants, without making them shareholders. So-called lifetime employment practice, seniority pay practice, and strong employment protection law make it possible for management to commit to employees' long-term rewards. *See* Zenichi Shishido, *Japanese Corporate Governance: The Hidden Problems of Corporate Law and Their Solutions*, 25 DEL. J. CORP. L. 189, 211–214 (2000).

[13] *See* Acharya et al., *supra* note 4, at 713.

[14] *See* Zohar Goshen & Assaf Hamdani, *Corporate Control and Idiosyncratic Vison*, 125 YALE L. J. 125 (2016).

[15] *See* Benjamin Hermalin, *Transparency and Corporate Governance, in* ENTERPRISE LAW: CONTRACTS, MARKETS, AND LAWS IN THE US AND JAPAN 342 (Zenichi Shishido ed., 2014).

[16] *See* Zohar Goshen & Richard Squire, *Principal Costs: A New Theory for Corporate Law and Governance*, 117 COLUM. L. REV. 767 (2017).

on the characteristic and environment of each firm. The choice will also be made by the incentive bargaining among the four players.

1.3 Enterprise Law as an Infrastructure of the Incentive Bargaining

The system of incentive bargaining will be endogenously selected by the incentive bargaining, which is affected by exogenous factors that include markets (product, capital, and labor), social norms, and law. They complementarily affect the endogenous selection.

The law that is an infrastructure of the incentive bargaining is called "enterprise law" in this book. Enterprise law is a set of different areas of law, which will complementarily affect the incentive bargaining of the firm including corporate law, securities regulation, banking law, tax law, employment law, bankruptcy law, intellectual property law, antitrust law, and soft laws, such as corporate governance codes and stewardship codes.

Enterprise law affects bargaining between the four capital providers in three ways. First, it may directly affect the incentive of a specific player.[17] Second, it may affect the relative bargaining power between two players and consequently increase or decrease the risk borne by each player.[18] And third, it may affect the coalition between two players.[19]

While an adequate legislative policy will be able to stimulate the incentive bargaining among the four players, which will lead to maximizing the firm value, an inadequate legislative policy will distort some players' incentives and disturb the increase of the firm's value.

1.4 Three Incentive Patterns and Divergence of Internalized Governance

The differences between the functional corporate governance practices of different countries will be revealed as resulting from differences in the incentive bargaining practices among the four players in these countries, particularly in the way coalitions are constructed among the four players.

17 For example, subjecting management to strict liability will give management an incentive to take less risk.

18 For example, shareholders' voting rights provided for by corporate law strengthen shareholders' bargaining power with management and decrease the risk of providing monetary capital to corporations.

19 For example, strong employment protection laws encourage employees and management to create a coalition.

The optimal internalized governance system, that is, incentive patterns, will diverge depending upon exogenous factors, namely, markets (capital, labor, and product); social norms; and laws. There is also the possibility of the coexistence of multiple internalized governance systems in a single country, depending upon the industry sector and the growth stage of the company. Different degrees of significance of firm-specific investment in each industry sector will be particularly influential on the choice of optimal internalized governance system.

1.4.1 Balancing Image

The basic incentive pattern is the balancing image, in which no coalition can be organized. Each player monitors management to maximize their own interest. Management will accordingly try to balance the pressure from different players and, as a consequence, run the firm toward the direction in which the compound vectors of monitoring points. The length of each vector, which indicates the strength of pressure, depends upon the overall bargaining power of the relevant player, which is in large part determined by markets, social norms, and law. *See* Figure 1.3.

The balancing image is the prototype of the public corporation because it can flexibly take dispersed interests into account. In many respects, this is similar to Berle and Means' "management control" company.[20] Management will be strong as a single window of the incentive bargaining, and it is not necessarily neutral, but has its own private benefit.

In large German companies, the incentive bargaining process seems to be in line with the balancing image introduced in this chapter. Co-determination law requires large corporations to have a supervisory board of which half of its members are representatives of shareholders and the other half are representatives of employees. In practice, most German listed companies have controlling shareholders, and it is considered necessary to counterbalance employee interests on the board.[21] The German supervisory board is the formal place of balancing incentive bargaining.

[20] Adolf A. Berle & Gerdiner C. Means, The Modern Corporation and Private Property (1932).

[21] *See* Franz Waldenberger, *Management in Germany – Control and Incentive Mechanism* (German Institute for Japanese Studies Working Paper, 2017).

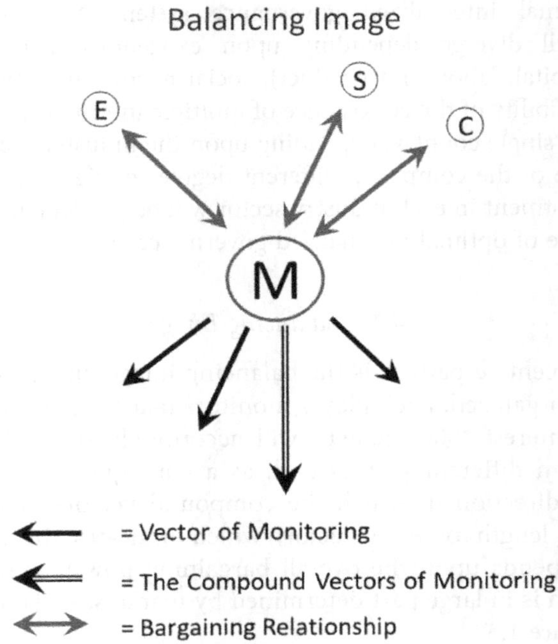

Figure 1.3 The balancing image incentive pattern.

1.4.2 *Monitoring Image*

In the monitoring image incentive pattern, shareholders and management create a coalition. Creditors and employees are motivated via markets and are not involved in corporate governance. *See* Figure 1.4.

In most public companies in the United States, the incentive bargaining seems to be in line with the monitoring image. The United States utilizes the agency model as a social norm and views shareholders as the owners who monitor their agent management to ensure that the firm is being run in the best interest of the shareholders. Liquid capital markets and external labor markets also utilize the monitoring image to work efficiently. The monitoring image incentive pattern best fits industries with low necessity of firm-specific investments.

1.4.3 *Bargaining Image*

In the bargaining image incentive pattern, there are two coalitions: the coalition between management and employees (the team of human

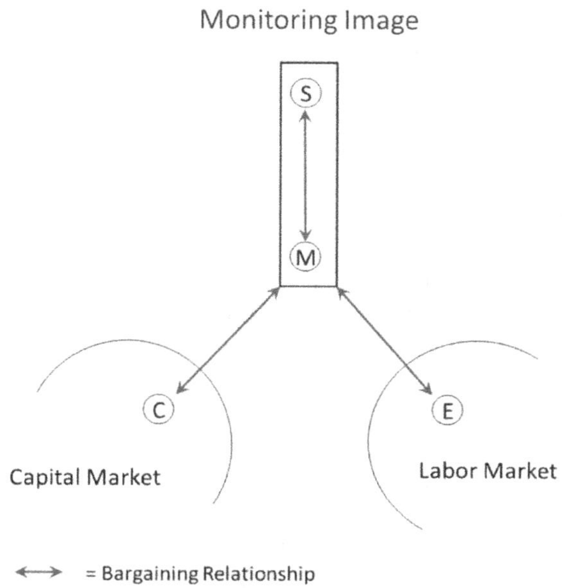

Figure 1.4 The monitoring image incentive pattern.

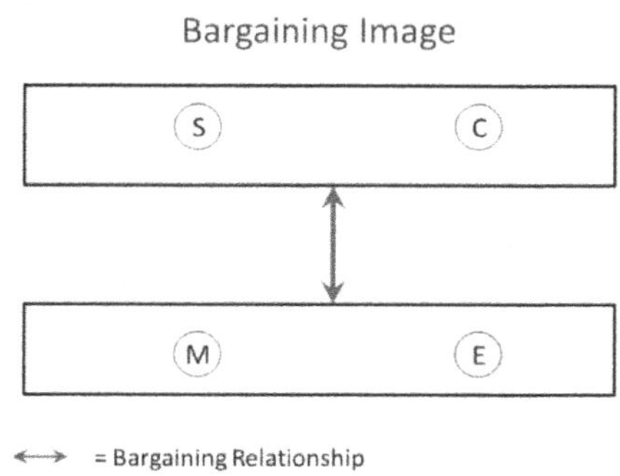

Figure 1.5 The bargaining image incentive pattern.

capital providers) and the coalition between shareholders and creditors (the team of monetary capital providers). The two teams bargain with each other via the representative of each team. *See* Figure 1.5.

The typical bargaining image incentive pattern can be found in venture capital investments in Silicon Valley and the Japanese main bank model. It fits industries with a high necessity of firm-specific investments and high-growth companies. It cannot be maintained when the cost of creating and maintaining these coalitions becomes too expensive.

1.5 Repeated Game

The incentive bargaining of the firm is a repeated game. In Stage 0, the four players design contracts establishing incentive patterns. They also agree on methods for sharing control and value added. In Stage 1, each player provides their own capital while management executes the business plan. In Stage 2, the players monitor each other and share the realized value added. Management also proposes financing and business plans for the next stage. And in Stage 3, the players usually return to Stage 1, but in end game scenarios, they return to Stage 0 if shareholders assess and find that the investment was not profitable in a way that risks a hostile takeover or insolvency. *See* Figure 1.6.

Stage 0 is the bargaining stage before contracts are entered into. Which incentive patterns a firm adopts is largely influenced by the importance of firm-specific investments in the industry, the liquidity of the external labor markets, social norms, and laws and practices that encourage or discourage coalitions among the players. Sharing control among the players in a way that reduces the risk to each player is particularly influenced by corporate law, bankruptcy law, and labor law. Sharing value added in a way that creates positive incentives between each of the players is influenced by each player's market power and characteristics prior to contract formation.

Stage 0 – Bargain before Contract

- Design contracts establishing incentive patterns
- Agreements for sharing control and sharing value added

Stage 1 – Execution

- Each player provides capital
- Execution and monitoring

Stage 2 – Monitoring

- Players share value added
- Management proposes plan for next stage

Stage 3 – End Game

- Usually, start again from Stage 1
- Possibly, return to Stage 0

Figure 1.6 Stages of the incentive bargaining repeated game.

Stage 1 is the execution stage. Each player provides capital to the firm based on the agreements made in Stage 0. However, the potential for renegotiation in the future will distort the incentive of the players, particularly employees, when they provide their capital. Management then executes the business plan.

Stage 2 is the after-contract stage of bargaining, which includes both monitoring and renegotiation. The provision of human capital needs to be monitored; employees are monitored by management, and management is monitored by shareholders and creditors. Overly aggressive monitoring, however, discourages human capital providers from making firm-specific investments. Furthermore, balancing autonomy and monitoring is important, and renegotiations are frequently necessary. Changing employment contracts is a typical form of renegotiation. Financing decisions also involve an aspect of renegotiation, including the choice between debt finance and equity finance and the choice between distributing dividends and retaining earnings.

Stage 3 is possibly the end-game stage between human capital providers and monetary capital providers. Legal regulation is indispensable here because serious conflicting interests will occur at this stage. Legislation plays a vital role in maintaining a good balance between buyers and sellers in takeover regulations, and between the *ex ante* and *ex post* incentives of the players in bankruptcy regulations.

1.6 State/Government's Role

This book will include the state/government (herein after the state)[22] as the fifth player of this game in the sense that the state provides indispensable resources (physical and legal infrastructures) to the firm, shares the pie as tax, and bargains with the other four players. The state is, however, a unique player, compared with the other four players, because of its unique channels of bargaining and its macro-level incentive. Therefore, this book will view the firm as a forum for incentive bargaining among the four players and consider that the state participates in the micro-level incentive bargaining from outside the forum. The state needs to provide the optimal infrastructure for incentive bargaining among the four

[22] Although the term "government" is usually used to represent the public actor that influences the incentive bargaining in the business sector, this book will uniformly use the term "state" to represent the public actor that participates the incentive bargaining of the firm in the three countries. *See* Chapter 2, n.1.

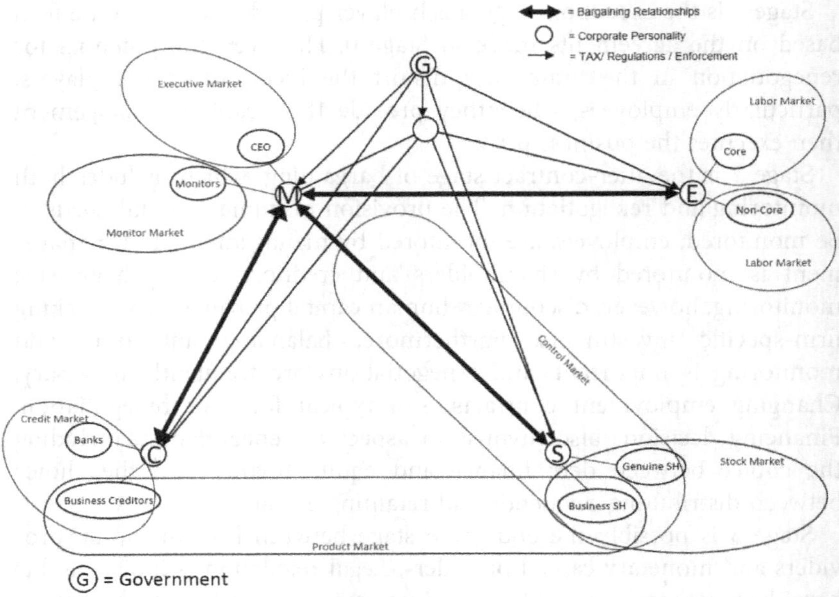

Figure 1.7 The image of the incentive bargaining, including the state/government. SH = Shareholders.

players of a firm to maximize the firm value, as a result, it could maximize economic value at the macro level (*See* Figure 1.7).

In the previous analysis by one of the authors of this book, what the state provides – such as taxation, regulation, and enforcement, as given foundational components of the incentive bargaining among the four players – and the state does not act as a fifth player.[23] In the real world, however, the four players could influence decision-making of the state. Also, for making the state create a legal system which stimulates an efficient incentive bargaining at the firm level and enhances the efficiency of the whole economy, we need to consider how to lead the state to take the ideal legislative policy. For that purpose, we need to take the state as the fifth player.

In Chapter 2, this book will adapt this framework to the three countries and provide the image of incentive bargaining with the state as the fifth player. In Chapter 11, this book will introduce the arguments of the political economy of law-making and analyze the incentives of lawmakers.

[23] *See* Shishido, *supra* note 1, at 11.

2

Corporate Governance and State

Section 1.6 of Chapter 1 provides the framework to analyze the incentive bargaining of the firm, including the state, or the government,[1] as the fifth player, that is a framework to view the firm as a forum for incentive bargaining among the four players and to consider that the state participates in the micro-level incentive bargaining from outside of the forum. Chapter 2 will adapt the framework to the three countries and compare the three different incentive mechanisms of the firm, including the state.

Section 2.1 compares the role of the state that directly affects the incentives of management, particularly through industrial policy in the three countries. Section 2.2 provides the images of the three different business systems including the state of the three countries, focusing on the incentive patterns.

2.1 The Role of the State in the United States, Japan, and China

The role of the state is very wide, including national security, road construction, water and sewage, coin mining, court system, social welfare, education, etc. Although these roles influence business corporations by providing the infrastructures for doing business in the country, this chapter focuses on the role of the state that directly affects the incentive bargaining of the firm, particularly, the incentive of management, such as regulations on corporate governance, regulation on employment, taxes, subsidizations, procurements, antitrust policy, and industrial policy.

[1] Although the term "government" is usually used to represent the public actor that influences the incentive bargaining in the business sector, the major public actor of each country is different: the Congress and each state are important actors in the United States; ministries of central government are most influential in Japan; and the Communist Party and the State inseparably exercise overwhelming influence in China. Therefore, this chapter will uniformly use the term "state" to represent the public actor that participates in the incentive bargaining of the firm in the three countries.

2.1.1 The United States

2.1.1.1 Federal Government's Support

The United State's industrial policy can be traced back to the New Deal initiated by Franklin Roosevelt during the great depression in 1933. The main theme of the New Deal is coordinated economic growth and industrial cooperation.[2] Roosevelt installed a new set of industrial policies. The passage of the National Industrial Recovery Act (NIRA) on June 16, 1933, created the National Recovery Administration (NRA), which encouraged firms to form federally backed industry cartels that would write "codes of fair competition" composed of pricing agreements and production restrictions.[3] The NRA was tasked to set up an industry section paralleling each major industry group that had written a code (e.g., steel and textiles) to oversee the operation of the code and to regulate production practices across enterprises.[4] Every code was required to include provisions ensuring workers' minimum wage and maximum hours, as well as a Section (7a) guarantee of the right of employees, "to organize and bargain collectively through representatives of their own choosing."[5] Moreover, a new agency was created, the Federal Emergency Relief Administration (FERA), to distribute $500 million in aid over two years to existing state and local public relief agencies.[6]

During the Cold War, the military played an essential role in connecting key industrial actors.[7] For example, new nuclear weapons labs, including Lawrence Livermore and Sandia, pushed atomic development, and the need for an air defense system accelerated real-time computing through the Whirlwind and SAGE (Semi-Automatic Ground Environment) projects.[8] The 1957 Sputnik crisis led to the creation in 1958 of the National Aeronautics and Space Administration (NASA) and the Defense Advanced Research Projects Agency (DARPA). NASA's

[2] *See* Frank R. Dobbin, *The Social Construction of the Great Depression: Industrial Policy during the 1930s in the United States, Britain, and France*, 22 Theory & Soc'y 1, 13 (1993).

[3] *Id.*

[4] *See id.*

[5] Theda Skocpol & Kenneth Finegold, *State Capacity and Economic Intervention in the Early New Deal*, 97 Pol. Sci. Q. 255, 256 (1982).

[6] Philip Harvey, *Learning from the New Deal*, 39 Rev. Black Pol. Econ. 87, 91 (2012).

[7] *See* William B. Bonvillian, *Emerging Industrial Policy Approaches in the United States*, Info. Tech. & Innovation Found. (Oct. 4, 2021), https://itif.org/publications/2021/10/04/emerging-industrial-policy-approaches-united-states/.

[8] *Id.*

push for moon landings through the Apollo Mission also created a major space technology and satellite communications sector that has been commercialized on a large scale.[9] This system of defense support for technology development and follow-on product procurement played a significant role in most of the major technology innovations in areas such as aviation, space, nuclear power, electronics, computing, and the Internet.[10]

The research and development (R&D) tax credit was enacted in 1981 to incentivize innovation by US companies, rewarding them for increasing their investment in R&D in the current tax year.[11] The Small Business Innovation Research (SBIR) program was introduced in 1982, which offers competitive R&D grant funding to small and startup companies. A related program, the Small Business Technology Transfer (STTR) program focuses on university-originated startups.[12] SBIR and STTR distribute over $3 billion to small businesses annually.[13]

2.1.1.2 Federal Regulations and Legislation

The Department of Labor's amendment of the Employee Retirement Income Security Act (ERISA) in 1979 to the "prudent man" rule governing pension fund investments significantly increased funds flowing into the venture capital (VC) industry during the late 1970s and early 1980s.[14] Before 1979, ERISA prohibited pension funds from investing vast amounts of money into venture capital or other high-risk asset classes.[15] The Department of Labor's clarification of the rule explicitly allowed pension managers to invest in high-risk assets, including venture capital.[16] Initially, corporate pension funds made small allocations to venture capital in the 1980s.[17] This was followed a decade later by US public pension funds.[18] The significant size of the assets held by corporate and public pension funds suggests that even a small share of

9 *See id.*
10 *See id.*
11 *See id.*
12 *See id.*
13 *Id.*
14 Samuel Kortum & Josh Lerner, *Assessing the Contribution of Venture Capital*, 31 RAND J. ECON. 674, 676 (2000).
15 *See id.*
16 *See id.*
17 *See* William H. Janeway, Ramana Nanda & Matthew Rhodes-Kropf, *Venture Capital Booms and Start-up Financing*, 13 ANN. REV. FIN. ECON. 111, 116 (2021).
18 *See id.*

their portfolio allocation to venture capital could mean a substantial amount of funds raised by venture capital investors.[19]

The Bayh-Dole Act of 1980 assigned ownership of federally funded research results to the universities where the research was carried out and gave universities a stake in its commercialization.[20] The Act facilitates the growth of the biotech sector since biotech companies frequently originate from university research.[21]

The Creating Helpful Incentives to Produce Semiconductors and Science Act of 2022 (CHIPS Act) was signed into law on August 9, 2022, to stimulate investments in US domestic semiconductor manufacturing capacity.[22] The CHIPS Act directs $280 billion in spending over the next decade;[23] $200 billion is for scientific R&D and commercialization.[24] $52.7 billion is for semiconductor manufacturing, R&D, and workforce development, with another $24 billion worth of tax credits for chip production. $3 billion is for programs aimed at leading-edge technology and wireless supply chains.[25]

2.1.1.3 Individual States' Industrial Policy

Many proposals for a national industrial policy appeared in the 1990s in the United States in response to slow economic growth, international competition, and the restructuring of production, the decline of Keynesianism, and the claims of supply side economics.[26] Some state governments, faced with declining federal transfers and a severe recession, acted on their own to stimulate economic development.[27]

One example of a comprehensive state-level industrial policy is Rhode Island's Greenhouse Compact, a $750 million comprehensive economic development plan designed to create 60,000 new jobs and raise average

[19] *See id.*
[20] *See* Bonvillian, *supra* note 7.
[21] *See id.*
[22] *See* Justin Badlam, Stephen Clark, Suhrid Gajendragadkar, Adi Kumar, Sara O'Rourke & Dale Swartz, *The CHIPS and Science Act: Here's What's in It*, McKinsey & Co. (Oct. 4, 2022), https://www.mckinsey.com/industries/public-sector/our-insights/the-chips-and-science-act-heres-whats-in-it.
[23] *Id.*
[24] *Id.*
[25] *Id.*
[26] *See* Hilary Silver, *Is Industrial Policy Possible in the United States? The Defeat of Rhode Island's Greenhouse Compact*, 15 Pol. & Soc'y 333, 333 (1987).
[27] *See id.*

wages in the state.[28] The Greenhouse Compact consists of strategic planning and calls for the cooperation of groups with roles in production, particularly labor, and business, to reach a consensus on how to revitalize Rhode Island's struggling economy.[29]

Individual states also offer a variety of incentives to persuade companies like automakers to locate manufacturing facilities within their borders. For example, California's Manufacturers' Investment Credit (MIC) offers a credit against California income tax based on the purchase and use of property in a manufacturing process in California.[30] Furthermore, in 1980, Tennessee gave the Nissan Motor Manufacturing Company an economic incentive package worth $33 million ($11,000 per employee) to locate its operations in the state.[31] In 1985, Kentucky entered into a bitter competition with several other states and provided Toyota Motor Manufacturing USA with a package worth $149.7 million ($49,900 per employee).[32] In 1996, Alabama provided a total incentive, including land, worker training, site improvement, and purchase of Mercedes Benz vehicles from Mercedes Benz to host the first Mercedes plant outside of Germany.[33]

2.1.2 *Japan*

Japan's industrial policies already started around 1890, aiming for economic growth to catch up with Western countries.[34]

Before World War I, the industrial policy targeted capital-intensive industries, such as steel and shipbuilding, by using subsidization and nationalization.[35]

[28] *Id.*

[29] *Id.* at 334.

[30] *See* Juan Luis Jay Ramirez, Anwar Y. Salimi & Hassan Hefzi, *The Impact of Tax Incentives on the Location of Manufacturing Facilities*, 5 J. Bus. & Acct. 76, 76 (2012).

[31] Andrew Kolesar, *Can State and Local Tax Incentives and Other Contributions Stimulate Economic Development*, 44 Tax Law. 285, 285 (1990).

[32] *Id.*

[33] Alabama offered $77.5 million for sewer, water, and other utility improvements, $92.2 million to buy and develop the site, and about $5 million annually for employee training and other programs. Additionally, Alabama agreed to buy 2,500 Mercedes utility vehicles for use by everyone from highway construction supervisors to agricultural agents. Allen R. Myerson, *O Governor, Won't You Buy Me a Mercedes Plant?*, N.Y. Times (Sept. 1, 1996).

[34] *See* Hideaki Miyajima, Sangyo Seisaku to Kigyo Toch no Keizaishi [Economic History on Industrial Policy and Corporate Governance] 32–35 (2004).

[35] *Id.* at 467.

In the 1920s, the industrial policy targeted the industries with economies of scale, which were under control by the international oligopolistic enterprises, by using subsidization and tariffs. It was a rather liberal policy that considered the economies of trade.[36]

In the 1930s, the military point of view overwhelmed the consideration of the economies of trade. The industrial policy turned from liberalism to developmentalism and targeted auto, aluminum, and airplane.[37]

During World War II and just after the war, resource allocation was restricted by the economic plans. The free-market economy was regained from 1949, and the industrial structure reformation that planned to transfer resources to the target industries restarted. In 1955, the five-year economic independence plan was made and targeted the growth industries, which were steel, oil, chemical, artificial fiber, auto, electric machinery, and machine tools. The protectionist policy by shutting out foreign competitors, offering low-interest loans, tax exemptions, etc. decreased the risk of business corporations and incentivized them to make capital investments in industries with economies of scale.[38]

Although the economic growth got on the right track from 1956 until the middle of the 1960s some factors of the post-war controlled economy remained, particularly regulation on imports for decreasing the deficit of the international balance of payment.[39]

From the middle of the 1960s to the recovery from the oil shock, which occurred in 1973, the administrative guidance[40] was the major tool of industrial policy. Then the focus of industrial policy gradually turned toward the improvement of market rules.[41]

In the 1970s, pollution turned to be a serious problem and the administrative guidance aimed to change the industrial structure

36 *Id.* at 467–468.

37 *Id.* at 468.

38 *Id.* at 469.

39 *See* Konosuke Odaka, Tsusho Sangyo Seisakushi 1980–2000 Soron [Political History of the Industrial Policy 1980–2000 General Remarks] 311 (2013).

40 According to Chalmers Johnson, the administrative guidance refers to "the authority of the government, containing in the laws establishing the various ministries, to issue directive (*shiji*), requests (*yobo*), warning (*keikoku*), suggestions (*kankoku*), and encouragements (*kansho*) to the enterprises or clients within a particular ministry's jurisdiction. . . .although it is not based on any explicit law, it cannot violate the law." Chalmers Johnson, MITI and the Japanese Miracle: The Growth of Industrial Policy, 1925–1975 265 (1st ed., Tuttle 1986).

41 Odaka, *supra* note 39, at 311.

from the energy-intensive industries to the knowledge-intensive industries.[42]

In the early 1980s, the industrial policy targeted specific industries as a whole being accompanied by exemptions of the Anti-Monopoly Act. Such a traditional industrial policy was criticized as unfair by foreign countries along with the increased presence of the Japanese economy.[43]

Because of international criticism and the Japanese government's principle of international cooperation, the Japanese industrial policy has been changed since the late 1980s.[44] The Act of Streamlining the Change of Industry Structure of 1987 targeted not a specific industry as a whole, but a specific enterprise and a specific region, without using the exemption of the Anti-Monopoly Act. Such characteristics have been succeeded by the industrial policy in the 1990s.[45]

After the 1990s, the focus of the industrial policy has moved from nurturing specific industries and specific enterprises to the reforming economic structure by deregulation and improvement of institutional infrastructures.[46]

Serious deregulation was started by the Hashimoto administration from 1996 to 1997 and accelerated by the Koizumi administration from 2001 to 2006, including the privatization of the post office and enactment of the Companies Act of 2005, which changed the nature of corporate law from mandatory law to enabling law.[47]

The Abe administration (the second to the fourth) from 2012 to 2020 tried to improve the institutional infrastructure of corporate governance. It initiated the "Corporate Governance Reform" in 2013 and published the Stewardship Code of 2014 and the Corporate Governance Code of 2015, which pushed Japanese management toward shareholder primacy.

The Abe administration also actively expanded the industrial policy, aiming for economic growth by using the "new targeting policy," which

42 *Id.* at 311, 313.

43 *See* Tetsuji Okazaki, Keizaishi kara Kangaeru Hatten to Teitai no Ronnri [Considering the Logic of Development and Stagnation from the Perspective of Economic History] 121 (2017).

44 *See* U.S.-Japan Structural Impediments Initiative (1989–1990). Odaka, *supra* note 39, at 312.

45 Okazaki, *supra* note 43, at 121–122.

46 Odaka, *supra* note 39, at 312; Okazaki, *supra* note 43, at 122.

47 The Companies Act of 2005 deregulated the stock option and the preferred stock, which enabled Japanese startup and VC industry to use Silicon Valley type equity incentive. *See* Zenichi Shishido, *Does Law Matter to Financial Capitalism?: The Case of Japanese Entrepreneurs*, 37 Fordham Int'l L. J. 1087, 1094–1098 (2014).

means the revival of the traditional industrial policy, aiming at nurturing specific industries.[48]

Such a new trend of targeting policy is observed not only in Japan, but also in the United States, which disclosed the direction to nurture innovation in specific areas, such as clean energy, biotechnology, and medical care.[49] It is economically reasonable for the government to subsidize for stimulating the incentive of capital investment to the specific technologies that are associated with economic externality.[50]

The Kishida Administration, starting from 2021, initiated the Five-year Program of Promoting Startups in 2023, which tries to improve the institutional infrastructure of startups and VC investments, including a one-trillion-yen (approximately $67 billion) budget for subsidizing the VC industry.

Comparative to the United States, the Japanese government has historically taken strong leadership.[51] The Japanese government has exercised a greater degree of both intervention and protection for the shift of industrial structure.[52]

Regarding the government approach to private enterprises, the US government focuses on monitoring and revealing misconduct of private enterprises, whereas the Japanese government focuses on providing a private enterprise environment to develop long-term projects.[53] In other words, the United States is a regulatory, or market-rational, state that concerns itself with the rules but does not concern itself with substantive matters, whereas Japan is a developmental, or plan-rational, state that has its dominant feature the setting of substantive social and economic goals.[54]

In the post-war development stage, the Japanese government did not normally give direct orders to private enterprises, but those enterprises that listened to the signal coming from the government and then

48 Okazaki, *supra* note 43, at 120, 122.

49 *See* National Economic Council, Council of Economic Advisers & Office of Science and Technology Policy, A Strategy for American Innovation: Securing Our Economic Growth and Prosperity (Feb. 2011).

50 Okazaki, *supra* note 43, at 123–124.

51 *See* Ezra F. Vogel, Japan as Number One: Lessons for America 24 (1979).

52 *See* Johnson, *supra* note 40, at 31.

53 Vogel, *supra* note 51, at 91–92.

54 *See* Johnson, *supra* note 40, at 19. That difference relates to the difference of governmental decision-making in the both countries: an elite bureaucracy centered in Japan and a parliamentary assembly centered in the US. *Id.* at 22,

responded were favored with easy access to capital, tax breaks, and approval of their plans to import foreign technology or establish joint ventures. However, an enterprise did not have to respond to the government.[55]

Regarding the relationship between central government and local governments, the United States is a state with decentralization of government to local jurisdiction, while Japan is a state with centralized government. The central government shows guidelines to local governments and allows local governments autonomy for execution.[56]

2.1.3 China

Modern Chinese industrial policy started much later compared to the United States and Japan because China had not adopted the market economy until the Reform and Opening Up of 1978. Although the Chinese government started launching some national industrial policies in the late 1980s, the quantity and sectoral coverage of national industrial programs remained quite limited.[57]

To achieve rapid industrial development, Chinese leaders from the late 1970s actively sought policy advice, advanced technology, and investment capital from abroad, particularly in Japan because Japan was widely seen as being closer and more compatible with the Chinese setting than most Western economies.[58] The perception that government guidance through non-imperative, indicative planning and industrial policies had contributed to Japan's rapid economic rise made Japanese experiences attractive to state-centric policy-makers in China.[59] A market-oriented approach to industrial policy was proposed by the Economic Structural Reform Institute (ESRI) founded in 1982 as a think tank for reformist Premier Zhao Ziyang and affiliated with the State Structural Reform Commission.[60] ESRI borrowed and pushed the particular Japanese institution of government-business "deliberation councils" (*shingikai/shenyihui*) with the aim of informal, non-hierarchical coordination of

[55] *See id.* at 24.
[56] *See* VOGEL, *supra* note 51, at 116–118.
[57] *See* Sebastian Heilmann & Lea Shih, *The Rise of Industrial Policy in China, 1978–2012*, 17 HARVARD-YENCHING INST. WORKING PAPER SER. 1, 3 (2013).
[58] *See id.* at 5.
[59] *Id.*
[60] *Id.* at 8.

economic policies.[61] China's first industrial association in 1979 and a more comprehensive one, mimicking Japan's Keidanren, in 1988 (the China Federation of Industrial Economics) serve as links between government bodies and enterprises.[62]

Industrial policy was elevated to an official instrument of economic reform already in China's seventh five-year plan for the 1986–1990 period.[63] In 1989 and 1994, the newly founded Industrial Policy Division of the State Planning Commission issued two pioneering programs that aimed at a comprehensive restructuring and upgrading of industrial organization.[64] However, due to a lack of prerequisites and expertise, the explorative industrial policy programs of the 1980s and 1990s failed at an early stage.[65] Despite these implementation failures, research on sectoral restructuring and upgrading was energetically pursued and deepened during the 1990s, in the reformed State Planning Commission, the newly merged State Economic and Trade Commission (SETC).[66]

Apart from Japan, China also learned industrial policy from Singapore via several national collaboration projects, and Singapore became the largest foreign direct investor in China since 2014.[67] These projects include China–Singapore Suzhou Industrial Park (SIP) in 1994, the Sino-Singapore Tianjin Ecocity in 2007, Sino-Singapore Guangzhou Knowledge City in 2010, and Chongqing Connectivity Initiative in 2015.[68]

[61] *Id.*
[62] *Id.*
[63] *Id.* at 10.
[64] *Id.*
[65] *Id.*
[66] *Id.*
[67] *See* Hong Liu & Ting-Yan Wang, *The Institutionalization and Effectiveness of Transnational Policy Transfer: The China–Singapore Suzhou Industrial Park as a Case Study*, 41 Pub. Admin. & Dev. 103, 103 (2021).
[68] The SIP's GDP in 2018 reached 257 billion RMB (approximately US$38.8 billion), contributing to 14 percent of Suzhou's total GDP, although the SIP only occupies 3.4 percent of Suzhou's land areas. By the end of 2017, the SIP had a population of 813,000, with 774,259 being fully employed, much higher than the initial employment projection of 360,000. SIP is a successful example of transnational policy transfer from Singapore to China in terms of economic performance and job creation. The Chinese State Council designated in 2015 the SIP as the country's first "open innovation" pilot zone, with the expectation that it would serve as a pioneering example of industrial upgrading and an innovation-driven economy for the rest of the country. The key to the success of SIP is its combination of "hardware" and "software." In terms of hardware, many advanced

Singapore's capability in attracting foreign investors, managing a self-contained industrial and residential district, pro-business regulations, proactive marketing skills, service-oriented attitudes toward investors, people-centered social management, and even officials' behaviors in daily work suited China's needs at that time.[69] More than 110 regulations, rules, and standards – covering economic development, urban planning, and management and public administration – were transferred and adapted to China's local context from 1994 to 2019.[70] Many of these regulations and practices were later applied in other cities nationwide.[71] By 2019, about 3,800 Chinese officials[72] (in 200 batches) had been trained in Singapore.[73] They not only brought back marketing knowledge and management skills, but also helped formulate policies and standards modeled after Singapore's practice.[74]

The change of top government leaders in 2002–2003 and the massive stimulus packages in the context of the global economic downturn in 2008–2009 led to a significant rise in national programs from 2004 and from 2009 onwards.[75] China's modern domestic industrial policies have expanded with three observable trends.[76]

First, recent industrial policies have increasingly focused on technologies centered around artificial intelligence, 5G telecommunications, and smart networks.[77] China began a significant mobilization of resources for

infrastructure building standards and principles from Singapore were adopted in the SIP, such as the "ready-built factories," and the principles of "master planning for the whole zone." The SIP even built a power substation and water treatment plant for the estate's exclusive use. The high-quality urban design and infrastructure not only attracted investment and companies, but also facilitated talent attraction and retention. Liu & Wang, *supra* note 67, at 105–106.

69 China's business climate in the early 1990s was hampered by hidden regulations, and local officials had little experience in dealing with foreign investors. *See id.* at 106.

70 *Id.* at 109.

71 *See id.*

72 The recipients of training are beyond the SIP officials. While about 60 percent of the trainees were public or managerial officials from the SIP, the remainder of the participants came from various government departments and companies in Suzhou city and Jiangsu province. The trainees were required to write a report after training and to undertake sharing sessions across departments to ensure the newly acquired knowledge could spread widely. *Id.*

73 *Id.*

74 *Id.*

75 Heilmann & Shih, *supra* note 57, at 3.

76 Barry Naughton, *Chinese Industrial Policy and the Digital Silk Road*, 15 Asia Pol'y 23, 24 (2020).

77 *Id.*

industrial policy in the 2000s, starting with the 2006 Medium and Long-Term Plan for Science and Technology.[78] Since that time, the efforts and government resources going into high-tech industrial policy have steadily increased.[79] In June 2014, the Chinese Government released Guidelines to Promote National Integrated Circuit Industry (National IC Plan) which articulates a well-defined strategy that identifies "national champions" supported by sufficient funds and bolstered by policies promoting inbound and outbound foreign direct investments that are designed to accelerate technology transfer and elevate China's semiconductor industry to the same level as other leading international competitors.[80]

Apart from the National IC Fund, multiple local and regional governments have established their own IC-related funds, received capital from the National IC Fund, or invested in the National IC Fund.[81]

In 2015, the Chinese government released "Made in China 2025," an initiative designed to develop select manufacturing sectors into worldwide industry leaders.[82] A series of national and provincial funds were established to facilitate indigenous R&D, acquisition of technology from overseas, and cultivate the technology, intellectual property, and brand identity necessary to achieve this goal.[83]

The government also provides subsidies to boost the semiconductor industry, which are taken in the form of regional, provincial, and

[78] *Id.* at 27.

[79] *See id.*

[80] Notably, the 2014 Guidelines called for the establishment of a National Integrated Circuit Investment Fund (National IC Fund) endowed with $150 billion in funds from the central and provincial governments and tasked with acquiring companies throughout the semiconductor supply chain. John VerWey, *Chinese Semiconductor Industrial Policy: Past and Present*, 2019 J. Int'l Com. & Econ. 1, 13 (2019).

[81] For example, both Beijing E-Town International Investment and Development Co. (an investment vehicle owned by the municipality of Beijing) and Shanghai Guosheng Group (an investment vehicle owned by the municipality of Shanghai) have invested in the National IC Fund, while regional governments in Hubei, Fujian, and Anhui provinces have stood up IC-related investment funds of their own. As of 2017, while the National IC Fund had secured roughly $21 billion in funding, provincial and municipal IC-related funds have raised over $80 billion and are well on their way to reaching the goal of $150 billion. In 2018 news reports indicated that the National IC Fund was in talks with the Chinese government to establish a second investment vehicle valued at $47 billion. *Id.*

[82] Ten sectors, which cumulatively constitute 40 percent of China's value-added manufacturing, were identified: next-generation information technology, controlling instruments and robotics, aerospace and aviation equipment, maritime equipment and shipbuilding, railway equipment, energy-efficient and new-energy vehicles, electrical equipment, new materials, medical devices, and agricultural machinery. *Id.* at 14.

[83] *Id.*

national funds (such as the National IC fund); investment vehicles; and policies that incentivize industry investment,[84] such as tax incentives.[85] National, provincial, and city-level funding made available through the National IC Plan and Made in China 2025 has incentivized multinational corporations to establish joint ventures or expand existing partnerships.[86] Intel, SK Hynix, and Samsung are all taking advantage of subsidized loans from the Chinese government to expand their existing operations in China, while the world's three leading foundries, Global Foundries, Taiwan Semiconductor Manufacturing Company (TSMC), and United Microelectronics Corporation (UMC), have announced their intention to set up new fabrication facilities in China.[87]

Second, while policies are still state-led, the successful implementation of these policies relies on close partnerships with private firms such as Alibaba, Baidu, and Tencent.[88] China's industrial policies have increasingly involved both state-owned enterprises (SOEs) and privately-owned enterprises (POEs).[89] Chinese policymakers have been willing to support successful national champions without much concern about whether the companies are SOEs or POEs.[90] Baidu, Alibaba, Tencent, and Byte Dance are dominant Internet firms in China, and an industrial policy based on cooperating with and promoting them as national champions has gradually formed.[91]

The dominant Internet firms possess technical expertise that government agencies do not have, and the government could easily exert

[84] VerWey, *supra* note 80, at 15.

[85] According to the Notice by the State Council of Issuing the Several Policies for Promoting the High-Quality Development of the Integrated Circuit Industry and the Software Industry in the New Era issued in 2020, IC manufacturers or manufacturing projects with IC line width of twenty-eight nanometers or less and been operated for more than fifteen years shall be exempted from enterprise income tax from the first to the tenth year. IC manufacturers or manufacturing projects with an IC line width of sixty-five nanometers or less and having been operated for more than fifteen years shall be exempted from enterprise income tax from the first to the fifth year, and pay enterprise income tax at half the statutory rate of 25 percent from the sixth to the tenth year. PRC Government, The State Council Issued the Notice on Several Policies for Promoting the Integrated Circuit Industry and Developing High-Quality Software Industry (Aug. 2020), https://www.gov.cn/zhengce/content/2020-08/04/content_5532370.htm.

[86] *Id.* at 17.

[87] *Id.*

[88] Naughton, *supra* note 76, at 24.

[89] *See id.* at 28.

[90] *See id.*

[91] *Id.*

influence over these dominant Internet firms, which in turn can exert control over the entire Internet field.[92] The tripartite combination of government regulation of information, industrial-policy protectionism, and dynamic and competitive enterprises means that Chinese cyberspace is almost entirely separate from the US-dominated Internet.[93] All of the largest social media platforms used worldwide are blocked by the Chinese firewall, and their alternatives are owned and operated by Chinese companies.[94] This creates the basis for a commonality of interests and interdependence between the Chinese government and the platform companies.[95]

Third, a new wave of regional policies aims to create urban clusters that will be more efficient and less congested than regions dominated by the single large cities.[96] China has launched major redevelopment initiatives within each of the three primary urban areas that form the core of the Chinese economy.[97] These programs seek to connect multiple medium-to-large cities instead of allowing a single megacity to develop.[98]

The Chinese government's involvement in the economy is more direct compared to both the United States and Japan. While both the Chinese government and the US government seek to provide funding and tax benefits to support targeted industries, the US government seldom creates a government-owned company to participate directly in the industrial program. The Chinese government, with the participation of SOEs, sometimes directly owned a significant share of key players in the targeted industry. For example, in 2012, a consortium led by the China Investment Corporation, a SOE, raised $7.1 billion to buy back half of the 40 percent share of Alibaba owned by Yahoo.[99]

92 *Id.*
93 *See id.*
94 *See id.* at 29.
95 *See id.*
96 *See id.* at 24.
97 One industrial area is the greater Beijing–Tianjin–Hebei (Jingjinji) region, a less centralized but more integrated megalopolis. Another industrial area is the Greater Bay Area, which links Hong Kong, Shenzhen, Dongguan, Guangzhou, and Macao into a single, tightly integrated region. The third industrial area is the Yangtze River Delta Region, which includes Shanghai, Jiangsu, and Zhejiang. *See id.* at 30; *see* Mark Preen, *The Yangtze River Delta Integration Plan*, China Briefing (June 6, 2018), https://www.china-briefing.com/news/yangtze-river-delta-integration-plan/.
98 Naughton, *supra* note 76, at 31.
99 *Id.* at 30.

Moreover, while provinces in China sometimes compete with each other to attract major enterprises, their competition is much less severe compared to the individual states in the United States because Chinese provinces are still subjected to strong control of the central government. Like Japan, China is a state with a centralized government, and individual provinces are obligated to follow the central government's guidelines. Thus, the Chinese government is able to easily coordinate different provinces to form integrated industrial regions that are absent in the United States.

2.1.3.1 Legal Nature and Theoretical Justification of Chinese Industrial Policy

Industrial policies in China usually have a dual nature. First, they set concrete goals of strengthening a specific industry or sector by enhancing the overall innovative and/or production capability, preferably by establishing domestic companies that would be competitive on a global scale.[100] Second, they have more politically oriented long-term goals that characteristically involve lofty ideals aiming at self-sufficiency, technological advancement, economic sufficiency, and global leadership in technology and manufacturing.[101] The concrete, short-term goal that includes detailed, numerical targets can be understood as the stepping stone that facilitates accomplishing the long-term goal. The dual nature also manifests the Chinese Communist Party's (CCP's) latest self-conception, which philosophizes the CCP as a leader that will help China achieve modernization and rejuvenation.[102] The successful implementation of industrial policies, therefore, reinforces the moral, political, and legal legitimacy of the CCP as the ruling party in China. They are economic and industrial instruments that ultimately serve ideological and political ends.

[100] *See, e.g.*, Made in China 2025 [hereinafter MIC 2025], The National IC Plan [hereinafter IC Plan]; *see also* US Chamber of Commerce, China's Approval Process for Inbound Foreign Direct Investment: Impact on Market Access, National Treatment and Transparency, 10–11 (2012), https://www.uschamber.com/sites/default/files/final_made_in_china_2025_report_full.pdf [hereinafter US Chamber Report].

[101] MIC 2025, Art. 1(3); IC Plan, Art. 1.

[102] Chang Xuemei & Cheng Hongyi, *What Is the Resilience of the Chinese Communist Party?*, People (July 3, 2017), http://theory.people.com.cn/n1/2017/0703/c40531-29377703.html.

There are three prevailing theoretical justifications for adopting various industrial policies that facilitate the development of infant or innovative industries, and China usually cites those three in its industrial policy announcement. First, the positive spillover of knowledge, where the promotion of industries can generate substantial learning by doing economies, and it contributes to the human capital formation in developing countries.[103] Second, there can be coordination failures that justify government intervention.[104] Third, a country is capable of creating new comparative advantages and moving up along the global supply chain, thereby obtaining leadership in high value-added industries.[105]

2.1.3.2 China's Industrial Fund in the Context of Industrial Policy

Along with the industrial policy, the government funds are formed to implement the industrial policy. As far as local government funds are concerned, complex choices have to be made, such as who should be empowered to make such decisions, what sectors to invest in, and what safeguards are placed to ensure due process and fair distribution, among others.

At the central level, the government typically rallies SOEs to contribute money to form a large pool of industrial funds. The companies that have received funding are predominantly Chinese domestic companies, many of which are new players in the market dominated by established and sophisticated high-tech companies.

At the local government level, China has also witnessed an explosive growth in both the number and size of industry guiding funds. This matches administrative decentralization, which has been spotted to be the key institutional feature to shape China's taxation system[106] and

103 *See* Patricia Succar, *The Need for Industrial Policy in LDC's – A Restatement of the Infant Industry Argument*, 28 INT. ECON. R. 521 (1987).

104 *See* Howard Pack & Kamal Saggi, *The Case for Industrial Policy: A Critical Survey* 3 (Policy Research Working Paper Series 3839, The World Bank, 2006), https://siteresources.worldbank.org/INTRANETTRADE/Resources/Internal-Training/HowardPack_KamalSaggiPaper.pdf.

105 *See* Lin Yifu, *New Structural Economics: A Framework for Rethinking Development* (WORLD BANK OPEN KNOWLEDGE REPOSITORY, 2010), https://openknowledge.worldbank.org/bitstream/handle/10986/19919/WPS5197.pdf?sequence=1&isAllowed=y.

106 Wei Cui, *Administrative Decentralization and Tax Compliance: A Transactional Cost Perspective*, 65 UNIV. OF TORONTO L. J. 187, 238 (2015).

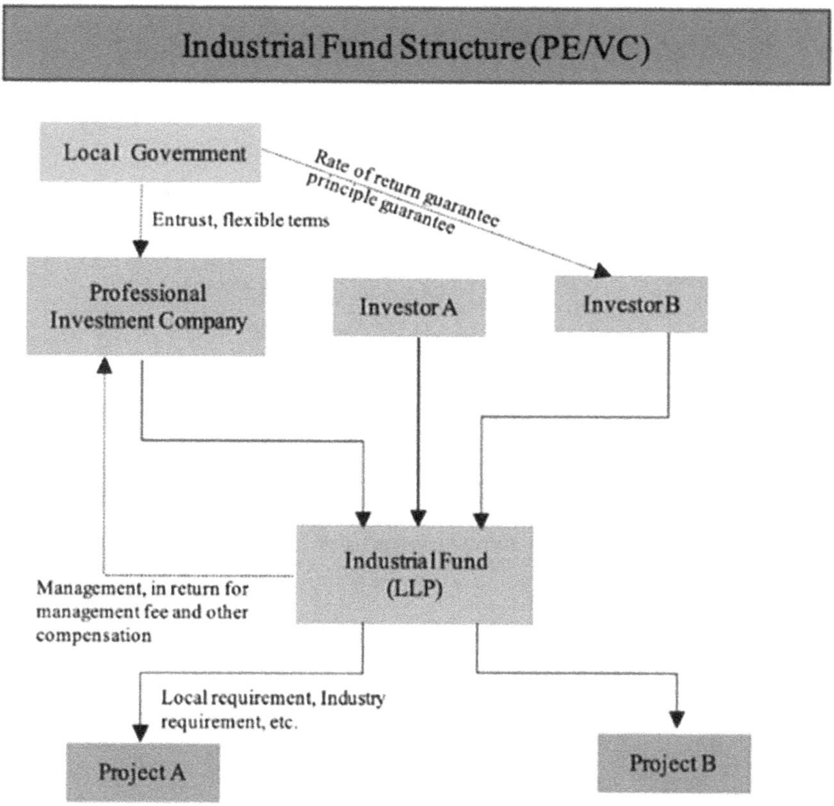

Figure 2.1 Structure of government guiding fund as PE/VC.

local spending behavior.[107] There are primarily two kinds, though their difference ultimately is negligible. The first (see Figure 2.1) is a venture

107 There are two dimensions along which a local government fund can be divided. The first dimension is the choice of entity. Just like any other investment companies, the local government funds can be organized either as a company limited by shares, a partnership or by contractual arrangement. Numerous considerations will go into the choice of entities, some of them are shared by private entities: tax, governance, control, division or responsibility and rights, which are the major considerations in choosing an appropriate business vehicle. The second dimension is the kind of investment the fund is conducting. PEZaoCan, *Analysis of Government Industrial Fund Policy and Practice Operation (Part II)*, SinaFinance (Oct. 27, 2017), https://cj.sina.com.cn/article/detail/6390473642/454172?column=fund&ch=9.

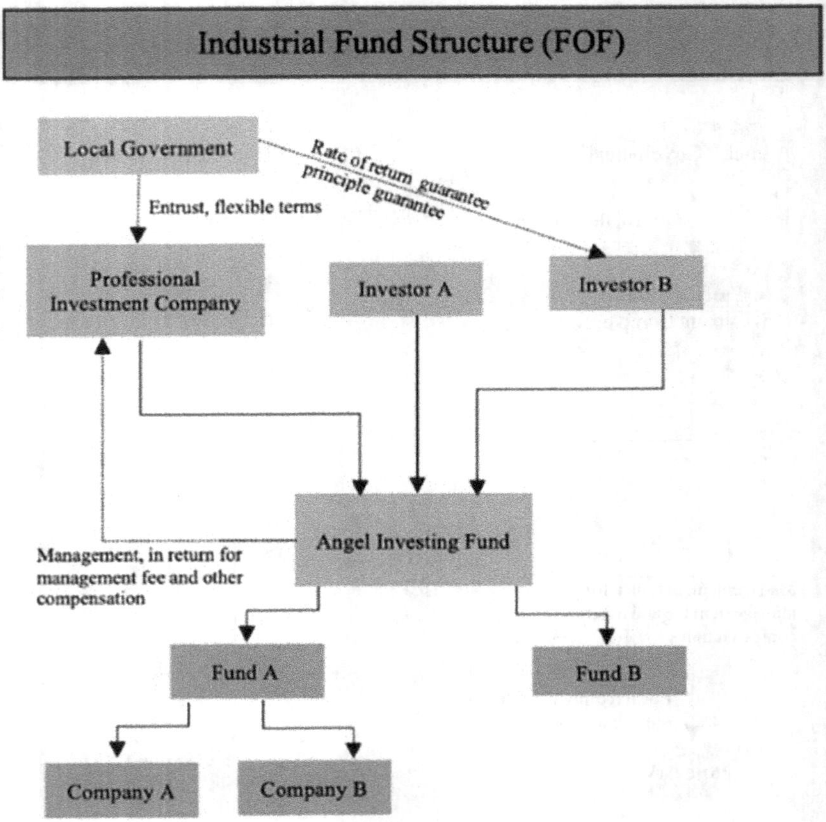

Figure 2.2 Structure of government guiding fund as FOF.

capital or private equity (VC/PE) fund that invests directly in the target companies.[108] The second kind (see Figure 2.2) takes the form

[108] The RMB20 billion Wuxi Integrated Circuit Industry Investment Fund (Wuxi IC Fund) is such an example. The government contributes 20 percent to the fund and encourages private entities to participate in the fund. The fund entrusts the daily management and operation to professional investment entities. Leng Yu, *Wuxi IC Industry Development Has Won 20 Billion "Big Red Envelopes,"* Wuxi Daily (Jan. 25, 2017), http://www.wxrb.com/news/wxxw/201701/t20170125_1264722.shtml; Wuxi Municipal People's Government, Notice of the Municipal Government on Printing and Distributing the Opinions on Accelerating the Development of the Integrated Circuit Industry, Art. 4, http://www.wuxi.gov.cn/doc/2016/12/30/1225272.shtml.

of a fund of funds (FOF) that invests in other angel investment companies.[109]

The structural difference between these two kinds of funds is ultimately negligible, because in both cases, the government itself is not running the fund. Instead, in both cases, the local governments entrust the fund to professional investment companies. The more meaningful differences, which also illustrate the flexibility of the fund and the creativity of local governments, come as the degree of "marketization" or, on the flip side, the degree of direct government shareholders' participation in the operation of the fund. Terms vary greatly, reflecting a spectrum of various relevant considerations, including the availability of highly skilled professionals, the purpose of the fund, the willingness of capital contribution by other limited partners (LPs), and even the local political culture.[110]

109 One example is the Hangzhou Angel Investment Guiding Fund (Hangzhou Guiding Fund). In the case of Hangzhou Guiding Fund, the Hangzhou Hi-Tech Investment Co. is the managing company primarily in charge of making investment decisions to other funds. While Hangzhou Guiding Fund retains the "right to monitor," without a clear instruction regarding its meaning or scope, and the investment company is responsible for establishing a reviewing committee that reviews the investment projects proposed by the angel investment company, making investment decisions, making periodic reports to Hangzhou Guiding Fund, the overall managerial the operational aspects of running a fund. Here, the government also subcontracts the operation and managerial function of the fund to a professional investment company, with conditions and incentive structures that monitor the performance of the company. HANGZHOU MUNICIPAL FINANCE BUREAU, HANGZHOU ANGEL INVESTMENT GUIDING FUND MANAGEMENT MEASURES (2021).

110 For example, if the government chooses to be more involved in the fund operation, it can require the prospective target projects or fund to be registered locally, ask for information or reviewing rights over the investment decision made by the entrusted investment company, veto power on material decisions, and ultimate authority on making investment decisions. On some occasions, the government is also willing to transfer, in part or in whole, of its own portion of pecuniary returns to other LPs. On the other extremity, the government can adopt a very hands-off approach. For example, it can inform the entrusted investment company (as an FOF) to participate solely as an ordinary LP in a sub-fund, without participating in the daily operation and management of the sub-fund, and enjoy same-share-same-right (tonggu tongquan) with other LPs, who can be other SOEs, private entities, or individuals. The government LP can further stipulate that it will neither transfer its own portion of distribution to other LPs nor guarantee other LPs' principals. The government can also put no preconditions, such as the locality requirement, on the sub-fund or project to be invested. Li Jie & Cheng Qian, *Zhengfu Chuangye Touzi Yindao Zijin de Zinfazhan yu Wenti Fenxi – Yi Jiangsusheng Weili [New Development and Problem Analysis of Government Venture Capital Guiding Fund – Taking Jiangsu Province as an Example]*, 6 JINGJI YANJIU CANKAO 80 (2016), https://tinyurl.com/nhk2z5kk; Sun Wei, *Zhengfu he Shichang Guanxi Shijiao xia de*

2.2 Incentive Patterns Including State

Section 1.4 of Chapter 1 provides the images of three incentive patterns: the balancing image for German corporations; the monitoring image for the US corporations; and the bargaining image for Silicon Valley and Japanese corporations. These incentive patterns do not include the state, but only include the four players: management and employees as human capital providers, shareholders and creditors as monetary capital providers. However, to provide the image of the incentive pattern of Chinese corporations, it is inevitable to include the state as the fifth player.

To compare the incentive patterns, including the state, this section uses more complicated pictures than those in Section 1.4 of Chapter 1.

2.2.1 The United States

Section 1.4 of Chapter 1 describes the US incentive pattern among the four players as the monitoring image, or principal-agent model.[111] Among the four players, shareholders and management create a coalition, and shareholders, as the owners, monitor their agent management. Creditors and employees are motivated via markets and are not involved in corporate governance.[112]

Figure 2.3 shows the US monitoring image by using a pyramidal shape for the corporate governance and another pyramidal shape for the hierarchy of employees, and several squares for several markets.

The new player, the state, is located outside of the forum and participates in the micro-level incentive bargaining, basically via management. The state tries to lead management toward the direction of its policy goal ("policy push"), particularly by tax policy, and management tries to lead the state to take the policy fulfilling its business demands ("demand pull").

Zhengfu Yindao Jijin Guifan Fazhan Yanjiu [Research on Normative Development of Government Guiding funds from the Perspective of Government and Market Relationship], 21 JINGJI YANJIU CANKAO 72 (2018), https://tinyurl.com/3y6fw2ch (mentioning that Shandong provincial government has the veto power in the provincial government guiding fund).

111 Besides the monitoring image, the principal-agent model for large corporations, the bargaining image, the Silicon Valley model that is optimal for growth co-exist in the United States, although the Silicon Valley model does not appear in Figure 2.3.

112 *See* Chapter 1, Figure 1.4.

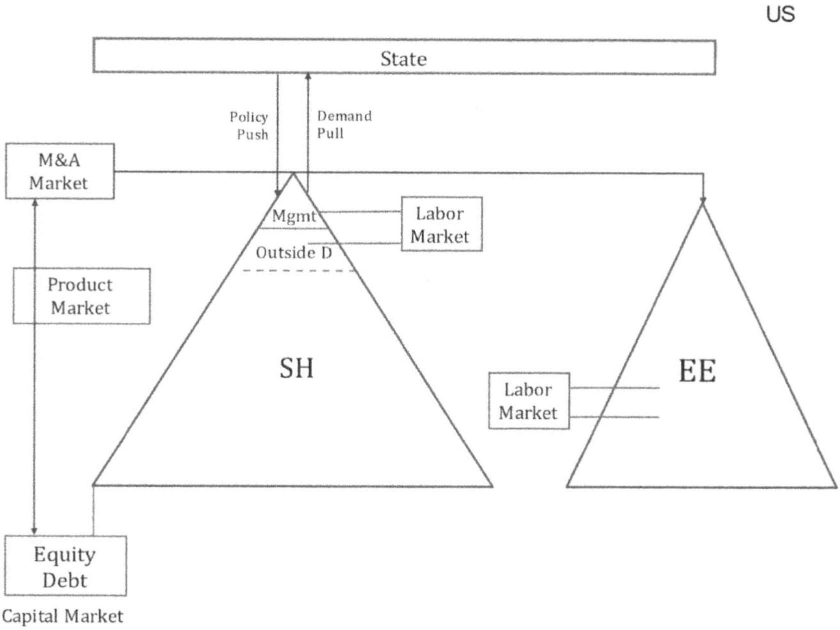

Figure 2.3 The US incentive pattern including state.

Regarding corporate governance (the left pyramidal shape), shareholders are located in the core of corporate governance as the residual claimant and the residual controller. Outside directors, as representatives of shareholders, monitor management. Neither employees nor creditors affect corporate governance as long as the firm is solvent.[113]

All markets are free liquid markets (squares with solid lines).[114]

For all human capital providers – management, directors, and employees – there are liquid external labor markets. They are strongly motivated by monetary incentives.

Management needs to seriously compete in free product markets where antitrust law is enforced generally stricter than in Japan, although the degree of strictness depends on the president and the economic era. Looser firms' stock prices and interest rates will be reflected in liquid

[113] Debt governance can be important for stagnant firms even before become insolvent. *See* Chapter 8, Section 8.1.

[114] The United States is a market-rational state, and an important role of the government is to keep competition in the markets.

capital markets and will easily be takeover targets in liquid mergers and acquisitions (M&A) markets.[115]

The state is the least interventionist among the three economies, but still plays important policy roles. The state is generally considered to be better not to intervene in individual business corporations based on the market-oriented social norm, but to stimulate competition among them via strong antitrust policy. The state sometimes adopts, however, strong industrial policies to back up a specific industry.[116] For example, the state played an important role in making the startup industry, such as in Silicon Valley, flourish through procurement for defense[117] and deregulation of pension funds' investment policy,[118] etc. State also sometimes rescues a giant corporation, of which failure will cause serious social damage, such as GM,[119] and bailout a financial institution, such as Silicon Valley Bank.[120]

The state consists of many actors.

First, as a federalist country, not only the federal state but also each local state participates in the micro-level incentive bargaining of a firm. The local states are competing with each other. For example, the state of Delaware strongly influences corporate governance and management incentives mostly via its courts, and the SEC has been trying to intervene in the incentive bargaining between the Delaware courts and business corporations.[121]

[115] Although the combination of poison pills and staggered boards is a strong anti-takeover measure, there is still room for raiders to take over a target company via proxy fight. *See* Curtis J. Milhaupt & Zenichi Shishido, *The Enduring Relevance of the Poison Pill: A U.S.–Japan Comparative Study*, 28 STAN. J. L. BUS. & FIN. 336, 349 (2023).

[116] *See supra* notes 2-6 and their accompanying texts. *See also supra* notes 27–33 and their accompanying texts.

[117] *See supra* note 10 and its accompanying text.

[118] *See supra* notes 14–19 and their accompanying texts.

[119] In December 2008, president George W. Bush on Friday announced $13.4 billion in emergency loans to prevent the collapse of General Motors and Chrysler. David M. Herszenhorn & David E. Sanger, *Bush Approves $17.4 Billion Auto Bailout*, N.Y. TIMES (Dec. 19, 2008), https://www.nytimes.com/2008/12/19/business/worldbusiness/19iht-20autoB.18826530.html.

[120] In March 2023, the Treasury and Federal Reserve stepped in to contain the financial damage from the closure of Silicon Valley Bank by guaranteeing even uninsured deposits and offering loans to other banks so they don't have to take losses on their fixed-income assets. This is seen as a de facto bailout of the Silicon Valley Bank. Editorial Board, *The Silicon Valley Bank Bailout*, WALL ST. J. (Mar. 12, 2023), https://www.wsj.com/articles/the-silicon-valley-bank-bailout-chorus-yellen-treasury-fed-fdic-deposit-limit-dodd-frank-run-cc80761e.

[121] *See* Chapter 11, nn.1–3 and their accompanying texts.

Second, both the federal state and each local state have independent actors: the government, which consists of the president (governor), ministries, governmental independent agencies, such as the SEC and the FTC, Congress, and the courts. Business corporations and industry groups try to incentivize those actors to take a favorable policy either for an individual corporation or for an industry by lobbying.

2.2.2 *Japan*

Section 1.4 of Chapter 1 describes the Japanese incentive pattern among the four players as the bargaining image. Management and employees create a coalition as the team of human capital providers. Shareholders and creditors create a coalition as the team of monetary capital providers. The two teams bargain with each other via the representative of each team: management and main bank.[122]

Figure 2.4, just as Figure 2.3 shows the image of the US monitoring model by several figures that indicate state, markets, and hierarchies, shows the image of the traditional Japanese bargaining model, which is referred to as the "main bank model" in general, that existed from the 1960s to the 1990s.[123]

The biggest difference between Figures 2.3 and 2.4 is that Figure 2.4 has only one pyramidal scheme, while Figure 2.3 has two pyramidal schemes. In the traditional Japanese model, employees, who are located outside of the corporate governance in the US model, are located at the center of the corporate governance.

Management, most board members, and full-time regular employees organize the company community.[124] They share an identity as "company

[122] *See* Chapter 1, Section 1.4, Figure 1.5.

[123] *See* Masahiko Aoki, Hugh Patrick & Paul Sheard, *The Japanese Main Bank System: An Introductory Overview, in* THE JAPANESE MAIN BANK SYSTEM: ITS RELEVANCE FOR DEVELOPING AND TRANSFORMING ECONOMIES 3 (Masahiko Aoki & Hugh Patrick eds., 1995).

[124] The company community consists of management, inside directors, and core employees who share an identity as "company men." Members of the company community share strong incentives to keep their autonomy against external governance. The company community norm works complementarily with the practice of "life-time employment," seniority-based promotion, internal promotion of management, company labor unions, cross-shareholding, and main bank monitoring. Although during Japan's economic growth, the company community created a growth bias, which was also beneficial to shareholders, its conflicts of interest based on agency cost of free cash flow turned out to be obvious after Japan's economic growth ended in the mid-1980s. *See* Zenichi Shishido,

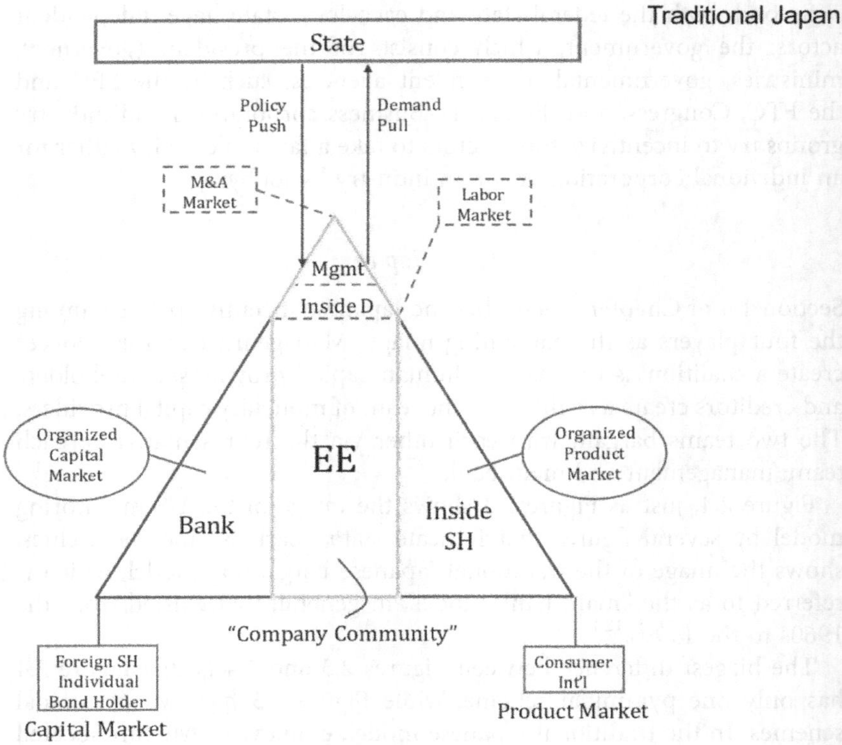

Figure 2.4 The traditional Japanese incentive pattern including state. EE=employees; SH=shareholders.

men." Being hired by a company as a full-time regular employee means belonging to the company community. The members of the company community are instantly given tenure when they are employed as freshmen, ensuring "lifetime employment."[125] It is against the company community social norm for a regular employee to move to another company, which means changing communities. The existence of the company community concept itself has limited the development of the external labor market, which is indicated as the square with dotted lines (illiquid market).

Seniority and egalitarian systems also support the concept of company community. Typically, for the first fifteen years after hiring, that is just

Japanese Corporate Governance: The Hidden Problem of the Corporate Law and Their Solutions, 25 DEL. J. CORP. L. 189, 201–205 (2000).

125 "Lifetime" means until a certain compulsory retirement age. *See id.* at 203.

after graduation from college, the distribution of positions and pay is basically equal among regular employees with the same seniority. This practice avoids excessive dissension among the members and keeps the community stable.

The internal governance, that is, the bottom-up monitoring of top management by its subordinates,[126] is much stronger in Japan than in the United States. First, the scope of internal governance is much wider in Japan than in the United States.[127] While in the United States, not ordinary employees but only junior managers participate in the internal governance, all company community members, including freshmen, participate in Japan because all regular employees care for the future of the firm on the premise of lifetime employment. Second, the time horizon of the future of the firm, which they care about, is longer in Japan than in the United States. And third, the company labor union, not the industry labor union, plays an important role as the mechanism of exercising voice by ordinary employees.

Not all shareholders, but only inside shareholders – which consist of cross-shareholding partners, such as financial institutions and business corporations – are involved in the corporate governance. They hold the stock not to maximize the investment return, but to keep their long-term transaction with the issuing company.[128] Cross-shareholding partners implicitly agree not to intervene in each other's corporate governance, more specifically, exchange blank proxies for the shareholders' meeting each other, and not to sell the stock without agreement by the issuing company, even if a raider offers a high price. Until the end of the twentieth century, in most listed companies, the majority of stocks were stabilized by cross-shareholdings, and there was no room for hostile takeovers. The illiquid M&A market is indicated as a square with the dotted line in Figure 2.4.

Outside shareholders whose objective is to maximize investment return, such as foreign institutional investors and individuals, are located not in the corporate governance, but in the free capital market. They cannot exercise their voice but only exit, which will reflect the stock price but not cause a takeover.

[126] *See* Viral V. Acharya, Stewart C. Myers & Raghuram G. Rajan, *The Internal Governance of Firms*, 66 J. Fin. 689 (2011).

[127] *See* Hokuto Dazai, Takuji Saito, Zenichi Shishido & Noriyuki Yanagawa, *Japanese Corporate Governance from the Perspective of Family Firms*, SSRN, 3–4 (2016), https://papers.ssrn.com/sol3/papers.cfm?abstract_id=2811069.

[128] *See* Shishido, *supra* note 124, at 204.

In most listed companies, the board of directors consists exclusively of insiders, that is, ex-employee company community members, without outside directors who represent the interest of shareholders. Therefore, neither hostile takeovers nor outside directors function as the scheme of external governance.[129]

The major scheme of monitoring management by monetary capital providers, or external governance, is the main bank monitoring. Typically, each company has its main bank, which generally lends the largest loans and holds the largest stocks among other banks. The main bank is responsible for monitoring the client company on an everyday basis, but does not intervene in its business and corporate governance as long as it keeps profitability (no red ink). If the client company continues to be red ink, the main bank intervenes in its corporate governance by exercising its voice. In serious financial situations, the main bank is expected to rescue the client company by sending personnel and offering financial support. It is called "contingent governance." The main bank is the representative of monetary capital providers, including other financial institutions and inside shareholders. It is called the "delegated monitor."[130]

In the premise of such strong internal governance and weak external governance, management can keep autonomy as long as it keeps company community norms, particularly protects the employment of regular employees, and shows prospective of growth. Actually, not only employees but also banks and shareholders share the same interest in growth, rather than profitability, during Japan's economic growth era. As a result, Japanese traditional corporate governance was not shareholder-oriented but stakeholder-oriented, particularly employee-oriented.

There are almost no labor and M&A markets. Most business-to-business (B2B) transactions are made in organized markets. A free capital market for outside shareholders and a free product market for consumers and international customers keep the economic efficiency.[131]

As in Figure 2.3, the state is located outside of the forum and participates in the micro-level incentive bargaining, basically via management. The state and management make incentive bargaining in the manner of policy push and demand pull, as in the United States.

[129] *See id.* at 208.
[130] *See* Aoki et al., *supra* note 123.
[131] *See* Shishido, *supra* note 124, at 205–208.

Japan does not have a federal system but rather a centralized political system. There are not as many actors of the state, which participate in the micro-level incentive bargaining of individual firms, as in the United States. Neither the diet nor local governments are active players. Basically, the central government ministry in charge of the industry, such as the Ministry of Finance for financial institutions and the Ministry of International Trade and Industry (MITI, now Ministry of Economic, Trade, and Industries [METI]) for manufacturing companies, is the exclusive window of bargaining for a specific company and a specific industry association.[132]

The state is interventionist between the United States and China. In the 1960s and 1970s, in particular, the government, mostly via the ministry in charge, played important policy roles, such as concentrating the limited monetary capital to several important industries via banks, taking protectionist policy against foreign competitors, subsidizing weak industries, and leading industries to the governmental policy goals by using the "administrative guidance" without legal basis. The government not only permitted but lead cartels. The US type antitrust policy was foreign to the Japanese traditional social norm, which prioritizes cooperation rather than competition.[133]

Listed companies, which share the same main bank, organize a horizontally integrated business group via their main bank-centered cross shareholdings (horizontal keiretsu). There is no linkage among different keiretsu groups.[134]

Although the traditional Japanese model (Figure 2.4) effectively worked during Japan's economic growth era from the 1960s to the middle of the 1980s, it turned to malfunction after the economic growth stopped, evidenced by the emergence of the economic bubble in 1985. Japanese companies lost their frontiers, i.e., they had no more new

[132] The governmental decision-making system in Japan is an elite bureaucracy-centered system, whereas it is a parliamentary assembly-centered in the United States. *See* JOHNSON, *supra* note 40, at 19.

[133] A high-ranked civil servant of the Ministry of International Trade and Industry (MITI, now METI) criticized antitrust law as a foreign protein that caused a shock reaction in Japan. *See* Naohiro Amaya, *The Ethics of Harmony and the Logic of the Antimonopoly Law*, *in* JAPANESE LAW IN CONTEXT: READING IN SOCIETY, THE ECONOMY, AND POLITICS 597, 599 (Curtis J. Milhaupt et al. eds., 2001).

[134] In China, plural SOEs organize a vertically integrated business group, and business groups are strategically linked to other business groups by the state. *See infra* notes 156–157 and their accompanying texts.

markets to invest even though they had a lot of cash. Many Japanese companies wasted their free cash flow, and Japanese traditional external governance was not able to monitor such waste without hostile takeovers and shareholder activism. Main banks had no incentive to monitor the use of free cash flow, but rather encouraged its waste.

Since the bubble burst in 1990, the Japanese economy has struggled with its low growth for three decades (the "lost three decades"). During the "lost three decades," the major players of Japanese corporate governance, including the state, have been searching for a new Japanese corporate governance model. As a result, Japanese corporate governance has been gradually changing. Although the reformation has not yet been completed, in other words, Japan is still changing; Figure 2.5 sketches out the current Japanese corporate governance in 2025.

The biggest difference between Figure 2.5 (New Japan) and Figure 2.4 (Traditional Japan) is that a new pyramidal figure appears on the left in Figure 2.5. The new pyramidal scheme indicates a startup company. Japanese large listed companies (the left pyramidal figure in Figure 2.5) finally recognized that disruptive innovations cannot be made without startups and now consider startups as their alliance partners and M&A targets. Startups become an important part of the Japanese business system.[135]

Although the company community is still the core of Japanese corporations, outside shareholders are now involved in their corporate governance with inside shareholders. Shareholders' interest is recognized as the most important among other stakeholders' interests, while employment protection is still important.[136] The percentage of outside directors are gradually increasing by the government-led corporate governance code and the pressure of institutional investors, although the boards with majority outside directors are still small numbers.[137]M&A markets and

[135] *See* ZENICHI SHISHIDO & VENTURE LAW FORUM (VLF), SUTA-TOAPPU TOSHI KEIYAKU: MODERU KEIYAKU TO KAISETSU [JAPANESE START-UP FINANCING DOCUMENTS: ANNOTATED MODEL CONTRACTS] 6 (2020).

[136] The "Corporate Governance Reform" from 2013 by the second Abe administration contributed to the change. *See* Zenichi Shishido, Sadakazu Osaki, Nobuyuki Kinoshita, Hirohiko Nakahara, Yuichiro Mizumachi & Tetsuya Watanabe, *Zadankai: Kigyo no Issho Purojekuto [Discussion: The Life of An Enterprise Project]* (Sadakazu Osaki) 1180 NBL 63, 64 (2023); ZENICHI SHISHIDO, SADAKAZU OSAKI, NOBUYUKI KINOSHITA, HIROHIKO NAKAHARA, YUICHIRO MIZUMACHI & TETSUYA WATANABE, INSENTHIBU BAGENINGU TO KIGYO HO: KIGYO NO ISSHO PUROJEKUTO [INCENTIVE BARGAINING AND ENTERPRISE LAW: THE LIFE OF AN ENTERPRISE] 425 (2025).

[137] In 2023, 72.3 percent of all listed companies to Tokyo Stock Exchange have more than one third independent outside directors, but only 11.3 percent have majority independent outside directors. TOKYO STOCK EXCHANGE, STATUS OF APPOINTMENT OF OUTSIDE

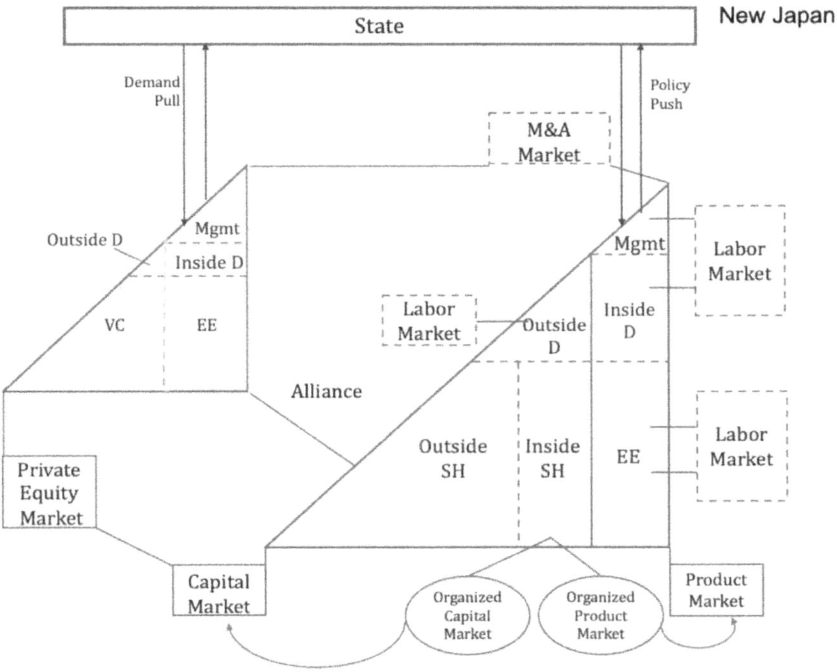

Figure 2.5 The new Japanese incentive pattern including state.

labor markets – both for employees, management, and outside directors – are still immature, although their liquidity is gradually increasing.

The organized capital market for inside shareholders and banks is gradually turning toward free market. The cross-shareholding rate has been steadily decreasing and foreign shareholders' share has been increasing to more than 30 percent. The share of outside shareholders overwhelmed that of inside shareholders in 2000.[138] The main bank monitoring has been weakening and has ended its role at least for the top listed companies.[139] The bond market has been enlarged.

Directors and Establishment of Nominating and Compensation Committee at Listed Companies (July 31, 2023), https://www.jpx.co.jp/equities/listing/ind-executive/nlsgeu000005va0p-att/aocfb40000003dlj.pdf.

[138] *See* Hideaki Miyajima, *Corporate Governance Reform, and Ownership, and Control: Perspective from Japan*, 30 Asian J. Pol. Sci. 3 (2023), http://doi/org/10.1080/02185377.2022.2159177.

[139] *See* Yasuhiro Arikawa & Hideaki Miyajima, *Relationship Banking in Post-Bubble Japan: Co-Existence of Soft-and Hard-Budget Constraints*, *in* Corporate Governance in

Organized product markets are also gradually turning toward free markets, particularly in industries where manufacturing architecture has been highly modularized, such as electronics.[140]

Administrative guidance is weakening; instead, ministries in charge try to lead industries by soft laws, named either codes or guidelines. The second Abe administration declared the "Corporate Governance Reform" in 2013 and tried to change the Japanese traditional stakeholder-oriented corporate governance to the Anglo–American style shareholder-oriented corporate governance. The Kishida administration tries to implement the Silicon Valley model to the Japanese startup industry with a one-trillion-yen (approximately $67 billion) subsidization budget.

Since the second Abe administration, the prime minister and the cabinet office play an important role in policy making regarding corporations and industries. For individual corporations and industries, the bargaining window of the states has been pluralized, in addition to the ministry in charge. The lobbying industry has emerged.

2.2.3 China

In China, there are two categories of listed companies: the SOE and the privately owned enterprise (hereinafter, POE).[141] Although for the corporate governance of both types of corporations, the Communist Party and the state, which are called the party-state because they function inseparably, are very influential, the ways of influencing are different in SOEs and POEs. We will use two different figures (Figures 2.6 and 2.7) to show the images of corporate governance of SOEs and POEs.[142]

The biggest difference between Figure 2.6 and Figures 2.3, 2.4, and 2.5 is the position of state in the corporate governance. While the state is located outside of the forum and participates in the micro-level incentive

JAPAN: INSTITUTIONAL CHANGE AND ORGANIZATIONAL DIVERSITY 79 (Masahiko Aoki et al. eds., 2007); *see* Miyajima, *supra* note 138, at 2.

140 *See* Zenichi Shishido, *Specificity, Enforceability, and Stickiness of Contracts,* 57 INT'L LAW. 475 (2024).

141 *See* Curtis J. Milhaupt & Wentong Zheng, *Beyond Ownership: State Capitalism and the Chinese Firm*, 103 GEO. L. J. 665, 667 (2015).

142 Although an influential view considers there is no fundamental difference between the corporate governance of SOEs and POEs, *see id.* at 669, we consider there to be structural differences between the two, particularly, the location of the party-state in their corporate governance and its way of influencing the incentive bargaining of the firm.

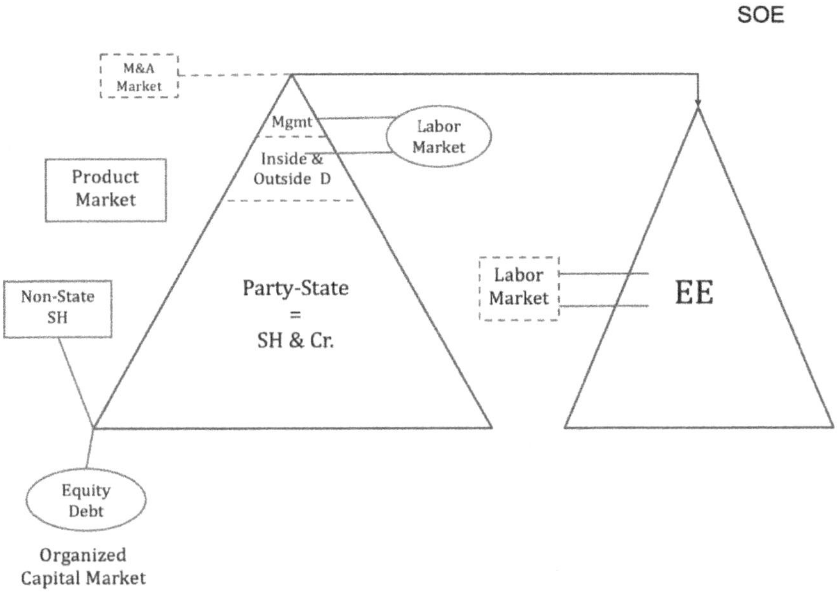

Figure 2.6 The Chinese SOE incentive pattern including state.

bargaining, basically via management in the US model and the old and new Japanese models, the party-state is in the corporate governance in the Chinese party-state model for SOEs.

The party-state is located at the center of SOEs' corporate governance in the three meanings.

First, the party-state is the major monetary capital provider, as the controlling shareholder[143] and the debt capital provider via state-owned banks. The party-state also provides subsidies and favors SOEs for governmental procurements.

Second, the party-state controls the nominations and compensation of top managers and directors of SOEs.[144] The party-state plays an

[143] The governmental holding company, SASAC, owns controlling shares of all central SOEs. The routine exchange of personnel between SASAC and the central SOEs is made to build SASAC capacity and promote cooperation between the SOE sector and the government. *See* Lin-Wen Lin & Curtis J. Milhaupt, *We Are the (National) Champions: Understanding the Mechanism of State Capitalism in China*, 65 Stan. L. Rev. 697, 711, 716, 726–727 (2013).

[144] *See id.* at 707, 711, 727, 737–738. An example of a significant degree of state control over managerial incentives is the cap of executive compensation at the central SOEs at twenty

equivalent role as the nominating and compensation committees in US corporations and as the strong human resources department of Japanese corporations.[145]

And, third, SOE managers are at the same time the party-state members and given hierarchical positions that are equivalent to those in a business organization.[146] Leaders are also rotated across the spheres of business, government, and the Party.[147] This is an interesting parallel to the Japanese company community model, in which managers, board members, and regular employees are at the same time the company community members and given seniority positions that are almost equivalent in the business organization (seniority system).[148]

Although the Chinese party-state model shares such a similarity with the Japanese company community model, Figure 2.6 is different from Figure 2.4 in the number of pyramidal schemes: Figure 2.6 has two pyramidal schemes, while Figure 2.4 has only one pyramidal scheme. Employees are located in the hierarchical pyramid outside of the corporate governance, as in the US principal-agent model (Figure 2.3), not as in the Japanese company community model, since human capital providers do not organize a team.

Management keeps autonomy as long as it keeps party-state norms and prospective of growth, even some SOEs do not adopt some "mandatory" party-building amendments to their charters.[149] Although this is another similarity with the Japanese company community norm,[150] it is

times the average employee's compensation. However, private benefit extraction by executives can be made by the practice of "on-duty consumption." *See* Milhaupt & Zheng, *supra* note 141, at 680.

145 The Party-State controls the selection and appointment of SOE executives. *See* Kasper Ingeman Beck & Kjeld Erik Brødsgaard, *Corporate Governance with Chinese Characteristics: Party Organization in State-Owned Enterprises*, 250 China Q. 486, 488 (2022).

146 *See* Lin & Milhaupt, *supra* note 143, at 700, 727. An implicit rule in China, the so-called Princelings, that the children of high-ranking party officials hold positions of authority in major enterprises, was introduced by the US scholars. *See* Ronald J. Gilson & Curtis J. Milhaupt, *Economically Benevolent Dictators: Lessons for Developing Democracies*, 59 Am. J. Comp. L. 227, 265–268 (2011).

147 *See* Lin & Milhaupt, *supra* note 143, at 741.

148 *See supra* notes 123–125.

149 Milhaupt & Zheng, *supra* note 141, at 678; Lin & Milhaupt, *supra* note 143, at 726; Lauren Yu-Hsin Lin & Curtis J. Milhaupt, *Party Building or Noisy Signaling? The Contours of Political Conformity in Chinese Corporate Governance*, 50 J. Legal Stud. 187, 189 (2021).

150 Management of Japanese large companies care to keep support by the company community by showing the community members, that is, junior management and all regular

not a result of internal governance by the human capital providers, but a result of external governance by the party-state as the major monetary capital provider.[151]

The party-state incentivizes the management of each company to keep growing by allowing private benefits and party-state positions.[152] Unlike the Japanese company community model, the Chinese party-state model is non-egalitarian (disproportional distribution),[153] high incentive,[154] and competitive,[155] which is similar to the US principal-agent model. It is a Pareto efficiency world.[156]

The party-state is also the industry policy engineer, which pushes individual companies and industries to realize rapid economic growth.[157] Plural SOEs organize a vertically integrated business group,[158] and

employees, the prospect of growth and committing long-term employment and egalitarian compensations and promotions. *See infra* note 124 and its accompanying text.

151 Gilson and Milhaupt analogize the role of the party-state to private equity general partners in Silicon Valley in the sense that the party-state has an incentive to monitor management of the portfolio companies to grow the business because they will obtain a significant portion of the gain from growth. Management gets rich if they successfully grow the business, but are removed if they fail. Gilson & Milhaupt, *supra* note 146, at 262.

152 *See* Lin & Milhaupt, *supra* note 143, at 744.

153 Although the state formally controls executive pay for SOEs, private benefit extraction is available both to SOE managers and to Party elites. *See* Gilson & Milhaupt, *supra* note 146, at 262; *see* Milhaupt & Zheng, *supra* note 141, at 680; *see* Lin & Milhaupt, *supra* note 143, at 744.

154 Milhaupt & Zheng, *supra* note 141, at 701–702; Lin & Milhaupt, *supra* note 143, at 707.

155 *See* Gilson & Milhaupt, *supra* note 146, at 262.

156 Parato efficiency is a situation where no action or allocation is available that makes one individual better off without making another worse off. *See* Robert D. Cooter & Thomas S. Ulen, *An Economic Case for Comparative Negligence*, 61 NYU L. Rev. 1067, 1098 (1986). If some agents will gain, and no agents will lose, a Pareto improvement can be achieved. The Chinese party-state model, as well as the US principal-agent model, looks like to try to achieve a Pareto improvement by making some agents better off, while the Japanese company community model looks like to prevent some agents from being better off, even if a Pareto improvement can be achieved. "The gains from growth, while improving the lives of millions, were disproportionately distributed within the party/state apparatus itself or to close relatives and associates of senior Party members." Gilson & Milhaupt, *supra* note 146, at 262.

157 *See* Lin & Milhaupt, *supra* note 143, at 751.

158 A national business group has four main components: the core holding company, whose shares are wholly owned by SASAC; one or more listed subsidiaries, a majority of whose shares are held by the core company; a finance company, which has certain parallels with Japanese main banks; and a research institute. *See id.* at 711. Business groups are not purely contract-based collaborations, but use organizational structures based on shareholding to link firms. *See id.* at 714.

business groups are strategically linked to other business groups by the state.[159] It is like the strong Japanese MITI and MOF in the heyday of their administrative guidance. Management of each company incentivizes the party-state not to intervene in the business by showing prospect of growth and loyalty to the party-state norm.[160]

China is economically a quasi-federal country,[161] although its political system is centralized. Not only the central government, but also local governments participate in the micro-level incentive bargaining of a firm.[162] Local governments are competing with each other.[163] It is different from Japan and similar to the United States.

The labor market for managers and directors is an organized market since the party-state controls their appointments and compensations. The labor market for employees is illiquid. Employees of SOEs seldom move to other companies because of the strong employment protection.[164]

Product markets are very competitive. Although the capital market for state capital is organized, as a matter of course, the capital market for non-state minority shareholders is a free liquid market. The M&A market for SOEs is very illiquid.

Chinese SOEs, according to their nature, are classified into two types: commercial SOEs and public service SOEs. Commercial SOEs would be fully operated on a commercial basis with the for-profit purpose of enhancing efficiency and maximizing the value of state assets. Such firms are all required to be restructured into joint stock companies with a view to being listed on a stock market in the future. The state can be the dominant controller, a majority shareholder, or even a minority shareholder in these firms. On the other hand, the public service SOEs are

159 *See* Lin & Milhaupt, *supra* note 143, at 707, 711.

160 *See* Gilson & Milhaupt, *supra* note 146, at 261; *see* Milhaupt & Zheng, *supra* note 141, at 670–671, 697.

161 *See* Gilson & Milhaupt, *supra* note 146, at 269–270. *See also* Yongnian Zheng, *China's De Facto Federalism, in* Federalism in Asia 213–241 (Baogang He, Brian Galligan & Takashi Inoguchi eds., 2007).

162 The township–village enterprise (TVE) gives local governments a "carried interest" in economic growth. The importance of TVEs to local governments' revenues provides local governments with a strong incentive to secure the property rights of private enterprises. Private entrepreneurs from outside the local area use the local government officials in the host jurisdiction to serve as their "agent for contract enforcement." However, TVEs are less relevant nowadays. Gilson & Milhaupt, *supra* note 146, at 263.

163 *See* Milhaupt & Zheng, *supra* note 141, at 695–706.

164 *See* Chapter 5, Section 5.1.3.

expected to provide public goods and services in a price-regulated environment in order to enhance the people's standard of living. Such firms can be solely owned by the state, and will be evaluated by cost control, product quality, operational efficiency, and capacity in delivering the necessary products or services.

The role of the state owner in enterprises, exercised by the State-owned Assets Supervision and Administration Commission (SASAC) at the central and local levels, will shift from "asset management" to "capital management." Specifically, state capital investment/management companies will be established to serve as the state shareholder in SOEs. SASAC, in turn, will become the state shareholder in such capital investment/management companies. The rationale for creating such state capital companies is to establish a firewall between SASAC and the SOEs so as to stop the "tendency for SASAC to become increasingly involved in the business operation of SOEs." Arguably, this policy move brings China's SOE supervision model closer to Singapore's Temasek model. The Temasek model is intended to create a level of separation between the Singapore government and government-linked companies so as to facilitate commercial decision-making that is insulated from the dictates of government policy.[165]

After the global financial crisis in 2007–2008, China had a huge debt overhang and some major companies were defaulting on their debt.[166] The debt has made massive SOEs sluggish and unproductive. The conventional bailout scheme executed by the government (through its central bank or Ministry of Finance) or state-owned banks no longer works due to the mounting nonperforming loans accumulated by the state-owned banks.

State ownership leads to political dominance, which makes SOEs less efficient and profitable. Studies show that listed companies with politically connected CEOs actually performed worse than their counterparts.[167]

[165] *See* Curtis J. Milhaupt, *The State as Owner – China's Experience*, 36 OXFORD REV. ECON. POL'Y 362, 368, 375 (2020).

[166] Since 2008, there has been an increase of credit to GDP of about 150 percentage points, roughly from 126 percent to around 277 percent at the end of 2018. Cindy Li & Tierno Paul, *The Role of Debt and Shadow Banking in China's Economy*, FED. RSRV. BANK OF S.F. (Jan. 14, 2019), https://www.frbsf.org/banking/asia-program/pacific-exchanges-podcast/role-of-debt-and-shadow-banking-in-chinas-economy/.

[167] Joseph P. H. Fan, T. J. Wong & Zhan Tianyu, *Politically Connected CEOs, Corporate Governance, and Post-IPO Performance*, 84 J. FIN. ECON. 330–357 (2007).

An earlier study surveyed the firm performance of all companies listed on the Shenzhen Stock Exchange (SZSE) and Shanghai Stock Exchange (SSE) and found a positive co-relationship between government ownership and firm performance.[168] In other words, "partial government ownership has a positive impact on SOE performance." However, the authors discovered that the relationship was nonlinear and followed "an inverted U-shape pattern." In other words, "100% government ownership is not good, but no government ownership is not good either. The optimal government ownership may be somewhere in between," although the authors did not address what was the "optimal" percentage of state ownership.

The Chinese government, in 2015, put forward the so-called mixed-ownership reform[169] to "invigorate torpid SOEs,"[170] which is motivated by the benefits of improved corporate governance and performance in SOEs through the sharing of control between the controlling state shareholders and non-state shareholders. The program encourages POEs to participate in the reform through various means, such as buying stakes and convertible bonds from or conducting share rights swaps with the SOEs. Selling shares to SOEs' own employees is also listed as one of the means.[171]

The new policy follows the spirit of the Third Plenum Decision that, for the first time, advocated for "the market to play a decisive role in the allocation of resources" and the state would refrain from exercising excessive intervention. The state promises to "respect" the principles of the market economy and allow the enterprises to be the central players in the mixed ownership reform process. In addition, a vow is made to protect the property rights of all forms of ownership,[172] enforce

[168] Qian Sun, Wilson H. S. Tong & Jing Tong, *How Does Government Ownership Affect Firm Performance? Evidence from China's Privatization Experience*, 29 J. Bus. Fin. Acct. 1, 3 (2002).

[169] Guidelines of the CCP Central Committee and the PRC State Council to Deepen Reform of the State-owned Enterprises (promulgated on August 24, 2015); Opinions of the State Council on the Development of Mixed-ownership Reform in SOEs, NDRC 2015 No. 54 (promulgated on September 23, 2015).

[170] The State Council of the People's Republic of China, China Issues Guideline to Deepen SOE Reforms (2015), http://english.www.gov.cn/policies/latest_releases/2015/09/13/content_281475189210840.htm.

[171] *Id.*

[172] Before China has a formal Property Law in 2008, foreign and private investors took advantage of other mechanisms such as contracts and corporations to create substitutes for property institutions in China. However, this may sustain in a long run as foreign

contracts, and encourage fair competition. On the other hand, the CCP has also stressed that the state sector should retain "dominance" and play the leading role by enhancing the "state sector vitality, controlling capacity and influence" in the Chinese economy. In this spirit, the general policy design of the mixed ownership reform program suggests that the state sector can involve private investment.[173]

Mixed-ownership reform of SOEs can be roughly divided into three categories: (a) to dilute state-owned capital in SOEs, leading to a reduction of the shareholding ratio of state-owned holding companies by means of receiving investments from non-state-owned strategic investors; (b) to separate ancillary business from the key business and then introduce private capital to invest in the ancillary business in the form of new businesses; and (c) to incorporate a joint venture and to invite the investment made by non-state-owned capital.

> A mixed economy with cross holding by and mutual fusion between state-owned capital, collective capital, and non-public capital is an important way to materialize the basic economic system of China. It is conducive to improving the amplification function of state-owned capital, ensuring the appreciation of its value and raising its competitiveness, and it is conducive to enabling capital with all kinds of ownership to draw on one another's strong points to offset weaknesses, stimulate one another and develop together.

While the mixed ownership reform may bring out more efficient corporate performance of SOEs, evidenced by the enhancement of

and private investors need a more solid and formal legal infrastructure to stabilize their property rights. Weitseng Chen, *Arbitrage for Property Rights: How Foreign Investors Create Substitutes for Property Institutions in China*, 24 Wash. Int'l L. J. 47–97 (2015).

173 The Third Plenum Decision confidently stated this objective as follows:

> A mixed economy with cross holding by and mutual fusion between state-owned capital, collective capital, and non-public capital is an important way to materialize the basic economic system of China. It is conducive to improving the amplification function of state-owned capital, ensuring the appreciation of its value and raising its competitiveness, and it is conducive to enabling capital with all kinds of ownership to draw on one another's strong points to offset weaknesses, stimulate one another and develop together.

On this basis, the CCP declared that it "will allow more SOEs and enterprises of other types of ownership to develop into mixed enterprises" and "non-state-owned capital to hold shares in projects invested by state-owned capital," as well as "mixed enterprises to implement employee stock ownership plans (ESOP) to form communities of capital owners and laborers."

productivity and profitability and the elimination of monopolies by SOEs due to the wider market access to private and foreign players, a more immediate effect may be the procurement of more funds for investment through the use of non-state-owned capital. In practice, healthy private companies are encouraged to invest in debt-laden SOEs. This may help curb SOEs' dependency on debt issuance and bank loans. For example, Alibaba, Baidu, JD.com, China Life Insurance Co., and Tencent, among others, raised US$10 billion in cash to invest in China Unicom in exchange for 35 percent equity. However, the SOEs may take advantage of this policy to shift non-performing business segments to private investors, even though this is not an intended policy purpose. The mixed ownership reform has been taken advantage of by some SOEs and local governments, with a short-termist vision, to secure more liquidity.[174]

However, mixed ownership reform may not fundamentally transform SOEs for two reasons. First, as long as the SOEs are controlled by the State (either through bureaucrats or state-owned arms), the controlling state ownership would not resolve but worsen the agency problem between the majority and minority shareholders. Second, achieving the intended policy targets of mixed ownership reform heavily depends on the reform of institutional mechanisms such as corporate governance, minority shareholder protection,[175] and contractual enforcement, which are critically important to the rights protection. The introduction of private capital into SOEs alone will not alter the relationship between the state and SOEs. China's institutional framework blurs the boundary between the SOEs and the state, and consequently, private firms are often marginalized due to the strong state influence over firms. What is needed is a freer and fairer competitive environment.

174 The mixed ownership reform was made in response to various policy concerns. First, this is a short-term solution to the non-performing loans accumulated by the SOEs and the inefficiency of the SOEs. Second, this may leave a better impression to the outside world that the government is not heavily or directly involved in the business operation of SOEs. Then, the huge difference between China and its Western counterparts may be narrowed somehow. Third, from the government's perspective, this would allow the government to devote more limited resources to more fund-needed sectors.

175 Yu-Hsin Lin & Yun-Chien Chang, *Do State-Owned Enterprises Have Worse Corporate Governance? – An Empirical Study of Corporate Practices in China*, 23 Eur. Bus. Org. L. Rev. 711 (2021) (claiming, on the basis of hand-coded data set on corporate charter provisions of 300 publicly listed Chinese companies that SOEs controlled by the central government with over 30 percent of shares are more pro-minority shareholders than are privately owned firms and have higher firm value), https://link.springer.com/article/10.1007/s40804-021-00223-1.

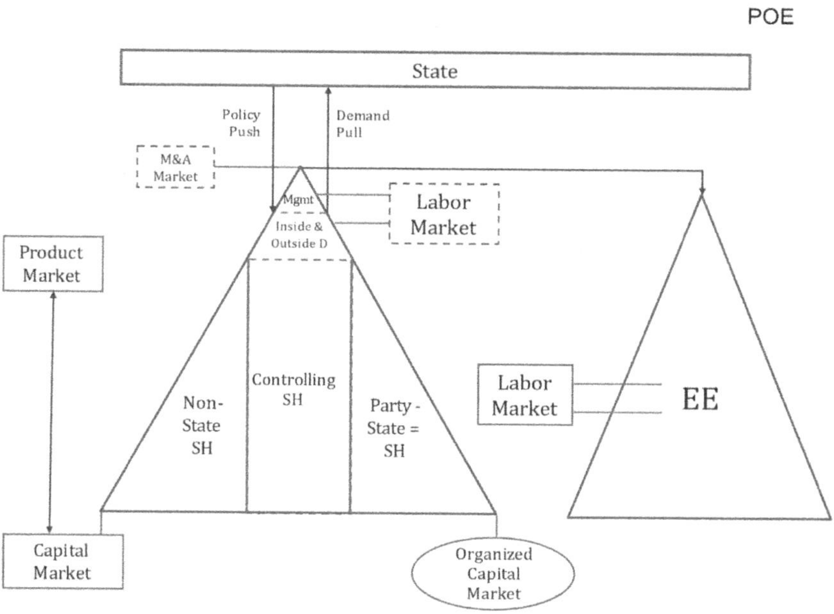

Figure 2.7 The Chinese POE incentive pattern including state.

Compared to Figure 2.6 for SOEs, in Figure 2.7 for POE, the state is not at the core of the corporate governance, but is located outside of the forum and participates in the micro-level incentive bargaining, basically via management, as in the United States and Japan. Chinese party-state is, however, exercises much stronger and more perversive influence than US and Japanese states.[176]

The corporate governance of Chinese POEs can be expressed as the owner management model. Most listed POEs are still first-generation companies, and their founders are top management and controlling shareholders. Management, as the controlling shareholder has a strong equity incentive while it cares about keeping a good relationship with the state.[177] There is little vertical agency problem between shareholders and

[176] *See* Milhaupt & Zheng, *supra* note 141, at 701–702. Although Milhaupt and Zheng emphasize that the party-state influence over SOE has important limits, the line between SOEs and POEs is blurry. Milhaupt & Zheng, *supra* note 141, at 669. We consider the structures of party-state influence on SOEs & POEs as fundamentally different.

[177] *See* Milhaupt & Zheng, *supra* note 141, at 669.

management, but a huge horizontal agency problem between minority shareholders and the controlling shareholder.[178]

Both state and non-state investors participate as minority shareholders.[179] There is a liquid capital market with non-state shareholders and free competitive product markets.

The M&A market is not as developed as in the US, but recently several M&As by high-tech companies are observed.[180]

Although the labor markets for ordinary employees and mid-managers are liquid, the labor market for top managers did not emerge yet probably because most listed POEs are still first-generation companies.

The state is both a shareholder and a policy engineer.[181] The state is ordinarily not a strong interventionist in POEs, but sometimes forces individual POEs to make or stop M&As along with its policy needs[182] and strongly intervenes in the corporate governance of individual POEs if

178 *See* Fuxiu Jiang & Kenneth A. Kim, *Corporate Governance in China: A Survey*, 24 REV. FIN. 733, 733 (2020).

179 The state, institutional investors, and individual investors, each holds one-third of listed companies in China. Milhaupt & Zheng, *supra* note 141, at 673, footnote 28. The private sector's share of China's largest listed companies reached its peak (55 percent) in 2021 and gradually decreased to 43 percent at the end of 2022. Tianlei Huang & Nicolas Véron, *The Private Sector's Share of China's Largest Listed Companies Continued to Decline to 43 Percent in the Second Half of 2022*, PIIE (Feb. 2, 2023), https://www.piie.com/blogs/realtime-economics/2023/private-sectors-share-chinas-largest-listed-companies-continued.

180 For instance, e-commerce giant Alibaba acquired Chinese video streaming giant Youku Tudou for $5.4 billion in 2016. Patrick Frater, *Alibaba Completes $4 Billion Takeover of Youku Tudou*, VARIETY (Apr. 5, 2016), https://variety.com/2016/biz/asia/alibaba-completes-youku-tudou-takeover-1201746908/.

181 *See* Gilson & Milhaupt, *supra* note 146, at 260–261, 268; *see* Milhaupt & Zheng, *supra* note 141, at 694.

182 One example is the aftermath sanctions against key players in the takeover war between Vanke (target) and Baoneng Group (bidder). After Baoneng Group initiated the takeover war, another POE, Anbang Group, joined the contest by purchasing a significant amount of Vanke shares. Wu Xiaohui, Chairperson of Anbang, was investigated and sentenced to eighteen years in prison. The government also imposed sanctions against Anbang and effectively seized control over Anbang. One possible reason for the punishment against Anbang is the Chinese government's efforts to restrict outbound M&As. The Chinese government was concerned about the capital flight (China lost a significant amount of its international reserve) and depreciation of RMB (which could facilitate capital flight further). Capital flight can occur in the process of outbound M&As. Anbang has been a very aggressive acquirer in outbound M&A markets. In the United States, for instance, Anbang purchased the Waldorf Astoria Hotel and Strategic Hotels & Resorts from Blackstone. In Korea, Anbang acquired two insurance companies. Sang Yop Kang, *The Vanke-Baoneng Case and Beyond: Hostile Takeover and Corporate Governance in China*, PEKING UNIV. SCH. TRANSNAT'L. L., RSCH. PAPER 6 (2018).

their management does not look loyal to the party-state norm.[183] Extralegal influence on POEs by the party-states can be exercised in a variety of ways, including "interviews" of firms or via industrial associations.[184] The party-state enjoys broad discretion in setting administrative rules.[185] Milhaupt and Zheng describe such a phenomenon as "capture." By aligning themselves with the political leadership's interests, goals, and priorities, firms obtain special advantages from the national or local governments, or state-generated rents, such as access to financing, being favored in stock listing, and state-sanctioned monopolies.[186]

2.2.4 Summary: Comparison among the Three Economies

The US monitoring image incentive pattern, or the principal-agent model, is closest to the normative model of corporate law and traditional economics theory: shareholder-oriented and market-oriented.

The internal governance is weak, and the external governance is strong. The US system is not good at incentivizing human capital providers to make relation-specific investments, but it is good at monitoring management for maximizing shareholder value. Its growth bias is weak.

The US system uses strong equity incentives. It is not an egalitarian, pro-Pareto efficiency model.

At the same time, the bargaining image incentive pattern, which is optimal for growth, is co-existing for startups.

The "paradigm shift"[187] occurs in the 2020s. ESG and the "purpose" movement caused the shift from extreme shareholder-oriented corporate governance to moderate stakeholder-oriented corporate governance.[188]

[183] Jack Ma, the founder of Alibaba, is considered to have been forced to resign the CEO position by the party-state because of his "improper statement." *See* George Calhoun, *The Sad End of Jack Ma Inc.*, FORBES (June 7, 2021), https://www.forbes.com/sites/georgecalhoun/2021/06/07/the-sad-end-of-jack-ma-inc/?sh=5928988b123a.

[184] Milhaupt & Zheng, *supra* note 141, at 685–687.

[185] See *Id.* at 691.

[186] *Id.* at 688–690. *See also* Haitian Lu, Hongbo Pan & Chenying Zhang, *Political Connectedness and Court Outcomes: Evidence from Chinese Corporate Lawsuits*, 58 J. LAW & ECON. 829–861 (2015); Lin & Milhaupt, *supra* note 149, at 189.

[187] *See* Martin Lipton, *It's Time to Adopt the New Paradigm*, HARV. L. SCH. F. CORP. GOVERNANCE (Feb. 11, 2019), https://corpgov.law.harvard.edu/2019/02/11/its-time-to-adopt-the-new-paradigm/.

[188] *See* BUSINESS ROUNDTABLE, STATEMENT ON THE PURPOSE OF A CORPORATION (Aug. 19, 2019), https://purpose.businessroundtable.org/. *See also* Elizabeth Pollman, *The Making and Meaning of ESG*, 14 HARV. BUS. L. REV. 403 (2024).

The United States is a federalist country and both politically and economically decentralized. Competition exists among federal and local states.

The Japanese bargaining image incentive pattern, or the company community model, is contrary to the normative model of corporate law and traditional economics theory: stakeholder-oriented and not market-oriented with a lot of organized markets. The social norm prioritizes cooperation rather than competition.

The internal governance is strong, and the external governance is weak. The Japanese system is not good at monitoring management for maximizing shareholder value, but good at incentivizing human capital providers to make relation-specific investments. Its growth bias is strong.

The Japanese system uses weak equity incentives. It is an egalitarian, anti-Pareto efficiency model.

Japan is now struggling with its low-growth economy. Although the government is trying to change from stakeholder-oriented corporate governance to shareholder-oriented corporate governance, the company community norm, which used to be the engine of growth, turns out to be the anchor resisting change.

Japan is both politically and economically centralized. There is only weak competition among regions.

The Chinese SOEs' party-state model is, in two senses, similar to the Japanese company community model. Not only the double appointment of managers at the business corporation and the party-state, or the company community, but also strong growth bias and the importance of continuity of the party-state, or the company community, are similar.

However, contrary to Japan, the internal governance is weak and the external governance by the party-state as the controlling shareholder is strong. The party-state is a kind of parallel to the private equity general manager in Silicon Valley.[189]

China is politically stakeholder-oriented and economically shareholder-oriented. It is not an egalitarian, pro-Pareto efficiency model, which is similar to the US principal-agent model.

The Chinese POEs' owner management model is closest to the startup model in Silicon Valley.[190] The owner-manager and state and non-state

[189] *See* Gilson & Milhaupt, *supra* note 146, at 262.

[190] The struggle between the invisible hand and visible hand is a long-time controversy in China's economic growth and development. The transition experiences in other emerging states proved the greater relevance of the invisible-hand model to the vibrant entrepreneurial sector. Timothy Frye and Andrei Hand, *The Invisible Hand and the Grabbing Hand*, 87 AM. ECON. REV. 354–358 (1997).

minority shareholders share the strong equity incentive. Labor markets for employees and middle managers are liquid in POEs. The M&A market, particularly for high-tech companies, has gradually developed. It is shareholder-oriented and market-oriented.

China is politically centralized and economically decentralized. There is strong competition among local governments.

The Japanese system and the Chinese system are both good at expanding the pie during a high-growth economy. While the US system is good at sharing a limited pie during a low-growth economy, the Silicon Valley model that is optimal for growth is co-existing.

PART II

Management

Executives and Monitors

3

Incentive of Management

Among the four players within a firm's incentive bargaining, management is the key player because it is the only window to the incentive bargaining.[1] How the firm's other three players – shareholders, creditors, and employees – incentivize management will determine the firm's direction. Government, as the fifth player, also influences the incentive of management either directly or via the corporate personality. Therefore, this chapter will provide readers with an overview of this book.

Because markets, social norms, and laws influence the incentives of management, corporate governance has a country-specific character. As comparative analysis will show, management's incentive structure in the United States, Japan, and China is different from one another because of dissimilar exogenous factors.

By virtue of the individuals that comprise it, management is not monotonously motivated by only one incentive, such as money. This chapter will also analyze management's incentives by categorizing them into three separate types: the power-related incentive, the reputational incentive, and the monetary incentive. Of course, all three are correlated with one another. The general characteristic of each country's management incentives is best understood by examining the sum of the three different incentive types.

Although, in the United States, the monetary incentive is generally considered the most important to motivate management, both in Japan and China, the monetary incentive does not play the leading role. Therefore, Section 3.1 starts with the power-related incentive of management. Section 3.2 refers to the reputational incentive of management. Section 3.3 examines the monetary incentive of management. Section 3.4 shows complementary results of the three different types of incentives in each country and the direction in which management incentive leads management to run the company.

[1] *See* Chapter 1, Section 1.4.

3.1 The Power-Related Incentive

Management's basic power-related incentive is to maintain autonomy from the firm's other three players as well as the government. Although a certain degree of autonomy is necessary to give management the incentive to initiate and execute long-term projects – in other words, to let management pursue its "idiosyncratic vision"[2] – an incentive to maintain autonomy is easily turned into an incentive to entrench themselves.[3] The degree of management's autonomy is influenced by its relative bargaining power with other players and possible coalitions with other players.[4]

Empire building is another power-related incentive. Management naturally has the incentive to increase the size of the firm it manages. In empire building, this typically happens through mergers and acquisitions (M&A), even if such attempts will detriment the firm's value. Management may feel that the larger the firm's size, the larger the prestige that comes with it. Employees, as another human capital provider, generally share the same feeling. The firm's size also correlates with the amount of managerial compensation in most countries. This is a typical agency problem between management and shareholders.

A major role of the board of directors, which will be discussed in detail in Chapter 4, is to monitor the two problematic power-related incentives, entrenchment and empire building. Different board laws and practices in each country affect its actual monitoring power and, thus, the incentive of management.

3.1.1 The United States

In the United States, management and shareholders create a coalition.[5] Based on the shareholders' interest-maximizing norm, management, as the shareholders' agent, bargains with creditors and employees via the

[2] Zohar Goshen & Assaf Hamdani, *Corporate Control and Idiosyncratic Vision*, 125 YALE L. J. 560 (2016).

[3] As symbolized in the argument on market myopia vs. management "hyperopia," the tendency of management to persist in failing strategies in the name of an always receding future. *See* Ronald J. Gilson & Jeffery N. Gordon, *Board 3.0: What the Private-Equity Governance Model Can Offer to Public Companies*, 32 J. APPLIED CORP. FIN. 1 (2020).

[4] *See* Zenichi Shishido, *The Incentive Bargain of the Firm and Enterprise Law: A Nexus of Contracts, Markets, and Laws*, *in* ENTERPRISE LAW: CONTRACTS, MARKETS, AND LAWS IN THE US AND JAPAN 1, 3 (Zenichi Shishido ed., 2014).

[5] *See* PETER A. GOUREVITCH & JAMES SHINN, POLITICAL POWER AND CORPORATE CONTROL: THE NEW GLOBAL POLITICS OF CORPORATE GOVERNANCE 22–26 (2005).

capital and labor markets. Creditors' and employees' bargaining power with management is weak as long as the firm is profitable. Although shareholders are recognized as the firm's owner, their bargaining power with management was not necessarily strong before the institutionaliza tion of the stock ownership structure.[6] Management enjoyed strong autonomy due to this dispersed ownership and proxy machinery. The US government does not often intervene in private firms' incentive bargaining, except for national security matters.

In the United States, the possibility of a hostile takeover has been very real. Therefore, a major concern for management was the risk of being taken over by a majority shareholder. This incentivized management to safeguard its autonomy by implementing defensive measures, typically the combination of poison pills and staggered boards.[7]

Since the late 1970s, the government (the US Securities and Exchange Commission, in particular), the corporate bar, and shareholders (institutional investors, in particular) have been trying to strengthen the board's independence from management by utilizing the monitoring model.[8] The Delaware case law has also been incentivizing management to organize an independent board.[9] The number of cases where a supermajority of independent directors replaced a firm's management, leading to falling stock prices, has increased.[10] Although the monitoring board looks to prevent management from entrenchment and empire building, some commentators criticize that

[6] *See* Mark J. Roe, Strong Managers, Weak Owners: The Political Roots of American Corporate Finance (1994).

[7] *See* Shishido, *supra* note 4, at 33; Curtis J. Milhaupt & Zenichi Shishido, *The Enduring Relevance of the Poison Pill: A U.S.–Japan Comparative Analysis*, 28 Stan. J. L. Bus. & Fin. 336, 347 (2023).

[8] *See* Jeffery N. Gordon, *The Rise of Independent Directors in the United States, 1950–2005: Of Shareholder Value and Stock Market Price*, 59 Stan. L. Rev. 1465, 1516–1518 (2007).

[9] *See* Curtis Milhaupt, *Takeover Law and Managerial Incentives in the United States and Japan, in* Enterprise Law: Contracts, Markets, and Laws in the US and Japan 189 (Zenichi Shishido ed., 2014).

[10] For example, following recommendations from a special committee of independent directors, Cutera Inc. fired CEO David Mowry and Executive Chairman Daniel Plants, which prompted a nearly 30 percent drop in its share price. Svea Herbst-Bayliss, *Cutera Fires CEO, Stock Tumbles and Large Investor Speaks Out*, Reuters (Apr. 12, 2023, 04:24 PM), https://www.reuters.com/business/cutera-fires-ceo-exec-chairman-after-their-push-board-shakeup-2023-04-12/; *see also* Jeffrey Sonnenfeld, *Another Suicidal Board?: How DuPont's Directors Failed Ellen Kullman*, Fortune (Oct. 13, 2015), https://fortune.com/2015/10/13/dupont-board-ellen-kullman/.

the current US boards are too interventionist and prone to making management more short-sighted.[11]

Around the turn of the twenty-first century, major US firms' stock ownership structures have dramatically changed. So-called "institutional ization" has gained momentum, and a couple of major investment funds have become majority shareholders in a growing number of large listed firms.[12] As a result, shareholders' bargaining power with management is substantially strengthened. Because of pressure from institutional investors, a substantial number of managements are forced to accept outside directors recommended by activist funds and remove their entrenchment devices.[13] Now, people are more concerned about the growing short-termism rather than managerial entrenchment.

Since the 1990s, the number of hostile takeovers has decreased and shareholder activism by hedge funds has turned to play a major role in monitoring management by shareholders. Since around 2010, environmental, social, and governance (ESG) activism has increased rapidly and influenced management from the stakeholders' interests point of view. Accordingly, anti-activist pills and anti-ESG pills turn to play an important role and stimulate debates.[14]

3.1.2 Japan

In the traditional J-model, management and employees create a coalition.[15] Based on the company community norm, management, as the representative of human capital providers, bargains with the representative of monetary capital providers, which used to be the main bank.

The main bank is usually the largest creditor and, at the same time, one of the largest shareholders. It is responsible for day-to-day

[11] *See* Benjamin E. Hermalin, *Trends in Corporate Governance*, 60 J. FIN. 231 (2005); Benjamin E. Hermalin & Michael S. Weisbach, *Information Disclosure and Corporate Governance*, 67 J. FIN. 195 (2012); Benjamin E. Hermalin & Michael S. Weisbach, *Understanding Corporate Governance through Learning Models of Managerial Competence*, 48 ASIAN-PACIFIC J. FIN. STUD. 7 (2019); *See* Sonnenfeld, *supra* note 10.

[12] *See* Ronald J. Gilson & Jeffrey N. Gordon, *The Agency Costs of Agency Capitalism: Activist Investors and the Revaluation of Governance Rights*, 113 COLUM. L. REV. 863 (2013).

[13] *See* Zohar Goshen & Sharon Hannes, *The Death of Corporate Law*, 94 NYU L. REV. 263 (2019).

[14] *See* Jeffrey N. Gordon, *The Rejected Threat of Corporate Vote Suppression: The Rise and Fall of the Anti-Activist Pill*, 2022 COLUM. BUS. L. REV. 206 (2022). *See also* Chapter 6, nn.163–164 and their accompanying texts.

[15] *See* Shishido, *supra* note 4.

monitoring on behalf of all monetary capital providers. The main bank is known as the "delegated monitor." The main bank is expected to rescue the firm in case of any financial difficulty. The main bank does not generally intervene so long as the firm is profitable, but strongly intervenes with management if the firm dips into the red (known as "contingent governance").[16] The main bank story, however, gradually ended in the mid-1980s and completely ended, at least for the top listed companies, after the banking crisis of 1997.[17]

Japanese management enjoyed strong autonomy from monetary capital providers, particularly shareholders, through their social norms (i.e., the company community) and stock ownership structure (i.e., cross-shareholding). Japanese management did not care about returns on equity (ROEs) and stock prices. Instead, it cared about keeping the firm profitable and out of the red in order to prevent bank intervention and maintain autonomy.

Since the "corporate governance reform" of 2013 by the second Abe administration, such a situation has rapidly changed, and now Japanese management is forced to take shareholders' interests into consideration seriously.[18] Particularly, the two soft laws had significant impacts on Japanese corporate governance and increased the relative bargaining power of shareholders against management. The so-called Ito Report of 2014 placed ROE as a major benchmark for management to care for the cost of capital,[19]

[16] MASAHIKO AOKI & HUE PATRICK, THE JAPANESE MAIN BANK SYSTEM: ITS RELEVANCE FOR DEVELOPING AND TRANSFORMING ECONOMIES (1995). *See also* Chapter 8, nn.16–17 and their accompanying texts.

[17] *See* Yasuhiro Arikawa & Hideaki Miyajima, *Relational Banking in Post-Bubble Japan: Co-existence of Soft – and Hard Budget Constraint, in* CORPORATE GOVERNANCE IN JAPAN: INSTITUTIONAL CHANGE AND ORGANIZATIONAL DIVERSITY 51 (Masahiko Aoki et al. eds., 2007).

[18] *See* JAPANESE CORPORATE GOVERNANCE CODE OF 2015. The results of a survey asking senior managers at a sample of major corporations in 1995 shows that 97% chose "A company exists for the interest of all stakeholders" and only 3% chose "Shareholder interest should be given the first priority" in Japan; 24% chose the former and 76% chose the latter in the United States. *See* Masaru Yoshimori, *Whose Company Is It?: The Concept of the Corporation in Japan and the West*, 28 LONG RANGE PLAN. 33 (1995). *See also* Franklin Allen, Elena Carletti & Robert Marquez, *Stakeholder Governance, Competition, and Firm Value*, 19 REV. FIN. 1315 (2015).

[19] METI, Jizokuteki Seicho heno Kyosoryoku to Insenthibu – Kigyo to Toshika no Nozomasii Kankei Kochiku Purojekuto [Project of Competitiveness and Incentive for Sustainable Growth: Building Normative Relationship between Enterprises and Investors] ITO REPORT (Aug. 2014).

and the Tokyo Stock Exchange demands that its listed companies make an effort to increase their PBR concern.[20]

Employees share management's interests as members of the company community. Japanese labor unions, which are mostly company unions, have not generally been adversarial with management, though they exercise a strong voice in crises.

Japanese management generally has a strong incentive to pursue empire building due to the growth bias of Japanese firms' strong internal governance.[21] Top management often assures its subordinates of the firm's bright future by increasing the firm's size. A symbolic example can be seen in the general waste of free cash flow during the Japanese economic bubble of the late 1980s and early 1990s.[22] Still today, Japanese firms tend to acquire companies at too expensive prices.

Before 2000, few Japanese listed firms had outside directors on their boards. A typical Japanese board was not, and still is not, a monitoring board. Instead, they are a managerial board, which consists mostly of inside executive directors who make all of the important business decisions. The company auditor (*kansayaku*), a quasi-board member and the only specialized monitor on the board, is expected to play the compliance monitor role, but not necessarily an entrenchment- or empire building-monitor role. Even after the Corporate Governance Code of 2015 strongly recommended that listed firms have at least two outside independent directors, the major role of independent directors is still advisory. The board seldom replaces top management.[23]

Although the possibility of a hostile takeover in Japan has not been a reality since the creation of cross-shareholding networks in the early 1960s,[24] Japanese management has been very sensitive to the risk.

[20] PBRs of majority listed companies of Tokyo Stock Exchange are lower than 1. *See* JPX, JPX Prime 150 Index (Jan. 30, 2024), https://www.jpx.co.jp/english/markets/indices/jpx-prime150/index.html; Kazuaki Nagata, *TSE Finally Ramps Up Market Reform One Year after Questionable Restructuring*, JAPAN TIMES (Apr. 18, 2023), https://www.japantimes.co.jp/news/2023/04/18/business/tse-market-reform-ramp-up/.

[21] See Viral V. Acharya, Stewart C. Myers, & Raghuram G. Rajan, *The Internal Governance of Firms*, 66 J. FIN. 689 (2011); Hokuto Dazai, Takuji Saito, Zenichi Shishido & Noriyuki Yanagawa, *Japanese Corporate Govenance from the Perspective of Family Firms*, SSRN (2016), https://papers.ssrn.com/sol3/papers.cfm?abstract_id=2811069.

[22] *See* Shishido, *supra* note 4, at 32.

[23] *See* Zenichi Shishido, *The Monitoring Board Revisited*, *in* CORPORATE LAW AND ECONOMICS (Adam B. Badawi ed., 2023). *See* Chapter 4, Section 4.3.2.

[24] *See* Zenichi Shishido, *Reform in Japanese Corporate Law and Corporate Governance*, 49 AM. J. COMP. L. 653 (2001).

In particular, it is wary of hostile activities by shareholders and has been trying to implement defensive measures such as Japanese-type poison pills[25] and reinforce cross-shareholding to maintain stable shareholders.[26]

Since around the turn of the twenty-firsy century, this environment, which affected management's power-related incentives, has changed a lot, particularly after the 1997 Japanese financial crisis.[27] Japanese banks lost their power to continue playing the role of "main banks."[28] Cross-shareholdings decreased.[29] Instead, institutionalization has gathered momentum in Japan.[30] The internationalization of corporate governance, such as the Corporate Governance Code of 2015, forced Japanese firms to accept outside independent directors, remove poison pills,[31] and decrease cross-shareholdings.[32] Institutional investors now exercise their voice by voting against management's proposals and engagement, as encouraged in the Stewardship Code of 2014 and 2017.

25 *See* Milhaupt & Shishido, *supra* note 7.

26 *See* Sho Ho & Wataru Tanaka, *Baishu Boeisaku in za Shado obu Kabushiki Mochiai – Jirei Kenkyu* [*Anti-Takeover Measures in the Shadow of Cross-Shareholding: A Case Study*], 1885 SHOJIHOMU 4 (2009).

27 *See* Zenichi Shishido, *The Turnaround of 1997: Changes in Japanese Corporate Law and Governance*, *in* CORPORATE GOVERNANCE IN JAPAN: INSTITUTIONAL CHANGE AND ORGANIZATIONAL DIVERSITY 310, 320, 322 (Masahiko Aoki et al. eds., 2007).

28 *See* Arikawa & Miyajima, *supra* note 17. *See* Chapter 8, Section 8.1.2

29 The ratio of shares held by commercial banks, insurance companies, and non-financial firms (business partners and the parent company) to total shares issued by listed firms decreased from 69.8 percent in the 1990s to 31.7 percent in 2021. Kengo Nishiyama, *Kabushiki Hoyukozo no Henka ga Unagasu "Kigyo to Kabunushi • Toshika tono Atarashii Kankei" Kochiku* [*Change of Stock Ownership Structure Urges to Build the "New Relationship between Companies and Shareholders/Investors"*], NOMURA SUSTAINABILITY QUARTERLY, 2022 Autumn, 179, 181. *See also* Hideakai Miyajima & Fumiaki Kuroki, *The Unwinding of Cross-Shareholding in Japan: Causes, Effects, and Implications*, *in* CORPORATE GOVERNANCE IN JAPAN: INSTITUTIONAL CHANGE AND ORGANIZATIONAL DIVERSITY 79 (Masahiko Aoki et al. eds., 2007). *See* Chapter 7, Section 7. 1. 2.

30 *See* Wataru Tanaka & Gen Goto, *Nihon ni okeru Akuthibizumu no Chokiteki Eikyo* [*The Long-term Effect of Hedge Fund Activism in Japan*] *in* JSDA Capital Market Forum (Dai-2-ki) Kenkyu Ronbunsyu [The 2nd JSDA Capital Market Forum Research Papers] (Nihon Shokengyo Kyokai, 2020) 115, https://www.jsda.or.jp/about/kaigi/chousa/JCMF/gototanakaronbun2.pdf.

31 *See* Alan K. Koh, Masafumi Nakahigashi & Dan W. Puchniak, *Land of the Falling "Poison Pill": Understanding Defensive Measures in Japan on Their Own Terms*, 41 U. PA. J. INT'L L. 687 (2020).

32 *See* The Council of Experts Concerning the Corporate Governance Code, Japan's Corporate Governance Code, FSA (Mar. 5, 2015), https://www.fsa.go.jp/en/refer/councils/corporategovernance/20150306-1/01.pdf.

Since 2021, the Japanese landscape of hostile takeovers and shareholder activism has radically changed[33] and now Japanese management is forced to consider shareholder interest seriously and care about stock price and ROE.

The Japanese government has been paternalistic to businesses through what is known as "administrative guidance."[34] Each government ministry monitors firms in the industry it is responsible for, and sometimes strongly recommends a policy that private firms are hard-pressed to object to. In that sense, Japanese management has the incentive to maintain autonomy from the government, gather governmental information, and sustain good relationships with government officers at the ministry in charge.[35]

The power balance inside the government has also changed. Although bureaucrats used to play a leading role in lawmaking, policymaking, and administrative guidance, politicians have become much more influential, particularly the Prime Minister's office. Management, therefore, has an increased incentive to lobby multiple players.

3.1.3 China

In the Chinese context, the most important agency problem is between the minority shareholders (principal) and the majority shareholders (agent), due to Chinese companies' concentrated shareholding structure.

In China, there's not always a clear coalition between managers and employees, as they may have divergent interests. In privately owned enterprises (POEs), shareholders and management may constitute a coalition if managers are also shareholders. Ultimately, the Chinese Company Law may give more weight to shareholder protection. In both state-owned enterprises (SOEs) and POEs, shareholders determine how corporate power is divided. Although the Chinese Company Law appears to adopt the norm of corporate social responsibility based on the stakeholder theory, the Chinese Company Law is more concerned with the protection of shareholders' rights. This often makes sense given

[33] *See* Chapter 6, Section 6.4; Chapter 7, Section 7.1.

[34] Ezra F. Vogel, Japan as Number One: Lessons for America 65–84 (1979); Chalmers Johnson, MITI and the Japanese Miracle: The Growth of Industry Policy, 1925–1975 265–274 (1986); Takehisa Nakagawa, *Administrative Informality in Japan: Governmental Activities Outside Statutory Authorization*, 52 Admin. L. Rev. 175 (2000).

[35] *See* Vogel, *supra* note 34, at 74–76; *see* Johnson, *supra* note 34, at 265–266.

the fact that China is a less-developed country whose economic growth is the first priority. As a result, the protection of shareholders' rights may be more important to promote and attract investment, thereby increasing social well-being.

The shareholder-centric Company Law is also evidenced in the dual-board structure.[36] The director or executive's fiduciary duty is a legal concept largely transplanted from common law jurisdictions. Chinese case law (in the form of so-called "guiding cases") on fiduciary duty is still under development. Partially borrowing from other civil law countries, the Chinese Company Law adopts a dual-board system: having a board of directors and a board of supervisors.[37] The function of the board of supervisors is to supervise the performance of the directors' and senior managers' fiduciary duty.[38] This suggests a further division of corporate power between directors and supervisors, and, consequently, diminishes the likelihood of seeing a coalition at the manager level.

Employees do not share much power in the Chinese context.[39] This may sound ironic since a socialist country is powerfully rooted in its workers and rural farmers. The Company Law, on its face, stresses the concept of corporate social responsibility, even though the concept has never been adjudicated in Chinese courts. More recent cases seem to align the concept of corporate social responsibility with the corporate's compliance with laws and regulations. It is fair to say that the value of this corporate social responsibility norm is only symbolic.

Employees are given some power in corporate governance. The Company Law reformation of 2023 not only enables companies to choose between a one-tier board and a two-tier board, but also adds a requirement of 300 employees. Therefore, for a limited liability company or a company limited by shares (including joint ventures[40]) with more than 300 employees, the board of directors must include employee

[36] *See* Virginia Harper Ho, *Corporate Social Responsibility in China: Law & the Business Case for Strategic CSR*, 12 S.C. J. Int'l L. & Bus. 1, 35 (2015).

[37] *See* Chapter 4, nn.23–25 and their accompanying texts.

[38] *Id.*

[39] *See* Wei Zhang, *Learning from Your Rival? A Surprising Convergence of Chinese and American Corporate and Securities Laws*, 9 UC Irvine J. Int'l, Transnat'l, & Compar. L. 77, 91–92 (2024).

[40] A joint venture in China is a business agreement where one or more foreign investors and at least one Chinese company combine for a specific purpose. Under the Company Law of 2023, the joint venture can choose a one-tier board even though it has more than 300 employees. However, it needs to have one or more employee representative directors in the one-tier board.

representative director(s), unless the company has established a board of supervisors which includes employee representative supervisor(s) (Company Law 2023, Arts. 68 and 120). Under the Company Law 2023, it is mandatory for companies with more than 300 employees to have either employee director(s) or employee supervisor(s) to participate in democratic management.

Engaging professional managers to run companies has a short history among SOEs and POEs. Historically, SOEs were established, invested, owned, and run by the State or the State's financial or investment arms.

Due to the high inefficiency and great waste of resources, however, the State has changed the way it controls SOEs. State control now is largely reflected in two activities. First, the State largely controls SOEs by focusing on dividend payments as the key parameter of corporate performance, just as an investor would. The State may also impose hard figures on the top management in charge of disciplining managers or directors in order to improve corporate performance. Second, and more importantly, the State controls SOEs by appointing key personnel. This is particularly true for the SOEs controlled by the central government.

The chairman or general manager of a central government-controlled SOE enjoys a senior ranking equivalent to the minister or deputy minister of a ministry under the State Council, that is, the cabinet. Both the Chinese Communist Party (CCP)'s Organization Department and the State Council have the power to appoint or remove the CEO (chairman or general manager) of the SOE. At that level, a more important criterion than corporate performance may be political correctness, as defined by one's loyalty to the Party's policies and willingness to enforce them. This scheme incentivizes SOE management to advance to a higher position,[41] such as a minister in the cabinet. The Chairman of Sinopec[42] was once appointed as Minister of Industry and Information Technology. The Chairmen of Big Four banks are usually promoted to be the head of the China Banking Regulatory Commission (CBRC), the China Securities Regulatory Commission (CSRC), or the China Insurance Regulatory Commission (CIRC). In that sense, the incentive scheme is a political reward rather than a money-based compensation package.

[41] Promotion in SOEs includes promoting to a higher position in the SOEs and increasing rank within the communist party.

[42] Yizhong Li served as chairman of Sinopec between 2000 and 2003. He was appointed as the minister for the State Administration of Work Safety in 2005 and the minister of Industry and Information Technology in 2008.

While the personnel appointment is used as a vehicle for state intervention in corporate governance, the intervention usually strays away from shareholder wealth maximization. The government may pursue and promote national interests other than profit maximization[43] though both may be aligned together. The personnel appointment can be viewed as the continuation of the government's goal-setting and monitoring. As a result, SOE's senior executives and directors would have an additional duty to achieve the government's goals in practice, apart from the conventional duties of loyalty and diligence imposed by the Company Law.[44]

From the Chinese government's perspective, the power to appoint senior executives is a more efficient, effective, and superior means for policy promotion and execution, generating the loyalty of senior executives to comply with and implement government policies. This dual goal, that is, profit maximization and welfare maximization, of SOE's directors and executives also raises controversy over the performance of fiduciary duties under the Company Law due to the possible conflicts between these two goals.[45] The profit-maximization goal often clashes with the welfare goal, which causes a paradoxical dilemma in corporate governance.

For POEs, engaging professional managers to run the business also has a short history. Recently, the demand for professional managers has increased. POEs have their own logic in terms of an incentive scheme. Compared to SOEs, economic returns are certainly more important. However, that does not suggest that loyalty toward the majority shareholders or the business's controlling family is any less important. Along with economic growth and the development of corporate governance, there has also been a floating market for professional managers.

43 *See* Amir N. Licht, *State Intervention in Corporate Governance: National Interest and Board Composition*, 13 Theoretical Inquiries L. 597–622 (2012).

44 For instance, the Commercial Banking Law sets out the commercial bank's obligation to maintain financial stability. This was once the dispute between the US and China in a WTO case. The US government's view is that the maintenance of financial stability is not supposed to be in the usual scope of duty for a commercial bank. Therefore, Chinese commercial banks should be viewed as the government's department, and their lending should be viewed as a subsidy scheme. The Chinese government, however, only recognizes the government function doctrine, and even Chinese commercial banks do not play the government's function, albeit the financial stability obligation imposed on commercial banks.

45 *See* Zhaofeng Wang, *Corporate Governance under State Control: The Chinese Experience*, 13 Theoretical Inquiries L. 487–502 (2012).

However, the market may not be as floating as we expect due to various legal restrictions. For instance, there are qualifications imposed on managers or directors in some specialized industries such as banking, insurance, securities, and other financial sectors. That means that all candidates for a manager or director position in these sectors must satisfy certain qualifications. There are also other regulatory restrictions that may inhibit the floating of specialized managers. The best example is the restriction imposed by the Anti-Competition Law that disallows managers or directors from working for their former company's competitors for a period of time after their employment ends. While this restriction may protect the fairness and competitiveness of the market, it also inhibits the floating of professional managers or directors.

For SOE managers, the power of control associated with the position is an important source of incentives. SOE managers can obtain not only useful information from closed networks with other SOE managers and party officials but also the attention of other members of the network when dealing with personal matters such as personal and family friends (such as children's education, job opportunities, medical resources, etc.).[46] The ability of an SOE manager to obtain returns from the political system is closely related to his or her position (control).[47]

Similar to Japan, Chinese POE managers also have an incentive for empire building, especially those managers with political connections.[48] One popular means utilized by politically connected top POE managers for empire building is conducting cross-border M&A.[49]

3.2 Reputational Incentive

Management, as a human capital provider, cares about its reputation both in the labor market, that is, the external manager market, and in the organization, that is, among its subordinates. Management, specifically in a large firm, may also care about its reputation with the government. As a result, these reputational concerns affect the direction management pursues.

46 *See* Qingquan Xin, Anze Bao & Fang Hu, *West Meets East: Understanding Managerial Incentives in Chinese SOEs*, 12 China J. Acct. Rsch. 177, 184 (2019).

47 See *id.*

48 *See* Denis Schweizer, Thomas Walker & Aoran Zhang, *Cross-Border Acquisitions by Chinese Enterprises: The Benefits and Disadvantages of Political Connections*, 57 J. Corporate Fin. 63, 63 (2019).

49 *See id.* at 77.

3.2.1 *The United States*

Management in the United States cares about its reputation in the external manager market much more than within the organization. Management turnover is quite high in the United States,[50] which means the external manager market is quite liquid. Reputation in the external manager market directly relates to each individual member of management's price tag as well as their professional pride. Management in the United States does not care as much about its reputation among subordinates as Japanese management does.[51] It also generally does not care about its reputation with the government, unless it is large enough to actively lobby on behalf of the firm and/or its industry.

This strong incentive to maintain a good reputation in the external manager market motivates management to increase major key performance indicators (KPIs), such as ROE and stock price. Weak incentive to maintain a good reputation within the organization, however, leads to weak internal governance.[52]

3.2.2 *Japan*

Management in Japan cares about its reputation in the organization much more than in the external manager market. Management is generally groomed internally.[53] As a result, most members of top management in Japanese firms have no experience in changing firms. Therefore, the external manager market is quite illiquid. This gives management a strong incentive to maintain a good reputation in the organization, that is, among its subordinates, which leads to strong internal governance, which has, by its nature, a growth bias.[54]

Management also cares about its reputation in business roundtable-type associations in order to obtain honorable positions within them, as

50 For instance, from January to September 2023, 1,425 CEOs in the US left their positions. Tom Chapman, *Why Is CEO Turnover in the US So High?*, BUSINESS CHIEF (Nov. 10, 2023), https://businesschief.com/leadership-and-strategy/why-is-us-ceo-turnover-so-high.

51 However, even in the United States, management must care for its reputation among subordinates to a certain degree because management needs to incentivize its subordinates to follow its direction. *See* Acharya et al., *supra* note 21.

52 *Id.*

53 *See* Atsushi Yashiro, *Selection and Promotion of Managers in Japanese Companies: Present and Future Perspectives*, 10 JAPAN LAB. REV. 25 (2013).

54 *See* Acharya et al., *supra* note 21.

well as in the government, in order to obtain imperial awards. Some observers claim the reputational incentive to obtain honorable positions and imperial awards makes Japanese management risk-averse since it avoids negative press.

3.2.3 China

Reputation-based incentives work both in the context of SOEs and POEs. As explained earlier, the reward system differs based on the nature of the firm's ownership. State ownership often makes the reward system more politics-biased while private ownership makes the system more investment return-favored. As a result, this means the reward system should be designed separately and accordingly.

Managers in SOEs have their own market. These managers usually float among SOEs. Although they may leave an SOE for a better compensation package at a POE, their most valuable asset is sometimes the strong political connections forged outside of corporate operations. Within an SOE, a senior manager may give instructions to junior managers or employees at a lower level by command. A command's enforcement in the form of instructions is quite different from the enforcement of a contractual responsibility. Command enforcement depends on the seniority and implied authority of the manager. When corporate governance is not mature, a command system may work better or more effectively if managers possess seniority and authority. When this executive moves to a POE, however, their skill, expertise, and experience may have more force in leading business operations than their seniority or authority. This does not suggest the irrelevance of political connection if the manager works in a POE. Political connection still matters in the sense that the government may offer implicit or explicit incentives (which is a form of subsidy). The political connection can also be monetized. For instance, commercial banks' lending and supply chain networks may be dependent on strong political connections.

Managers who used to work in SOEs may certainly bring other values or assets to POEs. For example, their previous political connections and skills would be valuable in dealing with government authorities if the private enterprise occasionally works with the government. In China's government-dominated market economy, these political connections and skills can be useful assets.

Since SOE managers' political promotion is tied to their reputation within the corporate group, especially how their supervisors view them,

SOE managers prefer to take actions that can attract the attention of their superiors.[55] Researches show that SOE managers have a strong incentive to build image projects to achieve political promotion, including public welfare donations and media promotion reports to enhance the personal image of a company or executive in the short term.[56]

POE managers also have an incentive to maintain a good reputation because management reputation is an important competitive advantage for the firms. Empirical research shows that firms managed by CEO with good reputations receive cheaper credit than others because reputable CEOs are associated with decreased default risk and risk associated with information asymmetry.[57]

3.3 Monetary Incentive

Monetary incentive, that is, various compensations, is management's basic economic incentive. Managing a firm is a difficult task, and managers face the legal risk of being sued. As a result, other players must agree on an amount of compensation that managers would be willing to accept for the job.

Each player also prefers a management compensation package that gives management an incentive to maximize its own payoff. Shareholders, in particular, would like to organize the compensation package, most of which is equity, to better align management's incentives with their own.

Monetary incentive correlates with both power-related incentives and reputational incentives. On the one hand, a large compensation increases the entrenchment incentive. On the other hand, further monetary incentive schemes, such as a "golden parachute,"[58] decrease the entrenchment

[55] *See* Xin et al., *supra* note 46, at 186.

[56] *Id.*

[57] The sample of the study is 403 Chinese CEOs who have won prestigious media awards. Examples of awards are the Man of the Year in the Chinese Economy award from China Central Television, the Most Influential Business Leaders in China award from Fortune, the Best Business Leaders in China award from China Business News, Best CEOs of Chinese Listed Companies award from Forbes, China's Most Valuable CEOs award from Manager. *See* Xiaofeng Quan, Cheng Xiang & Ru Gao, *Reputation Is Golden: Superstar CEOs and Trade Credit*, 51 J. Bus. Fin. & Acct. 631, 631, app. B (2024).

[58] A golden parachute is an agreement between a company and upper-level executives that substantial financial benefits will be given to these executives if the company is taken over by another firm. *See* Lucian A. Bebchuk, Alma Cohen & Charles C. Y. Wang, *Golden Parachutes and the Wealth of Shareholders*, 25 J. Corp. Fin. 140 (2014).

incentive by motivating management to accept takeovers. Generally, the amount of managerial compensation correlates with the firm's size,[59] which may encourage empire building. Increasing perks, a hidden aspect of management's compensation package, is also a symbolic empire building activity. The amount of compensation as a whole is an indicator of reputation in the external manager market. In this regard, reputational incentives and monetary incentives coexist.

3.3.1 The United States

Management compensation in the United States is generally high and also highly incentivized.[60] Management's incentive to increase its own price tag in the external manager market has kept compensation amounts skyrocketing. Neither supermajority independent boards nor their compensation committees can stop it.[61] The perks are big, too, such as insurance (e.g., health insurance and life insurance) and perquisites (e.g., club/gym membership, personal use of the company aircraft, use of a company car and driver, and security services).

Most of management's compensation package consists of equity-related items, such as restricted stock and stock options. This means the major KPI of incentive compensation is the stock price. Golden parachutes are popular, too. Management compensation in the United States is generally organized to solve the agency problem between management and shareholders.

[59] *See* Lucian A. Bebchuk & Jesse M. Fried, Pay without Performance: The Unfulfilled Promise of Executive Compensation (2004); Minoru Nakazato, J. Mark Ramseyer & Eric Rasmusen, *Executive Compensation in Japan: Estimating Levels and Determinants from Tax Records*, 20 J. Econ. & Mgmt. Strategy 843 (2011).

[60] Statistics showed that total compensation paid to large company CEOs in the United States was more than two times higher than in the UK, Germany, France, and Japan. Approximately 90 percent of the total compensation paid to large company CEOs in the United States is incentive pay. *See* Takaaki Kushige, Yuki Sato, Johnathon Brown & Keiko Kanda, *Executive Pay in Japan Seeks to Improve Corporate Value*, WTW (Jan. 18, 2024), https://www.wtwco.com/en-hk/insights/2024/01/executive-pay-in-japan-seeks-to-improve-corporate-value#about-the-study.

[61] *See* Jeffery N. Gordon, *Shareholder Activism, the Short-Termist Red-Herring, and the Need for Corporate Governance Reform*, The CLS Blue Sky Blog (Mar. 28, 2016), https://clsbluesky.law.columbia.edu/2016/03/28/shareholder-activism-the-short-termist-red-herring-and-the-need-for-corporate-governance-reform/.

3.3.2 *Japan*

Management compensation in Japan is generally low and also weakly incentivized.[62] Because of the illiquid external manager market, Japanese management almost never cares about its price tag in the market. Because of the company community norm,[63] Japanese management is afraid of being criticized as greedy by its subordinates. Therefore, Japanese management has a weak incentive to increase its compensation and is always against disclosure regulations of management compensation.[64] Since monetary compensation is so low, perks are relatively significant and believed to be a major incentive for managerial entrenchment.

Incentive pay, particularly equity compensation, has not been used much because shareholders were not sensitive to aligning management's incentives with their own. Additionally, both main banks and labor unions had no incentive to make management more risk-neutral. Recently, however, the percentage of incentive pay has gradually increased due to institutionalization and trending corporate governance reform.[65] Golden parachutes have never been used not only because the possibility of a hostile takeover has not been real,[66] but also because it is a concept foreign to the company community norm.

62 Statistics showed that total compensation paid to large company CEOs in Japan was 15% of the total compensation of CEOs in the United States, and 33% of the total compensation paid to large company CEOs in Japan is base salary. Compensation for outside directors in Japan is 100% cash compensation with no equity. *See* Kushige et al., *supra* note 60.

63 *See* Chapter 2, n.124 and its accompanying text; Zenichi Shishido, *Japanese Corporate Governance: The Hidden Problems of the Corporate Law and Their Solutions*, 25 Del. J. Corp. L. 189, 201–205 (2000).

64 Japanese securities regulations require individual disclosure of directors' compensation over 100 million yen (about US$0.67 million) per year. There is a strong tendency to set management compensation at just less than 100 million yen. Recently, there has been an increase in the number of executives in Japan with compensation over 100 million yen. In 2023, the median CEO compensation in Japan was 271 million yen. *See* Kushige et al., *supra* note 60.

65 Statistics show that the percentage of incentive fees for CEO compensation in Japan has increased from 42% in 2015 to 60% in 2019, and to 67% in 2022. *See* Sumio Morita, Naoto Ogawa, Yuki Sato & Johnathon Brown, *CEO Pay Landscape in Japan, the U.S. and Europe – 2020 Analysis*, WTW (Dec. 9, 2020), https://www.wtwco.com/en-in/insights/2020/12/ceo-pay-landscape-in-japan-the-us-and-europe-2020-analysis; *See* Kushige et al., *supra* note 60.

66 *See* Koh et al., *supra* note 31. *But* regarding recent change in hostile takeovers and poison pills, see Chapter 7, n. 25 and its accompanying text.

3.3.3 *China*

In China, the compensation scheme is quite different from Japan and the United States.

The basic norm is that a monetary package may not be the most valuable thing to offer. Instead, a senior ranking position in the SOE may roll out a roadmap for a political appointment in the government. Such an opportunity itself is priceless and attracts substantial talent.

After Xi Jinping's anti-corruption campaign, there has been a pay cut to senior ranking managers or executives with political ranks equivalent to those in the government. This creates a uniform pay package at an annual salary of 600,000 yuan (approximately US$84,000). In commercial banks, insurance companies, and oil companies, mid-level managers may occasionally have higher pay based on their company ranking and seniority.

The government allows higher-ranking managers to lower their political rank within the communist party if they wish to take more pay. However, there is no reported case of a high-ranking manager lowering his political rank for more money. This suggests that at least some senior managers favor potential political promotion over money. The government ranking can be viewed as a long-term compensation measure as a mandatory way to limit managerial opportunism and excessive risk-taking.[67]

The rationale behind this uniform pay package for senior executives has never been explained or clarified by the government. There is no reason to believe that an annual salary of 600,000 yuan guarantees no corruption. Removing the heavy reliance on incentive compensation may be a way of controlling agent behavior because incentive compensations are said to make agents more self-interested.[68] This may only ensure that a senior executive in an SOE with an equivalent ranking in the government should not be overpaid while at the same time being entitled to political benefits, creating a "clean" image of SOEs and government officials to the general public.

Nevertheless, it is worth noting that Chinese firms suffer from institutional weaknesses. For instance, empirical research has confirmed a negative effect of entertainment and travel costs (a standard expenditure

[67] *See* Xin et al., *supra* note 46, at 185.

[68] *See* Nina Walton, *Crowding Theory and Executive Compensation*, 13 THEORETICAL INQUIRIES L. 429–455 (2012).

item for Chinese firms) on firm productivity.[69] This means institutional deficiencies like expropriation or corruption undermine the firms' efficiencies (in the form of profitability or transaction costs).

POEs design their compensation packages largely based on monetary value and stock options. The stock option is usually 20–25 percent of the entire package.[70] To attract talent, private enterprises often offer better pay, including stock options, to potential candidates.

3.4 Complementary Results: Direction of Management

The three different types of management incentives correlate with one another and complementarily affect the firm's direction. This section will show the complementary results of the power-related incentive, the reputational incentive, and the monetary incentive in the three countries, focusing particularly on entrenchment, balancing different interests, and risk-taking. This section will also compare the influence of markets, social norms, and laws on management's incentive structure in each of the three countries.

3.4.1 The United States

US shareholders and the US government have put a great deal of effort into implementing monitoring systems, particularly the monitoring board, in order to prevent managerial entrenchment. The liquid external manager market gives management incentive to maintain a good reputation and increase its compensation, which is each individual member's market price tag. As a reputational incentive and heavily equity-oriented compensation package, the external manager market also aligns management's incentives with shareholders' due to shareholders' interest-maximizing norm.[71]

[69] Hongbin Cai, Hanming Fang & Lixin Colin Xu, *Eat, Drink, Government: An Investigation of Corruption from Entertainment and Travel Costs of Chinese Firms*, 54 J. L. & ECON. 55 (2011).

[70] The percentage of stock options for POE management will be much higher. For example, the percentage of stock options in Tencent's directors' and executives' packages in 2022 ranged from 48 percent (Xiulian Zhang) to 86 percent (Ian Charles Stone). *See* Tencent, 2022 Annual Report (Apr. 6, 2023), https://static.www.tencent.com/uploads/2023/04/06/214dce4c5312264800b20cfab64861ba.pdf.

[71] Recently, however, the shareholder primacy norm began to be criticized and a high profile debate is taking place over for whom the corporation should be managed. *See*

Consequently, current management in the United States generally has an incentive to maximize shareholder value, especially stock prices. Management has little discretion to balance the different interests of other players with shareholders' interests because of shareholders' strong bargaining power and the Delaware case law of fiduciary duty requiring management to maximize shareholders' interests.[72] Management's approach to risk-taking is risk-neutral due to stock market pressures, although some commentators believe that the SOX actually creates risk-averse management.[73]

In sum, in the United States, monetary incentive is the most important. Management's compensation package is heavily equity-related so that management has a strong incentive to increase the stock price of its firm. Management is risk-neutral. Management cares about its reputation in the external manager market much more than it does within the internal organization. Management creates a coalition with shareholders and, at the same time, has traditionally enjoyed strong autonomy. Now, however, independent directors and institutional investors strongly monitor management's incentive to pursue entrenchment and empire building.

3.4.2 *Japan*

Neither Japanese shareholders nor the Japanese government were sensitive to the agency problem between management and shareholders.[74] Employees and creditors shared an interest in empire building with management during the Japanese economic growth period. Based on

Business Roundtable, *Statement on the Purpose of a Corporation* (Aug. 2019); Edward Rock, *For Whom Is the Corporation Managed in 2020?: The Debate Over Corporate Purpose*, 76 Bus. L. 363 (2021); Lucian A. Bebchuk & Roberto Tallarita, *The Illusory Promise of Stakeholder Governance*, 106 Cornell L. Rev. 91 (2020).

72 Particularly, in the sale of company context where the conflict between shareholders' interests and other stakeholders' interests is inescapable, Delaware courts have kept the "Revlon rule" that the board should be required to seek the highest value reasonablly available for shareholders. Revlon, Inc. v. MacAndrews & Forbes Holdings, Inc., 506 A.2d 173 (Del. 1985). *See* Rock, *supra* note 71.

73 *See* Zenichi Shishido & Sadakazu Osaki, *Reverse Engineering SOX versus J-SOX: A Lesson in Legislative Policy*, *in* Enterprise Law: Contracts, Markets, and Laws in the US and Japan 349 (Zenichi Shishido ed., 2014).

74 *See* John Buchanan, Dominic Heesang Chai & Simon Deakin, *Agency Theory in Practice: A Quantitative Study of Hedge Fund Activism in Japan*, 22 Corp. Gov.: Int'l Rev. 296 (2014).

the company community norm, all major players, including shareholders, creditors, employees, and the government, supported management's entrenchment scheme, that is, cross-shareholding. All were also strongly against hostile takeover attempts. Management cared about its reputation only in the organization, that is, within the company community. The typical compensation package did not give management any equity incentive.[75] Therefore, Japanese management generally did not have an incentive to maximize shareholder value either. Instead, it had an incentive to keep the firm profitable in order to prevent layoffs and intervention by the main bank. Banks supported such a policy and encouraged management to stay risk-averse. However, management had wide discretion to balance the different interests between shareholders and employees. This was due to strong Japanese employment protection law and the Japanese corporate law of fiduciary duty that vaguely requires management to pursue corporate interests.[76]

The market environment, which supported management's traditional incentive structure, has changed since Japanese economic growth ended in 1985.[77] However, actual changes revealed that after 2013. Institutional shareholders and the government aggressively pursued corporate governance reform that was more oriented to shareholders' interests.[78] Corporate governance reforms such as the Corporate Governance Code of 2015, 2018, and 2021, and the Stewardship Code of 2014, 2017, and 2020, as well as the institutionalization of stock ownership structure, complimentarily affected management's incentives. Japanese management now cares about shareholders' interests.[79] At the same time, it also maintains discretion in order to balance the different interests of major players.

In sum, in Japan, monetary incentive is weak. Management's compensation is low and weakly equity-related. The external manager market is limited. Management creates a coalition with employees and cares about

[75] *See* Hokuto Dazai, Takuji Saito, Zenichi Shishido & Noriyuki Yanagawa, *Corporate Governance and Firm Performance: An Implication from Japanese Listed Family Firms* 16 Asian J. L. & Econ. (forthcoming 2025).

[76] *See* Toru Kitagawa, *Complementarity among the Abusive Dismissal Rule, Company Community Norms, and Illiquid External Labor Market: Transformation of Directors' Fiduciary Duty under Japanese Corporate Law*, *in* Enterprise Law: Contracts, Markets, and Laws in the US and Japan 70 (Zenichi Shishido ed., 2014).

[77] *See* Shishido, *supra* note 63, at 215–217.

[78] *See* Chapter 2, n.137 and its accompanying text.

[79] Compare with an interview paper by an economist thirty years ago. *See* Yoshimori, *supra* note 18, at 2; *see also* Allen et al., *supra* note 18, at 1317.

its reputation in the organization, that is, the company community.[80] Management has a strong incentive to maintain the company community's autonomy against monetary capital providers. The monitoring mechanisms of management's entrenchment and empire building pursuits are underdeveloped. Management tends to be risk-averse.

3.4.3 *China*

Empirical studies have supported the view that social norms, that is, corporate social responsibility, are valued by Chinese companies seeking to shape and improve corporate image. Corporate social responsibility diffuses into various dimensions of corporate operations such as economic responsibility, organizational responsibility, employee responsibility, environmental responsibility, community responsibility, and product responsibility, which in turn form a social context for corporate practices.[81] These dimensions have contributed varying cognitive and affective images to the overall corporate image, triggering a demand for further corporate reforms.

Social capital appears to be an indispensable element in a social network-based society, which once viewed enterprises as "danwei" or units.[82] Social capital could mean social ties, civic involvement, or "social holes" within a human system.[83] In China, social capital is as important as business, which is often, if not largely, conducted in a social network. An SOE's senior executive's capability and ability to secure scarce resources depend on their hierarchical, inter-organizational, and social connections.[84] Legal scholars[85] have termed China's business model as

80 *See* Chapter 2, n.124 and its accompanying text; Shishido, *supra* note 63, at 201–205.

81 *See* Weiping Yu & Hao Hu, *Corporate Social Responsibility in Shaping Corporate Image: An Empirical Study of State-owned Enterprises in China*, *in* CORPORATE SOCIAL RESPONSIBILITY IN ASIA: PRACTICE AND EXPERIENCE 3–17 (Kim Cheng Patrick Low et al. eds., 2013).

82 STOYAN TENEV, CHUNLIN ZHANG & LOUP BREFORT, CORPORATE GOVERNANCE AND ENTERPRISE REFORM IN CHINA: BUILDING THE INSTITUTIONS OF MODERN MARKET 10 (2002).

83 Thomas W. Lee, *The Management of People in Chinese Enterprises*, *in* THE MANAGEMENT OF ENTERPRISES IN THE PEOPLE'S REPUBLIC OF CHINA 51 (Anne S. Tsui & Chung-Ming Lau eds., 2002).

84 *See* Yanjie Bai, *Social Capital of the Firm and Its Impact on Performance: A Social Network Analysis*, *in* THE MANAGEMENT OF ENTERPRISES IN THE PEOPLE'S REPUBLIC OF CHINA, ch. 12 (Anne S. Tsui & Chung-Ming Lau eds., 2002).

85 YONGQIN WANG, DEMYSTIFYING THE CHINESE MIRACLE: THE RISE AND FUTURE OF RELATIONAL CAPITALISM (2013); SHAOMIN LI, MANAGING INTERNATIONAL BUSINESS IN RELATION-BASED VERSUS RULE-BASED COUNTRIES (2009).

relational contracts or relational property, which departs fundamentally from a rule-based society. While some advocate a transition from "status" to "contract," others insist on the advantages of a relation-based governance regime.[86] Therefore, social capital may have a sizable impact on firm performance over and above the effects of shareholding control, industrial sector, and managerial skills.

The Chinese government plays a critically important role in the context of capital contribution. The government provides public capital. The government may also form SOEs or sovereign wealth funds using public capital. However, this can be quite a controversial topic in political economy, political science, or law and economics. Relying on public capital for investment can create both positive and negative results.[87]

The Chinese government seems sensitive to the agency problem, both the vertical agency problem between management and shareholders and the horizontal agency problem between majority and minority shareholders.

Corporate governance reform was a priority for the government as it pushed forward market-oriented corporatization and SOE improvement, in particular. This was because the government was keenly aware of the harm the vertical agency problem between management and shareholders might bring to SOEs and listed companies. As a result, it initiated various reform strategies. For instance, for listed companies, the government transplanted the concept of independent directors and required listed companies to have a minimum number in 2001.[88] For SOEs, it

86 *See* Kun Luen Alex Lau & Angus Young, *Why China Shall Not Completely Transit from a Relation Based to a Rule Based Governance Regime: A Chinese Perspective*, 21 Corp. Gov.: Int'l Rev. 577–585 (2013).

87 Chinese state-owned banks certainly benefited from government capital. When China joined the WTO, China's Big Four banks were almost on the edge of technical bankruptcy. The government injected US$400 billion into them in order to polish their balance sheets. Thereafter, the Big Four banks were listed on Chinese and overseas stock exchanges. Now they have become the most profitable and largest commercial lenders in the world, even defeating their major counterparts in the United States, Japan, and the European Union. Capital from the government is an implicit guarantee for that business's safety and soundness. State ownership in the banks in this sense is an implicit security, giving sufficient comfort to depositors and investors. Nevertheless, moral hazard may make these banks engage in riskier behaviors as managers and executives feel less burdened by compliance. Path dependency may also see Chinese banks continue their lending irregularities and policy-based lending business, accumulating mounting non-performing loans and thereby creating a threat to the safety and stability of China's financial system.

88 China's independent director system was officially established in 2001 when the CSRC issued Guidance Opinions Regarding the Establishment of the Independent Directors

ensured that directors and executives performed their fiduciary duty as an effective means of reducing vertical agency costs.

Amid these efforts, the Chinese government was constrained to deal with the horizontal agency problem between majority and minority shareholders. This was largely due to the vested interest the government itself has in relation to many SOEs. SOEs, in more recent years, have seen growing importance and control in more industrial sectors.[89] POEs, on the other hand, have been experiencing a retreat from more industrial sectors. This is one institutional reason for a distorted balance between SOEs and POEs. When they come to compete in the marketplace, the horizontal agency problem inhibits fair competition and effective allocation of resources.[90] The government has been trying to rebalance this through various legal and institutional means. However, the vested interest of the government and the ruling party and the prohibitively high switching cost due to path dependency made this effort less meaningful.

In the Chinese context, incentives of management in SOEs in a corporation involve three aspects. First, as the dominance of majority shareholding is the key source of the horizontal agency problem, diversifying ownership appears a solution to giving more incentives to management. This may not work, at least for SOEs, as the state may not be willing to dilute its majority shareholding control. Second, in a party-state, the authoritarian framework stresses positive incentives for compliance since the management is politically dependent on the Chinese Communist Party. The Party's power to appoint key personnel to SOEs is an effective

System in Listed Companies, which required that at least one-third of the directors of listed companies be independent directors by the middle of 2003. Wei Shen, Corporate Law in China: Structure, Governance and Regulation 226 (2015).

89 In recent years, because the government has strengthened its stance of supporting SOEs in the name of "fostering large and internationally competitive" SOEs, POEs are increasingly at a disadvantage in market competition. *See* Chi Hung Kwan, *Can China Reform State-Owned Enterprises without Privatization? – Creation of a Fair and Competitive Market Environment as the Second-Best Option*, RIETI (Mar. 13, 2020), https://www.rieti.go.jp/en/china/19041101.html.

90 For instance, SOEs can set the prices of raw materials they supply at a high level by exploiting their monopoly position in the upstream sector, and they enjoy high profitability despite their low efficiency. In contrast, as POEs in the downstream sector must purchase raw materials at high prices, their profitability is deteriorating. When SOEs seek to become stronger, they usually receive governmental support instead of exercising their own capabilities. Furthermore, many POEs are concerned about the risk that they may become subject to stronger regulation because they compete with SOEs or that they may be nationalized in a worst-case scenario. *Id.*

means to exert control in a clientelist system.[91] In institutional terminology, a centralized mode of the regulative process may affect corporate governance and corporate disciplines. The third device is to rely on the firm's internal monitoring mechanisms, which have been proven to be weak and ineffective, however.[92] There is no way to prioritize these devices as the SOE reform in the Chinese context interacts deeply with China's societal governance and political system.

In contrast, managers in POEs share common strategic orientations with their counterparts in the US and have a strong motivation to innovate and a high propensity to take risks.[93] Because profits accrue directly to them, managers in POEs have a much greater incentive to accept risk than managers of SOEs.[94] For managers in POEs, goal accomplishment is not predicted on uniformity, stability, or predictability, but on complexity, dynamism, and hostility.[95] In addition, entrepreneurs tend to be overly optimistic in analyzing environmental information, particularly when they are relatively unfamiliar with the problem and /or substantial uncertainty exists.[96] As a result, managers in POEs were more likely to identify a market opportunity, move in quickly, and gain rapid returns compared to their SOE counterparts.[97]

In sum, in China, the incentive of management is different between SOEs and POEs.

In SOEs, the incentive of political promotion is much more important than a monetary incentive.[98] Managers in SOEs are politically risk-sensitive because they must maintain a good relationship with the party representatives in their firms and are typically cautious in their interpretation of policy guidelines issued by the party and state ministries.[99] Managers in SOEs care about their political reputation in the Chinese

[91] *See* W. Richard Scott, *The Changing World of Chinese Enterprises: An Institutional Perspective, in* The Management of Enterprises in the People's Republic of China 65 (Anne S. Tsui & Chung-Ming Lau eds., 2002).

[92] *See* Dennis K. K. Fan, Chung-Ming Lau & Shukun Wu, *Corporate Governance Mechanisms, in* The Management of Enterprises in the People's Republic of China, ch. 10 (Anne S. Tsui & Chung-Ming Lau eds., 2002).

[93] Justin Tan, *Innovation and Risk-Taking in a Transitional Economy: A Comparative Study of Chinese Managers and Entrepreneurs*, 16 J. Bus. Venturing 359, 370 (2001).

[94] *Id.*

[95] *Id.*

[96] *Id.*

[97] *Id.*

[98] *See* Chapter 2, nn.144–147 and their accompanying texts.

[99] *See* Tan, *supra* note 93, at 372.

Communist Party, which remains a crucial form of capital within the nonmarket sector of the economy.[100]

In POEs, the monetary incentive is important, and stock options are popular. Because profits accrue directly to them, managers in POEs have a much greater incentive to take risks to generate greater returns.[101] The external manager market is not as developed for the CEO level, probably because most POEs are still first-generation companies, but is rather developed for the mid-manager level. As a result, it does not give managers an incentive to care about their reputation.

100 *Id.*
101 *Id.*

4

Board Systems

A board of directors is required by corporate laws in almost all major countries as the organ, placed between shareholders and management, that makes important business decisions. Its organizational composition and functions, by law and in practice, however, are varied among countries, including the United States, Japan, and China.

The board of directors in most countries currently consists of inside (executive) directors and outside (non-executive) directors. The significance of the role of independent outside directors enormously varies among the three countries. This chapter will view the board of directors as an intersection of internal governance, that is, monitoring management by subordinates, and external governance, that is, monitoring management by shareholders,[1] and compare the role of independent outside directors in the United States, Japan, and China.

Section 4.1 compares board systems of the three countries, particularly from the point of view of one-tier boards and two-tier boards. Section 4.2 compares definitions of independent outside directors, which are influenced by different stock ownership structures and agency problems of the three countries. Section 4.3 compares the roles of independent outside directors in the three countries by categorizing their roles into the roles of decreasing agency cost and the role of creating value.

4.1 General Comparison

Board systems across the globe can be categorized into two kinds from an organizational structure point of view: one-tier boards and two-tier boards.[2] The two-tier board consists of the management board, whose

[1] *See* Viral V. Acharya, Stewart C. Myers & Raghuram G. Rajan, *The Internal Governance of Firms*, 66 J. FIN. 689 (2011). *See also* Chapter 6, Figure 6.1.

[2] *See* REINIER KRAAKMAN & JOHN ARMOUR, THE ANATOMY OF CORPORATE LAW: A COMPARATIVE AND FUNCTIONAL APPROACH 50–51 (3d ed. 2017).

members are all executive directors, and the supervisory board, whose members are all non-executive directors. A typical example of a two-tier board is the German board system. In contrast, one-tier boards feature both executive directors and non-executive directors on a single board. A typical example is the US board system. Most one-tier board systems utilize several board committees, such as an audit committee, a nomination committee, and a compensation committee. The Japanese board system and the Chinese board system are located between the US and German systems: the Japanese one is closer to the US system, and the Chinese one is closer to the German system.

The board of directors' decision-making power, that is, how it shares decision-making with shareholders' meetings and management, varies among the countries, although the principle that important business decisions should be decided by the board is shared by most countries.

It is not easy to categorize the world's board systems from a functional point of view because most boards are multifunctional, performing managerial, advisory, and monitoring functions. Relative weight among those functions varies from country to country. In general, US boards are monitoring-intensive, Japanese boards are currently transitioning from managerial-intensive to managerial- and advisory-mixed, and Chinese supervisory boards are statutorily tasked with monitoring the performance and fiduciary duties of managing board members, but their actual monitoring function is questionable.

4.1.1 The United States

In the United States, independent outside directors, who occupy all seats of the board but a chief executive officer (CEO) in most listed companies, play the leading role in corporate governance, as the major compliance monitor, the reliable conflicts of interest solver, and the strong efficiency referee. The independent director is not required to be independent of controlling shareholders, but only of management.

The board of directors in the United States is a one-tier board with committees.[3] US corporate laws, particularly Delaware corporate law, are based on a board-biased principle of control that requires board involvement for important business decisions while restricting shareholders'

[3] *See* Jeffery N. Gordon, *The Rise of Independent Directors in the United States, 1950–2005: Of Shareholder Value and Stock Market Price*, 59 Stan. L. Rev. 1465, 1490–1491 (2007).

decision-making power.[4] At the same time, the board is widely allowed to delegate managerial decisions to management, except for decisions that include conflicts of interest and corporate general policy.[5]

The mainstream practice in the United States during the 1950s was an advisory board, in which CEOs chose the outside directors who would advise them. After many large companies had "questionable payment" scandals in the 1960s, the monitoring board, in which independent outside directors monitor management by selecting and firing the CEO, became rapidly accepted.[6]

Currently, a typical US board is a place of external governance rather than an intersection of internal governance and external governance. Most boards of large listed companies in the United States now consist of all outsiders but one insider, who is the CEO.[7] There is no subordinate of the CEO, and no room for bottom-up monitoring on the board. Independent outside directors who represent shareholders' interests monitor the CEO on the board.

4.1.2 *Japan*

In Japan, monitoring the "company community"[8] has been the most important issue of corporate governance. Few companies had independent outside directors before around 2000, and insiders have been reluctant to accept outsiders of the company community on the board. Although the importance of independent outside directors has been gradually recognized since the Japanese Corporate Governance Code of 2015, independent

[4] Although Delaware corporate law is based on strong shareholder primacy that requires the board of directors to maximize shareholders' interest only, it does not let shareholders decide important business issues by themselves, but instead allows directors who have more information and ability than shareholders to decide issues. *See* Stephen M. Bainbridge, *The Board of Directors, in* THE OXFORD HANDBOOK OF CORPORATE LAW AND GOVERNANCE 275, 282 (Jeffery N. Gordon & Wolf-Georg Ringe eds., 2018).

[5] The agenda setting of the US monitoring board is generally abstract and focuses on the general direction of the firm. Independent directors do not commit to specific projects. *See* Jeffery N. Gordon, *Shareholder Activism, the Short-Termist Red-Herring, and the Need for Corporate Governance Reform*, THE CLS BLUE SKY BLOG (Mar. 28, 2016), https://clsbluesky.law.columbia.edu/2016/03/28/shareholder-activism-the-short-termist-red-herring-and-the-need-for-corporate-governance-reform/.

[6] *See* Gordon, *supra* note 3 at 1516–1518.

[7] *Id.* at 1476.

[8] *See* Chapter 2, n.124 and its accompanying text; Zenichi Shishido, *Japanese Corporate Governance: The Hidden Problems of the Corporate Law and Their Solutions*, 25 DEL. J. CORP. L. 189, 201–205 (2000).

majority boards are still few, and their major role is advisory. Their efficiency referee role is not yet taken seriously in practice.

The Japanese board system is claimed to be hard to understand by foreign observers because there are three alternative board systems and the traditional board system among the three, that is, the board with company auditors (*kansayaku*) is unique in the world. First, we will explain the board with company auditors, which is still used by majority listed companies,[9] and then explain two other relatively new alternative board systems.

Although Japan's board of directors with a board of company auditors (*kansayaku*) is often categorized as a two-tier board by foreign observers, it is actually a one-tier board.[10] There is no hierarchical relationship between the board of directors and the board of company auditors, both of which are composed of members elected by the shareholders' meeting. Although it is called a "board" of company auditors, most of its compliance monitor functions – such as its inspection right and right of injunction – can be exercised by an individual *kansayaku* acting as an independent corporate organ. As such, a *kansayaku* attends the board of directors meetings and participates in discussions with directors. Functionally, the board of company auditors is closer to the audit committee in a one-tier board, rather than to the supervisory board of a two-tier board.[11]

The monitoring role of non-executive quasi board members, the *kansayaku*,[12] focused on compliance monitoring.[13] The *kansayaku* has been criticized as a useless monitor by foreign observers because it has no voting rights. In Japanese practice, however, the chairman of the board seldom proceeds with a resolution if a single *kansayaku* expresses a strong objection to a proposal.[14]

[9] *See* Zenichi Shishido, *The Monitoring Board Revisited*, *in* Corporate Law and Economics 35, 44, nn.31, 56 (Adam B. Badawi ed., 2023).

[10] *See* Kraakman & Armour, *supra* note 2, at 50.

[11] *Id.* at 50, n.5.

[12] Companies Act, Art. 2 (10). The *kansayaku* has several English translations. The traditional translation is "statutory auditor." The Japan Federation of Kansayaku defines it as an "audit and supervisory board member." The official translation by the Ministry of Justice is "company auditor" (www.japaneselawtranslation.go.jp). In this book, we will use "*kansayaku*" as it is and, if necessary, use "company auditor" as its English translation.

[13] Companies Act, Art. 384. *See* Kenjiro Egashira, Kabushiki Kaisha Ho [Laws of Stock Corporations] 560 (9th ed., 2024).

[14] *See* Bruce E. Aronson, *Japanese Corporate Governance Reform: A Comparative Perspective*, 11 Hastings. Bus. L. J. 85, 101 (2015).

Relative to the United States, the Japanese Companies Act, which is based on a shareholder-biased principle of control, gives shareholders much wider decision-making power than their US counterparts. Under the Companies Act, shareholders can decide anything if a company's charter allows it without the initiation or consent of the board of directors. Therefore, the decision-making power of Japanese boards of directors vis-à-vis the shareholders' meeting is weaker than that of US boards. On the other hand, the Companies Act limits the board of directors' ability to delegate its decision-making power to management.[15]

The traditional board is legally premised to be a managerial board that makes not only important business decisions, but also many managerial decisions, such as buying and selling important assets, appointing and removing important employees, changing important company divisions, and large-amount debt financing.[16] The advisory board's function was weak because only a few companies had outside directors on their boards before 2000. There was no concept of a "monitoring board" that would monitor management from a shareholders' interest-maximization point of view. A typical Japanese board was not an intersection of internal governance and external governance, but a place of internal governance.[17]

In 2002, a board of directors with three committees[18] was implemented as an alternative board system to the traditional board with a board of company auditors. It was the first legislative attempt to introduce the US monitoring board model. However, only a small number of companies have chosen this new alternative.[19]

[15] The traditional board is legally premised to be the managerial board that makes important business decisions. Companies Act, Art. 362 IV.

[16] Companies Act, Art. 362 IV.

[17] Because a typical Japanese board consisted mostly of insiders, *i.e.*, the CEO and his subordinates, and a few outsiders, it had a capacity of internal governance, but was not a place of external governance.

[18] Companies Act, Arts. 2(12), 326 II.

[19] According to the data by the Japan Corporate Directors Association (JACD), the number of Tokyo Stock Exchange listed companies with a board of directors with three committees is ninety-two at the end of 2023. *See* Tōkyō Shōkentorihikijo Jōjō Kigyō Shimeiiinkaitō Setchigaisha Risuto [List of Companies with Nominating Committee, etc. for Listed Companies on the Tokyo Stock Exchange], https://www.jacd.jp/news/iinkaisecchi2.pdf.

Lawmakers implemented a board of directors with an audit and supervisory committee as a third alternative board system in 2014.[20] A board with an audit and supervisory committee is a hybrid between a board with a separate board of company auditors and a board with three committees. This hybrid makes it more flexible than a board with three committees. The number of listed companies that adopted this structure has increased rapidly.[21]

While a board of directors with a board of company auditors is required to make several managerial decisions under the Companies Act, a board of directors with three committees and a board of directors with an audit and supervisory committee are allowed to delegate most managerial decisions to management. The Companies Act aims to allow the board to concentrate on policy matter discussions while introducing the monitoring board model to Japanese companies. Although many large companies have decreased the weight of their board's managerial functions, the current mainstream practice is a mixture of a managerial board and an advisory board rather than a monitoring board.

4.1.3 China

In China, because of its concentrated stock ownership, the agency problem between minority shareholders and majority shareholders is the most important issue of corporate governance. Although Chinese listed companies are required to have both a supervisory board and independent directors on the management board, neither supervisors nor independent directors substantially monitor majority shareholders to protect minority shareholders' interests because most of them are elected by majority shareholders. Their ability to effectively monitor management is also doubtful because the majority shareholders exercise excessive control. Not only SOEs but also POEs with concentrated stock ownership have this issue as well.

Regarding the sharing of decision-making power among the management board, the supervisory board, and the shareholders' meeting,

[20] Companies Act, Arts. 2(11-2), 326 II.

[21] In 2016, 676 (18.7% of all listed companies) listed companies adopted the board with an audit and supervisory committee, 831 (22.8%) in 2017, and 927 (25.1%) in 2018. In 2022, 1,392 (36.9% of all listed companies) listed companies adopted the board with an audit and supervisory committee. *See* Zenichi Shishido, *supra* note 9, at 44 n.56.

the general shareholders' meeting is the power and decision-making organ of the company and has decision-making power concerning major issues.

The board of directors is the operational implementation organ of the company, is responsible for the general shareholders' meeting, and has the decision-making power concerning management issues under the authority of the general shareholders' meeting. The board of directors may, according to the resolution of the general shareholders' meeting, set up special committees, such as a strategy committee, an auditing committee, a nomination committee, a remuneration and assessment committee. The management is responsible to the board of directors and is in charge of the daily operation and management of the company.[22]

The supervisory board is the supervision organ of the company, which supervises whether directors and managers violate laws or articles of association of the company when accomplishing their corporate duties, and is entitled to inspect the company's financials. More specifically, the board of supervisors is in charge of reviewing and monitoring the activities of directors, the general manager, and company affairs in general.

The uniqueness of Chinese corporate governance and management structure lies in the existence of a supervisory board (or the board of supervisors).[23] Separate from and parallel to the board of directors, the board of supervisors exercises supervisory powers, that is, monitoring the conduct of directors and other senior managerial personnel, which differs from the executive powers exercised by the board of directors. This creates an additional layer of checks on management. It is widely accepted that China transplanted the idea of this "supervisory board" from Germany.

The Company Law used to require all corporations[24] to establish a board of supervisors.[25] Supposedly, Chinese corporations will not set a limit on

[22] Corporate Governance in China FAQs Format, Lehman, Lee & Xu, https://www.lehmanlaw.com/resource-centre/faqs/corporate-social-responsibility/corporate-governance-in-china-faqs-format.html.

[23] Company Law 2023, Art. 130. It is important to note that prior to the reformation of the Chinese Company Law of 2023, Chinese companies are required to establish a two-tier board (with a supervisory board). Chinese Company Law of 2023 allows limited liability companies and joint stock limited companies to choose between either a one-tier board (without a supervisory board) and a two-tier board (with a supervisory board). *See infra* note 107 and its accompanying text.

[24] Corporations is a subset of companies with limited liabilities. Under Chinese company law, the type of company closest to the US corporations is named company limited by shares. In this book, we will use corporations to refer to companies limited by shares.

[25] The board of supervisors shall be composed of not less than three members. Where a corporation has a relatively small number of shareholders and is relatively small in scale,

the number of supervisors, although the law requires that at least three supervisors, including one chairperson, be appointed if a full board is formed.[26] A board of supervisors should be composed of representatives of the shareholders and employees, and at least one-third of the supervisors on the board must be employee representatives elected by the company's employees' assembly or the employee representatives' assembly.[27]

Employee supervisors are theoretically more familiar with the business operations of the company than other supervisors. It is thought that they are better able to supervise the board of directors. In reality, however, employee supervisors may be the weakest members, since their promotion and salaries are decided by the board of directors or senior managers. The goal of having employee supervisors serve as strong supervisors cannot be easily fulfilled in the Chinese context due to their lack of neutrality. In listed companies, it is unrealistic to expect employee supervisors to protect minority shareholders from oppression. Having employee supervisors on the board of supervisors may even complicate the corporate governance mechanism due to their focus and agenda. As a result, it may also create conflicts with better corporate governance or burden other players.[28]

Shareholders elect members to the board of supervisors through straight voting in companies limited by shares.[29] This rule places minority shareholders in a more disadvantaged position. In addition, supervisors in Chinese companies cannot act separately and independently. Instead, they are required to act collectively, except when attending a meeting of the board of directors.[30] As supervisors are appointed and controlled by majority shareholders, it is no surprise that a board of supervisors is much weaker than it seems.

Since a board of supervisors is tasked with supervising directors and managers, it should not include any member from the board of directors

it may have one or two supervisors instead of a board of supervisors. Company Law 2023, Art. 130. Under Company Law 2018, the board of supervisors shall be composed of not less than five members. Company Law 2018, Art. 70. Regarding the reformation of 2023, which enables companies to choose between a one-tier board and a two-tier board, *see infra* notes 107 and 108 and their accompanying texts.

26 Company Law 2023, Art. 130.

27 *Id.*

28 Let us imagine a scenario in which employee supervisors put forward a proposal to increase salaries for employees. This proposal would therefore place a new financial burden on the company. There are no clear guidelines as to how employee supervisors should perform their own fiduciary duty in navigating these complications.

29 Company Law 2023, Arts. 111 and 116.

30 *Id.*, Arts. 130–133.

or senior management. Like a director's term, a supervisor's term is three years with re-election allowed under the Company Law.[31]

The major function of a board of supervisors is to monitor the company's finances as well as the directors and senior managers personally in the performance of their duties. Although the supervisors or the board of supervisors are granted a wide range of powers,[32] their role in corporate governance is very limited. Most commentators are critical of the corporate governance role performed by a supervisory board in practice.[33] Some factors that contribute to the "figurehead" status of typical Chinese supervisory boards include limited disclosure of

[31] *Id.*, Art. 130. Additionally, the Company Law outlines the procedural rules for boards of supervisors. The board of a company limited by shares is required to hold a meeting at least once every six months. Company Law 2023, Art. 132. The supervisors can also initiate extraordinary meetings. Apart from these rules, the company may provide for detailed meeting and voting procedures in the articles of association.

[32] In order to strengthen the supervisory power, the supervisors or the board of supervisors are empowered: (i) to inspect a company's financial accounts; (ii) to oversee the conduct of directors and managers in their performance of duties and to ensure compliance with laws; (iii) to recommend the dismissal of directors or senior managers who act in breach of laws, regulations, articles of association, or shareholders' resolutions; (iv) to take legal actions against directors and managers for their wrongdoing at shareholders' request; (v) to demand directors or senior managers make corrections or to rectify their actions if such actions damage the company's interests; (vi) to call for shareholders' extraordinary meetings; and (vii) to exercise other powers provided by the articles. The articles may also grant additional powers to the board of supervisors or to the supervisors themselves. Supervisors are entitled to propose interim shareholders' meetings and put forward resolutions at such meetings, as well as to attend the meetings of the board of directors, raise concerns, and make proposals. In dealing with unusual circumstances in company operations, the board of supervisors is granted the power to engage an external accounting firm to investigate the matters (at the company's expense). *See* Company Law 2023, Arts. 77–80, 131. These powers enhance the board of supervisors' ability to get information about the company, help the board better understand corporate information, and set priorities for supervision. Supervisors can even make requisitions to the board of directors for an extraordinary general meeting and convene the meeting on their own if the board of directors fails to. *Id.*, Arts. 62, 63, 113. These powers strengthen the board of supervisors' role as a watchdog, making it possible for the board of supervisors to be involved in the business decision-making process. The power to propose, convene, and preside over a shareholders' meeting, and report what it has found augments the links between the board and shareholders. The board of supervisors or individual supervisors have the power to initiate legal action against the directors and senior managers. This power to sue provides greater deterrence to illegal behavior by management and fortifies the protection for minority shareholders.

[33] *See* Stefan C. Peij, Pieter-Jan Bezemer & Gregory F. Maassen, *The Effectiveness of Supervisory Boards: An Exploratory Study of Challenges in Dutch Boardrooms*, 7 Int'l J. Bus. Governance & Ethics 191 (2012); Xiangang Tian, *Analysis of the Functions of Supervisory Board System in Modern Chinese Companies*, 51 Int'l J. L. & Mgmt. 153 (2009).

company information, lack of attendance requirements for board meetings, and inability to consult with outside experts.[34]

The two-tier board structure in China resembles the German model, where a management board makes decisions on daily operations while a supervisory board oversees the management board and approves major business decisions. The difficulty resides in the supervisory boards' lack of appointment or removal power over the management board members, which starkly differs from the German system in which a board of supervisors has the statutory power to appoint or remove management board members. Under the Chinese Company Law, the oversight function is delegated to the board of supervisors, but the board is without meaningful powers. This again confirms the relatively stronger managerial role played by the board of directors in Chinese Company Law and dictates the destiny of the board of supervisors as a decorative creature with no teeth. The weak supervisory board of Chinese listed firms is problematic.[35] The challenge is in ensuring supervisory boards function properly and effectively.

[34] Xi Chao, *In Search of an Effective Monitoring Board Model: Board Reforms and the Political Economy of Corporate Law in China*, 22 Conn. J. Int'l Law 1, 3–7, 12–13 (2006). Foreign Investment Enterprise Laws are silent about the supervisory board, but it has long been the practice that FIEs do not form a board of supervisors. The State Administration for Industry and Commerce (SAIC) released an interpretation in September 2006 indicating that foreign invested enterprises (FIEs) formed on or after January 1, 2006, must establish either a board of supervisors or appoint individual supervisors (depending on the size of the FIE) in accordance with the Company Law. The interpretation stemmed from an earlier implementing opinion jointly issued by the SAIC, the Ministry of Commerce (the MOFCOM), the State Administration of Foreign Exchange (the SAFE), and the General Administration of Customs that requires the corporate structure of FIEs to comply with the Company Law. According to the SAIC's interpretation, all FIEs established on or after January 1, 2006, must set up a board of supervisors or appoint individual supervisors. Meanwhile, the SAIC leaves companies the discretion to decide whether to establish a board or name individual supervisors, whether supervisors will be appointed or elected, the length of their term, and the scope of their authority. A small FIE may appoint or elect one or two individual supervisors. An FIE is deemed small if the FIE has a small number of investors or a small investment. The satisfaction of these requirements is evidenced by the articles of association. If the articles of an FIE do not contain any provision in relation to the board of supervisors, the SAIC may demand that the application for the establishment of the FIE be amended. The SAIC also has the discretion to deny the FIE registration if the legal requirement of forming a board of supervisors or naming one or two is not satisfied.

[35] *See* Yong Kang, Lu Shi & Elizabeth D. Brown, *Chinese Corporate Governance – History and Institutional Framework*, 618 RAND Corp. (2008), https://www.rand.org/content/dam/rand/pubs/technical_reports/2008/RAND_TR618.sum.pdf. The Code of Corporate Governance clarifies the duties and responsibilities of a supervisory board (Code of Corporate Governance, ch. 4). The supervisory board of a listed company shall be accountable to all shareholders. The supervisory board shall supervise the corporate

The power of supervisory boards in China is gradually increasing. Prior to 2005, the supervisory board in China did not have any power to discipline poorly performing executives and only played an advisory role.[36] In October 2005, CSRC's amendment in the Company Law granted the supervisory board the power to "recommend the dismissal of directors or senior managers who act in breach of laws, regulations, articles of associations or shareholders' resolutions." (Art. 54) and the supervisory board role gained more importance.[37]

4.2 Stock Ownership Structure and the Definition of Independent Outside Directors

Independent outside directors are expected to play an important role in modern corporate govrnance in the world. However, the law and

finance; oversee the legitimacy of directors, managers, and other senior management personnel's performance of duties; and protect the company's and the shareholders' legal rights and interests. However, it only has a loosely defined monitoring role over the board of directors and managers. Given the overwhelming influence of governmental authorities on boards of directors, the supervisory boards in China have yet to play a significant and effective role in governance. *See* On Kit Tam, *Ethical Issues in Evolution on Corporate Governance in China*, 37 J. Bus. Ethics 303–320 (2002). A 1999 survey shows that the board of supervisors in some companies had difficulty performing their supervisory duties. *See* Tenev Stoyan, Chunlin Zhang & Loup Brefort, Corporate Governance and Enterprise Reform in China – Building the Institutions of Modern Markets (2002). Supervisors have little authority in major corporate decisions, particularly when their responsibility to oversee the board of directors has been only vaguely defined in the Chinese Company Law. Moreover, no law gives supervisors the right to take civil action against board directors or senior managers when company misconduct is detected, and supervisors often lack the knowledge and experience to make contributions. These difficulties make the monitoring role of a supervisory board illusionary. *See* Cindy A. Schipani & Junhai Liu, *Corporate Governance in China: Then and Now, in* Corporate Governance (Lawrence E. Mitchell ed., 2009). To strengthen the role of supervisors, Art. 61 of the PRC Corporate Governance Code states that a listed company shall adopt measures to ensure supervisors' right to learn about company matters and shall provide necessary assistance for the normal performance of their duties. Additionally, no one shall interfere with or obstruct the supervisors' work. The supervisory board may report directly to securities regulation authorities as well as other related authorities, and may report to the board of directors and shareholders' meetings when it learns of any legal violations, regulations, or articles of association by directors, managers, or other senior management personnel.

36 *See* Guanggui Ran, Qiaoling Fang, Shuai Luo & Kam C. Chan, *Supervisory Board Characteristics and Accounting Information Quality: Evidence from China*, 37 Int'l Rev. Econ. & Fin. 18, 18 (2015).

37 *Id.* at 19. This change shows that Chinese legal reformation regarding the power of supervisory boards is converging with German law. This trend parallels the reduction of shareholding requirement for proxy proposals in Company Law 2023, which converges with the US law. *See* Chapter 6, n.22 and its accompanying text.

practice of independent outside directors are significantly different among the three countries.

Although the independent outside director aims to have "independence" as an "outsider," they are mostly used interchangeably in contrast to employees who are neither outsiders nor independent of management. Therefore, we will compare the independence element, that is, independent of whom, in the three countries, and refer to different nuances of "independent" and "outside"in each country by its culture and business practice.

There are two agency problems that independent outside directors are expected to solve: the agency problem between shareholders and management (vertical agency problem), and the agency problem between minority shareholders and the controlling shareholder (horizontal agency problem).[38] To solve the former, outside directors should be independent of the management, particularly the CEO. To solve the latter, outside directors should be independent of the controlling shareholder.

In countries with a dispersed stock ownership structure, independence from management is more important. In countries with a concentrated stock ownership structure, the independence from controlling shareholders is more important.[39] However, it is questionable whether "independent directors," who are elected by the controlling shareholder, can monitor the controlling shareholder and protect the interests of minority shareholders.[40] The radical change in stock ownership structure in the twenty-first century, described as "institutionalization," requires independent outside directors to play more complicated roles.[41]

4.2.1 The United States

Stock ownership structure in the United States was the most dispersed in the world, although there are a substantial number of companies with

[38] Currently, the third agency problem, between stakeholders and the firm itself, attracts lots of attention, and accordingly, independent directors in turn are expected to solve multiple agency problems. Multiple principals will face, however, information and coordination costs. *See* KRAAKMAN & ARMOUR, *supra* note 2, at 30; Lucian A. Bebchuk & Roberto Tallarita, *The Illusory Promise of Stakeholder Governance*, 106 CORNELL L. REV. 91 (2020).

[39] *See* Dan W. Puchniak & Luh Luh Lan, *Independent Directors in Singapore: Puzzling Compliance Requiring Explanation*, 65 AM. J. COMP. L. 265 (2017).

[40] *See* KRAAKMAN & ARMOUR, *supra* note 2, at 65.

[41] Ronald J. Gilson & Jeffery N. Gordon, *Board 3.0: What the Private-Equity Governance Model Can Offer to Public Companies*, 32 J. APPLIED CORP. FIN. 1 (2020).

controlling shareholders, such as family firms[42] and listed subsidiaries (equity carve-outs[43]). Since the 1990s, the institutionalization of stock ownership has rapidly increased, and the controlling block for many large companies is owned by a few institutional investors.[44] Because of this radical change in stock ownership structure, the role of independent outside directors is expected to change from a collective action problem solver to an intermediary between management and institutional investors.[45]

Reflecting such a stock ownership structure and the US philosophy of principal-agent theory, listing rules for US stock markets regarding independent directors do not require independence from controlling shareholders, but only require independence from the company and its top management.[46]

4.2.2 *Japan*

Japanese stock ownership structure is widely dispersed, although approximately one-third of listed companies have controlling shareholders that are either founding families[47] or parent companies.[48] Cross-

[42] For example, the Walton family is the largest shareholder of Walmart, holding 50 percent of the company's shares. *See* Chapter 10, Section 10.1.

[43] *See* Benjamin C. Powell, *Equity Carve-Outs as a Technology Commercialization Strategy: An Exploratory Case Study of Thermo Electron's Strategy*, 30 TECHNOVATION 37 (2010). Examples of equity carve-outs where the parent company holds more than 50 percent shares include Trex Medical Corporation, etc. *See* Patricia Anslinger, Dennis Carey, Kristin Fink & Chris Gagnon, *Equity Carve-outs: A New Spin on the Corporate Structure*, 33 MCKINSEY Q. 165, 172, http://www.denniscarey.com/publications/Equity%20Carve%20Outs%20A%20New%20Spin%20on%20Corporate%20Structure.pdf.

[44] *See* Ronald J. Gilson & Jeffrey N. Gordon, *The Agency Costs of Agency Capitalism: Activist Investors and the Revaluation of Governance Rights*, 113 COLUM. L. REV. 863 (2013); Zohar Goshen & Richard Squire, *Principal Costs: A New Theory for Corporate Law and Governance*, 117 COLUM. L. REV. 767 (2017).

[45] *See* Gordon, *supra* note 5.

[46] *See* Puchniak & Lan, *supra* note 39.

[47] Although there are substantial numbers of listed family companies with founding families as controlling shareholders, more than 20 percent ownership, at the same time, there are many listed family firms with family senior managers without family's controlling shareholdings, less than 5 percent, in Japan. *See* Hokuto Dazai, Takuji Saito, Zenichi Shishido & Noriyuki Yanagawa, *Corporate Governance and Firm Performance: An Implication from Japanese Listed Family Firms* , 16 ASIAN J. L. & ECON. (forthcoming 2025).

[48] The number of listed subsidiaries has decreased since the middle of the 2000s and now is 209 at the end of 2023, which is about half of the number at the end of 2006. *See* Kengo Nishiyama, *Oyako-jojo no Jyokyo (2022 Nendomatsu)* [*The Current Situation of Parent-Subsidiary Double-Listing at the End of March 2023*], NOMURA INST. CAP. MKT RSCH,

shareholdings among corporate shareholders are used to stabilize majority shareholdings in most listed companies, preventing corporate shareholders from exiting or exercising their voice.[49] Since the 1997 financial crisis, however, cross-shareholdings have gradually dissolved, and since the early 2000s, foreign institutional investors have owned more than 30 percent of Japanese listed companies' stocks.[50]

The concept of the outside director was first stipulated in corporate law in 2002. Outside directors under this legislation were not required to be independent of management or controlling shareholders, but were only required to have never worked for the company or its subsidiaries. Foreign observers criticized this definition of outside directors as too broad. However, this definition makes sense, at least in the first stage of Japan's corporate governance reform, because the primary function of the independent outside director in Japan was – and probably still is – not to monitor management or controlling shareholders but to monitor the "company community."[51]

In 2014, the Companies Act modified its definition of "outside" directors and *kansayaku* by introducing a ten-year cooling-off period instead of the "never worked for the company" requirement. Now, controlling shareholders, directors, employees of a parent or sister company, as well as close relatives of directors or officers, are excluded from being considered "independent."[52]

4.2.3 *China*

Several empirical studies confirm the concentration of equity ownership of Chinese listed companies. One study suggested that the five largest

http://www.nicmr.com/nicmr/report/repo/2023_stn/2023sum11.html. It is mainly because the conflict of interests problem of the parent-subsidiary double listing has been pointed out and criticized by foreign institutional investors. *See* METI, *Guru-pu Gabanansu Shisutemu ni kansuru Jitsumu Shishin* (*Guru-pu Gaidorain*) [*Practical Guidelines for the Corporate Group Governance System*] (July 28, 2019).

49 *See* Zenichi Shishido, *The Incentive Bargain of the Firm and Enterprise Law: A Nexus of Contracts, Markets, and Laws*, *in* Enterprise Law: Contracts, Markets, and Laws in the US and Japan 1, 35 (Zenichi Shishido ed., 2014).

50 Hideakai Miyajima & Fumiaki Kuroki, *The Unwinding of Cross-Shareholding in Japan: Causes, Effects, and Implications*, *in* Corporate Governance in Japan: Institutional Change and Organizational Diversity 79 (Masahiko Aoki et al. eds., 2007); Hideaki Miyajima & Ryo Ogawa, *Convergence or Emerging Diversity?: Understanding the Impact of Foreign Investors on Corporate Governance in Japan*, RIETI Discussion Paper (2016), https://www.rieti.go.jp/jp/publications/dp/16e053.pdf.

51 *See supra* note 8.

52 Companies Act, Arts. 2 (15), 2 (16).

shareholders held 49.7 and 53.3 percent of the average POE and SOE, respectively, between 2010 and 2019.[53] As far as POEs are concerned, the average stakes of the largest shareholders in listed POEs in China maintained a level of 55 percent from 2010 to 2017. This demonstrates the prevalence of concentrated stock ownership among listed POEs and highlights the importance of minority shareholder protection.[54]

There has been a trend of more dispersed equity holding structure[55] and SOEs are more decentralized.[56] Still, some listed companies are completely owned and controlled by one or several of the largest shareholders. SOEs on the Chinese Fortune Global 500 are mostly owned and supervised by the State-owned Assets Supervision and Administration Commission (SASAC), the so-called world's largest controlling shareholder.[57]

While Chinese SOEs on the Chinese Fortune Global 500 – for example, Sinopec or China Mobile – are listed on stock exchanges in Shanghai, Hong Kong, or other world financial capitals, they are nested within vertically integrated groups.[58] Each company's majority shareholder is the core (parent) company of the group – which is itself 100 percent owned by SASAC.[59]

With the pyramidal organizational structure, albeit its agency costs, the government separates firms from political interference.[60] However, this does not change the fact that the government, through the SASAC or other investing vehicles, is the controlling shareholder of the SOEs. Although the government supports the "non-public sector" by making sure it "enjoys equal rights and opportunities and is subject to equal

[53] Kim Choi, Ju Hyun, Jungwon Suh & Shuilian Yu, *Ownership Concentration and Financial Policy of China's Listed Firms*, 79 China Econ. Rev. 1, 2 (2023).

[54] *Id.* at 99.

[55] Wenge Wang, *Ownership Concentration and Corporate Control in Chinese Listed Companies*, 11 US-China L. Rev. 57, 70–80 (2014).

[56] Zhangkai Huang, Lixing Li, Guangrong Ma & Lixin Colin Xu, *Hayek, Local Information, and the Decentralization of State-owned Enterprises in China* (WBG Dev. Rsch. Grp. Fin. & Priv. Sector Dev. Team, Policy Research Working Paper No. 7321, June 2015).

[57] Marcos Aguiar et al., *SASAC: China's Megashareholder*, BCG Persp. (Dec. 1, 2007), http://www.bcgperspectives.com/content/articles/globalization_strategy_sasac_chinas_megashareholder.

[58] Li-Wen Lin & Curtis J. Milhaupt, *We Are the (National) Champions: Understanding the Mechanisms of State Capitalism in China*, 65 Stan. L. Rev. 700 (2013).

[59] *Id.*

[60] Joseph P. H. Fan, T. J. Wong & Tianyu Zhang, *Institutions and Organizational Structure: The Case of State-Owned Corporate Pyramids*, 29 J. L. Econ. & Org. 1217, 1244 (2012).

regulations," the governmental policy still tends to maintain the dominance of state ownership.[61]

The concept of "independent director" was first introduced to listed companies by the CSRC (China Securities Regulatory Commission, China's equivalent of the US SEC) in 2001 according to the Guidance Opinions on the Establishment of an Independent Director System in Listed Companies (the Guidance Opinions),[62] which required that at least one-third of the directors of listed companies be "independent" by the middle of 2003, including at least one registered accountant.[63]

According to the Guidance Opinions, an independent director owes a fiduciary duty and duty of diligence to the listed company and all of its shareholders.[64] Further, the Guidance Opinions (which are soft law in nature) provide that if a listed company establishes an auditing committee, a nomination committee, or a remuneration and assessment committee under the board of directors, both the majority members and the conveners of such committees shall be independent directors. It also adds that at least one independent director in the auditing committee shall be a professional accountant.[65]

Chinese law deplores stock ownership by independent directors.[66] It also prohibits an independent director from having any relationship with a larger shareholder that would compromise independence.[67] Chinese law denies "independent" status to any shareholders with at least 1 percent of company stock, any top ten shareholders, and any relative of the latter.[68] Similarly, the People's Bank of China (PBOC) also

[61] Asian Corporate Governance Association, *Hard Decisions: Asia Faces Tough Choices in CG Reform*, CG Watch 2018 Spec. Rep., 118 (Dec. 5, 2018), https://www.acga-asia.org/pdf/cg-watch-2018-fullreport.

[62] Issued by the CSRC on August 16, 2001.

[63] The Guidance Opinions on the Establishment of an Independent Director System in Listed Companies. The concept, generally, of independent director appeared for the first time in the Guiding Opinions for Listed Companies' Articles of Incorporation, issued by the CSRC on December 26, 1997. This piece of rules was succeeded by the Guidelines for the Articles of Association of Listed Companies, issued by the CSRC on March 16, 2006.

[64] Yuanshi Bu, Chinese Business Law, ch. 2 (2010).

[65] Guidance Opinions on the Establishment of an Independent Director System in Listed Companies [hereinafter Guidance Opinions], Art. 52.

[66] *Id.*, Art. 1(1).

[67] *Id.*, Art. 3(2). For example, PBOC (People's Bank of China, China's central bank)'s Independent Director Guidelines view stock ownership and lengthy service as "disqualifying factors" in electing independent directors. Commercial Bank Independent Director Guidelines, Art. 9.

[68] Guidance Opinions, Art. 2.

denies independent status to any employees or shareholders with at least 1 percent ownership.[69]

In addition to the normal board authority, independent directors are afforded special powers under Chinese law.[70] When independent directors want to exercise the special powers set forth under the Guidance Opinions, they must obtain the consent of at least one-half of all the independent directors.[71] They must also disclose their opinions separately if other independent directors have different opinions.[72]

A more stringent voting mechanism has been put in place for some transactions. For instance, in a management buyout, the takeover plan shall be carried out upon the resolution of the non-affiliated directors only. The resolution requires approval from two-thirds or more of the independent directors, and then it must be submitted to the shareholders' meeting for majority consent.[73]

A listed company needs to disclose relevant information when a request or proposal by independent directors is denied.[74] Independent directors have the right to request a deferment of the related discussion or the meeting as a whole if two or more independent directors determine that the materials presented at the board of directors meeting are not sufficient.[75]

One of China's chief and ongoing measures to improve corporate governance is encouraging listed companies to increase the number of independent directors on the management board. Independent directors are put in place to fight against majority shareholder-controlled directors. However, the effect of this legal requirement is minimal. A survey in 1999 showed that around 18 percent of surveyed companies had

[69] Guidelines on the System of Independent Directors and Outside Supervisors for Commercial Banks Under the Shareholding System, PBOC (effective as of June 4, 2002), Art. 2.

[70] The special powers include approving major related party transactions, putting forward the proposal to the board of directors relating to the appointment or removal of the accounting firm, proposing to the board of directors to call an interim shareholders' meeting, proposing to call a meeting of the board of directors, appointing the outside auditing or consulting organization independently, soliciting the proxies before the convening of the shareholders' meeting. Guidance Opinions, Art. 5(2).

[71] *Id.*

[72] Guidance Opinions, Art. 6(3).

[73] Measures for the Administration of the Takeover of Listed Companies, Art. 51.

[74] Guidance Opinions, Art. 5(3).

[75] *Id.*, Art. 7(1).

independent or outside directors.[76] After the issuance of the Guidance Opinions in 2001, there has been a steady increase in independent director engagement by listed companies.[77] It has been said, however, that companies facing the new legal requirements established by the CSRC were seeking methods for nominal compliance without implementing the system completely.[78] Because most Chinese companies do not have a formal system for setting up sub-committees under the board of directors, independent directors have few opportunities to exercise their independent judgment.[79]

Empirical research seems to confirm a positive correlation between Chinese listed companies' ratio of outside/inside directors and their market/book ratio.[80] In other words, a higher ratio of outside directors on the board may enhance a listed company's valuations. Therefore, Chinese investors are theoretically willing to pay a premium for having more independent directors.

In reality, the effectiveness of independent directors in protecting shareholders' interests is questionable.[81] This may be attributed to the

[76] Dongming Li & Shiqiang Deng, *An Empirical Study on the Structure and Power of Board of Directors in Listed Companies*, 10 Sec. Mkt. Rep. 25–30 (1999).

[77] Regulation No. 102 in 2001 by the Chinese Securities Regulatory Commission (CSRC). *See* Harjeet S. Bhabra & Tiemei Li, *Independent Directors and Corporate Performance: Evidence from Listed Firms in China*, 8 Corp. Ownership & Control 145 (2011).

[78] Tong Lu, *Development of System of Independent Directors and the Chinese Experience* (Inst. of World Econ. & Pol., 2003), Ctr. for Int'l Priv. Enter. http://www.cipe.org/china/development.htm.

[79] Chinese financial regulators also require financial institutions to appoint independent directors. For instance, the PBOC, China's central bank, issued both the Guidelines on the System of Independent Directors and Outside Supervisors for Commercial Banks Under the Shareholding System (Commercial Bank Independent Director Guidelines) and the Guidelines on Corporate Governance for Commercial Banks Under the Shareholding System (Commercial Bank Corporate Governance Guidelines), which prescribe stringent qualifications for such directors, on June 4, 2002. However, these guidelines fail to specify any powers that independent directors are to assume. The introduction of the independent director mechanism to China does neither stem from legislative action nor corporate governance's natural evolution. Instead, it was a unilateral movement taken by China's administrative branch. The Company Law of 2005 later formalized the mechanism for independent director appointment. *See* Donald C. Clarke, *The Independent Director in Chinese Corporate Governance* 31 Del. J. Corp. L. 125 (2005).

[80] Chong-En Bai, Qiao Liu, Joe Zhou Lu, Frank M. Song & Junxi Zhang, *Corporate Governance and Firm Valuations in China*, SSRN 19 (2002), http://ssrn.com/abstract=361660.

[81] *See* S. H. Goo, A. R. Carver & John Whitman, Corporate Governance: The Hong Kong Debate 320–321 (2003). For example, Yili, the country's dairy giant, removed an

fact that independent directors are more like "non-executive directors," whose role is closer to being a proxy of the controlling shareholders' interests against managerial attempts at shirking and embezzlement.[82] While the concept of "independent director" has been codified into Chinese law, the level of "independence" is not clear and shareholders have no way of claiming damages from the independent directors for lack of an appropriate level of "independence." Criticism of the independent director system seems to center on the powerlessness of independent directors in protecting the interests of small or medium shareholders. Reasons for the systems' low effectiveness include a concentration of ownership in listed companies, a strong tie between ownership and management, an unclear division of monitoring power between independent directors and the supervisory board, inefficiently equipped statutory powers, and a scarcity of eligible personnel.

4.3 Independent Outside Directors' Role of Monitoring and Creating Value

Just as the board of directors is multifunctional, so is the independent outside director. The roles of the independent outside director can be categorized into the role of decreasing agency costs (the monitoring role) and the role of creating value.

The role of decreasing agency costs includes compliance monitor, conflicts of interest solver, and efficiency referee.[83] The compliance monitor role ensures that there is no violation of law and corporate charter. The conflicts of interest solver role checks decisions that include aspects of conflicts of interest, such as self-dealing, rejecting shareholder derivative actions, and issuing poison pills.[84] The efficiency referee role

independent director from the board after he demanded an independent audit of the company's investment in government bonds, a program that caused suspicion among several independent directors. B. W. Yu, *My Suspicion Confirmed*, ZHENGQUAN SHIBAO [SEC. TIMES] (Dec. 12, 2004).

[82] *See* Clarke, *supra* note 79, at 125, 176–180. Other possibilities include a limited pool of paragons of virtue, lack of motivation, lack of detailed knowledge, lack of time, and fear of litigation on the side of independent directors, among others. *See* GOO ET AL., *supra* note 81, at 321–323. Therefore, independent directors in Chinese listed companies are less useful when it comes to protecting minority shareholders' interests and improving corporate governance.

[83] *See* Shishido, *supra* note 9, at 46.

[84] The decision on the issuance of a poison pill is not a genuine conflict of interest case, but includes a business judgment aspect. Therefore, in the United States, an "intermediate"

replaces incompetent management. Monitoring entrenchment and empire building would be included in the conflicts of interest solver and/or efficiency referee roles.

Although the first two, compliance monitor and conflicts of interest solver, are bottom-line roles for independent outside directors, the third role, efficiency referee, is not necessarily taken seriously in many countries outside the United States.

Independent outside directors not only monitor management but also create value for companies. Their value-creating roles include an advisory role, a catalyst role, a kingmaker role, and an intermediary role.[85]

Advice, which is provided by diversified outside directors with various backgrounds and expertise, must be valuable to management. Strong outside directors can also, as catalysts, stimulate debate among inside directors to induce synergistic value-creating discussion within the board. Outside directors are expected to be involved in the CEO's succession plan in many countries, although the exact degree of their involvement differs and depends on the country and company. Lastly, as a result of the institutionalization and rise of activist shareholders, outside directors are expected to play an intermediary role between management and institutional investors. They are now expected to analyze the current policy of incumbent managers against proposals advanced by activist shareholders and explain to mainstream institutional investors their support for or against new proposals.[86]

4.3.1 The United States

In the United States, independent outside directors are strongly expected to play all three decreasing agency-cost roles.

The Sarbanes-Oxley Act requires management to assess the effectiveness of internal control over financial reporting and requires the company's external auditor to confirm and report on such assessment. There is a single reporting line from the external auditor to the audit committee, which exclusively consists of independent outside directors.

standard of judicial review between the entire fairness standard and business judgment standard, which respects the decision by independent directors, has been established by case law. *See* William A. Klein & John C. Coffee, Jr., Business Organization and Finance: Legal and Economic Principles 202–207 (10th ed., 2007).

85 *See* Shishido, *supra* note 9, at 48–51.

86 *See* Gilson & Gordon, *supra* note 42.

As a result, independent outside directors carry a huge responsibility as the major compliance monitor.[87]

The role of independent outside directors as conflicts of interest solvers in cases of self-dealings, shareholder derivative actions, and defensive tactics against takeover attempts has always been important. Delaware courts have generally ruled to protect judgments made by truly independent directors, which in turn has encouraged US companies to increase the number of independent directors on their boards.[88]

US independent outside directors are the most advanced and radical as efficiency referees in the world. Such monitoring boards tend to replace CEOs quickly based on stock market performance, which some commentators criticize as "short-termism."[89]

The advisory role was the main function of outside directors during the 1950s and 1960s. However, the "monitoring board" model[90] was rapidly accepted by the late 1970s and, as a result, the advisory role of outside directors was minimized.[91]

The "super majority independent" board, which consists of all independent outside directors except the CEO, is now the mainstream board in the United States.[92] On such a board, independent outside directors cannot play the catalyst role to stimulate value-creating debate among inside directors.

[87] *See* Zenichi Shishido & Sadakazu Osaki, *Reverse Engineering SOX versus J-SOX: A Lesson in Legislative Policy, in* ENTERPRISE LAW: CONTRACTS, MARKETS, AND LAWS IN THE US AND JAPAN 349 (Zenichi Shishido ed., 2014).

[88] *See* Curtis Milhaupt, *Takeover Law and Managerial Incentives in the United States and Japan, in* ENTERPRISE LAW: CONTRACTS, MARKETS, AND LAWS IN THE US AND JAPAN, 189 (Zenichi Shishido ed., 2014).

[89] *See* Benjamin E. Hermalin, *Trends in Corporate Governance*, 60 J. FIN. 231 (2005); Benjamin E. Hermalin & Michael S. Weisbach, *Information Disclosure and Corporate Governance*, 67 J. FIN. 195 (2012); Benjamin E. Hermalin & Michael S. Weisbach, *Understanding Corporate Governance through Learning Models of Managerial Competence*, 48 ASIAN-PACIFIC J. FIN. STUD. 7 (2019); Jeffrey Sonnenfeld, *Another Suicidal Board?: How DuPont's Directors Failed Ellen Kullman*, FORTUNE (Oct. 13, 2015), https://fortune.com/2015/10/13/dupont-board-ellen-kullman/.

[90] It is a board model that Melvin Eisenberg proposed during the chaotic time of US corporate governance with many scandals of large companies. The monitoring board model defines the role of the board as a monitor of management by independent directors who are independent from the management. The monitoring model emphasizes the importance of selecting and firing the CEO by at least a majority of independent directors. *See* MELVIN A. EISENBERG, THE STRUCTURE OF THE CORPORATION 130–211 (1974).

[91] *See* Gordon, *supra* note 3, at 1511–1518.

[92] *See id.* at 1476.

In addition to their monitoring role, the kingmaker role is a major function of independent outside directors. In some ways, the kingmaker role may be understood as part of the monitoring role, that is, independent outside directors fire a poor-performing CEO to elect a better one. The kingmaker role is mainly performed by the nomination committee, which exclusively consists of independent outside directors.[93]

US independent outside directors are currently also expected to play an intermediary role because of the radical change of stock ownership structure, so-called institutionalization.[94]

Ronald Gilson and Jeffrey Gordon propose a new board model, so-called Board 3.0 for playing an intermediary role between management and institutional investors. The Board 3.0 is "composed of a workable number of thickly informed, well-resourced, and highly motivated directors who could effectively monitor managerial strategy and operational skill" and would persuade institutional investors to reject activists' contentions for the time being.[95]

4.3.2 Japan

In Japan, independent outside directors are newcomers. Although Japanese corporate law stipulates that directors have a duty to monitor each other regarding compliance and conflicts of interest,[96] all board members were executive directors in most companies before the 2000s, and it was not realistic to expect subordinate directors to monitor their boss, the CEO. Japanese corporate law requires large companies to have a board of company auditors (*kansayaku*), which must have a full-time member and more than half outside members, as a specialized compliance monitor.

In a company with three committees, which was introduced in 2002, and in a company with an audit and supervisory committee, which was introduced in 2014, the audit committee plays the compliance monitor role. Since Japanese securities regulation implemented the US-type compliance regulation (so-called J-SOX), which requires public companies to report on the effectiveness of their internal controls to a specific

[93] *See* NYSE Listed Company Manual 303A.04-05; NASDAQ Marketplace Rules 4350(c)(1); KRAAKMAN & ARMOUR, *supra* note 2, at 63.

[94] *See* Gordon, *supra* note 3.

[95] Gilson & Gordon, *supra* note 42. *See also* Shishido, *supra* note 9, at 57–58.

[96] Companies Act, Art. 362 II (2). *In re* Maruzen, 27-5 MINSHU 655 (Sup. Ct. May 22, 1973).

government entity, in 2006, company auditors and audit committees have turned to play a more important compliance monitor role, but not as much as their US counterparts.[97]

Independent outside directors' role as conflicts of interest solvers has been weak in Japan, relative to its US counterpart. Self-dealing transactions and competing transactions with the company must be ratified by the board of directors. The decision of whether the company accepts or rejects a shareholder derivative action is made by the board of company auditors (*kansayaku*). However, Japanese courts do not necessarily respect judgments by independent outside directors as compared to Delaware courts. Regarding whether the company issues a poison pill or not, Japanese case law[98] and government guidelines[99] strongly suggest that shareholders decide, not the board of directors.[100] Some commentators point out that such ignorance of independent outside directors by Japanese courts is a reason for the small number of independent outside directors at Japanese companies.[101]

Although the efficiency referee role on a board of directors, particularly of independent outside directors, is recognized in theory – after the Japanese Corporate Governance Code of 2015 – the role has not yet been taken seriously in practice. There are very few cases where CEOs are fired by the board through independent outside director initiatives.

The current major role of independent outside directors in Japan is the advisory role.[102] Although the catalyst role can also be played by independent outside directors since most boards of directors in Japan are insider majority-mixed boards, this role is not easy to realize because inside directors who are subordinates to CEOs seldom intervene in front of outsiders.

[97] There are three reporting lines in Japan: from external auditor to management, board of directors, and either corporate auditors or audit committee, while there is only a single reporting line from external auditor to audit committee in the US. *See* Shishido & Osaki, *supra* note 87, at 352.

[98] *See In re* Bulldog Sauce (Chapter 7, n, 17); *In re* Tokyo Kikai (Chapter 7, n. 25).

[99] Takeover Guidelines 2005 (Chapter 7, n. 21), 2023 (Chapter 7, n.111).

[100] *See* Curtis J. Milhaupt & Zenichi Shishido, *The Enduring Relevance of the Poison Pill: A U.S.-Japan Comparative Analysis*, 28 Stan. J. L. Bus. & Fin. 336 (2023).

[101] *See* Milhaupt, *supra* note 88.

[102] *See* Hideaki Miyajima, *The Diversification of Corporate Governance Arrangements: Ownership Structure and the Board of Directors, in* Enterprise Law: Contracts, Markets, and Laws in the US and Japan 267, 272 (Zenichi Shishido ed., 2014).

The incumbent CEO used to dominate the kingmaker role by simply nominating his successor.[103] The Japanese Corporate Governance Code of 2015 and 2018, however, requires the involvement of independent outside directors for CEO succession, on a "comply-or-explain" basis. Now, most large listed companies have nomination committees.[104] Although the CEO is a member or even the chairman of most committees and their decision is not binding but advisory, a CEO now must acquire a consensus among independent outside directors to choose his successor.

Institutionalization is ongoing in Japan, too.[105] Institutional investors are beginning to influence corporate governance. The possibility for independent outside directors to play the intermediary role may now materialize. Many institutional investors have already expressed their desire to have meetings with independent outside directors.[106]

4.3.3 China

While Chinese Company Law used to only allow a two-tier board system for corporate governance structure, the Chinese Company Law of 2023 enables limited liability companies and joint stock limited companies to choose between a one-tier board and a two-tier board.[107] Companies with more than 300 employees need to have employee representatives either on the board of directors or on the board of supervisors.[108]

Although the Company Law introduced the notion of "independent director" of management boards and the Guidance Opinion gave them substantial monitoring power, including compliance monitor, conflicts of interest solver, and efficiency referee,[109] the function and the role of an

[103] *See* Kenjiro Egashira, *Nihon no Kigyoshihai* [*Corporate Control in Japan*], 7 Kihon Hogaku: Kigyo [Basic Legal: Enterprise] 73, 93 (1983).

[104] In 2022, 83.6 percent of companies at Prime Market and 92.8 percent of companies at JPX-Nikkei 400 established statutory or voluntary nomination committees. Financial Services Agency, *Corporate Governance Reform in Japan* (June 21 2023), https://www.fsa.go.jp/singi/japan_corporate_governance_forum/06.pdf.

[105] *See* Miyajima, *supra* note 102, at 268.

[106] *See* Jeffrey N. Gordon et al., *Shareholder Activism and the Role of Independent Directors in Japan, Edited Transcript*, (Horoki Sampei) at 160, SSRN (2020), https://papers.ssrn.com/sol3/papers.cfm?abstract_id=3752246.

[107] Company Law 2023, Arts. 69, 121.

[108] Company Law 2023, Arts. 68, 120.

[109] The key powers of independent directors are provided in the Guidance Opinions as follows: (1) approving major-related transactions in amounts greater than RMB

independent director are not clear. One school of thought seems to suggest that the function of the independent director is to protect small shareholders against larger shareholders if the latter make use of their advantageous or predominant position at the minority shareholders' expense.[110] This is confirmed by the Guidance Opinions, which states that

> independent directors shall . . . protect the overall interests of the company, and shall be especially concerned with protecting the interests of minority shareholders from being infringed. Independent directors shall carry out their duties independently and shall not subject themselves to the influence of the company's major shareholders, actual controllers, or other entities or persons who are interested parties of the listed company.[111]

This, however, does not make sense because independent directors are elected by the majority shareholders, and minority shareholders will not be able to elect their representatives to the board in the first place. Self-election or nomination by the board without the support of controlling shareholders and management is rare for independent directors.[112] Controlling shareholders and management are more likely to choose those who have personal or financial connections with them to have allies in needed circumstances.[113]

3,000,000 (US$362,000) or exceeding 5 percent of the listed company's net assets before these transactions are submitted to the board for discussion; (2) requesting or convening a meeting with the board of directors; (3) requesting the board of directors to convene in an interim shareholders' meeting; (4) proposing an appointment or removal of the accounting firm to the board of directors; (5) retaining independent counsel; (6) soliciting proxies; (7) being part of the listed company's salary and remuneration, auditing, and nomination committees if these committees are established; (8) delivering independent opinions at shareholders' meetings or to the board of directors concerning the nomination and replacement of directors, the appointment and dismissal of important managing positions, directors' and high-ranking managers' compensations, major loans to "parties related to the listed company," and other occurrences that could damage the interests of minority shareholders; and (9) ratifying a management buyout (Measures for the Administration of the Takeover of Listed Companies, issued by the CSRC on July 31, 2006); and (10) proposing to call an interim shareholders' meeting (Guidance Opinions, Arts. 5, 6 & 7).

[110] María Gutiérrez, & Maribel Sáez, *Deconstructing Independent Directors*, 13 J. Corporate L. Stud. 63, 65 (2013).

[111] Guidance Opinions, Art. 1(2).

[112] Wei Shen, Corporate Law in China: Structure, Governance and Regulation 228 (2015).

[113] The Guidance Opinions of 2001 provide flexibility to majority shareholders and insider directors when intervening in the nomination process, as in the following steps: (1) independent directors are nominated by any of the following: (a) incumbent members of the board of directors; (b) the board of supervisors; or (c) a shareholder who owns more

Requiring more independent directors or outside directors seems to be built upon the flawed proposition that companies should be run in a "democratic" manner. This may be true if a company is a "political" enterprise. However, as a business enterprise, a collective decision-making process is less efficient and cost-effective.

A competing proposition is that independent directors are independent of management and shareholders and can thus mediate among various constituency interests. This seems to be a weak argument as most company outsiders, including creditors, employees, customers and suppliers, can protect themselves by negotiating more favorable contract terms.

The effectiveness of their role in reducing vertical agency cost, which is raised from the agency problem between shareholders and management, is doubtful, too. Some empirical studies[114] confirmed this ineffectiveness in terms of independent directors' agency cost-reducing capabilities and independence injection into the board's decision-making process. The failure to maximize the independent director function as an institutional mechanism is interconnected with the horizontal agency problem between majority and minority shareholders in the Chinese context. Majority shareholders exercise excessive control in many aspects of corporate governance, which effectively weakens other corporate governance rules, including independent directors. In practice, it is controlling majority shareholders who appoint (at least the majority of) independent directors to the board. Essentially, the majority of independent directors vote in the interest of the majority shareholders instead of their independent business viewpoints or the company's interest as a whole.

than 1 percent equity interest. Guidance Opinion Art. 4(1). (2) The listed company must pre-file the nomination information with the CSRC and the CSRC maintains the right to dissent within fifteen days after filing. Guidance Opinion Art. 4(3). And (3) approval will be made by the resolution of the shareholders' meeting. Guidance Opinion Art. 4(1).

[114] *See* Shaowei Lin & David Cabrelli, *Legal Protection for Minority Shareholders in China*, 8 Frontiers L. China 266, 297 (2013).

PART III

The Other Three Players and Incentive Bargaining

5

Employees

For maximizing firm value, incentive bargaining between management and employees is important, particularly in two aspects. One aspect is the bottom-up monitoring of the top manager by core employees, which is called "internal governance."[1] Another aspect is the top managers' commitment to maximizing long-term firm value, which will motivate employees to provide their human capital to the firm, particularly firm-specific human capital.[2]

Between employees and management, there is a natural coalition as human capital providers share the demand for autonomy from monetary capital providers.[3] The degree of the coalition is, however, different in different countries, depending on laws, markets, and social norms.

This chapter will focus on how different dismissal rules, compensation rules, and labor union laws will affect incentives of not only human capital providers, but also monetary capital providers, and create different practices, including corporate governance, complementarily with labor markets and social norms.

5.1 Employment Protection Laws

Among enterprise laws, the employment protection law is one of the most influential to the incentive bargaining of the firm, not only between management and employees but also between management and shareholders.

There is a vital path dependency in employment protection laws. In other words, employment protection is both tough to scrap and tough

[1] *See* Chapter 1, nn.10–11 and their accompanying text.

[2] *See* Chapter 1, n.12 and its accompanying text.

[3] Zenichi Shishido, *The Incentive Bargain of the Firm and Enterprise Law: A Nexus of Contracts, Markets, and Law*, *in* Enterprise Law: Contracts, Markets, and Laws in the US and Japan 1, 12–13, note 27 (Zenichi Shishido ed., 2014).

to get,[4] probably because employment laws reflect different social expectations about employment, rather than the other way around.[5]

5.1.1 The United States

The United States has the weakest employment protection law in the world. Under the "employment-at-will" rule, employees are presumed "at-will" unless their employment contract expressly provides the term of employment or expressly limits the employer's power to discharge the employee. An "at-will" employee can be discharged at any time for any legal reason and without cause.[6]

The at-will rule does not, however, guarantee US employers no-cost discharge. First, more than a third of US workers have some form of legal right against unjust termination because they are either covered by a union contract with express for cause protection, covered by an individual employment contract with express for cause protection, or civil service employees protected by federal or state law.[7] Second, federal and state laws prohibit discharge for a variety of "bad" reasons, such as racial or gender discrimination, or filing a workers' compensation claim.[8] Finally, the states have developed common law tort and contract causes of action for discharge in violation of public policy, for example where an employer fires an employee for refusing to violate the law, or for breach of the implied covenant of good faith and fair dealing, for example, firing a salesman for the purpose of not paying earned commissions.[9] Therefore, US law and practice are not so much different from both Japanese and European law as is commonly understood.[10]

However, there is a crucial distinction between US law and the Japanese law. US law almost always permits employment termination

[4] Bruce E. Aronson et al., *Enterprise Law Conference of 2014 Edited Transcript*, SSRN (2014), https://papers.ssrn.com/sol3/papers.cfm?abstract_id=2501143 [hereinafter Transcript] 23 (J. H. Verkerke).

[5] Transcript *id.* at 19 (Curtis J. Milhaupt).

[6] RESTATEMENT (THIRD) OF EMP'T LAW §2.01 (Am. Law Inst. 2015).

[7] J. H. Verkerke, *What We Know (and Don't Know) about How Employment Protection Law Affects Employment*, *in* ENTERPRISE LAW: CONTRACTS, MARKETS, AND LAWS IN THE US AND JAPAN 53, 56–57 (Zenichi Shishido ed., 2014).

[8] U.S. Civil Rights Act, 42 U.S. Code § 2000e-2 – Unlawful Employment Practices.

[9] KENNETH G. DAU-SCHMIDT, MATTHEW W. FINKIN, RUBEN J. GARCIA, & JASON R. BENT, LEGAL PROTECTION FOR THE INDIVIDUAL EMPLOYEE 338–353, 354–362 (6th ed., 2021).

[10] Verkerke, *supra* note 7.

for a legitimate business downturn, while Japanese law constrains the shrinkage of the workforce in a time of economic difficulty.[11]

5.1.2 *Japan*

Japan has one of the strongest employment protection laws in the world, which is called the "abusive dismissal rule,"[12] under which management cannot discharge employees without good cause, which has been strictly interpreted by the courts.[13]

Japanese courts require four requirements (or factors) for termination of employment for redundancy: (1) an unavoidable business necessity; (2) fulfillment of efforts to avoid dismissal; (3) selection based on objective criteria; and (4) due process before dismissal, such as bargaining with unions and laborers.[14]

Particularly, for the first requirement, the fact that the employer would be more profitable if the employees were dismissed is insufficient. Courts may intervene with business judgments regarding termination, even those prompted by a legitimate business downturn.[15]

The way of court enforcement is not flexible. Monetary damages are not available, but courts must decide whether a dismissal is nullified or not. It increases the unpredictability of the cost of discharge and discourages employers from making necessary shrinkage of the workforce during a business downturn.[16]

Several characteristics of the traditional Japanese employment system are said to compensate for the strong employment protection law.

First, employers use non-regular workers, who are not covered by strong employment protection, to adapt to fluctuations in product demand.[17] Non-regular workers are insecure and usually paid less than regular workers, even if they do the same jobs. Such a practice has been criticized recently as unfair discrimination, and employers have been obliged to pay equal compensation for the same jobs.[18]

[11] Transcript, *supra* note 4, at 23 (J. H. Verkerke).
[12] The abusive dismissal rule was originally based on case law and became statutory law in 2004. Labor Contract Act Article 16.
[13] Shishido, *supra* note 3, at 15.
[14] YUICHIRO MIZUMACHI, RODO-HO NYUMON [INTRODUCTORY LABOR LAW] 65 (2d ed. 2020).
[15] *Id.* at 60–61.
[16] Shishido, *supra* note 3, at 14, note 32.
[17] Verkerke, *supra* note 7, at 56.
[18] MIZUMACHI, *supra* note 14, at 27–28, 110–112.

Second, employers enjoy broad freedom of choice over the newly employed. Because once an employer employs a person as a regular worker, it will be hard for the employer to discharge the employee before his/her retirement age, courts are agreeable to employees' desire to select the right person with whom they can cope for decades, including from the perspective of thought and beliefs.[19]

Third, employers have wide discretion for relocating employees, both across geographical regions and across job classifications. If an employee rejects the relocation order, it will be a good cause for employment termination. Such a practice has been socially accepted because employers may need to relocate employees to meet the second requirement to terminate employment: fulfillment of efforts to avoid dismissal. In other words, Japanese employment is not for the job but for the membership of a firm.[20]

Fourth, although work rules, including compensation, can be changed unilaterally as long as the change is "reasonable," employers need to prove the reasonableness to the court, and it is not particularly easy to decrease compensation.[21] It may also be indispensable to avoid dismissal.

Finally, even regular workers have compulsory retirement ages. This practice is prohibited in the United States and the European Union (EU) as discrimination against age. Otherwise, it would be harder for young people in Japan to get jobs because Japanese workers generally do not retire voluntarily without compulsory retirement age.[22]

Japanese strong employment protection law is evaluated both positively and negatively.

The traditional positive view is that the regulation on lay-off legally supports the work practice of lifetime employment, and lifetime employment encourages employees to develop firm-specific skills.[23] In Japan, because workers seldom move even within the same industry,

[19] Mizumachi, *supra* note 14, at 77–78.

[20] Employment for the membership also reflects other practices: centralized labor management by human resource departments (*see* Sanford M. Jacoby, The Embedded Corporation: Corporate Governance and Employment Relations in Japan and the United States (2007)); and the employment of new graduates at the same time.

[21] Employers need to verify the reasonableness to the court. It is not easy particularly to decrease compensation. *See* Mizumachi, *supra* note 14, at 48–50.

[22] Mizumachi, *supra* note 14, at 75–76.

[23] Transcript, *supra* note 4, at 14 (Yohsuke Higashi).

accumulating industry-specific knowledge is the same as accumulating firm-specific knowledge, which is human capital.[24]

The recent negative view is that the great difficulty of dismissal in Japan is strongly and significantly related to the low profitability of Japanese firms.[25] One reason may be that the case law that prevents employers from laying off people has contributed to the paucity of hostile takeovers and hence harmed corporate governance.[26]

Another significant effect of the four-factor test on the incentive bargaining of the firm is that the rule has been making the discretion of management broader than provided for under corporate law because it gives management an excellent excuse to decrease dividends during downturns rather than laying off employees.[27]

5.1.3 China

Theoretically, the role of workers in the People's Republic of China (PRC)[28] is critical, given the nature of its communist founding. The Constitution of 1982 contains several provisions referring to workers' rights, duties, and aspirations.[29] Thus, it is of no surprise that China has extensively legislated on and tightly regulated employment and employee-related matters. Given the dynamics surrounding, China's transition form central planning to market economy, as well as from authoritarian rule to the rule of law (or rule by law), regulation of the employment relationship presents complicated legal, policy, and practical issues, not only for Chinese employers and employees, but also for the government and entire society.

24 Transcript, *supra* note 4, at 22 (Takaaki Eguchi).

25 Transcript, *supra* note 4, at 21 (Takuji Saito).

26 Transcript, *supra* note 4, at 22 (Takaaki Eguchi).

27 A survey of management in 1995 shows that 97 percent of Japanese management would choose job security over keeping dividends, while 89 percent of US management would choose to lay off employees to keep dividends. *See* Masaru Yoshimori, *Whose Company Is It? The Concept of the Corporation in Japan and the West*, 28 LONG RANGE PLAN. 33, 35 (1995). *See also* Toru Kitagawa, *Complementarity among the Abusive Dismissal Rule, Company Community Norms, and Illiquid External Labor Market: Transformation of Directors' Fiduciary Duty under Japanese Corporate Law*, *in* ENTERPRISE LAW: CONTRACTS, MARKETS, AND LAWS IN THE US AND JAPAN 70, 76–77 (Zenichi Shishido ed., 2014); Shishido, *supra* note 3, at 15.

28 For the purpose of this chapter, this refers to China, excluding the Hong Kong Special Administrative Region, Macau Special Administrative Region, and the territory of Taiwan.

29 Constitution of the People's Republic of China, Arts. 42–44.

Prior to the promulgation of the Labor Law, the basic employment system was a cradle-to-grave "iron rice bowl" system, under which the state-owned enterprises (SOEs), as the main employers, would not only hire all the employees in the urban areas but also take care of their social welfare and benefits. The uniqueness of this system was that employees had no right to choose or change a job, and employers were unable to fire employees except for gross misconduct or criminal acts. Even worse, the employees were attached to the employers for life, and the employers had to take care of the employees' welfare payments.[30]

The passage of the Labor Law of 1994 represents a critical movement from the planned economy to a market-oriented one, as well as an attempt to strike a balance between employee protection and employer needs. The Labor Law and its implementing rules offer more protections to employees, especially underage and female workers, given their relatively disadvantaged positions in negotiating employment contracts and labor relations.[31]

Meanwhile, the government has been steadily reforming the "iron rice bowl" system to a social insurance safety net covering employees' social insurance and welfare and freeing SOEs and employers from financial burdens. Along with these reformist movements, the PRC has implemented social insurance reform and enacted several key labor-related laws, such as the Labor Union Law. In recent years, the government has been switching its focus from labor protection to labor relation stability. The Labor Law and other labor-related rules and regulations cover almost all aspects of labor relations, such as employee promotion, career training, labor contract, collective contract, labor standards, labor protection, social insurance, and resolution of labor disputes.[32]

However, an increasing number of high-profile and eye-catching labor actions and strikes took place due to poor treatment and benefits received by the relatively low-skilled and poorly educated country workers. Migrant workers are also constantly abused and receive inferior and unequal treatment, including underpayment and excessive working hours.[33]

[30] *See* Wei Shen & Rohan Price, *Confucianism, the Rise of Worker Activism and Labor Law in China*, 12 China: An Int'l J. 115, 122 (2014).

[31] *See id.*

[32] *See id.* at 123.

[33] *See id.*

The central government has been taking meaningful actions to address the worsening labor conditions and benefits. The Labor Contract Law[34] can be seen as a critical attempt to address the deteriorating employment relationship in the marketplace.

Another piece of labor legislation is the Labor Disputes Mediation and Arbitration Law, under which mediation ranks first as the favored approach for resolving labor controversies, and arbitration as the final step in certain disputes, subject to the right of appeal to the courts. Encouraging the use of mediation and arbitration reduces the chances of worker protest, which may give rise to unrest, strikes, or even chaos. Both the Labor Contract Law and the Labor Disputes Mediation and Arbitration Law may help create a genuine collective bargaining system.[35]

5.1.3.1 Termination of Employment due to "Redundancy" before 1984

Legally speaking, redundancy (or mass lay-offs) is a type of termination. "Redundancy" is defined as a reduction in workforce of twenty or more persons or of several persons that is less than twenty but accounts for 10 percent or more of the total number of the enterprise's employees.[36]

Redundancy is justifiable where: (i) an employer is undergoing reorganization according to the enterprise bankruptcy law; (ii) an employer is facing severe difficulties arising from production or business conditions; (iii) an employer switches production, introduces a major technological innovation or revises its business method, and after the amendment of employment contracts, still needs to reduce its workforce; or (iv) other significant changes in the objective economic circumstances relied upon at the time of the conclusion of the employment contracts, rendering them not performable.[37] Under any of these circumstances, the employer needs to explain the situation to the labor union or all

[34] Labor Contract Law of the People's Republic of China (promulgated by Standing Committee of the National People's Congress on June 29, 2007, effective Jan. 1, 2008), LAWINFOCHINA, https://www.lawinfochina.com/display.aspx?id=6133&lib=law&EncodingName=big5.

[35] Dongfang Fan, *Labor Contract Law Strengthens Chinese Union*, 8 CHINA BRIEF (Feb. 4, 2008 03:04 PM), https://jamestown.org/program/labor-contract-law-strengthens-chinese-union/.

[36] WEI SHEN, CORPORATE LAW IN CHINA: STRUCTURE, GOVERNANCE AND REGULATION 248 (2015).

[37] *Id.* at 248–249.

employees thirty days in advance and to seek the labor union's or employees' opinions.[38] The employer may reduce employees after submitting a report to the local labor bureau.[39]

There is no legal requirement that a redundancy agreement must be prepared and signed, even though the employer is required to prepare a redundancy plan. After seeking opinions from the labor union, all the employees, and the labor bureau, the employer must make necessary modifications or improvements to the redundancy plan. The function of the redundancy plan is to provide a basis for employers in handling the redundancy.[40]

Chinese law lays down the criteria that an employer must satisfy to initiate a redundancy procedure.[41] Local legislation may outline more detailed criteria. For instance, Beijing lists some standards, which constitute "serious difficulties" to the enterprise. These factors include three years of continuous losses; insolvency; 80 percent of employees having no work to do; and inability to pay minimum living allowances to the employees for six months. There are no legal requirements or guidelines for deciding the number of employees to be reduced. In most cases, it is the employer who proposes the number of employees to be laid off.

The employer may be advised to consider the restrictions imposed on the types of employees who cannot be made redundant. In other words, the employer must retain some employees when making its redundancy plan. Employees to be retained include those employees: (i) who have concluded relatively long fixed-term employment contracts with their employers; (ii) who have concluded open-term employment contracts with their employers; or (iii) who are the only ones in their families that are employed and whose families have an elderly person or a minor for whom they need to provide.[42]

In a redundancy process, an employer is required to explain the situation to its labor union or all the employees thirty days prior to the reduction, and to provide them with relevant materials and information about the production and operation of the enterprise. A reduction plan needs to be prepared by the employer. The reduction plan should set out the names of the staff to be reduced, the time for reduction, the

[38] *Id.* at 249.
[39] *Id.*
[40] *Id.*
[41] *Id.*
[42] *Id.*

implementation process, the economic compensation payable to the reduced staff, etc.

Thereafter, the employer should seek opinions from the labor union and all the employees and make modifications to the reduction plan. The modified reduction plan, plus the employees' and labor union's opinions, should be reported by the employer to the local labor bureau. The local labor bureau will not give approval to the redundancy plan. However, it can object to the plan. With the green light from the local labor bureau, the employer can publish the reduction plan, proceed with the termination of the employment contracts, make severance payments, and finally issue the release certificates to the laid-off employees.[43]

As the number of laid-off employees must be agreed to by the labor union and local labor bureau, an employer should have a strong reason for making the proposed employees redundant. A labor bureau would prefer to see a smaller number of laid-off employees so that the lay-off will not create too great a burden on society. A labor union would play an active role in the redundancy process in addition to agreeing to or making proposals for the redundancy plan. A labor union can actually order its employer to rectify the violations if the employer violates laws and regulations.

5.1.3.2 Dismissal and Contract Termination in China after 1984

Prior to the 1980s, dismissing Chinese workers was difficult owing to the requirement of the local government's approval. However, after the 1980s, China focused on strengthening its market reforms to attract foreign investments, and consequently, Chinese employee protection regulations gradually relaxed to make terminating employee contracts much easier.[44]

The necessity of government approval was lifted in 1984, and other rights concerning personnel management were reconfirmed and expanded in 1986 and 1988, including the right to lay-off redundant workers.[45] For example, the legal procedure allowing Foreign Invested

43 *Id.* at 250.

44 Haiyan Wang, Richard P. Appelbaum, Francesca Degiuli & Nelson Lichtenstein, *China's New Labor Contract Law: Is China Moving towards Increased Power for Workers?*, 30 Third World Quarterly, 485, 489 (2009).

45 Mao-Chang Li, *Legal Aspects of Labor Relations in China: Critical Issues for International Investors*, 33 Colum. J. Transnat'l L. 521, 545 (1995).

Enterprises (FIEs) to dismiss employees without government approval was first established by the 1984 Implementation Provisions on Management of Labor in FIEs.[46] It stipulates that an FIE should consult the labor union and accord the employee an opportunity to defend themselves when it starts a disciplinary action against an employee.[47] The final decision rests with the FIE's management, but a dismissal must be filed with the government department in charge of the FIE and the labor bureau in the locality.[48]

The Labor Law enacted in 1994 marks a major shift in further relaxing the employment termination process. First, the 1994 Labor Law stipulates that companies can dismiss employees by terminating the employment contract and do not need to seek additional approval from the government.[49] Second, the Labor Law of 1994 set forth clearly the legal causes for employers to terminate employment contracts.[50]

An employment contract may be terminated after consultation with the labor union and a thirty-day notice to the employee, with severance pay due, in the following circumstances: (1) the employee, after medical treatment for sickness or injuries not suffered at work, is unable to resume his or her original job or take a new job designated by the employer; (2) the employee is incapable of discharging his or her duties, or unequal to his or her job even after training or change of post; (3) there is a major change of circumstances which makes the performance of the contract impossible and the two parties cannot agree on an amendment to the contract; and (4) when the company is reorganizing on the verge of bankruptcy or facing serious difficulties in their business operation after notice is given to the employees, consultations are held with the labor union, and a report is filed with the labor bureau.[51]

After the 2000s, China sought to shift from pursuing faster growth to improving the quality and efficiency of economic growth. This created additional space for the birth of the Labor Contract Law, which – in the process of protecting workers' rights and thereby reducing potential conflict – would raise wages, boost domestic consumption, and thereby reduce reliance on foreign investment as the sole source of China's

[46] *Id.*
[47] *Id.*
[48] *Id.*
[49] *Id.*
[50] *Id.*
[51] *Id.*

economic growth.[52] The global economic slowdown that began in 2008 provided another impetus to improve and perfect the labor contract system, and China enacted the Labor Contract Law of 2008.

Under the 2008 Labor Contract Law, after a worker completes two fixed-term contracts or ten years of employment, employment contracts must be made open-ended. If employers decide not to enter into a new contract, they also must pay severance for years worked from 2008.[53] Employees with open-ended contracts must be terminated for a cause.[54] Given that many employers in China had previously used the fixed-term contract system as a way to terminate employment without requiring a cause, these restrictions are significant.[55]

The 2008 Labor Contract Law also tightened the severance conditions. The Law requires a severance pay equal to one month's pay for each full year of service (a half month's pay for less than six months' service), and double severance pay for unfair dismissal.[56] The 2008 Labor Contract Law also provides significant penalties for failure to sign written contracts, pay wages on time, or provide required social insurance benefits; it increases the power of workers to participate in decision-making regarding rules and regulations that bear on employee welfare and enhances the power of the enterprise-level labor union/trade union[57] to ensure compliance with labor regulations.[58]

In comparison with the dismissal rule in the US and Japan, the ease of employee termination in China falls in between that of Japan and the US and has changed dynamically with the social and economic conditions. Prior to the 1980s, terminating employment contracts was difficult due to the requirement of the local government's approval. This was more similar to Japan's abusive dismissal rule. From the 1980s to 2008, Chinese employee termination regulations tended to emulate those of the US by making termination of employee contracts much easier. This was done to attract foreign investment, as evidenced by the 1994 Labor

[52] Wang et al., *supra* note 44, at 489.

[53] Mary Gallagher, John Giles, Albert Park & Meiyan Wang, *China's 2008 Labor Contract Law: Implementation and Implications for China's Workers*, 68 Human Relations 197, 198 (2015).

[54] *Id.*

[55] *Id.*

[56] *Id.*

[57] Labor unions in China are called trade unions. In this chapter, both trade unions and labor unions are referred to as labor unions in China.

[58] Gallagher et al., *supra* note 53, at 198.

Law. After 2008, the enactment of the 2008 Labor Contract Law tightened the requirement for terminating employees, and Chinese dismissal rules shifted closer to those of Japan.

5.2 Compensation and Work Rules

5.2.1 The United States

Employers subject to the Fair Labor Standards Act (FLSA) must pay covered employees the current Federal minimum wage of $7.25 per hour.[59] States can also set their minimum wage and currently twenty-eight states have set minimum wages above the federal minimum of $7.25 per hour.[60] For instance, the minimum wage in California is currently $15.50 per hour for all employers.[61] In cases where an employee is subject to both the state and federal minimum wage laws, the employee is required to pay the higher of the two minimum wages.[62] Employers subject to the FLSA must also pay covered employees time and a half for any hours worked in excess of forty hours a week.[63] Since most states now have minimum wages above the federal minimum wage, the federal minimum wage is becoming less relevant.

Firms in the US pay health insurance and defined pension benefits on a per capita basis, not on the level of earnings. Although the FLSA requires overtime payments, these don't apply to most salaried employees.[64] These characteristics of American law often make it more attractive for American employers to make their employees work long hours rather than hire new workers.[65]

The US companies are more market- and shareholder-oriented than their Japanese counterparts; they spend far less on training, and their

[59] Fair Labor Standards Act, 29 U.S. Code § 206 – Minimum Wage; U.S. Department of Labor, Minimum Wage, https://www.dol.gov/general/topic/wages/minimumwage.

[60] *See* e.g., State of California Department of Industrial Relations, Minimum Wage, https://www.dir.ca.gov/dlse/minimum_wage.htm.

[61] *Id.*

[62] U.S. Department of Labor, *supra* note 59.

[63] Fair Labor Standards Act, 29 U.S. Code § 207 – Maximum Hours; U.S. Department of Labor, Fact Sheet #22: Hours Worked under the Fair Labor Standards Act (FLSA), https://www.dol.gov/agencies/whd/fact-sheets/22-flsa-hours-worked (last visited Nov. 28, 2023).

[64] Fair Labor Standards Act, 29 U.S. Code § 213 – Exemptions.

[65] Jill Rubery & Damian Grimshaw, The Organization of Employment: An International Perspective 192 (2003).

employees are weak stakeholders at best.[66] To provide an incentive for employees to search out the best opportunities, US companies rely heavily on performance-based pay, which includes generous stock options.[67] The mean for performance-based pay was 55 percent in the United States and 30 percent in Japan.[68] To encourage maximal effort, the lion's share of the options went to the top performers.[69] The bonus multiples between those judged outstanding and those seen as only mediocre were considerable.[70]

As of 2022, the average bonus pay in the US is 11% of the salary for exempt employees, 6.8% for nonexempt salaried employees, and 5.6% for hourly employees.[71] Exempt employees are not entitled to overtime, while non-exempt employees are. The most common bonuses received are year-end bonuses (11% of employees), holiday bonuses (6% of employees), and cash profit-sharing bonuses (7% of employees).[72]

Thirty-five percent of non-listed companies and 43 percent of listed companies provide equity compensation to executives and all employees.[73] Thirty-five percent of US-listed companies are providing discounts for employee stock ownership plans.[74] Thirty-two percent of US-listed companies are offering shorter and more-flexible vesting schedules that cater to employees' needs.[75] For the average worker, the perceived benefit of a restricted stock unit (RSU) award is much higher than that of stock options because RSUs generally have value throughout the lifetime of the award while stock options are far more volatile and come with a risk of being worth nothing by the time employees are able to cash out.[76] This fuels a shift in the market where stock options are being phased out in

[66] Sanford M. Jacoby, The Embedded Corporation: Corporate Governance and Employment Relations in Japan and the United States, 129 (2005); Kenneth G. Dau-Schmidt, *Promoting Employee Voice in the American Economy: A Call for Comprehensive Reform*, 94 Marquette L. Rev. 765, at 769–772, 815–818 (2011).

[67] Jacoby, *supra* note 66, at 124.

[68] *Id.* at 143.

[69] *Id.* at 124.

[70] *Id.*

[71] Jack Flynn, *30 Average Bonus Statistics [2023]: What Is the Average Bonus Percentage?*, Zippia (Oct. 18, 2022), https://www.zippia.com/advice/average-bonus-statistics/.

[72] *Id.*

[73] Stephen Miller, *Companies Ramp Up Stock Compensation to Compete for Talent*, SHRM (Mar. 1, 2022), https://www.shrm.org/resourcesandtools/hr-topics/compensation/pages/companies-ramp-up-stock-compensation-to-compete-for-talent.aspx.

[74] *Id.*

[75] *Id.*

[76] *Id.*

favor of RSUs.[77] Companies are moving towards using RSUs to reward employees.[78] While private companies may use stock options to reward employees, as they move to go public, they are switching to RSUs.[79] RSUs are taxed when the shares are delivered, which is almost always at vesting. The taxable income is the market value of the shares at vesting.

5.2.2 *Japan*

The Minimum Wage Act provides a minimum wage, and the amount per hour depends on each prefecture.[80] The Labor Standard Act §24 provides four principles for paying wages: (1) by cash; (2) directly to the worker; (3) the whole amount of the wage; and (4) more than once per month on a specific date.[81]

Although traditional Japanese contract law prohibits an employer from changing working conditions that are part of a labor contract without the agreement of the worker (Labor Contract Law, Art. 9), the Labor Contract Law allows an employer to change working conditions by changing the *rules* of employment without the agreement of the worker, if the employer informs the worker of the changed rules and the change is reasonable (Labor Contract Law, Art. 10).[82] To verify the reasonableness of the change, the employer needs to show business necessity and provide due process of labor-management negotiation. Recent court cases are strict in reviewing whether the change was substantially informed.[83]

The typical wage for a regular worker consists of a fixed base salary, overtime pay, a bonus, and retirement pay. A unique characteristic of

[77] *Id.*
[78] *Id.*
[79] *Id.*
[80] *See* MIZUMACHI, *supra* note 14, at 132–133.
[81] *See id.* at 133.
[82] *See id.* at 130–132.
[83] *See* Zenichi Shishido, Sadakazu Osaki, Nobuyuki Kinoshita, Hirohiko Nakahara, Yuichiro Mizumachi & Tetsuya Watanabe, *Zadankai: Kigyo no Issho Purojekuto [Discussion: The Life of an Enterprise Project]* (Yuichiro Mizumachi) 1219 NBL 77 (2022). Ronald Gilson and Mark Roe argue that the promise of lifetime employment cannot be an effective commitment to encourage employees to make firm-specific human capital investment because management can renege on the promise by decreasing their compensation. *See* Ronald J. Gilson & Mark J. Roe, *Lifetime Employment: Labor Peace and the Evolution of Japanese Corporate Governance*, 99 COLUM. L. REV. 508 (1999). Although management can adjust bonuses and overtime according to market changes, it is very hard to decrease the base salary under the Japanese case law.

Japanese wages is that the portion of overtime pay and bonuses is large. In fact, it is hard for employers to decrease the fixed base salary and the retirement fee, because the calculation method is contractually fixed. Employers can decrease overtime and bonus pay to adjust to the market downturns because it is extremely difficult for a large company to lay off its regular workers, even when they turn out to be redundant.[84]

Although stock options are allowed as compensation for employees and directors by the Reformation of the Commercial Code (corporate law) of 1997, they are not widely used. Although stock options are a part of the rules of employment, the official interpretation is that they are not a wage that is regulated by the Labor Standards Act. Therefore, it would be a violation of the principle of paying all wages in cash to use a stock option to decrease the employee's fixed cash compensation.[85]

The most serious problem concerning Japanese labor conditions is long labor hours. Even death as a result of overwork is not rare. Although employers are basically prohibited from making employees work more than forty hours per week and eight hours per day (Labor Standard Act, Art. 32), there used to be no limitation on overtime if employers make an agreement with the majority representative of the workplace (Labor Standard Act, Art. 36).

Although US law does not restrict the upper limit of overtime, workers may quit a company that requires overwork and find another company. In contrast, it is not easy for Japanese regular employees to change their jobs to protect their health because of the long-term employment practice, company community norms, and the illiquid external labor market. Moreover, overtime pay is an important income source for workers.[86]

The Work Style Reform Law of 2018 reformed the Labor Standard Act Article 36 and provides the upper limit of overtime by the Article 36 agreement with legal punishment. Recently, in cases of death from overwork, a substantial number of court cases ordered not only the employer companies but also directors to pay damages because of the violation of the duty of care for workers' health.[87]

[84] *See* Shishido et al., supra note 83, at 77.

[85] Yuichiro Mizumachi, Shokai Rodo-ho [Detailed Guide to Labor Law] 655 (3d ed., 2023).

[86] Mizumachi, *supra* note 14, at 163–164.

[87] *Id.* at 161–162, 160–163. Companies Act Article 429 provides directors' liability for the "third parties." *See* Chapter 8, n.106 and its accompanying text.

The work style reform will restrict large companies' abilities to use overtime work by putting a legal cap, and non-regular workers by requiring "same pay for the same work," as buffers for adjusting the workforce with market changes. Large companies shift to using subcontracts and subsidiaries to decrease labor costs.[88]

5.2.3 *China*

In accordance with the trend of promoting worker rights, the Chinese labor laws make the hiring (and firing) of local employees more expensive and burdensome.[89] Chinese law provides that employees are entitled to and employers are liable to pay social insurance and welfare benefits such as retirement and pension benefits, medical care and disability benefits for injuries or diseases that are employment-related, unemployment benefits, worker compensation for job-related injuries and diseases; pregnancy and maternity benefits; and death benefits for survivors.

The level of these benefits needs to be consistent with the level of national (and local) economic development. The total amount of these benefits may amount to one-third of each worker's monthly salary in some localities. While an enterprise is allowed to independently determine its own method of wage distribution and wage level on the basis of its own productivity rate and economic results,[90] it is also required to take into consideration the consumer price index and wage guidelines for the region,[91] which set standard rates as well as upper and lower limits for annual wage increases, and the rate specified in the collective contract.[92] Equal pay for equal work is the general norm where there is no collective contract or where the collective contract is silent on the matter.[93]

While fixed salary, bonuses based on company performance, and benefits such as health insurance and retirement plans, are basic

88 *See* Shishido et al., *supra* note 83, (Mizumachi) 1220 NBL 58.

89 Wage pressure in China has made Vietnam an increasingly attractive option for direct investment projects by foreign investors. *See* Simon Mundy, *Samsung Reveals Chinese Labor Breaches*, FIN. TIMES (Nov. 26, 2012), http://www.ft.com/intl/cms/s/0/60bde16c-37a0-11e2-8edf-00144feabdc0.html#axzz3A3LjqVjY.

90 Labor Law, Art. 47.

91 According to a report issued by the State Statistics Bureau, twenty-eight of thirty-one provinces issued wage guidelines in 2008. *See* "Statement from Two National Ministries: Last Year 28 Provinces Nationwide Issued Wage Guidelines" (May 19, 2009), https://news.sohu.com/20090519/n264052486.shtml.

92 Labor Contract Law, Art. 11.

93 *Id.*

components of a salary package, performance-based bonuses play a significant role, especially for Privately Owned Enterprises (POEs). However, managers in SOEs may focus on other objectives, such as employment growth, instead of profit maximization.[94] In SOEs, senior managers' compensation is more likely to be related to the civil service pay scale rather than pay-for-performance.[95] In general, listed companies offer better benefits, such as additional insurance coverage and more equity incentive plans, than non-listed companies.[96]

5.2.3.1 Service Awards

The concept of "seniority allowance" is equivalent to the concept of "service awards." The employer has the discretion to offer a special bonus to a particular employee because of their long-term service. The seniority allowance is part of the employee's total wages.

5.2.3.2 Profit-Sharing Scheme

It is common in China to offer employees participation in an employee share plan (also known as an equity incentive plan). In 2021, over 800 domestic listed companies in China had equity incentive plans.[97] Among them, about 400 listed companies implemented equity incentive plans for the first time.[98] Equity incentive plans have become common and are considered an effective means for listed companies to improve corporate governance and enhance their governance capabilities.

Additionally, more non-listed companies are realizing the importance of equity incentive plans to improve their company's performance and their employees' loyalty, especially for start-up companies with limited capital in their early stages.[99] Non-listed companies frequently use equity incentive plans to attract and retain talent.[100]

94 *See* Lei Luo, *Determinants of Stock Option Use by Chinese Companies*, 31 J. APPLIED BUS. RSCH. 1355, 1357 (2015).

95 *See id.*

96 NNNEWS, 2022 NIAN SHANGSHIGONGSI RENCAI FAZHAN QUSHI BAOGAO [2022 Talent Development Trend Report of Listed Companies], http://www.nnnews.net/p/3160683.html.

97 Gordon (Minghao) Feng and Peter (Yi) Zhu, *Employee Share Plans in China: Regulatory Overview*, THOMSON REUTERS PRAC. L. (2025), https://uk.practicallaw.thomsonreuters.com/9-507-4557?transitionType=Default&contextData=(sc.Default)&firstPage=true.

98 *Id.*

99 *Id.*

100 *Id.*

Small enterprises are encouraged to adopt a profit-sharing scheme if their capital return ratio and net assets gain ratio are above the social average. The scheme should be approved by the employees' representatives committee or the labor union, as well as by the board of directors and the shareholders. The scheme should also be examined and approved by the labor bureau and the assets management department of the government before implementation.

Under the Company Law of 1994, adopting stock-based employee incentive schemes was problematic. Stock-based incentives were once a novel concept and practice in Chinese law, partly because the Chinese Labor Law only allowed payment of wages and bonuses to be made in cash. The Company Law of 1994 did not adopt the concept of share buy-backs, which made the adoption of the share option plan difficult.[101] Employees in SOEs were generally not permitted to hold stock options due to the regulatory control over the state's assets. Due to regulatory barriers, multinational companies were not able to include Chinese employees, working in their PRC subsidiaries, in their global stock-based incentive schemes.

The amended Company Law of 2018[102] and other regulations,[103] eventually eliminated major legal barriers and deregulated the overall legal environment for stock-based incentive schemes. The Measures for the Administration of Equity Incentives of Listed Companies (the "Measures") promulgated by the China Securities Regulatory

[101] The 2018 amendments to the Company Law allow share buy-back, which, however, only applies to listed companies. Even in the United States, share buy-backs can help companies offset the dilution caused by stock option issuance. The ability to buy back shares provides companies with an incentive to companies an incentive to "pay employees more in options instead of salaries." *See* Bolko Hohaus, *Share Buybacks and Employee Stock Options*, 16 CESIFO FORUM 79, 79 (2015).

[102] Company Law of the People's Republic of China was adopted on December 29, 1993, and had six amendments. The first amendment was on December 25, 1999. The second amendment was on August 28, 2004. The third amendment was on October 27, 2005. The fourth amendment was on December 28, 2013. The fifth amendment was on October 26, 2018. The sixth amendment was on December 29, 2023.

[103] Among others, these regulations include but are not limited to the Several Opinions on Promoting the Reform, Opening-Up and Stable Development of Capital Markets (issued by the State Council in 2004); the Guidelines for Reform of Segmented Shares of Listed Companies (issued by the China Securities Regulatory Commission [the CSRC]), State-owned Assets Supervision and Administration Commission, Ministry of Finance, the People's Bank of China (the PBOC) and the Ministry of Commerce (the MOFCOM); Tax Circular [2005] No. 35 (issued by the Ministry of Finance and the State Administration of Taxation).

Commission (the "CSRC") became effective on January 1, 2006. The Measures systematically provide, for the first time, detailed guidelines for the implementation of stock options and stock-based incentive schemes for employees in listed companies.[104] Since then, Chinese listed companies that have completed the share-trading reform are allowed to use option-based compensation for top management and employees.[105] However, several companies attempt to use stock options as a welfare system.[106] For example, some companies set option strike prices significantly lower than their prevailing market price; exercise standards are extremely lax for some option plans; some companies introduce incentive plans immediately before positive corporate information disclosure.[107]

Employees may acquire or be rewarded with stocks or stock options in a locally listed enterprise at which they work. The management personnel or employees with higher responsibilities may hold as much as five to fifteen times the stock held by other employees.[108]

In general, the Employee Stock Option (ESO) regulations in China are stricter than those in the United States and other developed economies.[109] Specifically, eligible recipients may include directors, senior executives, core technical personnel, and management backbones, but exclude supervisors[110] and independent directors.[111] The size of the option pool shall not exceed 10 percent of the company's total share capital, and a single grantee cannot hold more than 1 percent of the total share capital of the company.[112] In particular, for a senior manager of SOEs, the prospective equity incentive earnings shall be controlled within 30 percent of her total compensation (including the prospective option and equity earnings) during the validity period of an equity incentive plan.[113]

104 Luo, *supra* note 94, at 1356.
105 *Id.*
106 *Id.*
107 *Id.*
108 *Id.*
109 *Id.*
110 Supervisors refer to member of the supervisory board.
111 Guidelines for the Supervision of Unlisted Public Companies No. 6 – Supervisory Requirements for Equity Incentive and Employee Stock Option Plans (promulgated by China Securities Regulatory Commission on Aug. 21, 2020, effective Aug. 21, 2020), LAWINFOCHINA, https://lawinfochina.com/display.aspx?id=34406&lib=law&SearchKeyword=&SearchCKeyword=.
112 Luo, *supra* note 94, at 1356.
113 *Id.*

The employee's participation in the Employee Stock Ownership Plan is on a voluntary basis. The employer is required to discuss items such as the criteria of qualified employees, the number of shares to be purchased, and the plan of purchase with the employees collectively and to get approval from the shareholders. Employees can purchase shares or be awarded shares.[114]

5.3 Labor Union Laws and Labor-Management Relationships

Labor union laws provide rules for negotiations between employees and management, for example, the collective bargaining rule, in which labor unions play an important role.[115]

Labor union laws and practices also affect coalition building among the four players of corporate governance, particularly between management and employees, and so will affect the corporate governance of the country.

5.3.1 The United States

The unionized rate in the United States in 2020 was 10.8 percent overall and only 6.4 percent in the private sector.[116] Some commentators observe that labor unions are essentially a non-factor in US corporate governance.[117]

Overall, US labor laws are relatively restrictive to unions' ability to organize and inflict costs on their employers, and give employers relatively strong weapons to resist employee organization and strikes.

Regarding the definition of covered workers, the US labor law has broad exceptions, including exceptions for supervisors, managers, confidential employees, agricultural employees, and independent contractors.[118] Indeed, as "small businesses," independent contractors are

[114] *See* Lei Zhou, Feng Wei & Yu Kong, *Do Employee Stock Ownership Plans Affect Corporate Social Responsibility? Evidence from China*, 19 Int'l J. Env't Rsch & Pub. Health 1055, 1055 (2022) (stating that 430,000 ordinary employees in China have purchased shares in their companies through ESOPs as of December 2019).

[115] *See* Shishido, *supra* note 3, at 16.

[116] BLS, A Look at Union Membership Rates across Industries in 2020 (Feb. 25, 2021), https://www.bls.gov/opub/ted/2021/a-look-at-union-membership-rates-across-industries-in-2020.htm.

[117] Transcript, *supra* note 4, at 28 (Curtis Milhaupt).

[118] *Id.* at 25; 29 U.S.C. § 152 (3); Kenneth G. Dau-Schmidt & Michael D. Ray, *The Definition of "Employee" in American Labor and Employment Law*, 53 Bull. Comp. Lab. Rel. 59 (2004).

prohibited from organizing under American Antitrust law and are liable for triple damages for any collective action they take.[119]

US labor law provides a burdensome election procedure for employee organizations. Unions must make a sufficient showing of interests by collecting representation cards from employees to petition for a representation election.[120] The employer is free to campaign against the union and even compel employees to attend company "captive audience" meetings at which the union is disparaged.[121] The National Labor Relations Act (NLRA) sanctions for the employer commission of unfair labor practices, such as discharging union supporters are purely remedial (reinstatement and backpay) and do not provide deterrence for recalcitrant employers.[122]

Even if the employees successfully organize, the US labor law imposes restrictions on employee collective action while giving employers significant powers to resist employee collective action and destroy the union. Congress passed the Taft-Hartley and Landrum-Griffen Amendments to the NLRA with the specific purpose of reining in union power.[123] Secondary boycotts are prohibited, and partial slowdowns or partial work stoppages are unprotected.[124] US employers can permanently replace economic strikers and can engage in offensive lockouts[125]. Although there is an obligation on the parties to "bargain in good faith," there is no obligation to agree, and unions that win representation elections achieve a first contract only 63 percent of the time.[126]

The most successful American unions are organized more on a regional or market basis.[127] US unions are not strongly attached to the management of a specific company and sometimes don't compromise

119 Columbia River Packers Ass'n v. Hinton, 315 U.S. 143 (1942).

120 National Labor Relations Act, 29 USC § 159 (c)(1).

121 *In re* Livingston Shirt Corp., 107 N.L.R.B. 400, 405–406 (1953).

122 *See* Michael Weiner, *Can the NLRB Deter Unfair Labor Practices? Reassessing the Punitive-Remedial Distinction in Labor Law Enforcement*, 52 UCLA L. Rev. 1579 (2005).

123 See Kenneth G. Dau-Schmidt, Roberto L. Corrada, Christopher David Ruiz Cameron, César F. Rosado Marzán, Michael M. Oswalt & Rafael Gely, Labor Law in the Contemporary Workplace 68–74 (4th ed., 2024).

124 *See* Transcript, *supra* note 4, at 28 (Kenneth Dau-Schmidt).

125 *See id.* at 26.

126 *See* Paul Weiler, *Striking a New Balance: Freedom of Contract and the Prospects for Union Representation*, 98 Harv. L. Rev. 351, 353–355, tbl. 1 (1984).

127 *See id.*; NLRB v. Mackay Radio & Telegraph Co., 304 U.S. 333 (1938); Dau-Schmidt et al., *supra* note 123, at 854.

even when the company is in the zone of insolvency, although they don't necessarily want their members' employers to go bankrupt.

Although the NLRA has the stated purposes of promoting equality in bargaining power between employers and employees, and industrial peace,[128] labor relations in the United States are more adversarial than in other industrial countries. Section 8(a)(2) of the NLRA is premised on an adversarial relationship between labor and management, and prohibits employer-organized committees of employees that "deal with" terms and conditions of employment.[129] As a result, work councils are considered to be illegal, hampering communication and cooperation between employers and employees.[130]

Even with relatively weak bargaining power, US labor unions used to initiate a lot of work stoppages under the adversarial relationship with management.[131] The number of work stoppages per year has, however, dramatically declined from 200 in the 1970s to 20 in recent years, probably because the globalization of production and outsourcing to low-wage countries makes strikes a perilous undertaking.[132]

Recently, unions have enjoyed a modest resurgence in the US in the tight post-pandemic labor market. Organizing has increased, and American unions are enjoying success at the bargaining table.[133] On September 15, 2023, the United Auto Workers (UAW) staged an unprecedented strike against the Big Three Detroit automakers: Ford Motor Company, General Motors, and Stellantis. The US President Joe Biden visited autoworkers on the picket line as they entered the twelfth day of striking to show his support for union members.[134] After forty-one days on strike, the UAW and Ford Motor reached a tentative labor agreement that includes an 11 percent wage increase in the first year and

[128] 29 U.S.C. § 151.

[129] *See* DAU-SCHMIDT ET AL., *supra* note 123, at 440–457.

[130] *See* id.

[131] *See* Kenneth G. Dau-Schmidt, *Labor Law and Industrial Peace: A Comparative Analysis of the United States, the United Kingdom, Germany and Japan Under the Bargaining Model*, 8 TULANE J. INT'L & COMP. L. 117 (2000).

[132] *See* Transcript, *supra* note 4, at 27 (Kenneth Dau-Schmidt).

[133] *See* Robert Combs, *ANALYSIS: Unions, on a Roll, Are Reeling in the Workers*, BLOOMBERG NEWS (Aug. 21, 2023); https://news.bloomberglaw.com/bloomberg-law-analysis/analysis-unions-on-a-roll-are-reeling-in-the-workers.

[134] *See* Sara Powers, *UAW Strike 2023: Biden Joins UAW Picket Line, Trump Heads to Michigan*, CBS NEWS (Sept. 27, 2023, 3:23 PM), https://www.cbsnews.com/detroit/news/uaw-strike-2023-heres-what-to-know-as-biden-lands-in-michigan-heads-to-the-picket-line/.

totals 25 percent over a 4½-year contract, plus a $5,000 ratification bonus and cost-of-living adjustments.[135] Later, the UAW reached agreements with both Stellantis and General Motors that matched Ford's offer.[136]

5.3.2 Japan

Japan's unionized rate was 17.1 percent in 2020. However, in firms with more than 1,000 workers, the unionized rate is 41.8 percent. Labor unions are still an important player in corporate governance in Japan compared to the United States.

Overall, Japanese labor laws are relatively agreeable to unions' ability to inflict costs on their employers and give employers relatively weak weapons in a strike.[137]

Japanese law allows for the organization of a broader and more important array of employees than its US counterpart.[138]

Japanese workers can engage in any kind of "justifiable collective action." Although secondary actions are prohibited, the Japanese law has a very narrow definition of what constitutes a secondary action.[139]

Although Japanese employers have the right to continue operations during a strike, there are restrictions on permanently replacing workers, and Japanese employers are allowed to engage in only defensive lockouts.[140]

Japanese unions are organized largely on a firm-by-firm basis. Therefore, union members "ride on the same boat" with management and are not as adversarial as their US counterparts. Although Japanese unions legally have more bargaining power than American unions, they are less likely to use it because of the context of bargaining on a firm-specific basis.[141]

135 *See* Phoebe Wall Howard, Eric D. Lawrence & Jamie L. LaReau, *UAW President Shawn Fain: We've Reached a Tentative Deal with Ford after 41 Days on Strike*, Detroit Free Press (Oct. 25, 2023, 7:31 PM), https://www.freep.com/story/money/cars/ford/2023/10/25/uaw-strike-ford-reaches-tentative-deal-with-union-sources-say/71318908007/.

136 *See* David Shepardson & Joseph White, *UAW Reaches Deal with GM, Ending Strike against Detroit Automakers*, Yahoo Finance (Oct. 30, 2023), https://tinyurl.com/4cvu3f6d.

137 *See* Transcript, *supra* note 4, at 26 (Kenneth Dau-Schmidt).

138 *See id.* at 25.

139 *See id.* at 26.

140 *See id.*

141 *See id.* at 25.

The company union is an important channel of internal governance, that is, bottom-up monitoring management by employees.[142] There are two measures of communication between labor and management at an individual company level: collective bargaining and labor-management consultation. While collective bargaining is a legally supported measure, the results of which are formally concluded as a collective agreement in most cases, labor-management consultation is an informal voluntary negotiation, in which opinion sharing between labor and management is made regarding a wide range of issues, including management policy.[143]

5.3.3 *China*

5.3.3.1 Labor Unions in China

In China, official organizations like the US-type labor unions are called trade unions. In this section, both labor union and trade union refer to the same type of labor organization in Chinese companies. The labor union movement in China dates back to the early years of the twentieth century. The current labor union system is a relatively new system rebuilt in the 1980s. Although the labor unions have the right to carry out their work "independently and voluntarily," these rights are subject to the Labor Union Law and PRC laws enshrining the supremacy of the Chinese Communist Party (CCP) over the labor unions.[144]

On its face, the Chinese Constitution guarantees freedom of assembly and freedom of association.[145] However, these freedoms can only be exercised within certain boundaries. In other words, the union organizations are subordinated to the All-China Federation of Trade Unions (ACFTU) which is the sole government-backed and monitored union lawfully permitted to exist in China.[146] Self-run labor unions are currently not allowed in China because the CCP is afraid of the development of alternative centers of power.[147] This may be one of the key obstacles

[142] Regarding internal governance, *see* Chapter 1, nn.10–11 and their accompanying texts.
[143] *See* Mizumachi, *supra* note 85, at 1081.
[144] Labor Union Law of the People's Republic of China (promulgated by the Standing Committee of the National People's Congress on Dec. 24, 2021, effective Jan. 01, 2022), Lawinfochina, http://lawinfochina.com/display.aspx?id=37381&lib=law (*hereinafter* Trade Union Law), Art. 4.
[145] Constitution of the People's Republic of China, Art. 35.
[146] Labor Union Law, Art. 13.
[147] See Dennis Campbell, International Employment Law, ch. 23 (2012).

faced by China to join the Comprehensive and Progressive Agreement for Trans-Pacific Partnership (CPTPP), which requires the member states to respect the freedom of self-run labor unions.

In practice, labor unions in China continue to play the role of a "transmission belt" between the CCP and the working classes.[148] This role may well explain why there has been no significant labor union activity on an industry-wide scale or in a certain geographical area, even though the ACFTU has a nationwide network with branches at all levels.

The CCP and the Chinese government are well aware of the social need to have labor unions play a "communication" role. In recent years, the Chinese government has been pushing for a general unionization campaign, that is, a campaign to establish and utilize more labor unions in POEs. This campaign targets large multinational companies, particularly Fortune 500's subsidiaries in China.

China's labor unions are government-backed. Therefore, a labor union is not necessarily supportive of any industrial action. The primary function of a labor union is to improve employer-employee relationships and to preclude labor disputes from escalating into labor unrest, strikes, or even chaos.

In practice, however, "low union credibility contributes to unstable industrial relations."[149] A labor union is empowered with certain rights to uphold the interests of the workers.[150] From time to time, under the increasing social and political pressures from society and the CCP, labor unions are now more often involved in the negotiation of collective contracts, the resolution of labor disputes, and the negotiation of and adjustment to the resettlement plan of the enterprises, among other things. However, in practice, the role of labor unions is still less active (or less pro-employee) than anticipated.

5.3.3.2 Employee Participation in Labor Union

It is an employee's right to participate in a labor union.[151] However, this right to unionize is attached with some caveats. First, an employee refers to any individual in China whose main income is derived from wages. Second, an employee has the right to join an official labor union

[148] Labor Union Law, Art. 2.

[149] Patti Waldmeir, *China Workers Get to Grips with Rights*, FIN. TIMES (June 13, 2010), https://www.ft.com/content/eb955a12-770a-11df-ba79-00144feabdc0.

[150] Labor Union Law Arts. 20–21.

[151] Labor Union Law, Art. 3.

recognized by the government. In other words, there are no recognized self-governed labor unions in China. Third, a local-level union can be set up in its enterprise only. This suggests that employees from various employers cannot form a cross-employer labor union. Once a labor union is set up in an enterprise, it is open to all employees in the enterprise, including low, middle, and senior-level employees as well as expatriate employees.[152] Employees are not able to form separate labor unions in an enterprise. Fourth, the right to unionize is a right rather than an obligation. An employee is not subject to compulsory unionism and has the right to elect members or representatives of the committees of the labor unions.[153] Once an employee is a member of the union, he or she may be offered assistance or benefits by the labor union. An employer is under a legal obligation to guarantee the employee's right to participate in the labor union.[154] An employer is required to allow the labor union to organize events or activities for the members.

An employer is not allowed to terminate an employment contract simply due to the fact that the employee joined the labor union or has been involved in the labor union's activities. Otherwise, the employer will be ordered to reinstate the employment contract, to pay retroactively any remuneration due during the period of termination of the employment contract, and to make compensation that is double the annual income of the employee concerned (which is imposed by the labor bureau as it sees fit).[155] The labor administrative bureau is able to issue an order to the employer to correct the situation if the employer obstructs an employee's lawful participation in labor union activities. Additional administrative measures and penalties are available if the employer continues not to support the employee's participation. In the most extreme cases, an employer may be charged with criminal liabilities if the obstruction is in the form of violence or threats, which may constitute a criminal offense.[156]

5.3.3.3 Functions of Labor Unions

A labor union has a wide variety of rights and powers to represent all the employees, including senior management personnel and executives, as

[152] Measures of the Shenzhen Special Economic Zone for Implementing the PRC Labor Union Law (effective as of Aug. 1, 2008), Art. 55.
[153] Labor Union Law, Art. 9.
[154] *Id.*, Arts. 2 and 3.
[155] *Id.*, Art. 53.
[156] *Id.*, Art. 51.

well as grassroots and blue-collar employees. Under the Chinese Labor Union Law, a labor union can order the enterprise to make corrections if the employer terminates the employees' labor contracts because of the employees' participation in trade union activities,[157] voice its opinions if it believes that any employee was inappropriately penalized by the enterprise,[158] participate in the investigation of job-related accidents resulting in injury or death,[159] and assist employees in signing individual employment or collective contracts with the employer on behalf of the employees,[160] represent the employee in negotiations with the enterprise and request that the employer rectify the violations and appeal to the government if it is not satisfied with the rectification by the employer.[161]

A labor union is sometimes granted the right to participate in the decision-making process of the employer when the decision(s) will affect the immediate rights and interests of the employees. For instance, labor union representatives must attend the board, management, or even departmental level meetings when such meetings discuss issues such as wages, benefits, labor safety and hygiene, and social insurance, which involve the immediate interest of staff and workers.[162] The enterprise is also required to "listen to the opinions of the labor union" when it "considers" major operational, management, and development issues.[163] The participation level of the labor union may be lower as the enterprise is not required to have the labor union representative attend the meetings.

The labor union's right to participate in the company's management is also reflected in the Company Law, which requires the company to solicit opinions and suggestions from the labor union, workers, and staff members when it "considers a decision on restructuring its system, major issues on its business operations or the formulation of important internal rules and regulations."[164] This consultation process does not seem to grant the labor union the right to veto or obstruct the employer's decision. However, when the board of directors or senior management's decisions relate to employee rewards and penalties, wage systems, wage

157 *Id.*, Art. 20.
158 *Id.*, Art. 22.
159 *Id.*, Art. 39.
160 *Id.*, Art. 21.
161 *Id.*, Art. 23.
162 *Id.*, Art. 39.
163 *Id.*
164 Company Law, Art. 18.

benefits, labor protection, and labor insurance, the labor union may have a *de facto* veto, as the employer's decision without the labor union's attendance and cooperation may lead to the invalidation of the company action.

5.3.3.4 Collective Bargaining

Labor unions also bear responsibilities. A labor union's primary responsibility is to safeguard the employees' legal rights and interests.[165] To fulfill this responsibility, the labor union should: participate in the negotiation and collective contract system;[166] assist the employees when their interests are infringed upon by the employer;[167] make suggestions to resolve situations such as a work stoppage or a slowdown in the enterprise;[168] and participate in the labor dispute settlement process.[169] The labor unions are also subjected to a catch-all requirement that they should not act against the interests of the government, the CCP, and the people's interests as a whole.

More and more collective contracts are signed between the employer and labor unions or employees' representatives on behalf of the employees. The employer is not required to sign a collective contract unless the labor union makes such a request. The collective contract should cover matters such as labor compensation, working hours, rest, leave, work safety and hygiene, insurance, and benefits.[170] The collective contract may include provisions that do not usually appear in individual employment contracts. For instance, it may include provisions regarding the conditions and procedures for redundancy and for compensation for the reduced staff. However, it cannot include provisions that are only applicable to a particular employee. If the labor union is strong, more favorable

165 Labor Union Law, Art. 6.
166 *Id.*
167 *Id.*, Art. 21.
168 *Id.*, Art. 28.
169 *Id.*, Art. 29.
170 Under the Regulations for Collective Contracts (Jan. 20, 2004), the following should be contained in a collective contract: remuneration; working hours; rest and holidays; working safety and sanitation; supplemental insurance and welfare; special protection for female employees and employees who are minors; operational skill training; employment contract administration; award and punishment; redundancy; term of the collective contract (one-to-three years); procedures for modification and termination of the collective contract; provisions for the consultative handling of disputes arising from the performance of the collective contract; liabilities for breach of the collective contract; and other terms.

terms, such as additional compensation, may be incorporated into the collective contract.

Once the collective contract comes into effect, it is binding upon the employer and all employees in the company. Nevertheless, an individual employee may still bargain for better terms and conditions in their individual employment contract. As the law only requires that the terms and conditions in the individual labor contract are no less favorable than those in the collective contract, the latter is signed in conjunction with, rather than to replace, the individual employment contract.

Collective bargaining was once effective in setting labor standards and strengthening labor protections involving the associations of employers and employees. However, the use of collective representation has recently declined and is gradually replaced by new forms of association, e.g., NGOs.

In general, collective bargaining is weak in China due to two factors. First, most blue-collar laborers are poorly educated, unskilled, and less informed in labor representation. The majority of laborers' low education, poor remuneration, and tenuous residency status make them far more vulnerable than well-educated white-collar workers. Second, collective bargaining is not necessarily government-backed, which suggests that some collective bargaining is only an informal gathering in China's regulatory environment. As a result, the real function of collective bargaining is questionable and may even be compromised if activities cross the boundaries of a coordinated organization.

Currently, the ACFTU seems unable to interrupt the striking workers' momentum. Trade unions in China are usually a little more than arms of management run by party cadres. Some local authorities have started experiments designed to bring more consultation to the workplace. For instance, Guangdong province has proposed legislation to allow more labor rights by introducing collective bargaining and worker representation on company boards, which unsurprisingly encountered lobbying and resistance from Hong Kong businesses.

However, it is doubtful whether the government will back or tolerate an entirely independent labor union because of the political implications of such a body. The only reason that the government has lately been showing more tolerance for strikes is that the recent strikes and labor relations activities were not coordinated.[171] As a matter of fact, using

[171] *See* Tom Mitchell, *China: Strike Force*, FIN. TIMES (June 10, 2010), https://www.ft.com/content/a6aca74e-74c5-11df-aed7-00144feabdc0.

trade unions to expand collective bargaining power among workers is a practice disliked by local officials who fear worker activism and upward wage pressure.

5.3.3.5 Labor Strikes and the Involvement of Labor Union

Employees were once granted the right to strike under the 1975 and 1978 Constitutions.[172] However, the 1982 Constitution removed this right. The legality of striking is not clear under Chinese law: it is neither allowed nor forbidden.

The Labor Law provides an informal mechanism for dealing with a "work stoppage or work slowdown" in an enterprise – a labor union should represent employees in consultations with the enterprise, express the opinions and demands of the staff and workers, and put forward opinions on resolving the existing matter(s). Meanwhile, the labor union also needs to assist the enterprise in duly carrying out the work concerned and resuming production and work as quickly as possible.[173]

The Labor Union Law Article 28 actually outlines the role of labor unions in strikes or unrest: mediating the dispute rather than leading the dispute.[174] It is unclear as to what actions the employer can take or what remedies they have against strikers in the event of strikes, unrest, work stoppage, or work slowdown. Similarly, under the current law, neither an employer nor an employee is entitled to claim damages or compensation from the other side due to industrial actions (which is rarely seen in reality).

[172] Feng Chen, *Individual Rights and Collective Rights: Labor's Predicament in China*, 40 Communist & Post-Communist Stud. 59, 70 (2007).

[173] Labor Union Law, Art. 28.

[174] *Id.*

6

Shareholder I

External Governance by Voice

In Chapter 5, we observed the incentive bargaining between employees and management. In Chapters 6 and 7, we will examine the incentive bargaining between shareholders and management, particularly from the perspective of external governance.[1]

It is important to note that stronger monitoring by shareholders is not necessarily better, because excessive monitoring will distort the incentive of management to initiate and execute long-term plans to maximize corporate value. Likely, excessive monitoring increases compliance costs. There is a tradeoff between monitoring management and preserving management autonomy. Although the optimal balance is firm-specific, a country's enterprise law affects the balance of autonomy and monitoring. Chapters 6 and 7 will compare how enterprise law in the United States, Japan, and China, respectively, affects the balance within these countries' respective markets and social norms.

External governance, that is, the monitoring of management by shareholders, can be categorized into two types: external governance by voice and external governance by exit. These work together to affect the monitoring effect by shareholders. Although external governance by voice and exit is on a continuum and hard to distinguish, particularly in the era of shareholder activism, this chapter will focus on the former.

Figure 6.1 shows that internal governance (monitoring management by core employees) and external governance (monitoring management by shareholders) influence each other as indispensable mechanisms of corporate governance, figuratively speaking, the former acts as the engine and the latter acts as the brake. The two ways of external

[1] Regarding the framework of external governance and internal governance, *see* Chapter 1, nn.10–11 and their accompanying texts.

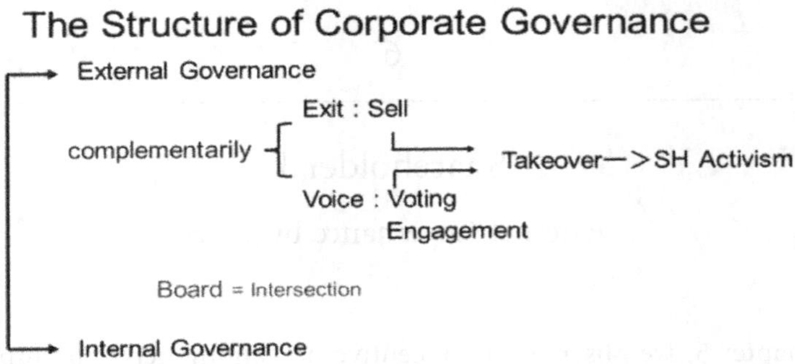

Figure 6.1 The relationship between external governance and internal governance.

governance – exit and voice – complementarily influence management and appear either as a threat of takeover or shareholder activism. Monitoring by the board of directors is positioned between external governance and internal governance.

This chapter will divide legal systems that affect the relative bargaining power of shareholders and management into three categories: Shareholders' voting and minority rights, and, in particular, their veto and proposal rights (Section 6.1); Disclosure regulations, including the 5 percent rule and proxy rule (Section 6.2); and Directors' and officers' fiduciary duties, the business judgment rule, and shareholder suits (Section 6.3). Finally, this chapter will examine how shareholder activism reflects an interplay of various legal systems, markets, and social norms in the United States, Japan, and China (Section 6.4).

6.1 Shareholders' Voting and Minority Rights

It goes without saying that a shareholder's right to vote is the most important legal foundation and mechanism that supports a shareholder's bargaining power against management. Although the effect of a single small shareholder's vote is negligible, a majority of votes is decisive on most agenda items in shareholders' meetings, including the selection of management.

Law can circumscribe the bargaining power of shareholders arising from their voting rights by either limiting the decision-making power of the shareholders' meeting or by requiring a special majority to discharge directors. Likewise, the law can expand the voting-based bargaining power by giving minority shareholders veto and proposal rights.

6.1.1 The United States

US law, and, in particular, Delaware law, requires management to obey its fiduciary duty to maximize shareholder interest. But as we will observe in Section 6.3, the US law at the same time limits shareholders' voting-based bargaining power by giving the board of directors wide decision-making power. This is called the "board primacy model," which flows from the principle that important business decisions aimed at maximizing shareholder interests should be made by the board of directors, not by shareholders.[2]

Delaware corporate law limits the scope of shareholders' intervention and initiatives. 8 Del. C. §141(a) provides that: the business and affairs of every corporation organized under this chapter shall be managed by or under the direction of a board of directors, except as may be otherwise provided in this chapter or in its certificate of incorporation. No such broad management power is statutorily allocated to the shareholders. Under the Delaware code, shareholder voting rights were essentially limited to the election of directors and approval of charter or bylaw amendments, mergers, sales of substantially all of the corporation's assets, and voluntary dissolution.[3] As a formal matter, only the election of directors and amending the bylaws do not require board approval, and shareholder action is possible.[4] In practice, of course, even the election of directors (absent a proxy contest) is predetermined by the existing board nominating the next year's board.[5]

In Delaware, shareholders have the right to remove annually elected directors without cause by a majority vote of the outstanding shares. Specifically, Section 141(k) of the Delaware General Corporation Law provides that "any director or the entire board of directors may be removed, with or without cause, by the holders of a majority of the shares then entitled to vote at an election of directors," subject to exceptions regarding classified boards and cumulative voting. In the case of a staggered or classified board, the removal of a director by shareholders during a director's term is limited to for-cause removal.

[2] *See* Stephen M. Bainbridge, *Preserving Director Primacy by Managing Shareholder Interventions*, *in* Research Handbook on Shareholder Power 231 (Jennifer G. Hill & Randall S. Thompson eds., 2015).

[3] *Id.*

[4] *Id.*

[5] *Id.*

Delaware corporate law's default special majority is a simple majority of all voting shares. In most cases, minority shareholders need more votes to exercise their veto on fundamental changes than their EU and Japanese counterparts.[6]

6.1.1.1 Minority Rights

The Delaware court has empowered minority shareholders' rights in a controlled transaction. In the *MFW Shareholders' Litigation*, the Delaware Chancery Court stated that the deferential business judgment rule would apply to the transaction if two conditions are satisfied: (1) negotiation and approval by a special committee of independent directors, and (2) approval by an uncoerced, fully informed vote of a majority of the minority investors.[7] In *Corwin v. KKR Financial Holdings LLC*,[8] the Delaware Chancery Court pronounced in the context of a non-controller transaction that the approval of a merger by a fully informed body of disinterested stockholders is a precondition to the application of the business judgment rule.[9]

Minority Shareholders can bring proposals that can be included in the firm's proxy materials under Rule 14a-8 of the Securities Exchange Act of 1934 if they have continuously held: (A) At least $2,000 in the market value of the company's securities entitled to vote on the proposal for at least three years; or (B) At least $15,000 in market value of the company's securities entitled to vote on the proposal for at least two years; or (C) At least $25,000 in the market value of the company's securities entitled to vote on the proposal for at least one year.

As a result of the limited voting power of shareholders, the subject of shareholders' proposal rights is limited compared to its Japanese counterpart. Shareholders cannot propose regarding dividends and corporate governance. Companies that adopt proxy access, by which certain

[6] In Germany, waiving shareholders' preemptive right needs a three-quarters majority vote (Aktiengesetz [Stock Corporation Act], §186(3)-(4)). In the UK, waiving shareholders' preemptive right needs a special resolution (at least three-quarters of shareholder votes), Companies Act 2006 §283(1). In Japan, fundamental structural changes, such as mergers and divisions, need a two-thirds majority vote (Companies Act, Arts. 783, 795, and 309 II (8)).

[7] *In re* MFW S'holders Litig., 67 A.3d 496 (Del. Ch. 2013), affirmed in Kahn v. M & F Worldwide Corp., 88 A.3d 635 (Del. 2013).

[8] Corwin v. KKR Fin. Holdings LLC, 125 A.3d 304, 312 (Del. 2015).

[9] *See* Umakanth Varottil, *Minority Shareholders Rights, Powers and Duties: The Market for Corporate Influence*, *in* COMPARATIVE CORPORATE GOVERNANCE 346, 352 (Afra Afsharipour & Martin Gelter eds., 2021).

minority shareholders can nominate their director candidate in the company's proxy solicitation document, are, however, increasing.[10] Moreover, the universal proxy card, in which all director candidates, including those proposed by shareholder, must be listed, was adopted by SEC Rule 14a-19 in 2022, which strengthens shareholder rights.[11]

Moreover, minority shareholders who are dissatisfied with a merger transaction can seek an appraisal from the court to sell their shares at a judicially determined fair price (Delaware General Corporation Law §262).

6.1.2 *Japan*

Although Japanese law imposes a relatively relaxed fiduciary duty on management to maximize corporate interest, courts have interpreted it to allow management to take into account stakeholder interest in addition to shareholder interest. This rule gives shareholders' meetings in Japan much wider decision-making power than US law. This is called the "shareholder primacy model," which flows from the principle that shareholders should decide by themselves matters that are relevant to their interests.[12]

Japanese corporate law does not limit shareholder intervention and initiatives. The corporation's charter can further enlarge the default decision-making power of the shareholders' meeting. The shareholders' meeting can decide dividends, stock buybacks, director compensation, and poison pills, all of which are exclusively decided by the board of directors in the United States. This means that minority shareholders can exercise their proposal right on those matters and offer an important weapon to activist shareholders. Minority shareholders can even propose charter amendments, which in the US requires a board's endorsement.[13]

Compared to the United States, Japanese corporate law is loyal to the stock majority rule on the election and discharge of directors. The

[10] *See* Holly J. Gregory, Rebecca Grapsas & Clair Holland, *The Latest on Proxy Access*, Harv. L. Sch. F. Corp. Governance (Feb. 1, 2019), https://corpgov.law.harvard.edu/2019/02/01/the-latest-on-proxy-access/.

[11] *See* Jeffrey N. Gordon, *The Rejected Threat of Corporate Vote Suppression: The Rise and Fall of the Anti-Activist Pill*, 2022 Colum. Bus. L. Rev. 206 (2022).

[12] *See* Olivier Weinstein, *The Shareholder Model of the Corporation, between Mythology and Reality*, 3 Acct., Econ. & L. 43, 43 (2013).

[13] There is no distinction between charter and bylaws in Japan. *See* Geeyoung Min, *Shareholder Voice in Corporate Charter Amendments*, 43 J. Corp. L. 289, 289 (2017).

election of directors must be made not by the plurality rule, but by the majority rule. A staggered board is not allowed. By default, the discharge of directors is done through a simple majority and does not require a cause.

Japanese corporate law requires a two-thirds majority vote of participating shares on fundamental changes, such as charter amendments, mergers and divisions, and issuing new shares to third parties at "particularly" favorable prices. Therefore, minority shareholders representing more than one-third of voting shares have veto rights on these issues, but unlike European shareholders, this one-third minority cannot veto the decision to waive preemptive rights.[14]

The dissenting minority shareholders' appraisal right, in cases of mergers and cashouts (Companies Act, Art. 262), is frequently exercised and plays an important minority protection role.

Japanese corporate law provides relatively more expansive minority shareholder rights, such as the inspection right of accounting books (Companies Act, Art. 433 I), the right of selecting inspector (Art. 358 I), and the right of calling shareholders' meetings (Art. 297), for stockholders who hold more than 3 percent of shares and continue to hold them more than six months. Stockholders who hold 1 percent or 300 votes of all shares and continue to hold them for more than six months enjoy shareholder proposal rights (Arts. 303 II, 305). Now, these minority shareholder rights are actually utilized by activist shareholders. Particularly, shareholder proposal right turns out to be a useful weapon for them because minority shareholders can propose any matters to be resolved at the shareholders' meeting, which is much wider than those of the US counterpart, including the increase of dividends and nominating director candidates.[15]

6.1.3 China

The effective company law in China until July 1, 2024 is the Company Law of the People's Republic of China amended in 2018 (*hereinafter* Company Law 2018).[16] On December 29, 2023, China enacted a newly

[14] *See* Reinier Kraakman & John Armour, The Anatomy of Corporate Law: A Comparative and Functional Approach 182 (3d ed., 2017).

[15] *See* Curtis J. Milhaupt & Zenichi Shishido, *The Enduring Relevance of the Poison Pill: A U.S.-Japan Comparative Analysis*, 28 Stan. J. L. Bus. & Fin. 336, 352 (2023).

[16] Company Law of the People's Republic of China (2018 Amendment) (promulgated by the Standing Committee of the National People's Congress on Oct. 26, 2018, effective

revised Company Law of the People's Republic of China (*hereinafter* Company Law 2023), which will become effective after July 1, 2024.[17] This book will refer to the relevant articles from both the Company Law 2018 and the Company Law 2023.

A shareholders' meeting has certain statutory rights and powers to control the operations of a company. These statutory powers include the determination of the business policy and investment plan of the company; examination and approval of the company's annual financial budget, final accounting, profit distribution plans, and plans for recovery of losses; approval of any increase or decrease of registered capital and issuance of corporate bonds.[18] In addition, shareholder approval is required to amend the articles of association and to make decisions regarding the merger, division, and dissolution of the company.[19]

The range of decisions that must be made by a shareholders' meeting under Chinese corporate law is extraordinarily large in comparison with other jurisdictions. As a result, the board is left with limited discretion. However, empirical research shows that the power of shareholders' meetings is weak in practice. Only 20 percent of company actions are voted upon at shareholders' general meetings in spite of the wide range of matters that legally require votes from such meetings.[20] The explanation for this reality is the collective action problem, which tends to suggest that such meetings cannot be relied upon (especially by minority shareholders) for shareholder protection.

Shareholders can benefit from the Company Law and be more deeply involved in the decision-making process of their company. Shareholders individually or collectively holding 10 percent or more of the voting rights and the shareholders separately or aggregately holding 10 percent of the shares can request to convene an interim shareholders' meeting in cases where the board of directors does not convene or preside over a shareholders' meeting.[21]

Oct. 26, 2018), LAWINFOCHINA, https://www.lawinfochina.com/display.aspx?id=29161&lib=law.

17 Company Law of the People's Republic of China (2023 Revision) (promulgated by the Standing Committee of the National People's Congress on Dec. 29, 2023, effective July 1, 2024), LAWINFOCHINA, https://www.lawinfochina.com/display.aspx?id=42338&lib=law.

18 Company Law 2018, Art. 37; Company Law 2023, Art. 59.

19 *Id.*

20 James V. Feinerman, *New Hope for Corporate Governance in China?* 191 CHINA Q. 590, 599 (2007).

21 Company Law 2018, Art. 101; Company Law 2023, Art. 114.

In addition, shareholders are granted an agenda-setting power. Shareholders individually or collectively holding 3 percent (down from 5 percent in the Company Law of 1995)[22] or more of a company's shares may submit, through the board of directors, a written interim proposal ten days before a shareholders' meeting is held.[23] Hence, this is a higher hurdle for shareholders to incorporate a proxy document to prove that the proxy initiator has a substantial interest in their firm compared to the United States.[24] The contents of an interim proposal shall fall within the scope to be decided by a shareholders' meeting, and the interim proposal shall have a clear topic for discussion and matters to be decided. The board of directors should notify other shareholders within two days and submit the interim proposal to the shareholders' meeting for deliberation.[25]

A minority shareholder may initiate a lawsuit against the controlling shareholder if the latter abuses his or her rights (or powers) and causes losses to other shareholders.[26] Shareholders may bring lawsuits against any person(s), including controlling shareholders, who encroach upon the lawful rights and interests of their company and cause losses to the company.[27] The Company Law provides both a standard and a legal basis for minority shareholders' right to sue, an expansion of the earlier law, which was even more ambiguous as to whether such a right even existed. However, it is still not clear what constitutes an encroachment or abuse of a shareholder's rights under the Company Law.

Proposal rights give minority shareholders[28] the chance to raise their concerns and agendas in shareholders' meetings, without which the agenda and content of the shareholders' meeting may be completely

22 The percentage requirement is further reduced to 1 percent in Company Law 2023. Company Law 2023, Art. 115.

23 Company Law 2018, Art. 102; Company Law 2023, Art. 115.

24 The US law requires shareholders who have held 1 percent of shares (or at least $2,000 in market value) for at least one year to include proxy documents at the company's expense with the general documents for voting proxies. *See* SEC Rule 14a-8(b) (1). Although, Chinese Company Law 2023 reduces the percentage of shares requirement to 1 percent which is the same as the US law, Chinese Company Law 2023 does not specify a cash amount threshold. Thus, the requirements to submit proxy documents in China are stricter for companies with many shares. *See* Company Law 2023, Art. 115.

25 Company Law 2018, Art. 102; Company Law 2023, Art. 115.

26 Company Law 2018, Arts. 20 and 151; Company Law 2023, Arts. 21 and 189.

27 Company Law 2018, Art. 152; Company Law 2023, Art. 190.

28 Minority shareholders who aggregately hold 3 percent or more (1 percent under Company Law 2023) of the shares of the company may put forward an interim proposal to the board of directors. *See* Company Law 2018, Art. 102; Company Law 2023, Art. 115.

controlled by the board of directors. In this sense, interim meetings can be useful devices to constrain the board of directors and managers. The availability of proposal rights also creates market power constraints, as outsiders are able to acquire the equity and replace directors before the expiration of the directors' tenure at the next annual shareholders' meeting. The market can help lower the costs of acquisition. However, there are some uncertainties surrounding the exercise of this agenda-setting power. First, it is not clear whether a company should reimburse the expenses involved in the whole process. Second, it is not clear if this may trigger frivolous litigation, which may delay the process and waste judicial resources.

Shareholders may also rely on cumulative voting to gain control and oust the management of a company limited by shares.[29] The Company Law incorporated a cumulative voting system[30] after it was first introduced in China (the Code of Corporate Governance), issued by the China Securities Regulatory Commission (the CSRC) on January 7, 2002.[31] Cumulative voting rights provide minority shareholders with large minority stakes a chance of securing the election of at least one or more directors,[32] thereby affecting board and management decisions and creating a more balanced corporate governance regime.

Some thresholds for passing shareholder resolutions, as codified in the Company Law, offer minority shareholders more protection. In interested (or related-party) transactions such as guarantees or investments by a company in related entities, a majority of voting rights by disinterested shareholders is required for a company's decision to provide security for its shareholders or its *de facto* controlling person(s).[33] This rule protects a company from being treated unfairly in such transactions[34] and precludes interested shareholders from engaging in

[29] Cumulative voting is not mandatory in China. Chinese company law offers cumulative voting as an option that can be adopted by Chinese companies. Company Law 2018, Art. 105; Company Law 2023, Art. 117.

[30] The adoption of a cumulative voting system is not mandatory. The Company law just says the shareholders' assembly "*may*, under the articles of association or resolution of the shareholders' assembly, adopt a cumulative voting system." Company Law 2018, Art. 105; Company Law 2023, Art. 117.

[31] Company Law 2018, Art. 105; Company Law 2023, Art. 117.

[32] *See* Jeffrey N. Gordon, *Institutions as Relational Investors: A New Look at Cumulative Voting*, 94 COLUM. L. REV. 124, 124 (1994).

[33] Company Law 2018, Art. 16; Company Law 2023, Art. 15.

[34] *See* JAMES D. COX, THOMAS HAZEN & F. HODGE O'NEAL, CORPORATIONS 204–215 (1997).

business misconduct. Similarly, directors of listed companies are ineligible to vote on matters in which they have an interest.[35]

Two-thirds of the voting rights of attending shareholders have to be secured in a shareholders' meeting if a company wants to acquire or sell major assets over a one-year period, the aggregate value of which exceeds 30 percents of the value of the company's total assets, or the company provides security over a one-year of a value exceeding 30 percent of the value of its total assets.[36] The 30 percent benchmark is lower than the 50 percent threshold set by the US law.[37] A lower benchmark may make it easier for firms' owners to reinforce their policing power over the management agency problem. These rules, also adopted in other regulations,[38] guarantee that minority shareholders have a say on at least some corporate matters.

6.2 Disclosure Regulations, Five Percent Rule, and Proxy Rules

Disclosure regulations could increase shareholder bargaining power against management by providing shareholders with information that is necessary to monitor management.

Although the major purpose of the 5 percent rule and the proxy rule is to protect minority shareholders by providing them with the information of large shareholders and activist shareholders, they also affect the relative bargaining power of activist shareholders and management by providing management with an alert and by incurring the cost of disclosure to activist shareholders. Both the 5 percent rule and the proxy rule not only regulate activist shareholders but also regulate buyers in the context of hostile takeovers. This section will briefly introduce their significant effects on shareholder activism, and their detailed explanation will be made in Section 7.2.

6.2.1 *The United States*

6.2.1.1 Disclosure Regulations

Under the Securities Act, the public offering was required to be registered, which involved filing a statement with the SEC that answered a

[35] Company Law 2018, Art. 124; Company Law 2023, Art. 139.
[36] Company Law 2018, Art. 121; Company Law 2023, Art. 135.
[37] Katz v. Bregman, 431 A2d 1274 (Del Ch. 1981).
[38] CSRC's Rules for Shareholders' Meetings of Listed Companies further facilitate minority shareholders' ability to call shareholders' meetings.

variety of disclosure-prompting questions.[39] Persons associated with the offering faced a comprehensive system of civil damage liability.[40] Absolute liability was imposed on the issuer for investors' damages arising from a material misstatement in the registration statement.[41] Absolute liability subject to a "due diligence" defense was imposed on the issuer's top officers and directors and banks underwriting the offering.[42] This imposition subject to a due diligence defense was intended to motivate non-issuer actors, particularly the lead underwriter, to investigate the issuer and participate actively in the registration statement.[43] Moreover, issuers with publicly traded shares were required on an ongoing basis to make periodic disclosures 10-Q, and 8-K filed pursuant to the Exchange Act.[44]

6.2.1.2 SOX

The US Congress enacted corporate governance regulations in the Sarbanes-Oxley Act of 2002 (SOX) as part of a new federal regulation on securities transactions, in response to major corporate and accounting scandals in 2001 that involved the Enron Corporation and WorldCom.[45]

Section 302 of SOX requires chief executive officers (CEOs) and chief financial officers (CFOs) of public companies to attest to the effectiveness of internal controls as well as the adequacy of financial statements. Section 404 requires that management assess the effectiveness of internal controls over financial reporting and requires the external auditors to attest to and report on such assessments. "Significant deficiencies" must be reported by management and by an independent auditor.[46]

SOX strengthened the bargaining power of the monitors, complementarily with the pre-existing independent boards, influential institutional investors, liquid external labor markets, and so on. At the same time, SOX made management more defensive.[47]

[39] *See* Merritt B. Fox, *Civil Liability and Mandatory Disclosure*, 109 COLUM. L. REV. 237, 241 (2009).

[40] *Id.*

[41] *Id.*

[42] *Id.*

[43] *Id.*

[44] *Id.* at 242.

[45] *See* Zenichi Shishido & Sadkazu Osaki, *Reverse Engineering SOX versus J-SOX: A Lesson in Legislative Policy*, *in* ENTERPRISE LAW: CONTRACTS, MARKETS, AND LAWS IN THE US AND JAPAN 349–351 (Zenichi Shishido ed., 2014).

[46] *Id.* at 351–352.

[47] *Id.* at 365–366.

6.2.1.3 Proxy Rules and 5 Percent Rule

In the United States, the proxy rules and the 5 percent rule (Rule 13D) are used to complementarily discourage shareholder activism.[48] The SEC, however, deregulated those rules in the 1990s and, as a result, opened the door to hedge fund activism.[49] The SEC stopped proxy material pre-screening and censorship in 1992. The SEC adopted the "free communication" rule (Rule 14a-2) in 1999. The SEC streamlined the Schedule 13D rules in 1998, which is short-form Schedule 13G. Since then, hedge funds with significant shareholdings have been able to use wolf-pack tactics. The willingness of institutional investors to follow the pro-shareholder, and proactive recommendations of ISS have helped make these tactics even more effective.[50]

6.2.1.4 Private Remedies

Both the Securities Act and the Exchange Act provide a variety of private remedies for disclosure violations. For example, Securities Act §11 establishes a right of recovery for purchasers of securities covered by a registration statement filed under the Securities Act. 15. Securities Act §12(1) provides purchasers with a remedy against sellers who violate the registration and prospectus delivery requirements of §5 of the Securities Act. Exchange Act §18 provides a remedy for purchasers and sellers who rely on a false or misleading statement contained in a document filed with the Securities and Exchange Commission (SEC) under the Exchange Act. 15 Exchange Act §20A provides purchasers and sellers of securities with an express right of action against persons who trade on inside information. Securities Act §-12(2) affords purchasers of securities a right of rescission (or damages as a rescissional equivalent) against a seller in a transaction involving an information failure.[51] Moreover, plaintiffs seeking redress from an issuer and other participating parties can file a Rule 10b-5 action, which mirrors in many respects the common law cause of action for deceit.[52]

48 *See* Bernard S. Black, *Shareholder Passivity Reexamined*, 89 Mich. L. Rev. 520 (1990).

49 *See* Thomas W. Briggs, *Corporate Governance and the New Hedge Fund Activism: An Empirical Analysis*, 32 J. Corp. L. 681 (2007).

50 *See id.*

51 Robert N. Rapp, *The Proper Role of Securities Act Section 12 (2) as an Aftermarket Remedy for Disclosure Violations*, 47 Bus. Law. 711, 712 (1992).

52 *See* Stephen Jung Choi & Adam C. Pritchard, Securities Regulation: Cases and Analysis 570 (2019).

Private securities legal actions are frequently utilized, encouraged by the class action system and the plaintiff attorney's contingent fee system. It is a unique characteristic of US securities regulation that private enforcement plays a very important role.[53]

6.2.1.5 Criminal Enforcement

Section 21(d) of the Exchange Act authorizes the SEC to refer criminal violations of the securities laws to the US Attorney General for prosecution.[54] Section 32(a) of the Exchange Act makes it a criminal offense to "willfully violate[...] any provision [of the Exchange Act] or any rule or regulation thereunder" or to "willfully and knowingly make[...], or cause[...] to be made, any statement in any application, report, or document required to be filed under [the Exchange Act] ... which statement was false or misleading with respect to any material fact."[55] Stiff penalties of up to $5,000,000 in fines and twenty years' imprisonment for natural persons, and $25,000,000 in fines for corporations will be imposed on those convicted.[56]

Congress added a separate securities fraud offense to the federal criminal code as part of the SOX: whoever knowingly executes, or attempts to execute, a scheme or artifice – (1) to defraud any person in connection with any security of [a reporting company]; or (2) to obtain, by means of false or fraudulent pretenses, representations, or promises, any money or property in connection with the purchase or sale of any security of [a reporting company]; shall be fined under this title, or imprisoned not more than twenty-five years, or both.[57]

6.2.2 *Japan*

6.2.2.1 Disclosure Regulations

In addition to the Companies Act which requires all corporations to report their balance sheets, profit and loss statements, business reports, and their detailed supplements to their annual shareholders' meetings for

[53] *See* John Armour, Bernard Black, Brian R. Cheffins & Richard Nolan, *Private Enforcement of Corporate Law: An Empirical Comparison of the United Kingdom and the United States*, 6 J. EMPIRICAL LEGAL STUD. 687, 711 (2009) (highlighting that 150–200 federal securities class actions are brought annually in the United States together with some number of non-class actions brought in state court.)

[54] CHOI & PRITCHARD, *supra* note 52, at 927.

[55] *Id.* at 928.

[56] *Id.*

[57] 18 U.S.C. §1348.

protecting shareholders and creditors, the Financial Instruments and Exchange Law requires listed companies to disclose their accounting information attested by Certified Public Accountants (CPAs) and corporate governance information, Management's Discussion and Analysis (MD&A), etc., by annual securities report for protecting investors.[58] In addition to the annual securities report, a semi-annual report is also required. Although the formal quarterly report was abolished in 2023, informal quarterly disclosure and timely disclosure are required by the Tokyo Stock Exchange.[59]

Disclosure regulations by the Financial Instruments and Exchange Law are publicly enforced with criminal punishment and surcharge. Investors who suffered losses due to the misrepresentation of the annual securities report can directly sue the company for damages. The burden of proof regarding negligence and the amount of damage is transferred from the plaintiff investor to the defendant company (Financial Instruments and Exchange Law §21-2 I, II).

6.2.2.2 J-SOX

A Japanese analog to the US SOX, J-SOX, was introduced into Japanese securities regulation in 2006, in response to a couple of fraudulent disclosure scandals in 2004.

J-SOX shares the object and basic structure of SOX. Both require that the management of listed companies certifies internal control disclosures and that independent auditors attest to preventing fraudulent accounting and increasing the reliability of disclosed information. In practice, however, they appear to have totally different effects. Although SOX improved the corporate governance of listed companies by strengthening the bargaining power of the monitors, it also had the serious side effect of making management more defensive. J-SOX, on the other hand, did not strengthen the bargaining power of monitors and failed to improve the corporate governance of publicly traded companies, but it did not create serious side effects.[60]

[58] Before owning the continuous disclosure duty, the issuing company is required to disclose the information in the securities registration statement and the prospectus at the initial public offering. Issuing companies' liability for misrepresentation of issuance disclosure is even stricter than that of continuous disclosure, including no-fault liability (Financial Instruments and Exchange Law §16).

[59] Financial Instruments and Exchange Law (prior to 2023 reformation) §24-4-7; Tokyo Stock Exchange Listing Rule §404.

[60] *See* Shishido & Osaki, *supra* note 45, at 365–366. Assessments of SOX and J-SOX are, however, very controversial in both countries.

Such divergent effects of two similar pieces of legislation are the result of the complementary effects of the law, markets, and social norms. J-SOX's indirect reporting system, the lack of a complete enforcement mechanism, the prevalence of insider-dominated boards, illiquid external labor markets, and the company community norm allow management and auditors to formally comply with the rules while concealing real problems.[61]

6.2.2.3 Proxy Rules and Five Percent Rule

Because proxy solicitation is rarely used in Japan, proxy rules have little effect on the relative bargaining power between shareholders and management.[62] In contrast, the 5 percent rule is much more significant.[63] While the 5 percent rule provides useful information to ordinary investors, it generally discourages institutional investors, who are forced to disclose their investment activities to the public, from purchasing more than a 5 percent share in a company.[64]

Before the 2006 amendment, Japanese securities regulation imposed relaxed reporting requirements on banks, securities firms, investment funds, etc. to reduce their administrative cost.[65] Since 2006, the amended securities regulation has restricted the availability of the relaxed reporting

[61] The fact that the first year "material weakness" report was only 2 percent, compared to 17 percent in the United States, can be seen as a result of the superficial efforts to comply with the law. *See* Shishido & Osaki, *supra* note 45, at 349, 362, 366.

[62] Japanese proxy rule was implemented by the reformation of the Securities Transaction Law of 1948 based on the US Securities Exchange Act of 1934, the major purpose of which was to prevent incumbent management's abusive use of the proxy machinery. *See* HIDEFUSA IIDA, FINANCIAL INSTRUMENTS AND EXCHANGE LAW 176 (2023). Solicitors must provide shareholders with reference documents for proxy solicitation that describe matters legally required to be included. Proxy documents must enable shareholders to select either approval or disapproval on each proposal (Financial Instruments and Exchange Act §194, Execution Order §§36-2–36-6, Cabinet Office Ordinance on Proxy Solicitations).

[63] The 5 percent rule was added to Japanese securities regulation in 1990 based on the US Williams Act of 1968. The main goal was to provide issuers time to prepare countermeasures against greenmailers, who had gained notoriety after T. Boon Pickens' attack on Koito Manufacturing Co. in 1989. *See* Zenichi Shishido, *A Texan Raid on a Japanese Company*, 16 JAPAN ECHO 61 (1989).

[64] *See* ZENICHI SHISHIDO & SADAKAZU OSAKI, JOJO KAISHA HO [LAWS OF LISTED COMPANIES] 163 (2023).

[65] For example, in 2005, the activist Murakami Fund took advantage of this relaxed rule and acquired large stakes in several companies without disclosure before surprising their boards with proposals for major business changes.

rule.[66] As a result, the Japanese 5 percent rule turns out to be the strongest regulation among major stock markets.[67]

Although the major purpose of the 2006 reformation was to restrain hedge fund activism, it has, in reality, not discouraged hedge fund activism because it simply made hedge funds disclose their purpose of making important proposals, but has discouraged large volume holding by traditional institutional investors that take a long-term investment policy.[68]

6.2.2.4 Private Remedies

Financial Instruments and Exchange Law provides no-fault liability and presumption of the amount of damages for the violation of disclosure regulation to encourage private enforcement (§§16, 19 I, II, 21-2, 21-2 III, V, VI).[69] Private enforcement has, however, played an unimportant role in Japan mainly because class action is not available and there is little incentive to sue for both the plaintiff investors and plaintiffs' lawyers.[70]

6.2.2.5 Criminal Enforcement

Misrepresentation in large volume holding reports and changing reports, and non-submission of these reports will be criminally punished and ordered surcharge payment (Financial Instruments and Exchange Law §§172-7, 172-8, 197-2 V, VI). Surcharge payment will come to the government, while the benefit of misrepresentation that is seized by SEC will be distributed to victims in the United States.[71]

6.2.3 China

6.2.3.1 Duty of Disclosure

Until a 1997 criminal law amendment, it was unclear under Chinese law who had the duty to disclose information, whether it was the company, its directors, or both. For instance, the 1993 Company Law only imposes the duty of disclosure on the company rather than its directors, officers,

[66] In particular, the rule is only available to investors who do not buy stocks for the purpose of making important proposals to the issuer, and the rule increases the frequency of compulsory reporting.

[67] *See* Shishido & Osaki, *supra* note 64, at 165.

[68] *See id.* at 165–166.

[69] *See id.* at 324–326. The existence of the presumption of the amount of damages is more investor-friendly than the US law.

[70] *See id.* at 327. Recently, however, quasi-class actions using the internet have increased.

[71] Financial Instruments and Exchange Law §172 I; Securities Exchange Act of 1934 §21 (d) (5).

or supervisors.[72] The Criminal Law (amended in 1999) finally filled the gap, by providing, for example, that companies making omissions or false statements in the prospectus; the subscription of shares, or the materials used in bonds issuances be fined 1–5 percent of the illegally raised funds; individuals engaged in the same conduct be penalized for imprisonment of no more than five years or detention. The companies and directors with inside information leaking such information, which fundamentally affects the prices of securities and causes serious effects, will be subject to detention or imprisonment for no more than five years.[73]

The CSRC issued the Provisional Enforcement Rules of Information Disclosure by Listed Companies in 1993. This piece of regulation primarily deals with the content and format of information disclosure by a listed company.[74] It laid down the principle that both the issuing company and the directors of the company must ensure that no false or seriously misleading information or gross omissions are included in disclosure documents. Failing to do so will make both the company and the directors jointly liable for violations.[75] The information disclosure regime, after almost thirty years' development, is now in a relatively stable shape. By mid-2009, the CSRC in total released twenty-nine pieces of rules dealing with the content and form of information disclosure.

6.2.3.2 Major Disclosure Laws and Regulations

The Code of Corporate Governance for Listed Companies in China has been developed and enforced since January 2002.[76] The code is

[72] Company Law 1993, Arts. 140, 153 and 156.

[73] In addition, these companies and directors will be fined between one and five times the amount of the illegal gains made through this conduct. In more severe circumstances, they will be sentenced to imprisonment of between five and ten years and will be required to pay a fine between one and five times the amount of the illegal gains from their misconduct. The amended Criminal Law imposes the penalty of imprisonment or detention on the directors if they are involved in the information leakage. The Company Law 2005 further confirms the general principle that both the company and directors are liable for the leakage of sensitive information to the market. Compensatory liabilities, for instance, are imposed by the amended Company Law 2005 on the company directors and other senior managers for breaches of laws and rules when the company violates laws and rules. Criminal Law 1997, Art. 180; Company Law 2005, Art. 150.

[74] CSRC released the Provisional Rule No. 1 on the Content and Form of Information Disclosure – Content and Form of Prospectus in 1993.

[75] CSRC's Provisional Enforcement Rules of Information Disclosure by Listed Companies (1993), Art. 5.

[76] CSRC, Code for Corporate Governance for Listed Companies in China, http://www.csrc.gov.cn.

mandatory for all listed companies and has been incorporated into the listing rules of two stock exchanges (plus the new one in Beijing). Information disclosure is an ongoing responsibility of all listed companies. All the shareholders in such companies have an equal right to receive correct, timely, and complete information, and regular disclosure of audited annual reports, mid-year reports, and unaudited quarterly reports. Disclosure of corporate governance practices is required in the annual report, along with disclosure of information on the controlling shareholder or the actual controller of the company.

The Company Law 2018 went a step further by entitling a shareholder of a company to examine the company's shareholders' meeting minutes, board resolutions, supervisory board minutes, and accounting books by submitting a request with reasons for such disclosure.[77] If the company refuses to do so, the shareholder may petition the court for an order.[78] The information rights would increase the deterrent effects of shareholder oversight. The right of a shareholder to examine accounting books, business records, vouchers, and documents will give a minority shareholder[79] significant rights. Directors, supervisors, and senior officers must attend shareholders' meetings upon request by shareholders and answer inquiries from the shareholders.[80] The shareholders are empowered to elicit accurate information from the directors, the senior officials, and the supervisors.[81]

The Securities Law prohibits fraud, insider trading, and securities manipulation.[82] The issuer is required to publish share issuing documents by public notice and display these documents in public

[77] Shareholders of a company can access the articles of association, corporate bond counterfoils, and list of shareholders (equivalent to the registrar of members), but not accounting books. Shareholders can also consult records relating to corporate bonds. Accounting books may contain some accounting anomalies that financial statements do not have. Nevertheless, given the number of shareholders, a company limited by shares may have, confining the right to access accounting books in LLCs can lower the administrative burden on companies limited by shares. Company Law 2018, Arts. 33 and 97; Company Law 2023, Arts. 57 and 110.

[78] *Id.*

[79] The Company Law does not set a minimum percentage of share requirement for shareholders to exercise their inspection right. The company says, "the shareholders recorded in the register of shareholders may, pursuant to the register of shareholders, claim to and exercise the shareholder's rights." *See* Company Law 2018, Arts. 32 and 33; Company Law 2023, Arts. 56 and 57.

[80] Company Law 2018, Art. 150; Company Law 2023, Art. 187.

[81] *Id.*

[82] Securities Law 1998, Art. 5.

places.[83] The share issuing documents should be true, precise, and complete.[84] The underwriter is under a legal obligation to examine the authenticity, precision, accuracy, and completeness of the issuing documents.[85] Disclosures should be timely and made in a manner prescribed by applicable laws and regulations.[86] Criminal punishment of securities-related offenses was introduced into the Criminal Law in its 1997 amendments, which contain some articles that impose criminal liabilities on companies and their employees who are directly involved in various forms of securities fraud.[87] Accordingly, companies and individuals that have omitted material information or made false statements in the prospectus or the subscription of shares will be heavily fined; individuals who have engaged in the same type of conduct and are directly in charge of the company's business will be subject to detention or imprisonment of up to five years.[88]

The CSRC released several rules governing information disclosure before the Company Law was enacted in 1993. For instance, the first piece of rule was the Implementing Rules on Information Disclosure by Listed Companies. The minimum required disclosure documents include the prospectus, the listing announcement, and the annual and semi-annual reports, as well as the interim report.[89] The duty to disclose is clearly imposed on the directors who are required not to disclose false or misleading statements or make gross omissions in the disclosed documents.[90] The directors and promoters are jointly liable for misconduct or violation. Some detailed requirements appeared for the first time as part of the disclosure rule. For example, in the takeover announcement, personal details and the shareholding of directors must be disclosed.[91]

The CSRC issued a total of twenty-four sets of Rules on Content and Format of Information Disclosure by Listed Companies from 1993 to mid-2009. These rules cover the main issues surrounding disclosure, including the initial public offering prospectus, annual reports, semi-annual reports, reports of changes in shareholding, share listing

[83] *Id.*, Art. 17.
[84] *Id.*, Art. 13.
[85] *Id.*, Art. 24.
[86] *Id.*, Arts. 61, 62, 110, and 177.
[87] Criminal Law 1999, Arts. 160 and 161.
[88] *Id.*, Art. 160.
[89] Implementing Rules on Information Disclosure by Listed Companies (for trial), Art. 4.
[90] *Id.*, Art. 5.
[91] *Id.*, Item 2 of Art. 22.

announcements, and prospectuses of issuing new shares. These rules form the core of the disclosure regime. The CSRC, from time to time, issued circulars or measures to regulate the disclosure regime. For example, it issued the Circular Concerning Engagement of Accounting Institutions by Companies to Issue Shares, which requires the issuing companies to provide profit-making forecasting materials. The CSRC also released the Questions and Answers Concerning Disclosure Standards by Listed Companies in April 2001. These provide guidance on particular questions raised by listed companies. Although not necessarily legally binding, these documents are still important in guiding listed companies in their business conduct. In order to facilitate compliance, the CSRC also published its administrative rules in 2001, increasing transparency of law enforcement and interpretation.

6.2.3.3 Proxy Rules and 5 Percent Rule

China's 5 percent rule is more effective in regulating a "creeping acquisition," rapid accumulation of a significant percentage of the company's stock in the open market, compared to its US and Japanese counterparts.[92] Details of the 5 percent rule will be explained in more depth in Chapter 7.

6.2.3.4 Remedies

Civil, administrative, or criminal remedies may be available to the investors who suffer losses from any breach of disclosure duties. Under the Securities Law, any violation may result in civil compensation liability.[93]

6.2.3.5 Private Actions

The form of private actions available to investors is limited to individual or joint action.[94] Joint action resembles the class action lawsuit under US

[92] Chinese Security Law not only requires the large volume holder to disclose within three days after holding more than 5 percent, but also prohibits trading of the company's stock for three days. If the large holder's stock holding either increases or decreases by more than 5 percent, she is required to disclose within three days and prohibited from trading the company's stock for three days. If the large holder's stock holding either increases or decreases by more than 1 percent, she is required to disclose it the next day. Securities Law of the People's Republic of China (promulgated by the Standing Committee of the National People's Congress on Dec. 28, 2019, effective Mar. 21, 2020), Art. 63, LAWINFOCHINA, https://www.lawinfochina.com/display.aspx?id=31925&lib=law.

[93] Securities Law 1998, Art. 207.

[94] The Several Provisions on Hearing Civil Compensation Cases Arising from False Statement on the Securities Market, Art. 12.

law in some respects. Nevertheless, there are differences with respect to the registration requirement, the plaintiff's rights, the representative's powers, and the binding effect of the court rulings.[95] This suggests that class actions in China are not a viable way to pursue securities claims, even though in theory the US-style class action lawsuit is more economic (in the cost-saving sense but not necessarily in the cost redistribution sense) for this type of litigation.[96] It is characteristic in China that parties involved in securities litigation are encouraged to use mediation or arbitration.[97]

6.2.3.6 Public Enforcement

CSRC has broad administrative powers to enforce securities laws and regulations, and may exercise its powers to supervise the securities market by imposing administrative liabilities on companies and management involved in misconduct or violations such as issuing stop order, confiscating profit from misconduct, imposing administrative fines up to renminbi (RMB) 300,000 on company officers, directors or supervisors who are directly involved, etc.[98]

Another resort available to CSRC may be criminal remedies available under the amended Criminal Law, which include criminal fines,[99] detention[100] and imprisonment,[101] and which may be imposed separately or jointly. Criminal fines range from 1 to 5 percent of falsely registered capital if a company manages to be registered with false documents.[102] The directly responsible officers of the company will be fined RMB 20,000–200,000.[103] These fines are not nearly large enough to discourage fraud. Likewise, prison terms are relatively short, with a maximum term of five years.[104]

[95] *See* Walter Hutchens, *Private Securities Litigation in China: Material Disclosure about China's Legal System?* 24 U. PA. J. INT'L ECON. L. 599, 641 (2003).

[96] *See* Susan V. Lawrence, *Shareholder Lawsuits: Ally of the People*, 165 FAR E. ECON. REV. 26, 27 (2002).

[97] The Several Provisions on Hearing Civil Compensation Cases Arising from False Statement on the Securities Market, Art. 4.

[98] Securities Law 2005, Arts. 179 and 189.

[99] Criminal Law, Art. 158.

[100] *Id.*, Art. 159.

[101] *Id.*

[102] *Id.*, Art. 158.

[103] *Id.*, Art. 161.

[104] *Id.*, Arts. 158, 159, 160, and 181.

6.3 Directors' and Officers' Fiduciary Duties, Business Judgment Rule, and Shareholder Suits

Shareholders can sue directors and officers for damages because of their breach of fiduciary duties. The legal system of shareholder suits as the enforcement mechanism of directors' and officers' fiduciary duties supports shareholders' bargaining power against management. On the other hand, the business judgment rule provides management with a safe harbor. Therefore, corporate law rules on fiduciary duties, shareholder suits, and business judgment rules will affect the relative bargaining power of shareholders and management.

6.3.1 The United States

US law, particularly Delaware corporate law, imposes on management a strict duty of loyalty to the shareholder while allowing management a wide safe harbor through the business judgment rule.

In the US, directors owe both the duty of care and the duty of loyalty to the shareholders. The duty of care requires directors and officers to exercise the degree of care that an ordinarily prudent person in a similar position under similar circumstances would exercise.[105] However, Delaware Law has a provision DGCL §102(b)(7) which allows shareholders to introduce a charter amendment that waives director liability for duty of care violation.[106]

For potential duty of care claims, directors are protected by the business judgment rule. The core idea for the business judgment rule is that Courts should not second-guess good-faith decisions made by independent and disinterested directors.[107] Under the business judgment

[105] *See* Marcia M. McMurray, *An Historical Perspective on the Duty of Care, the Duty of Loyalty, and the Business Judgment Rule*, 40 VAND. L. REV. 605, 609 (1987).

[106] DGCL §102(b)(7) can be seen as Delaware's response to its harsh ruling in Smith v. Van Gorkom where the Delaware Supreme Court found the directors breached duty of care and resulted in a 23 million settlement. DGCL §102(b)(7) helped alleviate the liability concerns of directors following Van Gorkom case; *see* Smith v. Van Gorkom, 488 A.2d 858 (Del. 1985); John L. Reed & Matt Neiderman, *Good Faith and the Ability of Directors to Assert 102 (b)(7) of the Delaware General Corporation Law as a Defense to Claims Alleging Abdication, Lack of Oversight, and Similar Breaches of Fiduciary Duty*, 29 DEL. J. CORP. L. 111, 113 (2004).

[107] *See* WILLIAM T. ALLEN, REINIER KRAAKMAN & VIKRAMADITYA S. KHANNA, COMMENTARIES AND CASES ON THE LAW OF BUSINESS ORGANIZATION 269 (2021).

rule, there is a presumption that the duty of care is fulfilled if there is no self-dealing, fraud, or illegality.

The duty of loyalty requires a corporate director, officer, or controlling shareholder to exercise their power over corporate processes or property (including information) in a good-faith attempt to advance the interests of the company and shareholders.[108] The standard of review for a duty of loyalty violation is entire fairness review. However, if directors can obtain an affirmative vote of a majority of disinterested directors, then the business judgment rule may apply.

US law provides shareholders with strong weapons to enforce management fiduciary duties: direct and derivative suits for damages.

Direct suits are available to shareholders who have suffered an injury specific to them, that other shareholders have not suffered. The existence of the class action system and the plaintiff attorney's contingent fee system encourages shareholders to raise direct suits.

In the United States, the number of shareholder direct actions overwhelms the number of shareholder derivative actions. The demarcation between the two types of shareholder suits is blurred, and the plaintiff can choose either type. The lower barrier to give for direct action than derivative action, and the availability of class action gives plaintiffs' attorneys an incentive to choose direct actions.[109]

Derivative suits are brought by shareholders on behalf of a corporation for an injury that the corporation has suffered as a whole. There is a significant procedural hurdle in filing a derivative lawsuit. Specifically, prior to the filing of a derivative lawsuit, the shareholders of the firm must first demand that the board of directors bring legal action against the wrongdoers.[110] In practice, the majority of board members (including the CEO) are often named as defendants in derivative lawsuits.[111] Naturally, the directors rarely want to approve the demand. If the board of directors disapproves the demand, a judge typically follows the board's decision and dismisses the lawsuit.[112]

108 *Id.* at 309.

109 *See* Elliott J. Weiss & Lawrence J. White, *File Early, then Free Ride: How Delaware Law (Mis) Shapes Shareholder Class Actions*, 57 VAND. L. REV. 1797, 1804 (2004).

110 *See* Thomas Bourveau, Yun Lou & Rencheng Wang, *Shareholder Litigation and Corporate Disclosure: Evidence from Derivative Lawsuits*, 56 J. ACCT. RSCH. 797, 802 (2018).

111 *Id.* at 803.

112 *Id.*

To mitigate the board of directors' conflict of interest arising from the demand requirement, many states follow the "demand futility" doctrine. The demand futility doctrine allows shareholders to bypass the demand requirement and file a derivative lawsuit without the directors' approval.[113] To do so, shareholders need to prove that the majority of the directors cannot impartially judge the necessity of initiating a derivative lawsuit. In deciding whether demand is futile, Delaware courts use a test requiring shareholders to allege "particularized facts" that cast a reasonable doubt on the directors' independence or on their exercise of business judgment.[114] Satisfying this test often poses a challenge, particularly because discovery (e.g., access to books and records) is not allowed at this stage.[115] Nevertheless, plaintiffs almost always argue that demand is futile rather than make a demand on the board.[116]

However, the availability of the "futility exception" caused abuse of derivative lawsuits, wasting time and money for courts and firms.[117] In response to the abuse of the "futility exception," US states from 1989 to 2005 adopted the Universal Demand (UD) laws that require the shareholders to make a demand on the board of directors prior to *every* derivative lawsuit. Delaware does not have a UD requirement until 2021.[118]

The adoption of UD laws thus restores the effectiveness of the demand requirement and helps directors regain control of derivative lawsuits.[119] Following enactments of UD laws, shareholders were deprived of the option to plead demand futility.[120] As a consequence, fewer derivative lawsuits are filed, and the litigation risk pertaining to derivative lawsuits is significantly reduced in the states that adopted the UD laws.[121] Some

[113] *Id.*

[114] *See* Ian Appel, *Governance by Litigation*, SSRN (June 2019) (manuscript at 8), https://ssrn.com/abstract=2532278.

[115] *See id.*

[116] *See id.*

[117] *See* Feng Chen, Qingyuan Li & Li Xu, *Universal Demand Laws and the Monitoring Demand for Accounting Conservatism*, 48 J. Bus. Fin. & Acct. 1246, 1250 (2020).

[118] *See* Appel, *supra* note 114, at 9; Erick M. Sandler, Jeffrey P. Mueller & Palak Sharma, *The Delaware Supreme Court Adopts a Universal Demand-Futility Test in Facebook Investors' Derivative Suit*, Day Pitney (Sept. 27, 2021), https://www.daypitney.com/insights/publications/2021/09/27-the-delware-supreme-court-adopts/.

[119] *See* Bourveau et al., *supra* note 110, at 803.

[120] *See* Chen et al., *supra* note 117, at 1250.

[121] *See* Bourveau et al., *supra* note 110, at 803.

have claimed that the laws probably make derivative litigation impossible to maintain.[122]

Meanwhile, the robust discovery system in US law helps shareholders to raise their suits, further supporting shareholders' bargaining power against management.

In derivative suits, plaintiffs and their lawyers often control the discovery agenda.[123] Accordingly, defendants must respond to every discovery request by the plaintiff (unless they succeed in convincing the court that it is improper), while it is left to the plaintiff to decide whether, when, and how to review the defendants' responses.[124] It is also usually less expensive to present discovery requests, especially document requests and interrogatories, than to respond to them.[125] These factors can render the pretrial discovery stage so much more cumbersome and expensive for the defendants than for the plaintiff that defendants may be induced to settle the case rather than going to trial, even though they might have a significant chance of winning on the merits.[126]

6.3.2 *Japan*

Japanese corporate law does not distinguish between the duty of care and the duty of loyalty. Japanese corporate law has a statute on the fiduciary duty of directors to the company (Companies Act, Art. 355). Although the statutory phrase "fiduciary duty to the company" has been generally interpreted by commentators to mean "duty to the shareholder,"[127] and a recent case ratified the view,[128] the prevalent view is that the fiduciary duty of directors does not prohibit directors to balance stakeholders' interests as well.[129]

122 Appel, *supra* note 114, at 10.

123 Tim Oliver Brandi, *The Strike Suit: A Common Problem of the Derivative Suit and the Shareholder Class Action*, 98 Dick. L. Rev. 355, 371 (1993).

124 *Id.*

125 *Id.*

126 *Id.*

127 Zenichi Shishido, *Japanese Corporate Governance: The Hidden Problems of Corporate Law and Their Solutions*, 25 Del. J. Corp. L. 189 (2000).

128 In *re Rex* Holdings Shareholder Litigation, 2190 Hanji 96 (Tokyo High Ct., April 17, 2013).

129 *See* Zenichi Shishido, *The Incentive Bargaining of the Firm and Enterprise Law: A Nexus of Contracts, Markets, and Laws, in* Enterprise Law: Contracts, Markets, and Laws in the US and Japan 15 (Zenichi Shishido ed., 2014); Toru Kitagawa, *Complementarity among the Abusive Dismissal Rule, Company Community Norms,*

The business judgment rule has been developed through case law for the last thirty years.[130] While Japanese courts allow management wide discretion, they check not only the procedure of the decision but also the substantial adequacy of the decision.[131]

Japanese corporate law also provides for shareholder derivative suits and direct suits for damages for duty breaches. Although the Japanese discovery system is weak, and plaintiff shareholders are unlikely to be economically compensated, particularly in derivative suits, shareholder suits are raised relatively often.[132]

Companies Act Article 429 provides, "If officers, etc., have acted in bad faith or with gross negligence in performing their duties, such officers, etc., are liable to a third party for damages arising as a result thereof." A third party includes not only a creditor but also a shareholder.

If directors and officers cause damage to the corporation, shareholders can raise a derivative suit only, and a direct suit is not available. Shareholders can use direct suit based on Article 429 if directors and officers cause damage to the individual shareholders. Recently, the Article 429 suit is used to recover individual damages suffered by unfair valuation in cases of cashout, such as for MBO.[133] This represents a new measure of private enforcement complementing the factual class actions via the Internet.[134]

Historically, the shareholder action seeking revocation of a resolution at a shareholders' meeting (Companies Act, Arts. 830 and 831) has played an important role in making management keep legal procedure and answer to shareholders' questions. As a side effect, however, it incurs too much cost to companies for the preparation of annual meetings.[135]

and am Illiquid External Labor Market: Transformation of Directors' Fiduciary Duty under Japanese Corporate Law, in ENTERPRISE LAW: CONTRACTS, MARKETS, AND LAWS IN THE US AND JAPAN 75–77 (Zenichi Shishido ed., 2014).

130 *See in re Nomura Securities Co.*, 1760 HANJI 144 (Tokyo District Ct. Jan. 25, 2001); Shishido, *supra* note 129, at 31.

131 *See in re Apaman*, 2091 HANJI 90 (Sup. Ct. July 15, 2010); Hatsuru Morita, *Wagakuni ni Keiei Handan Gensoku ha Sonzai Shiteitanoka* [*Has the Business Judgement Rule Existed in Japan?*] 1858 SHOJI HOMU 4 (2006).

132 *See* Mark D. West, *Why Shareholders Sue: The Evidence from Japan*, 30 J. LEGAL STUD. 351 (2001); Dan W. Puchniak & Masafumi Nakahigashi, *Japan's Love for Derivative Actions*, 45 VAND. L. REV. 1 (2021).

133 *See in re* Rex Holdings Shareholder Litigation, *supra* note 128.

134 *See* SHISHIDO & OSAKI, *supra* note 64, at 324.

135 *See* Hiroshi Mitoma, *Jojo Kigyo niokeru Teijikabunusisokai Unei no Jittai to Minaoshi no Hokosei [The Practice of Operating Annual Shareholders' Meetings of Listed Companies and a Suggested Revision], in* KOPORETO GABANANSU KAIKAKU NO TEIGEN – KIGYO

6.3.3 China

6.3.3.1 Duties of Directors and Managers

Article 148 of the revised Corporate Law 2005 stipulates that "the directors, supervisors and senior executives of a company shall comply with the laws, administrative regulations and the articles of association of the company and bear the duties of loyalty and due diligence towards the company."[136] In addition to assigning duties to directors, the revised Corporate Law outlines these duties in Articles 148(2) and 149 by proscribing illegal and punishable activities such as the acceptance of bribes, misappropriation of company funds, exploitation of company's business opportunities, certain transactions with the company, competition with the company's business, and disclosure of confidential information.[137] Finally, the revised Corporate Law adds a catch-all provision (Art. 149 (8)) prohibiting all other acts that are inconsistent with directors' duties.[138]

China Securities Regulatory Commission (CSRC) revised its Guidelines for Articles of Association of Listed Companies in 2016.[139] Article 97 introduces a duty of loyalty, and Article 98 introduces a duty of diligence.[140] Article 98 specifies that the duty of diligence includes treating all shareholders fairly and understanding the operations and management circumstances of the company.[141]

6.3.3.2 Shareholder Suits

Under the Company Law of 1994, shareholders may bring legal action directly against directors or other shareholders when a resolution of a shareholders' meeting or the board of directors violates any law, administrative regulations, or infringes the shareholders' rights.[142] This was a relatively restrictive cause of action because this covers only the resolution of shareholders' meetings or the board of directors and does not

KACHI KOJO • KEIZAI KASSEIKA HENO MICHISUJI [REFORMING CORPORATE GOVERNANCE: THE ROAD TO IMPROVING FIRM VALUE AND STIMULATING THE ECONOMY] 155 (Zenichi Shishido & Gen Goto eds., 2016).

136 *See* Guangdong Xu, Tianshu Zhou, Bin Zeng & Jin Shi, *Directors' Duties in China*, 14 EUR. BUS. ORG. L. REV. 57, 60 (2013).

137 *Id.*

138 *Id.*

139 *Id.*

140 *Id.*

141 *Id.*

142 Company Law 1995, Art. 111.

cover breach of directors' fiduciary duties that does not involve a resolution of either a shareholders' meeting or the board of directors. Basically, this cause of action needs an endorsement from the shareholders' meeting or board of directors, which technically is quite unrealistic given the fact that the majority shareholders dominate the shareholders' meetings or board of directors (through their appointed directors). The Company Law 2018 expands the existing provisions on shareholder actions, but it remains to be seen how helpful they will be in practice. There appear to be three available types of actions: shareholder lawsuits against void or voidable resolutions; derivative actions; and direct actions.

A shareholder can challenge in court shareholders' meetings and board resolutions that do not comply with the articles of association or that were passed at a meeting convened or conducted improperly. The lawsuit must be brought by the shareholder within sixty days of the resolution.[143] This rule forces both majority and minority shareholders to hold shareholders' meetings in an orderly, predictable, and lawful manner, thereby avoiding unnecessary disputes. This also incentivizes shareholders to strike a balance when they table their proposals at shareholders' meetings to ensure that mutually acceptable conditions can be satisfied. Evidently, the Company Law encourages minority shareholders to make use of shareholders' meetings as a valid platform to observe any irregular or illegitimate behavior of majority shareholders.

Shareholders' right to sue against a resolution of a general meeting is restricted to the procedurally and legally wrongful decisions made by the management. This suggests that shareholders cannot exert this right to fight for any value-decreasing decision if the decision itself is made without any procedural illegality. The court cannot rely on this rule to assess the fairness of a decision from the viewpoint of minority shareholders. Put differently, this right does not protect minority shareholders from the controlling agency problem. Unfortunately, the Company Law can put a shareholder at a procedural disadvantage in that the court may, at its discretion, require the shareholder to provide security for costs.[144]

[143] Company Law 2018, Art. 21; Company Law 2023, Art. 22.

[144] The practical difficulty here is at least twofold. First, it may be procedurally troublesome for a shareholder to bring a representative action on behalf of other shareholders. Second, legal costs for litigation in China consist of recoverable court fees (which are to be settled by the losing party in litigation) and attorney fees (which are not recoverable, no matter the result of the case). Therefore, the amount of attorney fees may prevent the grieving shareholder from initiating a shareholder action for a nominal

6.3.3.3 Derivative Actions

Derivative suits involving listed companies are said to be completely absent in the landscape of derivative actions in China. This phenomenon may be explained in different ways.[145] The most likely reason is perhaps a discouraging attitude the courts have taken toward derivative suits, either because of the complexity of derivative actions, politically advantageous controlling shareholders, or the possibly large number of parties involved in these cases.

Although the concept of derivative actions was not formalized and codified until the passing of the Company Law of 2005, administrative (non-legislative) bodies were not dormant on such matters. The CSRC, for example, adopted the concept in its Principles of Corporate Governance for Listed Companies of 2002 and allowed derivative suits.[146] The CSRC's green light to the derivative actions, nevertheless, was only a weak starting point for the implementation of derivative actions, as the Principles of Corporate Governance for Listed Companies were not legislation and did not provide a legislative or legal basis for the shareholders to pursue and the courts to accept claims. The Principles of Corporate Governance for Listed Companies contributed to the development of derivative actions by authorizing the shareholders to request that their company instigate a lawsuit. The way the Principles of Corporate Governance for Listed Companies phrased this authority as a power and made it a required step or prerequisite to initiating the derivative action, was different from the Company Law of 2005, which merely mentions a demand requirement.

amount of loss. WEI SHEN, CORPORATE LAW IN CHINA: STRUCTURE, GOVERNANCE AND REGULATION 307 (2015).

[145] It is possible that practical barriers to litigation and transaction costs block prospective plaintiffs in companies limited by shares from pursuing derivative suits. A cost-benefit analysis may easily disincentivize minority shareholders from taking this route for rights protection. Other explanations may be that companies may be managed better so as to reduce abuses that may trigger derivative actions, or disputing parties may more easily resolve their disputes through private means, owing to the availability of better information between disputing parties. *Id.* at 311.

[146] The relevant provision reads: "[t]he directors, supervisory board members, and managers of the company shall bear liability for compensation in cases where they violate law, administrative regulation or the Articles of Association and cause damages to the company during the performance of their duties. Shareholders shall have the right to request the company to sue for such compensation in accordance with law." CSRC's Principles of Corporate Governance for Listed Companies, Art. 4.

Before the passing of the Company Law of 2005, during the period from 2002 to 2004, higher courts in Zhejiang, Jiangsu, Shanghai, and Beijing all issued "opinions" permitting the use of the derivative suit mechanism in courts in their localities.[147] These opinions legitimize derivative suits with limited applicability and enrich the derivative suit concept and practice.[148]

A shareholder derivative action is viewed as a necessary part of China's effective corporate governance system and a tool for the protection of company shareholders, especially minority shareholders. Codifying shareholder derivative actions in the Company Law is reflective of a formal shift from conventional reliance upon *ex ante* supervision by administrative agencies to a greater emphasis on judicial power and *ex post* remedies. China's inadequate judicial system may explain the low number of derivative actions.

The SPC issued the Provisions on Several Issues Concerning the Application of the PRC Company Law I on April 8, 2006 to clarify certain procedural issues in connection with the standing requirement for shareholders who seek to initiate derivative actions. This clarification directs the courts to apply new rights from the Company Law of 2005 in cases involving transactions occurring before the new law came into effect.

Apart from the directors, supervisors, or senior officers, shareholders are also allowed to initiate derivative actions against any other persons

[147] These opinions include: Beijing Higher Court's Guiding Opinions on Several Issues on Adjudicating Corporate Dispute Cases 2004; Jiangsu Higher Court's Opinions on Several Issues on Adjudicating Cases Applying Company Law (Trial Implementation) 2003; Shanghai Higher Court's Opinions on Adjudicating Cases Regarding Corporate Litigation (I) 2003 (the Shanghai Opinions); and Zhejiang Higher Court's Understandings of Difficult Issues on Applying the Company Law 2002.

[148] The Shanghai Opinions affirms the inclusion of controlling shareholders and third parties as potential defendants; identifies the participation of the company as a "third party"; authorizes judicial determination of whether the company has been harmed, the causal connection between the defendants' actions and the harm, any good-faith defenses available to the defendants, and the degree of control exercised by the controlling shareholder defendant over the corporate entity inhibiting the underlying action; forbids settlement that all disadvantage the real parties in interest; empowers the court to annul offering transactions; and allow for damage awards against not only the defendants but also the company. The Shanghai Opinions have demonstrated a high level of sophistication in adjudicating derivative actions. The opinions rightly emphasize the preoccupation with shareholder oppression at the hands of controlling shareholders, and warns against court approval of pressurized settlements in derivative actions. This reflects the Shanghai Higher People's Court's awareness of the defect in the lopsided capital structure of controlled Chinese companies. SHEN, *supra* note 144, at 309.

who encroach upon the lawful rights and interests of a company, thereby causing losses to the company.[149] However, it is not clear whether and to whom a demand needs to be made. In addition, this expanded scope of possible defendants in derivative actions does not clarify whether controlling shareholders are included or not.

The financing mechanisms under the Chinese Civil Procedure Law are not necessarily supportive of the initiation of derivative actions. The basic rule is that the losing party pays various costs of litigation and court fees, and each party bears its own attorney's fees.[150] The courts are, in some cases, willing to award attorneys' fees to the winning parties as a matter of law. While all the arrangements for fees and costs have reasonable grounds, individual minority shareholder plaintiffs may have difficulty in financing all the costs for the proceeding. Funding through contingency fees has been accepted in practice since the National Development and Reform Commission (the NDRC) and Ministry of Justice issued the Measures on Fees for Lawyers' Services on April 13, 2006.[151]

6.3.3.4 Direct Actions

According to the Company Law, if a director violates the law, regulations, or articles of association and impairs the shareholders' interests, the shareholders may initiate a court proceeding.[152] This is a broad private right of action bestowed upon shareholders to sue for breaches by directors and executives that directly injure the interests of the shareholders. The availability of this private enforcement right may also help

[149] This rule may be interpreted broadly to cover an outsider who does not pay a debt to the company on time and is not sued by the directors and the supervisors. This rule may be used to prohibit majority shareholders from utilizing other companies as intermediaries to transfer interests in public companies. *Id.* at 315–316.

[150] State Council's Measures for the Payment of Litigation Costs, effective as of April 1, 2007. Filing fees are calculated as a fraction of the amount in controversy and are paid by plaintiffs upfront before acceptance of an action. Plaintiffs also need to pay a retainer of over half of the total predicted fees. Demanding shareholders may be required to post a bond as a pre-condition to bring a derivative suit. Posting security for defendants' reasonable litigation costs may inhibit nuisance suits in which initiating shareholders sue in bad faith. *Id.* at 316.

[151] Contingency fees are allowed to be up to 30 percent but not in specified classes of cases, including unpaid wages, spousal support, inheritance, marriage, and multi-plaintiff lawsuits. If a plaintiff shareholder is unsuccessful on the underlying claim, the loser will be deemed to be the company, which is supposed to pay the court fees. *Id.*

[152] *Id.* at 317.

obviate the need for derivative suits. This *ex post* enforcement right is echoed in other Chinese legislation as well.[153]

Both derivative and direct actions are alternatives to more specific regulatory monitoring. They have shifted from administrative and criminal penalties to the private enforcement mechanism, a self-enforcing model of corporate governance which is more popular and useful in the US and other common law jurisdictions.[154] The availability of derivative actions *per se* resets the balance between majority and minority shareholders and substitutes deterrence for prior supervision. These actions are important in the sense that procedural protections or bright-line prohibitions operate *ex ante* as substitutes for less predictable judicial standards, which are often created and applied *ex post*. It is worth noting that the operation of these actions depends on the effective involvement and functioning of the judiciary. In other words, the technical competence, institutional autonomy, and judicial independence give Chinese courts a final say on the operability of these designs in complex commercial disputes.[155]

For both derivative and direct actions, the Company Law does not provide statutory limitation provisions and the rule to split litigation expenses. According to the General Principles of Civil Law (the GPCL), the statutory limitation is two years and runs from the date when a company (in a derivative action) or a shareholder (in a direct action)

[153] For example, shareholders have the right to protect their interests through civil litigation or other legal means in cases where board resolutions are in violation of the law or infringe on the rights or interests of the shareholders. Shareholders are also allowed to initiate litigation against the directors of their company according to the articles of association of the company. The Code of Corporate Governance of Listed Companies, Art. 4. The Guidelines for the Articles of Association of Listed Companies, Art. 10. *Id.*

[154] *See* Bernard Black & Reinier Kraakman, *A Self-enforcing Model of Corporate Law*, 109 HARV. L. REV. 1911 (1996).

[155] Competence, autonomy, and independence have different meanings in Chinese parlance. Competence refers to the technical expertise of judges or judicial institutions in adjudicating cases. Autonomy refers to the judge's ability to act with his or her own authority, in particular, when the law does not provide a promulgated "legal bases" to him or her. Judicial autonomy, that is, in common law courts, allows a judge to create substantive legal principles which elaborate on or contradict regulatory or statutory norms. Judicial independence is probably the highest degree of autonomy and allows judges to act separately from and against the interest of political or military power. While judicial competence or autonomy is relatively easier to assess, the degree of judicial independence is hard to evaluate. Unconstrained judicial autonomy or independence may lead judicial institutions to avoid legal bases and regulatory controls owing to corruption, bribery, or *ex parte* pressures.

knows or should have known of the wrong done to the company or the shareholder.[156] The Company Law does not require plaintiffs to post security for litigation expenses, nor does it require a company to reimburse shareholder plaintiffs' litigation expenses. Without special rules, Chinese courts are likely to apply general rules and leave the company and the prevailing shareholder plaintiffs to decide how to split the expenses. This may discourage shareholders from pursuing *bona fide* or meritorious litigation, even though the traditional "security for expenses" rule can be utilized to strike out opportunistic derivative actions.

6.3.3.5 Class Actions

The concept of class actions has not been widely deployed in corporate law cases in China. However, it is clear that both individual actions and joint actions are acceptable to Chinese courts in civil compensation cases arising from false statements in the securities market. In other words, Chinese courts will not carry out a proceeding in the form of a class action, as class actions are not applicable to securities-related actions.[157] The number of plaintiffs in a joint action shall be determined before the hearing is held. Where there are a large number of plaintiffs in one case, the plaintiffs can appoint two to five litigation representatives, and each litigation representative may appoint one or two lawyers to represent him or her in the proceeding.[158]

6.4 Shareholder Activism

Shareholder activism is defined here as minority shareholders' attempt to monitor management not by exit, but by voice, including voting, raising suits, engagement, and proxy fights to nominte minority directors.

Although the activist shareholder includes individual shareholders, activism by institutional investors and hedge funds has particularly substantial effects on corporate governance because of their substantial stock ownership, that is, the rapidly increasing institutionalization of

[156] The two-year period starting from the date when the company is aware of the wrong to it may not be fair to minority shareholders, who may not have first-hand knowledge of the occurrence of losses, and the directors or managers have more incentives not to release such information or even proceed with the action.

[157] The Circular and Several Provisions of the Supreme People's Court on Handling Cases of Civil Compensation Arising from False Statement in the Securities Market, Arts. 4, 12 and 14.

[158] *Id.*, Art. 14.

stock ownership since the 1990s and hedge funds' sophistication in making persuasive proposals.

This section will compare the current situation of shareholder activism in the three countries as arising from the complementary effects of law, markets, and social norms.

6.4.1 The United States

Shareholder suits, both direct and derivative, are frequently raised in the United States by plaintiff attorneys, attracted by agreeable courts, contingency fees, director and officer insurance, the class action lawsuit, and the discovery system. Although such private enforcement plays an important monitoring role, many criticize the number of frivolous suits. Delaware courts have recently become reluctant to admit contingency fees of plaintiff attorneys for so-called peppercorn settlements[159] in merger litigation.[160]

Even in the United States, the relative bargaining power of shareholders and management was "strong manager, weak owner" until the 1980s.[161] Top managers enjoyed substantial autonomy based on dispersed stock ownership and proxy machinery.

The stock ownership structure, however, started to change in the 1990s, and now a few institutional investors control most large listed companies in the United States if they act in concert. Shareholder activism thus influences corporate governance: shareholders replace management, elect hedge fund-backed directors, and vote to abandon staggered boards and poison pills.[162]

Since the 1990s, there has been a shift from hostile takeovers to activist interventions by hedge funds, and the shift has accelerated since the 2010s.[163] Now, hedge fund activism plays a more important role than

159 *See* Jill E. Fisch, Sean J. Griffith & Steven D. Solomon, *Confronting the Peppercorn Settlement in Merger Litigation: An Empirical Analysis and a Proposal for Reform*, 93 Tex. L. Rev. 557 (2015).

160 *See* Zohar Goshen & Richard Squire, *Principal Costs: A New Theory for Corporate Law and Governance*, 117 Colum. L. Rev. 767 (2017).

161 *See* Mark J. Roe, Strong Managers, Weak Owners: The Political Roots of American Corporate Finance (1994).

162 *See* Maria Goranova & Lori Verstegen Ryan, *Shareholder Activism: A Multidisciplinary Review*, 40 J. Mgmt. 1230, 1233, 1241–1242 (2014).

163 *See* Milhaupt & Shishido, *supra* note 15, at 349; Ofer Eldar, Tanja Kirmse & Michael D. Wittry, *The Rise of Anti-Activist Poison Pills* 3 (Eur. Corp. Governance Inst., Working Paper No. 689, 2023), https://perma.cc/S6PC-WLMT.

hostile takeovers in corporate governance. Moreover, the surge of environmental, social, and governance (ESG) activism, whose objectives involve a broad set of stakeholders, turns out to be a major category of shareholder activism.[164]

The poison pill is evolving in response to the market shift, from hostile takeovers to hedge fund activism. The features of the anti-activist pill include a low share ownership trigger and acting-in-concert provisions. In the Williams Companies case of 2021,[165] the Delaware Chancery Court enjoined a typical anti-activist pill by applying the Unocal analytical framework of threat and proportionality.[166] Because the Williams Companies-type pill could operate not just against the hedge fund activists, but also against ESG activists, the Williams Companies Decision stirred up debates about assessment of anti-activist poison pill.[167]

6.4.2 *Japan*

Although shareholders rarely raised derivative actions against listed companies in the past, such actions have dramatically increased since the Commercial Code reformation of 1993 fixed court fees of derivative actions regardless of the amount of damages. Since then, shareholder derivative actions have played an important role in monitoring management in Japan.[168] At least, this has had the effect of making management more sensitive to compliance, but critics also point out the chilling effects of derivative suits.

The pioneer of shareholder activism by institutional investors in Japan was CalPERS. Since 1990, CalPERS has started to systematically vote by proxy in Japan, as it did in the United States. Its campaign in Japan is credited with having improved disclosure and dividend yields of Japanese listed companies.[169]

164 *See* Milhaupt & Shishido, *supra* note 15, at 349–350.

165 Williams Companies Stockholder Litigation, 2021 WL 754593 (Del. Ch. 2021).

166 *See* Milhaupt & Shishido, *supra* note 15, at 350.

167 *See* Jeffrey N. Gordon, *The Rejected Threat of Corporate Vote Suppression: The Rise and Fall of the Anti-Activist Pill*, 2022 Colum. Bus. L. Rev. 206 (2022); Caley Petrucci & Guhan Subramanian, *Pills in a World of Activism and ESG*, 1 Chi. Bus. L. Rev. 417 (2022); Zohar Goshen & Reilly S. Steel, *Barbarians Inside the Gates: Raiders, Activists, and the Risk of Mistargeting*, 132 Yale L. J. 411 (2022).

168 *See* West, *supra* note 132; Puchniak & Nakahigashi, *supra* note 132, at 1.

169 *See* Sanford M. Jacoby, *Convergence by Design: The Case of CalPERS in Japan*, 55 Am. J. Comp. L. 239 (2007).

A genuine Japanese institutional investor, the Pension Fund Association (PFA), also launched a surprising activism campaign in 2003. The overall ratio of negative votes by the PFA was 43 percent in 2003 and 25 percent in 2004. The impact of this campaign went far beyond that of foreign investors. For example, some 20 percent companies reduced the size of their boards in the 2004 season.[170]

Japan faced its first wave of hedge fund activism when The Children's Investment Fund (TCI) attacked J-Power in 2005. In 2007, Steel Partners attempted to take over Bulldog Sauce. Both attempts were, however, unsuccessful. In their wake, for a while, hedge fund activism had a limited impact in Japan. Some UK commentators theorized that this was because the hedge funds articulated their arguments under the logic of shareholder primacy, a logic that was explicitly rejected by managers and shareholders because, in Japan, shareholders do not act as principals and managers do not act as their agents.[171]

But the stance of Japanese shareholders and managers had changed since 2013, when the Abe administration started its Corporate Governance Reform. The first Japanese Stewardship Code was published in 2014, and the first Corporate Governance Code was published in 2015. Under these new soft laws, both domestic and foreign institutional investors are required to exercise their shareholder votes in the interest of their beneficiaries and to make efforts to engage with the boards of their portfolio companies. Likewise, the soft laws require that management take shareholder interests seriously and urge management to communicate with institutional investors, reform their boards, and dissolve their cross-shareholdings. In a sense, the new soft laws forced Japanese shareholders to behave as principals and Japanese managers to behave as their agents.

As a result, since around 2020, the scene of shareholders' meetings and the behind-the-scenes engagement between shareholders and management has radically changed when compared to the 1990s. Votes against management have increased, and shareholder proposals often obtain substantial support. Hedge fund activism has become increasingly influential. Both management and hedge funds jostle to seek the support of

170 *See* Takaya Seki, *Legal Reform and Shareholder Activism by Institutional Investors in Japan*, 13 Corp. Governance 377 (2005).

171 *See* John Buchanan, Dominic Heesang Chai & Simon Deakin, *Agency Theory in Practice: A Quantitative Study of Hedge Fund Activism in Japan*, 22 Corp. Governance: Int'l Rev. 296 (2014).

institutional investors and proxy advisors, based on the principal-agent theory. Sometimes, management is forced to accept hedge fund-backed directors.[172]

Such a radical change in the relationship between shareholders and management in Japan is accelerated by the changes in the stock market and labor market. Share crossholdings have decreased from more than 30 percent in the early 1990s to 9.6 percent in 2019. Foreign institutional investors own more than 30 percent of the shares of Japan's listed companies now. The increased percentage of non-regular workers in Japanese companies also works to improve the relative influence of activist hedge funds.[173]

ESG activism surged in 2022, partially because of the FSA mandating a report in line with the Task Force for Climate-related Financial Disclosure (TCFD) for all Prime market-listed companies in 2021. Twelve climate change proposals were subject to a vote. Proposals asking J-Power and Sumitomo Mitsui FG to align their operations with the Paris Agreement goals won 25 percent support.[174]

6.4.3 China

Historically, shareholder activism is nearly absent in Mainland China due to a combination of two factors. First, under the PRC laws framework, shareholders rather than the board of directors play the most important role in corporate governance and shareholders' meeting is the ultimate authority to approve all material matters and major transactions.[175] The second factor is the shareholder structure of listed companies. As of 2019, more than 90 percent of listed companies in both the Shanghai Stock

172 *See* e.g., Grace Huang & Kanoko Matsuyama, *Activist Fund Executives on Board Bolstered Olympus, CEO Says*, JAPAN TIMES (Mar. 28, 2022), https://www.japantimes.co.jp/news/2022/03/28/business/corporate-business/activist-fund-executives-bolstered-olympus/; Toshiba Shareholders Endorse Two Directors from Activist Hedge Funds, JAPAN TIMES (June 28, 2022), https://www.japantimes.co.jp/news/2022/06/28/business/corporate-business/toshiba-activist-directors/.

173 Changes of markets and corporate governance norms not only increased hedge fund activism but also successful hostile takeovers by competitor companies, which had not been attempted since Oji Paper failed to acquire Hokuetsu Paper. *See* Chapter 7, n.18, and its accompanying text.

174 *See* Insightia, Corporate Governance in Asia 2023.

175 See Jianwei Zhang, *Shareholder Activism in China*, N.Y. STATE BAR ASS'N 2 (2019), nysba.org/Sections/International/Seasonal_Meetings/Tokyo_2019/Coursebook/Panel_14_-_Zhang_-_China_-_Shareholder_Activism.html.

Exchange and the Shenzhen Stock Exchange are controlled by their controlling shareholders.[176] The Chinese state owns around 50 percent of all the shares of listed companies and selects, directly or indirectly, almost 70 percent of the directors of all Chinese listed companies.[177] There is thus less room for activist investors compared to the US market.

However, the landscape of shareholder activism has been slowly changing in recent years due to the establishment of the China Securities Investor Services Center (CSISC) .[178] The CSISC is a finance service institute set up in 2014, aiming to provide education, legal, information, and technology services to medium-to-small investors.[179] ISC usually becomes a shareholder of a listed company by holding 100 shares of the company and acts as the representative of minority shareholders to exercise its rights.[180] ISC has held shares in more than 3,000 listed companies.[181] ISC sends shareholder letters to listed companies urging the improvement of corporate governance and may sometimes bring lawsuits against majority shareholders or listed companies.[182] As of March 31, 2019, there are twenty lawsuits filed or backed by ISC.[183] ISC also acts as a mediator to settle disputes between investors and listed companies.[184] ISC has become more and more influential in the market, and an increasing number of listed companies have to take into account ISC's recommendation or opinion on corporate governance and the protection of minority investors very seriously.[185] Recently, scholars have observed that the number of activist campaigns in China has soared since 2019; these activist campaigns are not only initiated by ISC but also by private and state activist shareholders.[186]

176 *See id.*

177 *See* Grace Jinying Hu & Marc Goergen., *A Study of Ownership Concentration, Control and Evolution of Chinese IPO Companies*, SSRN (2001), http://ssrn.com/abstract=286612.

178 *See* Zhang, *supra* note 175, at 2.

179 *Id.*

180 *Id.*

181 *Id.*

182 *Id.*

183 *Id.* at 3.

184 *Id.*

185 *Id.* at 5.

186 *See* Dan W. Puchniak, Zhang Wei & Zhou Chun, *China's Rules-Based, Free Market, for Shareholder Activism: Overlooked Reality or Empirical Mirage?* 18–21, ECGI (Apr. 5, 2024), https://www.ecgi.global/content/china%E2%80%99s-rules-based-free-market-shareholder-activism-empirical-mirage-or-overlooked-reality.

7

Shareholder II

External Governance by Exit: Mergers and Acquisitions

Chapter 6 describes how shareholders monitor management by using their rights as minority shareholders, for example, through shareholder activism, in particular. This chapter describes how shareholders monitor management by selling off their stock to a raider who intends to gain corporate control, that is, the hostile takeover.

Now, in several countries, activist hedge funds can change the corporate governance of target companies without obtaining control, and some argue that shareholder activism can be a substitute for hostile takeovers. It is hard to identify whether an acquisition of substantial stock is for shareholder activism or for a hostile takeover. Defenses initiated by the management, typically poison pills, are not only used against hostile takeovers but also against shareholder activism. Regulations on buyers, such as the 5 percent rule, the proxy rule, and the takeover bid (TOB) rule, affect not only hostile takeovers but also shareholder activism. Explanations of poison pills, the 5 percent rule, the proxy rule, and the TOB rules are mainly made in this chapter, although they are also related to the subjects of Chapter 6.

Section 7.1 provides an overview of the history and current situation of the hostile takeover in three countries and examines its relationship with friendly takeover and shareholder activism. Section 7.2 compares regulations on buyers, that is, raiders, such as the TOB rule, 5 percent rule, proxy rule, antitrust regulation, and regulation from the national security point, from the perspective of their deterrent effect on buyers. Section 7.3 compares types of defense mechanisms against takeover attempts by sellers, that is, incumbent management, and regulations on these defenses in the three countries, particularly from the perspective of the board discretion and shareholders' involvement. Section 7.4 summarizes Sections 7.2 and 7.3 and examines the balance of autonomy and monitoring management by shareholders in each country. Section 7.5 focuses on the peculiar problem of the friendly takeover and legal remedies for the conflicts of interest problem from a comparative perspective.

7.1 The Significance of Hostile Takeovers and Their Continuity with Friendly Takeovers and Shareholder Activism

Friendly or hostile, a takeover means the change of control from dispersed ownership to a single controlling shareholder. The distinction between friendly takeovers and hostile takeovers depends on whether the incumbent management agrees to the change of control or not. But management is ultimately beholden to shareholders, so there is no clear line separating hostile takeovers and friendly takeovers.

The possibility of occurrence of takeovers, particularly the ones hostile in nature, is a source of shareholders' monitoring power against management, that is, external governance by exit. From an economic perspective, the takeover is useful as a scheme for efficient resource allocation[1] and for reducing the agency cost of free cash flow.[2]

Although takeovers play such significant roles in corporate governance and economic efficiency, most countries have various legal regulations on takeovers. There are three possible reasons for such regulations. First, takeovers, particularly hostile ones, cause significant conflicting interests among the four players – employees, management, creditors, and shareholders. Second, no corporate decision is necessary to make control transactions that make fundamental changes.[3] And third, the appearance of a new player, the buyer, causes special conflicts of interest problems: the agency problem of target boards to shareholders; the agency problem of buyers to shareholders; and the agency problem of controlling shareholders to minority shareholders.[4]

There are several comparative points of takeover practice in different countries.

First, who could be a buyer, and in which manner, friendly or hostile? How often are they business buyers (competitors) or financial buyers (funds)?

Second, what should/will the target board do in the face of a takeover attempt? Can the target board consider stakeholders' interests in the decision to exercise defenses? More specifically, can the target board

[1] *See* Michael C. Jensen, *Takeovers: Their Causes and Consequences*, 2 J. Econ. Persp. 21 (1988).

[2] *See* Michael C. Jensen, *Agency Cost of Free Cash Flow, Corporate Finance, and Takeovers*, 76 Am. Econ. Rev. 323 (1986).

[3] *See* Reinier Kraakman , et al., The Anatomy of Corporate Law: A Comparative and Functional Approach 205 (3d ed., 2017).

[4] *See id.* at 207.

defend against the offer if the buyer plans to increase firm value by laying off redundant workers?

Third, what defenses are used, and how can they be exercised? Different rules on what a board is permitted to do in the face of an unwanted offer might generate different incentives for management.[5]

The answers to these questions distinguish the markets and regulatory models into two groups. This distinction roughly is the one between financial markets in common law and civil law jurisdictions. It appears that financial markets in common law jurisdictions are more friendly to institutional investors such as funds due to the more dispersed capital markets and a liquid control market. By contrast, the civil law jurisdiction is more likely to see a more concentrated capital market and a less liquid control market. That is why Japan and China have a stronger lending market in terms of capital sources for enterprises. Accordingly, stronger rights protection in common law jurisdictions supports a shareholder-centric takeover regime. Civil law jurisdictions may be opposite, and a management-centric model may be more likely to exist.

7.1.1 The United States

The stock ownership structure of the United States used to be dispersed ownership before the institutionalization started in the 1990s, while listed companies in most countries in the world, except the United States and the United Kingdom, have controlling shareholders. In other words, only the United States and the United Kingdom had an environment, in which hostile takeovers can be successfully made. Actually, substantial numbers of hostile takeovers were observed in both countries.

Most buyers in the 1970s were competitors, both in a friendly way and hostile way. Buying oil on Wall Street was considerably cheaper than drilling in the ground in the late 1970s.[6] Now, financial buyers have increased.

The typical defense is a poison pill. If poison pills are implemented, the acquirer must talk to the board of the company first before going to the shareholders. Therefore, poison pills change the balance of bargaining

[5] *See* Bruce E. Aronson et al., *Enterprise Law Conference of 2014: Edited Transcript*, SSRN (2014), https://papers.ssrn.com/sol3/papers.cfm?abstract_id=2501143 [herein after Transcript] 111 (Curtis Milhaupt).

[6] *See* Jensen, *supra* note 1.

power among the players.[7] Poison pills can be implemented by the board in the United States.[8]

Normatively, in the United States, it is considered that directors should be provided an incentive to sell the business when a buyer makes an offer that is in the shareholders' best interests,[9] although there are some debates on the range of discretion on the boards.[10] Actually, target boards mostly try to maximize shareholder interest and use poison pills as leverage for price negotiation.[11] The attempt to utilize takeovers for maximizing shareholder interest is also revealed in the practice of golden parachutes.[12]

Since the 1990s, there has been a shift from hostile takeovers to activist interventions by hedge funds, and the shift has accelerated since the 2010s.[13] Now, hedge fund activism plays a more important role than hostile takeovers in corporate governance.

7.1.2 Japan

Japan is not a country without takeovers by its nature. Many takeovers were made during the *zaibatsu* era before the war, and raiders appeared just after the reopening of the Tokyo Stock Exchange (TSE) in the early

[7] *See* Transcript, *supra* note 5, at 110 (Akio Hoshi).

[8] *See* Moran v. Household Int'l, 490 A.2d. 1059 (Del Ch. 1985), aff'd, 500 A.2d 1346 (Del. 1985); Curtis J. Milhaupt & Zenichi Shishido, *The Enduring Relevance of the Poison Pill: A U.S.-Japan Comparative Analysis*, 28 STAN. J. L. BUS. & FIN. 336, 340–342 (2023).

[9] *See* Douglas G. Baird & Robert Rasmussen, *Private Debt and The Missing Lever of Corporate Governance*, 154 U. PA. L. REV. 1209, 1215 (2006); Frank H. Easterbrook & Daniel R. Fischel, *The Proper Role of a Target's Management in Response to a Tender Offer*, 94 HARV. L. REV. 1161, 1175 (1981).

[10] *See* Lucian Ayre Bebchuk, *The Case against Board Veto in Corporate Takeovers*, 69 U. CHI. L. REV. 973, 1012 (2002); Martin Lipton, *Pills, Polls, and Professors Redux*, 69 U. CHI. L. REV. 1037, 1059 (2002).

[11] *See* Marcel Kahan & Edward B. Rock, *How I Learned to Stop Worrying and Love the Pill: Adaptive Responses to Takeover Law*, 69 U. CHI. L. REV. 871 (2002); Ronald J. Gilson, *Reflections in a Distant Mirror: Japanese Corporate Governance through American Eyes*, 1998 COLUM. BUS. L. REV. 203 (1998). *But see* Air Prods. & Chems., Inc. v. Airgas, Inc., 16 A.3d 48 (Del. Ch. 2011).

[12] *See* Lucian Bebchuk, Alma Cohen & Charles C. Y. Wang, *Golden Parachutes and the Wealth of Shareholders*, 25 J. CORP. FIN. 140 (2014).

[13] *See* Milhaupt & Shishido, *supra* note 8, at 349; Ofer Eldar, Tanja Kirmse & Michael D. Wittry, *The Rise of Anti-Activist Poison Pills* 3 (EUR. CORP. GOVERNANCE INST., Working Paper No. 689, 2023), https://perma.cc/S6PC-WLMT.

1950s when individual shareholders own almost 70 percent because of the liquidation of *zaibatsu* families made by the occupation armies.

Against such hostile takeover attempts by domestic raiders and preparing for opening the stock market to foreign investors, business leaders started to organize cross-shareholdings among ex-zaibatsu member companies, which will be called horizontal *keiretsu*. As a result, stock ownership by insiders, such as financial institutions and corporations, mostly cross-shareholding members, overwhelmed stock ownership by outsiders, such as individuals and foreigners, in the late 1960s. Since then, the stock ownership rate by insiders, or stabilized shareholders, has been more than the majority until the late 1990s.

It is fair to say that there was no control market in Japan for the three decades, the 1970s, 1980s, and 1990s, mainly because of such a stock ownership structure. There are other reasons too. Strong employment protection laws transform full-time regular employees into "shark repellents."[14] A traditional justification for a takeover, changing bad management to good management, is not plausible because of the lack of an external manager market.

After the burst of the Japanese economic bubble in 1990, the rate of cross-shareholdings started to decline and, at the same time, the stock ownership rate by insiders also started to decline. Japanese financial crisis of 1997 accelerated the trend and the outsider stock ownership rate reversed the insider stock ownership rate in 2000. Now the outsider stock ownership rate is around 60 percent and the foreign shareholders rate is over 30 percent.[15]

In 2005, Livedoor, a rapidly growing IT startup company that had just made its initial public offering (IPO), announced its intent to seek majority control of Nippon Broadcasting, a traditional radio station. The board of Nippon Broadcasting decided to issue the warrants to Fuji Broadcasting, a traditional TV station and actual parent of Nippon Broadcasting, which would reduce Livedoor's stake substantially while raising Fuji's stake to 59 percent.[16]

[14] *See* Marco Pagano & Paolo Volpin, *Managers, Workers, and Corporate Control*, 60 J. FIN. 841 (2005).

[15] *See* Hideakai Miyajima & Fumiaki Kuroki, *The Unwinding of Cross-Shareholding in Japan: Causes, Effects, and Implications*, *in* CORPORATE GOVERNANCE IN JAPAN: INSTITUTIONAL CHANGE AND ORGANIZATIONAL DIVERSITY 79 (Masahiko Aoki et al. eds., 2007).

[16] *See* Sadakazu Osaki, *Regulation of Japan's Capital Markets and the Battle for Control of Nippon Broadcasting System*, 18 NOMURA CAP. MKT. REV. 25 (2005).

The defense taken by Nippon Broadcasting was substantially the same as the Japanese traditional *ex post* defense, issuing new stock to white knights. Before this case, although there were many cases in which buyers required an injunction against "unfair issuance of new stock" (Companies Act Art. 210) courts dismissed most cases with the reasoning that financing purpose overwhelmed entrenchment purpose (so-called principal purpose rule). In this case, which is similar to preceding cases, however, the Tokyo District Court and the Tokyo High Court issued three legal rulings, each judging the new rights issue as unfair, and ordering Nippon Broadcasting to desist.[17]

Livedoor v. Nippon Broadcasting (2005) seemed to open the door to the control market, but *Steel Partners v. Bull-Dog Sauce* (2007) closed the door again.[18]

In 2007, Steel Partners, a US-based investment fund, announced a tender offer to Bull-Dog Sauce, a dominant company in a niche food market and a relatively small-sized listed company. Steel was already the largest shareholder with 10.25 percent, and offered to buy all shares at 1,584 yen per share for cash. Bull-Dog issued three stock warrants for each share, which Steel could not exercise. Bull-Dog could acquire the stock warrants allotted to Steel at a price of 396 yen each. Shareholders' meetings approved both the change to the charter and the issuance of stock warrants with 83.4 percent of the vote. Steel requested an injunction.[19]

The Supreme Court dismissed the case for the following reason: If there is a risk that the acquisition of management control by a particular shareholder would damage the company's enterprise value, discriminatory treatment cannot be immediately construed as a violation of the principle of shareholder equality (Companies Act Art. 109 I). Whether shareholders' interests would be harmed should be decided by the shareholders themselves, and their decision should be respected unless the procedures were not reasonable. Bull-Dog Sauce Supreme

[17] Livedoor v. Nippon Broadcasting, 1213 KINHAN 6 (Tokyo High Ct., Mar. 23, 2005). *See* John Coffee Jr., *Expert Opinion for Livedoor v. Nippon Broadcasting*, 289 BESSATSU SHOJI HOMU 409 (2005).

[18] Steel Partners v. Bull-Dog Sauce, 61 MINSHU 2215 (Sup. Ct., Aug. 7, 2007). *See* also the failed hostile takeover attempt by Oji Paper against Hokuetsu Paper. *See* Milhaupt & Shishido, *supra* note 8, at 347, note 46 and its accompanying text.

[19] *See* Hwa-Jin Kim, Haruka Okihara & Stephen Woodcock, *Importing Hazardous Substances from the United States: The Poison Pill in Japan and Korea*, 10 J. KOREAN L. 1, 21–22 (2010).

Court decision fixed the rule of defense, that is, let shareholders decide who should obtain the control, or "no-frustration rule."[20]

Listed companies started to implement Japanese poison pills when the Ministry of Economic, Trade, and Industries (Japan) (METI) and the Ministry of Justice (Japan) (MOJ) issued the Defense Guideline of 2005, the same year of the Livedoor case. The Guideline permits defenses by using discriminatory warrants if they are reasonable from the perspective of keeping and increasing firm value.[21]

While poison pills in the United States can be implemented anytime by the board, Japanese poison pills are required to be implemented by the shareholders' meeting. While warrants are issued when poison pills are implemented, and the board has the discretion to erase the pills in the United States, warrants are issued when the board decides to exercise poison pills because warrants are not transferable with the underlying stock to which they were attached in Japan.[22] Therefore, Japanese poison pills have no legal effect even if the acquirer crosses the threshold, but they have a prior warning effect.

Target boards mostly prioritize company communities' interests over shareholders' interests and almost always resist hostile takeover attempts.

Although hedge fund activism in Japan until 2013 was mostly unsuccessful,[23] recent hedge fund activism, since the Abe administration's declaration of "Corporate Governance Reform" in 2013, publication of the Japanese Stewardship Code of 2014 and Japanese Corporate Governance Code of 2015, started to fill the vacancy of the hostile takeover, with supports of mainstream institutional investors. As an example of strengthened shareholder activism, non-renewals of pills have been increasing since 2013 because of the institutional investors' resistance.[24]

[20] *See id.* at 27 (2010); KRAAKMAN ET AL., *supra* note 3, at 212.

[21] Ministry of Economy, Trade and Industry and Ministry of Justice, Guidelines regarding Takeover Defense for the Purposes of Protection and Enhancement of Corporate Value and Shareholders' Common Interests (2005). *See* Curtis J. Milhaupt, *Bull-Dog Sauce for the Japanese Soul-Courts, Corporations and Communities – A Comment on Haley's View of Japanese Law*, 8 WASH. U. GLOBAL STUD. L. REV. 8 345, 353, 358 (2009).

[22] *See* Milhaupt & Shishido, *supra* note 8, at 345–346, notes 39–41 and their accompanying texts.

[23] *See* John Buchanan, Dominic Heesang Chai & Simon Deakin, *Agency Theory in Practice: A Quantitative Study of Hedge Fund Activism in Japan*, 22 CORP. GOVERNANCE: AN INT'L REV. 296 (2014).

[24] *See* Alan Koh, Masafumi Nakahigashi & Dan W. Puchniak, *Land of the Falling "Poison Pill:" Understanding Japanese Defensive Measures on Their Own Terms*, 41 U. PA. J. INT'L L. 687, 688 (2020).

The relevance of the Japanese poison pill, which was once considered to be dead, has substantially increased around 2020, both as an antitakeover defense and as a safeguard against activism.[25]

7.1.3 China

Takeover transactions involving state-owned enterprises (SOEs) are rare in China.[26] The number of takeovers, either tender offers or hostile takeovers, has been low. The key reason for this lack of takeover transactions is the China Securities Regulatory Commission (CSRC)'s pro-SOE approach when SOEs are acting as both sellers and buyers, which comes at the expense of non-state shareholders' opportunities for value maximization.[27] For instance, SOEs used to be exempted from the mandatory bid rule.[28] SOEs used to be able to buy or hold other SOEs' shares without making a unanimous offer, while POEs must follow the mandatory bid rules.[29] The pro-SOE stance in takeover laws effectively insulates SOE management from potential threats of being ousted by takeovers, thereby failing to enhance the corporate governance regime.

The main rules regarding the takeover of a Chinese public company are set forth in the Takeover Rules of Listed Companies (the "Takeover Rules"), first promulgated by the CSRC in 2006.[30] Since then, it has been revised thrice, in 2008, 2012, and 2014, respectively.

25 Particularly, the Tokyo Kikai Supreme Court decision (*In re* Tokyo Kikai, 1641 KINHAN 48 (Sup. Ct., Nov. 18, 2021) on a creeping control case and the Mitsuboshi Supreme Court decision (*In re* Mitsuboshi, 1667 KINHAN 56 (July 28, 2022)) on an anti-activist pill case are important. *See infra* notes 110–112 and their accompanying texts. *See* also Milhaupt & Shishido, *supra* note 8, at 14.

26 *See* Benjamin Chun, *A Brief Comparison of the Chinese and United States Securities Regulations Governing Corporate Takeovers*, 12 COLUM. J. ASIAN L., 99, 121 (1998); Sang Yop Kang, *Unravelling China's Hostile Takeover Landscape: The Reduced Significance of Corporate Governance* (PEKING UNIV. SCH. TRANSNAT'L. L., Working Paper 2024).

27 Takeovers involving state-owned assets have often encountered very strict government scrutiny and SOE-friendly takeover laws. As a result, non-controlling shareholders of SOEs often cannot obtain the best price for their shares due to more rigid markets. *See* Charlie Xiao-Chuan Weng, *Lifting the Veil of Words: An Analysis of the Efficacy of Chinese Takeover Laws and the Road to a Harmonious Society*, 25 COLUM. J. ASIAN L. 180, 182, 209 (2012).

28 It is important to note that the CSRC has recently modified regulations to remove the mandatory bid rule exemption for listed SOEs. *See id.* at 200, 202.

29 *See id.* at 200–201 (2012).

30 Shangshigongsi Shougou Guanli Banfa [*The Rules on the Takeovers of Listed Companies*] (Promulgated by the China Securities Regulatory Commission, May 17, 2006, effective Sept. 1, 2006) [hereinafter "Takeover Rules"].

7.2 Regulations on Buyers

Although takeovers may provide economic efficiencies, most countries have regulations on buyers because takeovers have several significant risks: risk of damaging firm value, risk of being coercive to minority shareholders; antitrust risk; and national securities risk.

Although how to decrease the risk of damaging firm value by takeovers is mainly tackled by sellers' board's discretion on defenses, the two major financial regulations that require buyers to disclose information: statements of large-volume holding (5 percent rule) and proxy rule, also play an essential role to decrease such a risk by disclosing information of buyers. To meet these disclosure regulations is costly to buyers, and strict regulations will discourage takeover attempts.

Protection of minority shareholders is always a big issue in takeover cases because takeovers without guaranteeing exit to all shareholders cause a coercive effect. Requiring buyers to purchase all stocks will discourage takeovers because of the cost. The takeover rules of each country vary by taking this tradeoff into consideration.

Takeovers may cause antitrust effects, particularly monopolies. Most countries have antitrust regulations of prior notification by buyers.

To deal with national securities risk, most countries have some regulations on foreign shareholders acquiring companies that produce products or provide services related to national securities. In the field of direct foreign investment, the national security review regime has gained popularity. The first Trump administration substantially revised the Committee on Foreign Investment in the United States (CFIUS) rules so as to block investment from China and other countries. China once became the largest investor in the United States in 2016. Due to the CFIUS reform initiated by the Trump administration, China's investment in the United States in the form of mergers and acquisitions (M&As) declined 90 percent in 2019. The United States also encouraged the European Union to adopt a similar regime for national security concerns. Now, the EU has adopted an EU-wide foreign direct investment (FDI) screening regime to scrutinize FDI from China, Russia, and other strategically important opponent countries. A large-scale national security review regime worldwide seriously worsens the FDI-related legal environment.

7.2.1 The United States

The Williams Act of 1968 imposed disclosure and procedural requirements for tender offers that eliminated many abuses thereof, such as the "Saturday Night Special," but did not require a mandatory bid.

The Williams Act sought to provide shareholders with sufficient time and information to make an informed decision about tendering their shares and to warn the market (or the target management) about an impending offer.[31]

Rule 13d-1(a) requires investors to file a 13D report within five days of acquiring more than 5 percent beneficial ownership.[32] Rule13d-1(b) allows certain "qualified institutional investors" to file a shortened 13G report (in lieu of the 13D report) within forty-five days of year-end and Rule 13d-1(c) permits passive but nonqualifying investors to file a 13G report (in lieu of the 13D report) within ten days of acquiring their holdings.[33]

§14(d)(1) mandates disclosure of the identity, financing, and future plans of a tender offeror, including plans for any subsequent going private transaction.[34] The regulations under these provisions include Rule 14d-3, which requires bidders to file and keep current 14D-1 reports for tender offers; Rule 14e-2, which requires the target's board to comment on the tender offer; Rule 13e-4, which requires companies to make much the same disclosures as third-party offerors when these companies tender for their own shares; and Rule 13e-3, which mandates particularly strict disclosure when insiders (including controlling shareholders) plan going-private transactions that would force public shareholders out of the company.[35]

7.2.1.1 Antitrust Laws

The most common antitrust review for an acquisition is a pre-closing review required under the Hart-Scott-Rodino Antitrust Improvements Act of 1976 ("HSR").[36] Before the adoption of HSR, the only way for the

[31] William T. Allen, Reinier Kraakman & Vikramaditya S. Khanna, Commentaries and Cases on the Law of Business Organization 489 (2021).

[32] The deadline for initial Schedule 13D filings used to be ten days. *Id.* In October 2023, the SEC amended the beneficial ownership reporting under Sections 13(d) and 13(g) of the Securities Exchange Act of 1934 and shortened the deadline for initial Schedule 13D filings from ten days to five days and the new amendment has now become effective. U.S. Securities and Exchange Commission, *SEC Adopts Amendments to Rules Governing Beneficial Ownership Reporting*, https://www.sec.gov/newsroom/press-releases/2023-219.

[33] Allen et al., *supra* note 31, at 489.

[34] *Id.* at 491.

[35] *Id.*

[36] Claire A. Hill, Brian Jose Miguel Quinn & Steven Davidoff Solomon, Mergers and Acquisitions: Law, Theory, and Practice 190 (2019).

government to enforce either the Sherman Act or Section 7 of the Clayton Act concerning mergers was by filing a lawsuit after a transaction considered to be anti-competitive had closed.[37] Such lawsuits took an extended period to prosecute, and during the ensuing time, the merged entities had time to establish themselves in the marketplace with customers, vendors, employees, etc.[38] Even if the government were ultimately successful in its antitrust claims, the preferred remedy, a divestiture, was not easily accomplished.[39]

The HSR Act established a premerger notification regime that requires that parties to M&As deals provide the Fair Trade Commission (FTC) and the Department of Justice (DOJ) with certain information about the deals before they close.[40] Such a transaction cannot close until the statutory waiting period of thirty days ends.[41] If the transaction is structured as a tender offer, then the statutory waiting period is only fifteen days.[42] The waiting period is intended to provide the government with sufficient time to study the competitive effects of the transaction and the opportunity to intervene before the transaction has closed.[43]

Once this waiting period has passed or the government has provided the parties with notice of an "early termination" of the waiting period, if the parties so request, then the parties are free to close the transaction.[44] If, during the course of the waiting period, the government believes the proposed transaction might violate the antitrust laws, the government can initiate a "second request" for information.[45] After a second request has been made, parties are not permitted to close the transaction until they come into "substantial compliance" with the government's subpoena, and the waiting period can extend for many months.[46]

Failure to comply with the requirements of the HSR Act can yield severe penalties.[47] The maximum penalty for a failure to file is $41,484 per day until the violation is remedied.[48] For example, MacAndrews &

[37] *Id.*
[38] *Id.*
[39] *Id.*
[40] *Id.*
[41] *Id.*
[42] *Id.* at 192.
[43] *Id.*
[44] *Id.*
[45] *Id.*
[46] *Id.* at 192–193.
[47] *Id.* at 196.
[48] *Id.*

Forbes acquired 800,000 shares of Scientific Games in early June of 2012.[49] MacAndrews & Forbes failed to make an HSR filing until August 16, 2012, and when it did, it was subject to a $720,000 fine.[50]

7.2.1.2 The Foreign Investment Risk Review Modernization Act (FIRRMA)

In the United States, the government is permitted to review – and reject – foreign acquisitions on national securities grounds.[51] A 1988 amendment to Section 721 of the Defense Production Act of 1950, known as the Exon-Florio Amendment, grants the President authority to block or suspend a merger, acquisition, or takeover by a foreign entity if there is "credible evidence" that a "foreign interest exercising control might take action that threatens to impair the national security" and existing provisions of law do not provide "adequate and appropriate authority for the President to protect the national security in the matter before the President."[52] The President has delegated this review process to the CFIUS, an interagency committee that conducts national security reviews of investments that may result in a foreign person's ability to control a US entity.[53] CFIUS is empowered to administer the Exon-Florio Amendment.[54] Exon-Florio was again amended in 2018 in the FIRRMA.[55] FIRRMA deals primarily with Chinese investment and technology transfer, particularly in artificial intelligence, augmented reality/virtual reality, robotics, and financial technology.[56]

CFIUS had the authority to initiate reviews of transactions and impose measures to mitigate national security concerns.[57] CFIUS, however, had jurisdiction solely over "covered transactions," which included a review

49 *Id.*
50 *Id.*
51 *Id.*
52 *Id.* at 199.
53 Zack Hadzismajlovic, *FIRRMA Becomes Law, Reforming CFIUS, Export Controls, and Forever Changing Diligence in Foreign Direct Investment and Structuring of Public and Private Equity Deals*, 30 Intell. Prop. & Tech. L. J. (2018), file:///C:/Users/81803/Downloads/FIRRMA%20Becomes%20Law,%20Reforming%20CFIUS,%20Export%20Controls,%20and%20Forever%20Changing%20Diligence%20in%20Foreign%20Direct%20Investment%20and%20Structuring%20of%20Public%20and%20Private%20Equity%20Deals.pdf.
54 Hill et al., *supra* note 36, at 199.
55 *Id.* at 199.
56 Hadzismajlovic, *supra* note 53.
57 *Id.*

of a specific subset of transactions that involved export-controlled commodities and technology.[58] FIRRMA sought to fill the gap by including emerging and foundational technologies not yet subject to US export controls that may have been transferred to China through foreign investments in the United States.[59] Moreover, FIRRMA converted the CFIUS review from a voluntary submission to a mandatory declaration requirement for certain covered transactions.[60] Covered transactions involving the acquisition of at least a 25 percent voting interest in a US business by a foreign person that is itself 25 percent or more owned, directly or indirectly, by a foreign government are now subject to a mandatory declaration.[61] This declaration is required to be submitted at least forty-five days before the closing of the transaction.[62]

7.2.2 Japan

Although the TOB regulation was implemented in Japan in 1971 based on the Williams Act of 1968 in the United States, TOB was rarely used because takeover attempts on listed companies were rare during the 1970s and the 1980s. After T. Boone Pickens's acquisition of Koito Manufacturing stock in 1989, the mandatory TOB rule, so-called the one-third rule, was implemented in 1990. Most TOBs during the 1990s were used for friendly takeovers. After 2000, several hostile takeover attempts were made, and the Nippon Broadcasting case in 2005 opened the door to the corporate control market in Japan. In 2006, the TOB regulation was strengthened, including a mandatory bid to all stocks, so-called the two-thirds rule.

Japanese TOB regulation used to require a mandatory bid not for acquisitions in stock exchanges but only for acquisitions outside of stock exchanges.[63] If a buyer is going to own more than one-third of the target company's stock by acquisition outside of stock exchanges,[64] the buyer must use TOB (Financial Instruments and Exchange Act, Art. 27-2). The

[58] *Id.*

[59] *Id.*

[60] Hill et al., *supra* note 36, at 201.

[61] *Id.*

[62] *Id.*

[63] As an exception, when a buyer who already owns more than one-third purchases more than 5 percent even from stock exchanges, he or she must use TOB.

[64] If a buyer is going to own 5 percent or more by acquisition outside of stock exchanges from more than ten people, the buyer also must use TOB.

reformed mandatory bid rule of 2024 incorporates acquisitions inside exchanges and decreases the threshold ownership from one-third to 30 percent (30% Rule) (Revised Financial Instruments and Exchange Act, Art. 27-2 (1) 1).

A partial bid is possible. However, if a buyer is going to own more than two-thirds, the buyer must offer to purchase all stock (Two-Thirds Rule) (Financial Instruments and Exchange Act, Art. 27-13 (4)).

The mandatory bid obligation arises when a buyer crosses the threshold point in Japan, while the obligation arises after crossing the threshold point in the UK. On this point, Japanese regulation is harder for buyers than UK regulation.

The requirement of statements of large-volume holding, so-called 5 percent rule (Financial Instruments and Exchange Act, Arts. 27-23–27-30), was implemented in Japan in 1990, at the same time as the implementation of the one-third rule. A large-volume holder of a listed company's stock is required to provide the large-volume holding report that prescribes the share of holding stock, the way of financing, the object of holding stock, etc., within five business days after the large-volume holder owns more than 5 percent stock. After providing the large-volume holding report, either if the holding share changed by 1 percent or more, or if an important item, such as the object of holding stock disclosed by the large-volume holding report changed, particularly, from "genuine investment" to "obtaining control," the large-volume holder needs to provide the report of change within five business days. In 2006, the rule was reformed to be stricter, and institutional investors turned to owe heavier disclosure obligations in Japan than those in the United States and European Union (EU).[65]

The 5 percent rule does not effectively restrict creeping acquisitions because there is a time lag between the arising of the reporting obligation and the actual disclosure of the report. In 2021, an investment fund purchased Tokyo Kikai stock from the TSE, owned 8.08 percent when its reporting obligation arose, and owned 26.50 percent when its large volume holding report was disclosed. Furthermore, the investment fund changed its object of holding stock from "genuine investment" to "obtaining control" by the report of change, which was submitted one day after the original large volume holding report. It owned 32.72 percent when the report of change was disclosed.[66] The same type of case also

[65] *See* notes 65–68 and their accompanying texts in Chapter 6.

[66] *In re* Tokyo Kikai, *supra* note 25. *See* Milhaupt & Shishido, *supra* note 8, at 352–354, footnotes 76–79 and their accompanying texts.

occurred in the United States, and the debate on the reform of Securities and Exchange Commission (SEC) rules is underway.[67]

Criminal punishment and surcharge will be imposed against the violation of TOB rules and the 5 percent rule (Financial Instruments and Exchange Act, Arts. 197; 197-2; 172-5; 172-6; 172-7; and 172-8). These penalties are necessary to protect shareholders of the target company because stock purchase in violation of these rules is not necessarily nullified. On the other hand, too strict criminal sanctions would cause chilling effects and have a substantial deterrent effect on the buyers.

7.2.2.1 Anti-Monopoly Act

Japanese competition law takes a similar approach to the US counterpart, that is, prohibition of anti-competitive M&As (substantive regulation) and requirement of prior notification to the FTC (prior notification regulation).[68]

In terms of substantive regulation, the Anti-Monopoly Act stipulates, "No company may acquire or hold shares of any other companies if its acquisition or holding of shares substantially restrains competition in any particular field of trade, nor may any company use unfair trade practices to acquire or hold shares in another company." (Art. 10 I).

Regarding the prior notification regulation, the Anti-Monopoly Act requires an acquiring company to give the FTC advance notification of the plan for the acquisition if the transaction meets certain criteria (Art.10 II) and prohibits the transaction until the expiration of the thirty-day waiting period from the date of acceptance of the notification, although the FTC may shorten the relevant period, if it finds it to be necessary (Art. 10 VIII).[69]

[67] *See* Wachtell, Lipton, Rosen & Katz, *Re: Petition for Rulemaking Under Section 13 of the Securities Exchange Act of 1934* (Mar. 7, 2011), https://www.sec.gov/rules/petitions/2011/petn4-624.pdf; Lucian Bebchuk & Robert Jackson Jr., *The Law and Economics of Blockholder Disclosure*, 2 HARV. BUS. L. REV. 39 (2012); Ronald Gilson & Jeffrey Gordon, *The Agency Costs of Agency Capitalism: Activist Investors and the Revaluation of Governance Rights*, 113 COLUM. L. REV. 863 (2013). For instance, the most recent revision of the Securities Exchange Act of 1934 shortened the deadline for initial Schedule 13D filings from ten days to five days, and the new amendment has now become effective. *See supra* note 32.

[68] *See* Mitsuo Matsushita, *The Antimonopoly Law of Japan, in* GLOBAL COMPETITION POLICY 151, 181–182 (Edward Montgomery Graham & J. David Richardson eds., 1997).

[69] *See id.*

7.2.2.2 Foreign Direct Investment Screening

The Foreign Exchange and Foreign Trade Act (FEFTA) requires foreign investors to file prior notifications before investing in Japanese companies that engage in certain businesses designated as sensitive to Japanese national security (§27). The FEFTA amendment of 2023 expands designated businesses to include those related to securing stable supply chains such as permanent magnets, machine tools/ industrial robots, semiconductors, storage batteries, natural gas, metals and mineral products, metal 3D printers, and drones.[70]

Japanese FDI screening is an *ex ante* screening based on mandatory prior notification. The basic review period is five months, although it may vary case by case. The ministry in charge may propose mitigation measures, and the petitioner may voluntarily withdraw the filing. So far, there has been only one suspended case.[71]

7.2.3 China

The Chinese Securities Law includes a "Five-percent Rule," which requires a purchaser to disclose every 5 percent increase in its ownership of a company's equity when acquiring a block of shares, whether or not the acquisition is part of a takeover.[72] This is to alert the market that there is a potential bidder. In China, additional purchases before the disclosure of large volume holding reports and reports of change are prohibited (Chinese Securities Law, Art. 63), which is a stricter regulation than in the United States and Japan.[73]

Chinese Takeover Rules include a mandatory bid rule. Under the Takeover Rules, a shareholder who holds over 30 percent of a company's voting power is considered a "*de facto* controller."[74] The Takeover Rules require an acquirer to make an offer to purchase the target shares from

[70] *See* METI, *Cabinet Decision on the Cabinet Order to Partially Amend the Export Trade Control Order*, METI (June 27, 2023), https://www.meti.go.jp/english/press/2023/0627_004.html.

[71] In 2008, the Japanese government ordered TCI Fund, a UK fund trying to acquire up to 20 percent of the shares in J-Power, to cease its investment in a Japanese company on the grounds of public order concerns. Hiroaki Takahashi & Koji Kawamura, *Foreign Direct Investment Regimes Japan 2024*, ICLG.com (Nov. 16, 2023), https://iclg.com/practice-areas/foreign-direct-investment-regimes-laws-and-regulations/japan.

[72] Securities Law, Art. 63.

[73] *Id.*, Art. 63; *See* Chapter 6, n.92 and its accompanying text.

[74] Takeover Rules, *supra* note 30, Art. 84.

the market when the beneficially owns over 30 percent of the shares of a listed target company.[75] Once a shareholder holds 30 percent of the issued shares of a listed company and intends to continue acquiring shares in the company, it must make an offer to all the other shareholders of the company. In this case, the proportion of the shares proposed for such acquisition shall be no less than 5 percent of the shares issued by the company.

Article 35 requires the offer to be at a price not less than the highest price the acquirer paid for such securities within the prior six months.[76] However, this rule does not require the acquirer to make an offer for *all* of the rest of the target shares. Thus, no "equal treatment" of the target shareholders is guaranteed.[77]

A shareholder making an offer is required to submit an acquisition offer report to the CSRC and the relevant stock exchange.[78]

At first glance, one would probably conclude that the Takeover Rules provide even more robust protection to target shareholders (at least against acquirers) than either the US or the UK model since it allows for both the protective mechanism under the US model (target board's authority to adopt defensive measures) and that under the UK model (the mandatory bid rule). However, neither of these two types of protections under the Chinese Takeover Rules is effective, and thus the Chinese shareholders face an even graver threat from an acquisition bid.[79]

[75] *Id.*, Art. 56.

[76] *Id.*, section 35.

[77] *See* Wei Shen & Colin Mengshan Xu, *Collective Action Problems in Chinese Takeover Rules: Deficiency and Difficulty in Protecting Target Shareholders in a Hybrid Regime*, 32 Eur. Bus. L. Rev. 905, 922 (2021).

[78] The report must contain particulars relating to the purpose, duration, price, number of shares, and total sum involved in the acquisition. The shareholder must then publicly announce the acquisition offer within fifteen days of submission of the report. The offer period shall not be shorter than thirty days or longer than sixty days. During the offer period, the shareholder may not withdraw its offer or acquire shares in the company by any other method or on terms different from those of the offer. Any amendments to the offer require approval from the CSRC and the relevant securities exchange. The shares of the listed company shall be terminated from the stock exchange if the distribution of the equities among the shareholders fails to meet the listing conditions after the expiration of the term of the takeover. However, before the completion of the takeover, holders of the remaining shares shall be entitled to require the shareholder to purchase their shares on the same terms as the offer, and the purchaser shall purchase such shares. Wei Shen, Corporate Law in China: Structure, Governance and Regulation 480 (2015).

[79] *See infra* notes 82–86 and 121, and their accompanying texts.

The Chinese mandatory bid rule is triggered when a shareholder acquires the "controller" status by owning over 30 percent of the target company. Article 56 of the Takeover Rules reads as follows:

> If the acquirer beneficially owns more than 30% of the outstanding stock of the target company, such acquirer shall make a *general tender offer* to all of the shareholders of the target company; if the acquirer estimates that it cannot make a general tender offer within 30 days after such acquirer triggers the 30% shareholding requirement, it shall divest its shareholdings in the target company to the extent that it beneficially owns less than 30% of the target company within those 30 days, and shall file a public notice within two days after such divesture; *afterwards*, the acquirer shall only further increase its shareholding in the target company through *tender offers*...[80] [emphasis added]

A "general tender offer" is a tender offer to all the target company's shareholders to purchase all of their shares.[81] In other words, if an acquirer is obligated under law to make a general tender offer, it has to make an offer to purchase *all* of the remaining shares of the target company.

At first glance, this looks very much like the UK mandatory bid rule. However, the word "afterwards" italicized in the language of Article 56 of the Takeover Rules, creates an ambiguity, which is exploited by the acquirers (and their lawyers) in China. Supposedly, the original intent of this "afterwards" language means that after the consummation of the general tender offer required by the first part (before the first semi-colon) of the quoted language(at this point, the acquirer owns way more than 30 percent of the target company), any further increase in shareholding must be conducted through a tender offer. However, the acquirers have been interpreting this "afterwards" language as "after the divesting (at this point, the acquirer owns less than 30%), any further increase in shareholding by the acquirer should be in the form of a tender offer, which could be either a general or a partial offer."[82] Under a partial offer,

80 Takeover Rules, *supra* note 30, Art. 56.

81 *Id.*, Art. 23.

82 *Id.*, Art. 23. Article 23 of the Takeover Rules states

> If an investor adopts the means of tender offer to purchase the shares of a listed company by itself, it can send out a tender offer to all the shareholders of the target company for purchasing all the shares they hold (hereinafter referred to as the general tender offer), or send out a tender offer to all the shareholders of the target company for purchasing part of the shares they hold (hereinafter referred to as the partial tender offer).

the acquirer shall make the offer available to all shareholders, but only has to purchase no less than 5 percent of the company's outstanding stock.[83] Therefore, in practice, the acquirers have been using a three-step process under Rule 56 to acquire over 30%: (1) the acquirer will acquire over 30%, (2)instead of making a general tender offer, the acquirer will divest its holding below 30% and file a public notice, and (3) further increase its holding over 30% using a partial tender offer for 5% of the target shares.[84]

Effectively, this loophole under the Chinese version of the mandatory bid rule only requires an acquirer who acquires control to purchase up to 35 percent of the outstanding shares of the company, instead of all the shares. Although this is only the acquirer's interpretation of the law, the CSRC has neither taken any actions against acquirers who engage in such practice nor issued any further interpretation on this issue. Thus, this practice remains and is now the prevailing common practice in the market for acquiring a controlling stake in a public company.[85]

Under this practice, however, the Chinese mandatory bid rule no longer effectively addresses the shareholder collective action problem due to the lack of "equal treatment" since 65 percent of the shares are potentially going to be left out and suffer a minority discount. Taking this factor into consideration, the target shareholders will likely be pressurized into tendering their shares in the first step tender offer, even if the offer price is somewhat inadequate.[86]

7.3 Regulations on Sellers

Regulations on sellers restrict the target company board's discretion to implement and exercise defenses against takeovers.

Defenses are categorized into *ex ante* defenses and *ex post* defenses. *Ex ante* defenses, such as staggered boards in the United States and cross-shareholdings in Japan, are traditionally not regulated by law but are now under pressure from institutional investors to be abolished. Most

[83] *Id.*, Arts. 23 and 25. Article 25 of the Takeover Rules states that "If a purchaser purchases the shares of a listed company by means of a tender offer according to Articles 23, 24, 47 and 56 of these Measures, the proportion of shares to be purchased shall not be lower than 5% of the issued shares of the said listed company." Hence, the acquirer only needs to bid for 5 percent of the shares via a partial tender offer.

[84] Shen & Xu, *supra* note 77, at 926.

[85] *See id.*

[86] *See id.*

countries have regulations on *ex post* defenses, such as poison pills in the United States[87] and issuing new stock to white knights and poison pills in Japan, because of their conflicts of interest or entrenchment nature.

Although ways of regulating *ex post* defenses vary in countries, they can be categorized into two directions: the joint decision-making model,[88] in which the decision of independent directors is respected, and the no-frustration model, in which the decision of shareholders is respected.[89]

7.3.1 *The United States*

In the United States, *ex ante* defenses include various shark repellents, particularly, staggered boards, which make buyers wait for three years to replace all directors even if they acquire majority stock, which is an effective defense. Now, because of institutional investors' pressure, many companies are forced to abolish staggered boards.[90]

Instead of a staggered board, now dual-class stock is the strongest *ex ante* defense in the United States. Dual-class IPOs have been increasing despite opposition from institutional investors.[91]

The US *ex post* defenses are poison pills. Warrants with extremely favorable terms will be allotted to all shareholders, but buyers when they cross the threshold of ownership. Boards can adopt and redeem poison pills at any time without shareholders' approval.[92] Buyers are forced to stop before crossing the threshold point, usually 15–20 percent, and negotiate with the target board. In most cases, target boards try to

87 Although the poison pill can be implemented *ex ante* "clear day pill," the poison pill can be implemented at any time by the board sole discretion in the United States. Therefore, the US pill's *ex post* nature is stronger than its *ex ante* nature.

88 *See* KRAAKMAN ET AL., *supra* note 3, at 224.

89 *See id.* at 212.

90 *See* Carol Bowie, *ISS 2016 Board Practices Study*, HARVARD L. SCH. FORUM ON CORP GOVERNANCE (June 1, 2016), https;//corpgov.law.harvard.edu/2016/06/01/iss-2016-board-practices-study.

91 *See* Dhruv Aggarwal, Ofer Eldar, Yael Hochberg & Lubomir P. Litov, *The Rise of Dual-Class Stock IPOs* (NAT'L BUREAU OF ECON. RSCH., Working Paper No. 28609, 2021).

92 In the wake of the poison pill, however, there was a serious debate on whether a shareholder vote should be required before the adoption of a poison pill. The SEC was, in particular, against the Moran decision (*infra* note 97). that validated the board's exclusive role in the adoption of the pill. *See* Milhaupt & Shishido, *supra* note 8, at 341–342, notes 18–22 and their accompanying texts.

increase the purchase price for shareholders, and once they have successfully done the deal, the boards redeem the pill.[93]

Regulation of sellers in the United States is based on a typical joint decision-making model.[94] The US standard places the board of directors in the position of gatekeeper without the participation of shareholders.[95] The US hostile takeover regime generates strong incentives for boards to be comprised of a majority of truly independent directors.[96]

The origin of the poison pill and its validation by the Delaware judiciary go back to *Moran v. Household International.*[97] Soon after that, Delaware case law developed a so-called intermediate standard of review,[98] which consists of the Unocal rule and the Revlon rule. Under the Unocal rule, the board must prove that the hostile offer was reasonably perceived as a threat to corporate value and policy, and that the board's selected defenses were not disproportionate to the threat.[99] Under the Revlon rule, when the board is pursuing a sale of control, the board's fiduciary duty is to sell the company to the bidder that offers to the shareholders the highest value reasonably available.[100]

The poison pill's power in the hands of the board of directors was confirmed by the Airgas case decision that affirmed the board's right to keep a poison pill when faced with a structurally non-coercive, all-cash, fully financed tender offer, and the stockholders were fully informed as to the target board's views.[101] The Airgas case made it clear that shareholders need to change the composition of the board by a proxy contest to challenge an incumbent board's power over the pill.[102]

In response to the market shift from hostile takeovers to activist intervention by hedge funds since the 1990s, the poison pill increased its

[93] *See* Gilson, *supra* note 11; Kahan & Rock, *supra* note 11.

[94] *See* Kraakman et al., *supra* note 3, at 215–223.

[95] It should be noted, however, that although the board may have unilateral control over the adoption of the D-Pill, a board seeking to maintain the pill in the face of a tender offer or committed activist campaign can be voted out of office by shareholders in a proxy contest. *See* Milhaupt & Shishido, *supra* note 8, at 344, note 34.

[96] *See* Curtis J. Milhaupt, *In the Shadow of Delaware: The Rise of Hostile Takeovers in Japan*, 105 Colum. L. Rev. 2171 (2005).

[97] Moran v. Household International, 490 A2d. 1059 (Del. Ch. 1985).

[98] It is an intermediate rule between the "business judgment rule" and the "entire fairness rule."

[99] Unocal Corp. v. Mesa Petroleum Co., 493 A.2d 946 (Del. 1985).

[100] Revlon, Inc. v. MacAndrews & Forbes Holdings, Inc., 506 A.2d 173 (Del. 1985).

[101] Air Products v. Airgas, 16 A.3d 48, 54 (Del. Ch. 2011).

[102] Airgas, 16 A.3d at 122 and note 430. *See* Milhaupt & Shishido, *supra* note 8, at 347–348.

anti-activist feature, such as a low threshold ownership and acting-in-concert provisions that broaden the definition of beneficial ownership.[103] In the Williams Companies case, the Delaware Chancery Court enjoined a typical anti-activist pill by holding that the pill's unusual features were not proportionate to the threat.[104] The Delaware Supreme Court affirmed the decision. The Williams Companies' decision sparked academic debate about the validity and role of the anti-activist pill in corporate governance.[105]

7.3.2 Japan

Japanese traditional *ex ante* defenses are cross-shareholdings and stabilized shareholding (restricted rate of stock liquidity). Since the financial crisis of 1997, because of the damaged assets of banks, the pressure from institutional investors and the Japanese Corporate Governance Code, many Japanese companies have been forced to decrease the rate of cross-shareholdings and the rate of stabilized shareholding.

Issuing new stock to white knights used to be the major *ex post* defense in Japan, and Japanese courts were agreeable to targets' boards to use this defense in most cases. The case law, however, was changed by the Nippon Broadcasting Tokyo High Court decision in 2005, which issued an injunction against the traditional defense. After that, the need for the poison pill were recognized, and at that time the stock option had already been introduced in Japanese corporate law.

The first poison pill was used by Nireko in 2005, but it was suspended by the court. The Nireco pill had similar features to the Delaware pill. However, under Japanese corporate law, warrants are not transferable with the underlying share to which they are attached. Therefore, the pill would discriminate, not only against the bidder, but also against ordinary shareholders who purchased shares after the warrants were issued. Since then, most Japanese pills have taken the form of a "pre-warning" pill, which is not an enforceable legal instrument, but a public statement that the company will issue the discriminatory warrants if a prospective bidder crosses the threshold ownership without providing certain information and allowing shareholders a certain time for consideration.[106]

[103] *See* Chapter 6, nn.165–166 and their accompanying texts.

[104] Williams Companies Stockholder Litigation, 2021 WL. 754593 (Del. Ch. 2021).

[105] *See* Chapter 6, n.167 and its accompanying text.

[106] *See in re* Nireco, 1900 Hanji 156 (Tokyo High Ct., 2005); Milhaupt & Shishido, *supra* note 8, at 346, note 42 and its accompanying text.

Besides such a difference of legal nature between the Delaware pill and the Japanese pill, there are two more differences. First, the Japanese pill is required to obtain shareholder approval at some point, while the Delaware pill can be adopted and exercised by the board's sole discretion without shareholder approval. Second, the theoretical justification for the use of the Japanese pill is based on the broad concept of "corporate value" while the justification of the Delaware pill is based on the board's fiduciary duty to protect shareholders and promote shareholder value.[107]

Now, Japanese poison pills play a major role in *ex post* defense, but they are not genuinely *ex post* defense but they also have *ex ante* defense nature because governmental guidelines and case law require shareholder approval for implementing Japanese poison pills.[108] Therefore, Japanese regulation on sellers is based on the no-frustration model. The current Japanese rules do not privilege the decisions of independent directors or committees, thus creating few legal incentives for their adoption.[109]

Recently, two important Supreme Court decisions regarding the poison pill were released. They raised new legal issues regarding the Japanese pill.

In a case of creeping acquisition, Tokyo Kikai, the defendant company, adopted a "pre-warning" pill, not on a "clear day" but post-bid, by obtaining shareholder approval via a modified version of the Majority of the Minority (MoM).[110] The plaintiff investment fund sued for injunctive relief, but the Tokyo High Court rejected it, and the Supreme Court affirmed the decision. The Tokyo Kikai case sparked the debate on whether the board should be allowed to use the poison pill with the MoM approval.[111]

[107] *See id.* at 343, notes 29–30 and their accompanying texts.

[108] *Ex ante* shareholders' approval of a defensive plan is encouraged by the Guidelines and the Bull-Dog Sauce case and is effectively required by the TSE rules. *See* Milhaupt, *supra* note 96. Recent cases require shareholder approval for implementing pills and allow boards to exercise pills. *See in re* Nippo Sangyo, 446 SHIRYOBAN SHOJIHOMU 130 (Nagoya High Ct., Apr. 22, 2021); *In re* Nihon Asia Group, 446 SHIRYOBAN SHOJIHOMU 154 (Tokyo High Ct. Apr. 23, 2021).

[109] *See* Milhaupt, *supra* note 96, at 2201, n.107.

[110] *In re* Tokyo Kikai, *supra* note 25. "First, the 'minority' only excludes shares held by the acquirer/interested shareholder and incumbent directors, not shares held by entities supportive of incumbent management, such as cross-shareholding partners; and it only includes 'minority' shares actually voted, not all outstanding 'minority' shares." Milhaupt & Shishido, *supra* note 8, at 338, note 4.

[111] Structurally coercive bids from which shareholders genuinely need protection, and disagreements over firm value, which, consistent with Japanese judicial rulings, should be decided by shareholders, could easily be confused by the courts, as they apparently were in the Tokyo Kikai case (*supra* note 25). If all bids are deemed "coercive" (regardless of the reason), incumbents will easily obtain shareholders' approval for

In 2022, the Supreme Court affirmed an injunction against an anti-activist pill issued by Mitsuboshi.[112] The pill was a "post-bid warning pill" with a 20 percent trigger and an acting-in-concert provision. The board exercised the pill with the approval of a slight majority of all shareholders (not MoM). The Osaka District Court and the Osaka High Court reasoned for the injunction that the Mitsuboshi pill excessively restricted plaintiffs' shareholder rights, such as transferring shares, making shareholder proposals, and calling special shareholders' meetings, also the Mitsuboshi board's process for determining that the investors were acting in concert with the investment fund was deemed to be arbitrary. The Mitsuboshi decision is important because it is the first case in which Japanese courts did not rubber stamp the approval of the shareholders.

METI released the New Takeover Guidelines of 2023,[113] which makes clear that hostile takeovers may increase firm value and require the management of target companies not to reject takeover proposals without rational reasons and to report to the board of directors upon receiving a takeover proposal.[114] The practical impact of the guidelines is significant, and several hostile takeovers were made by competitors immediately after their release.[115]

7.3.3 China

As to the target board's power to defend the company against a potential bid, Article 8 of the Takeover Rules imposes a general duty of care and

defensive measures via the modified version of MoM, particularly in Japanese small-cap companies, which still have a sizeable percentage of stable, friendly shareholders. Milhaupt & Shishido, *supra* note 8, at 353–354, notes 76–79 and their accompanying texts. *See* METI, *Guidelines for Corporate Takeovers – Enhancing Corporate Value and Securing Shareholders' Interests*, appendix 3, 1 (3) (2023).

112 *In re* Mitsuboshi, *supra* note 25. *See* Milhaupt & Shishido, *supra* note 8, at 354.

113 METI, *supra* note 111. *See* Reuters, *Japan Releases New M&A Guidelines to Promote Takeovers, Consolidation*, Reuters (Aug. 31, 2023, 12:41 PM PDT), https://www.reuters.com/markets/deals/japan-releases-new-ma-guidelines-promote-takeovers-consolidation-2023-08-31/.

114 *See* METI, *supra* note 111, 2.2, 3.1 (2023).

115 *See* e.g., Nidek's acquisition of Takisawa (Yuji Ohira, *Nidec to Buy Japan's Takisawa, Will Launch Tender Bid Thursday*, NIKKEI Asia (Sept. 13, 2023 18:08 PM JST), https://asia.nikkei.com/Business/Business-deals/Nidec-to-buy-Japan-s-Takisawa-will-launch-tender-bid-Thursday); Daiichi Life insurance's acquisition of Benefit One (Nikkei (Feb. 8, 2024), https://www.nikkei.com/article/DGXZQOUB085IR0Y4A200C2000000/); Brother' acquisition of Roland DG (Nikkei (Mar. 13, 2024), https://www.nikkei.com/article/DGXZQOUC135L20T10C24A3000000/).

loyalty on the target board.[116] It also makes a general statement that all resolutions and measures adopted by the target board in response to a TOB must be in the best interest of the target company and its shareholders, and the target board may not abuse its power and impose improper obstacles for a takeover.[117]

The Chinese model allows for the board to unilaterally adopt defensive measures that are not "improper," unless such defensive measures as disposal of the company's assets, outward investment, adjustment to the major business of the company, or any guarantee or loan that have a significant impact on the assets, liabilities, rights, and interest or business operations of the target company.[118] The target's board may engage an independent financial adviser to assess its financial conditions and opine on the fairness of the offer. The board needs to make a recommendation to the shareholders and make such a recommendation available to the public and the CSRC.[119]

Since Chinese Company Law was designed on the premise of shareholder primacy, the actions that a target board can take without the approval of the shareholders are actually much more limited than the Takeover Rules suggest.

Some commonly used defensive measures cannot be unilaterally adopted by the target board under Chinese law.

The shareholder rights plan (commonly known as the "poison pill"[120]) is an extremely effective defense against hostile acquirers, but it requires the issuance of new shares or warrants.[121] Unlike Delaware law, Chinese Company Law requires shareholder approval for the issuance of new shares.[122] Thus, the target board is not able to use a poison pill as a defense, unless the prior approval of its shareholders is obtained. The CSRC is granted the authority to overrule the poison-pill mechanism.[123] The "poison put" is not a valid defense under Chinese Company Law

[116] Takeover Rules, *supra* note 30, Art. 8.
[117] *Id.*
[118] Takeover Procedures 2002, Art. 33.
[119] *Id.*, Art. 31.
[120] "Poison pill" in the Chinese context refers to a strategy to discourage hostile takeovers by issuing new shares at a nominal price to all shareholders except the bidder. *See* SHEN, *supra* note 78, at 502.
[121] China Securities Regulatory Commission authorized the issuance of warrants in 2006. *See* The Administrative Measures for the Issuance of Securities by Listed Companies, Arts. 31–34.
[122] Company Law 2018, Art. 133; Company Law 2023, Art. 151.
[123] Takeover Procedures 2006, Art. 10.

either, because any issuance of corporate bonds will be subject to the approval of the shareholders.[124] Further, a poison put could substantially impact the liabilities of the target company, and thus would require prior shareholder approval under the Takeover Rules as well.[125]

The golden parachutes practice is not workable under Chinese law because all compensation packages of directors require the approval of the shareholders[126] and these parachutes have a substantial impact on the liabilities of the target company and thus also require shareholder approval under the Takeover Rules.[127] Shark repellent requires charter amendments, which require shareholder approval under the Company Law.[128] Crown jewel defense also cannot be adopted by the board unilaterally because the Company Law requires that the sale of significant assets of a listed company be approved by two-thirds of the shares voted thereon.[129] While defensive repurchase can be used as a defensive measure if the company can selectively repurchase those shares from shareholders that are identified as likely to sell to the hostile bidder, Chinese Company Law limits the circumstances under which a company can repurchase its own shares, and engaging in defensive measures is not one of those circumstances.[130]

The board of a Chinese company does not have the needed corporate power to unilaterally adopt these defenses. Moreover, the lack of clarity around the board's authority or power to adopt defensive measures also creates barriers. The US model is premised on a clear set of common law rules so that the directors can have certainty as to whether or not the adoption of certain defenses violates their fiduciary duty to the shareholders. However, the Chinese model sets the general principle that the board should not adopt any "improper" defensive measures, without giving any further interpretation, either statutory or judicial, as to what "improper" means.[131] This lack of certainty exposes the target directors to liability for violating their fiduciary duties, thereby giving them a

124 Company Law 2018, Art. 37(8); Company Law 2023, Art. 59(6).
125 Takeover Rules, *supra* note 30, Art. 33.
126 Company Law 2018, Art. 37(2); Company Law 2023, Art. 59(1).
127 Takeover Rules, *supra* note 30, Art. 33.
128 Company Law 2018, Art. 37(10); Company Law 2023, Art. 59(8).
129 Company Law 2018, Art. 121; Company Law 2023, Art. 135.
130 Company Law 2018, Art. 142; Company Law 2023, Art. 162.
131 Takeover Rules, *supra* note 30, Art. 8. *See* John Armour, Jack B. Jacobs, and Curtis J. Milhaupt, *The Evolution of Hostile Takeover Regimes in Developed and Emerging Markets: An Analytical Framework*, 52 HARV INT'L L. J. 219, 273 (2011).

disincentive to adopt any defensive measures, even when such a defense is necessary to protect the target shareholders against structural coercion. Thus, under the current legal structure regarding defensive measures, the target board's hands are tied even when the adoption of defensive measures is practically in the best interest of the target shareholders.

On the other hand, the implementation of the Chinese corporate law poses another challenge. The Chinese courts are extremely unwilling to take what they regard to be complex corporate law cases, making the enforceability for the law regarding takeover and anti-takeovers questionable.[132] This exacerbates the agency problem between the target board and its shareholders, since in a legal environment where there is no effective enforcement mechanism, target boards can get away with defensive measures that are employed only for the board's entrenchment purpose, as opposed to in the interest of the shareholders.

In summary, the Chinese law regarding the target board's authority to adopt defensive measures is flawed on both the black-letter law level and the enforcement level. On the black-letter law level, the Chinese model actually did not confer a lot of authority to the target boards to adopt defensive measures, and regarding the limited defensive measures that the target board might be able to adopt unilaterally, the lack of clarity in the statutory language discourages the board from adopting these defenses in times of need. On the enforcement level, the lack of enforcement of the law regarding takeovers in China grants a free pass for the target board to entrench itself, thus exacerbating the agency problem between the target board and the shareholders. In both cases, the shareholders bear the ultimate cost of such flaws in law or the enforcement of such law.

7.4 Balance of Autonomy and Monitoring

The optimal balance of autonomy and monitoring management is country specific. The balance is affected not only by the balance of regulations on buyers and those on sellers but also by other areas of law, particularly, employment law and tax law. Stock market development, labor market landscape, and social norms also complementarily affect the balance of autonomy and monitoring.

[132] *See id.*

7.4.1 The United States

Regarding regulations of the market for corporate control, the United States has weak regulations both on buyers and sellers: no mandatory takeover but only procedural regulations on buyers and allowing the sellers' board's discretion to exercise defenses with certain limitations.

The United States has the weakest employment protection, so-called employment at will, and the most liquid external labor market in the world. As Jean Tirol says, the negative externalities exerted by shareholders' control of employees are smaller in countries with liquid external labor markets, where the norm of shareholder value maximization is less controversial.[133]

The US tax-free reorganization rule attaches greater importance to continuity at the shareholder level than the corporate level, compared to Japanese law, and does not require continuity of employees and continuity of management, which will discourage buyers.[134]

Overall, the United States has a relatively buyer-friendly legal system while keeping a balance of autonomy and monitoring management in its own way.

7.4.2 Japan

Regarding regulation on the market of corporate control, Japan has relatively strong regulation on buyers initiating a mandatory takeover,[135] and US-type weak regulation on sellers. A robust company community norm prevents implementing the Revlon rule.[136]

Japan has one of the strongest employment protections in the world, the so-called abusive dismissal rule, and has an illiquid external labor

133 *See* Jean Tirole, The Theory of Corporate Finance 15-67 (2006).

134 *See* Tetsuya Watanabe, *Income and Incentives for Corporate Transactions: A Japanese Perspective, in* Enterprise Law: Contracts, Markets, and Laws in the US and Japan 150 (Zenichi Shishido ed., 2014).

135 It is stronger than the US takeover rule because of mandatory takeover for buyers who attempt to cross one-third voting rights, but not as strong as the UK takeover rule because of a mandatory offer to all stocks only for buyers who attempt to cross two-thirds voting rights.

136 However, the Revlon rule is gradually accepted as a norm in practice. *See* Masakazu Iwakura, *Kyogoteki Kokaikaitsuke Jokyo niaru Taisho Jojokigyo no Torishimariyaku no Kodojunsoku – Kihan to [Code of Conduct, Norms, Duties, Etc. of Directors of Listed Company Targets in Competitive Tender Offers]*, 20 Hitosubashi Hogaku 11, 23 (2021).

market. Strong employment protection law strengthens management autonomy against shareholders.[137] Long-term employment contracts effectively transform employees into "shark repellent," and employees will frequently act as "white squires."[138]

Tax law requirements for continuity of employees and continuity of management for qualified reorganizations discourage buyers' incentives.

Overall, Japan has a seller-friendly legal system.

7.4.3 China

Chinese Company Law pursues shareholder centralism albeit a corporate social responsibility provision which, however, has never been litigated in Chinese courts. As the company is a product of shareholder investment, shareholders deserve the final decision-making power on major issues of the company.[139] However, in listed companies, since many small and medium-sized retail investors (minority shareholders) do not participate in corporate governance at all, the management or majority shareholders of listed companies are the ultimate decision-makers.

In the decision-making on matters such as the means of defense against hostile takeovers, the shareholders' meeting is toothless. The anti-takeover defensive measures are almost always "proposed" by the board of directors. The shareholders have been suffering from information asymmetry and may often vote for a plan that may be unfavorable to them. In order to contain hostile takeovers "in advance" and consolidate their control of listed companies, the boards of Chinese listed companies have put anti-takeover clauses in their respective listed company constitutions. In less than two years after the Vanke case[140] occurred, more than 600 A-share listed companies have added

[137] *See* Toru Kitagawa, *Complementarity among the Abusive Dismissal Rule, Company Community Norms, and an Illiquid External Labor Market: Transformation of Directors' Fiduciary Duty under Japanese Corporate Law*, *in* ENTERPRISE LAW: CONTRACTS, MARKETS, AND LAWS IN THE US AND JAPAN 70 (Zenichi Shishido ed., 2014).

[138] *See* Pagano & Volpin, *supra* note 14.

[139] Company Law 2018, Arts. 36 and 98; Company Law 2023, Arts. 58 and 111.

[140] The Vanke takeover battle started on July 25, 2016, when Foresea Life Insurance Ltd (a subsidiary of Baoneng Investment Group) acquired 15.04 percent of Vanke's A shares. *See* Taurai Muvunza & Terrill Frantz, *Disturbing the Peace: Anatomy of the Hostile Takeover of China Vanke Co*, SSRN (Mar. 2, 2020), https://papers.ssrn.com/sol3/papers.cfm?abstract_id=3547244.

anti-takeover clauses in their articles of association.[141] The anti-takeover clauses in the articles of association of many listed companies are essentially at the expense of the interests of all shareholders. Many clauses restricting shareholders' freedom of decision-making and damaging the shareholder rights and interests of the acquired company are a stark violation of the Company Law, Securities Law, and the Measures for the Administration of Acquisitions of Listed Companies. Unfortunately, these clauses were passed without any difficulty.

The blurring of shareholder centralism is also evident in the use of post-event defensive measures. In many hostile takeover disputes, the board adopted defensive measures without obtaining *ex ante* authorization from the shareholders' meeting or seeking *ex post* ratification by the shareholders' meeting. Administrative intervention to quell hostile takeover disputes demonstrates a very important but long-standing issue in China's hostile takeover rules, namely, who should have the final say in hostile takeover disputes, and the division of power between the regulatory authority and courts has not yet been clarified. Past hostile takeover cases also exposed an important problem that the penalties imposed by the CSRC are not heavy enough on purchasers who failed to perform their information disclosure obligations, and did not restrict the voting rights of illegally acquired shares.

Moreover, in a Chinese takeover context, the acquirer potentially can treat holdout shareholders very differently due to the Chinese judiciary's underdeveloped (and as argued here, erroneous) method of determining the "reasonable price" of a company's stock ("appraisal"), thus the pressure to accept the acquirer's first offer can be extremely strong. Overall, China has a relatively buyer-friendly legal system under statutory law, but the actual implementation of the statutes varies case by case.

7.5 Friendly Takeovers and Their Conflicts of Interest Problem

In both interested transactions and arm's length transactions, target management's conflicts of interest are more serious in friendly takeovers than in hostile takeovers because instead of paying a premium to shareholders, the acquirer could bribe incumbent officers to let him have the

[141] *See* Economic Journal, *More than 620 Listed Companies Added Anti-takeover Clauses*, XINHUA (June 15, 2017), http://www.xinhuanet.com/politics/2017-06/15/c_129633097.htm.

firm at a cheaper price.[142] Therefore, legal rules that mitigate the conflicts of interest problem are necessary.

7.5.1 The United States

In arm's length cases, the business judgment rule will apply, and the arm's length transaction price will be respected. If target boards, however, commit to a change in corporate control and target shareholders lose the opportunity to obtain a control premium in the future, target boards will owe the Revlon duty, the duty to conduct an auction or, by some other means, seek to obtain the highest price reasonably available for shareholders.[143]

Regarding controlling shareholders cashing out minority shareholders, such as Management Buyouts (MBO), which are typical conflicts of interest cases, traditional Delaware case law applied the entire fairness rule.[144] Delaware courts have explored the measures to transfer from the entire fairness rule to the business judgment rule, such as the approval by the independent committee, the approval by the MoM, and the combination of the TOB and short-form merger. Finally, in 2014, the Delaware Supreme Court established the so-called MFW framework that applies the business judgment rule if the independent committee conducts price negotiation and the majority of independent minority shareholders, who are provided sufficient information, approve the transaction.[145]

Delaware General Corporation Law stipulates that the fair value in appraisal remedy does not include synergistic effects (§262 (h)). Although Delaware case law once tried to interpret the statute restrictively to include future value,[146] the Delaware Supreme Court clearly excluded synergistic effects from the fair value in the Verition case in 2019.[147]

In Delaware appraisal cases, the discounted cash flow (DCF) value has traditionally been used for the valuation of listed companies' stock.[148]

[142] *See* Transcript, *supra* note 5, at 108–109 (Mark Ramseyer).

[143] Revlon v. MacAndrews & Forbes Holding Inc., 506 A.2d 173 (Del. 1985). *See* William A. Klein & John C. Coffee, Jr., Business Organization and Finance 204 (10th ed., 2007).

[144] Sterling v. Mayflower Hotel Corp., 93 A.2d 107 (Del. 1952).

[145] Kahn v. M&F Worldwide, 88 A.3d 635 (Del. 2014).

[146] Weinberger v. UOP, Inc., 457 A.2d 701 (Del. 1983); Cede & Co. v. Technicolor, Inc., 684 A.2d 289 (Del. 1996).

[147] Verition Partners Master Fund Ltd. v. Aruba Networks, 210 A.3d 128 (Del. 2019).

[148] *See* R. Scott Widen, *Delaware Law, Financial Theory and Investment Banking Valuation Practice*, 4 N.Y.U. J. L. & Bus. 579 (2008).

The Delaware Supreme Court showed, however, the direction that the fair value is the deal price minus synergistic effects in 2019.[149] A Delaware Chancery Court used the market price that is not affected by the merger as the fair value.[150]

Although since the early 2000s, the appraisal arbitrage by activist hedge funds had increased, it turned to decrease after the two Delaware Supreme Court decisions in 2017,[151] which showed that the fair value can be lower than the merger price.[152]

7.5.2 Japan

Target directors owe a fiduciary duty to pursue the interest of shareholders as a whole, that is, "fair value transfer" duty. If directors breach their duty intentionally or with gross negligence, they need to pay damage directly to shareholders according to Companies Act Article 429. The "fair corporate value" equals to the shareholder value, which does not include the interest of employees and other stakeholders.[153] The Revlon duty has, however, not been accepted by Japanese courts.[154]

The MBO Guideline of 2007 and M&A Guideline of 2019 show normative procedures, such as implementing a special committee that has bargaining capacity with the buyer and consulting with financial advisors and law firms, for MBO and cash out by controlling shareholders as a safe harbor.[155]

The appraisal proceeding is more important in Japan, while the breach of fiduciary duty claim is more important in the United States. The burden of proof is on the shareholder in a fiduciary duty claim whereas,

149 Verition Partners Master Fund Ltd. v. Aruba Networks, 210 A.3d 128 (Del. 2019).

150 *In re* Appraisal of Jarden Corporation, Cons. C.A. No.12456-VCS (Del. Ch. 2019).

151 Dell, Inc. v. Magnetar Global Event Driven Master Fund, Ltd., 177 A.3d 1 (Del. 2017); DFC Glob. Corp. v. Muirfield Value Partners, L.P., 172 A.3d 346, 387 (Del. 2017).

152 *See* Wei Jiang, Tao Li, & Randall Thomas, *The Long Rise and Quick Fall of Appraisal Arbitrage*,100 Boston Univ. L. Rev. 2133 (2020).

153 *See in re* Rex Holdings Shareholder Litigation (Chapter 6, n. 128).

154 *See* Transcript, *supra* note 5, at 122–123 (Hidefusa Iida). In the Tecmo case, no court considered the fact that Tecmo's board rejected the tender offer price of 920 yen (by Square Enix) a relevant factor to appraise the fair price of Tecmo's share (in the merger with Koei). (Transcript, supra note 5, at 124 (Wataru Tanaka) II-17). But regarding recent change in practice, *see* Milhaupt & Shishido, *supra* note 8, at 355, note 85 and its accompanying text.

155 *See* Ministry of Econ., Trade and Indus., Fair M&A Guidelines Enhancing Corporate Value and Securing Shareholders' Interests 42–44 (June 28, 2019).

in appraisal proceedings, the court has wider discretion to determine fair value. The deterrent effect of the appraisal remedy would be less than that of the fiduciary duty claim.[156] The Japanese Companies Act requires implementing synergistic effects into the "fair value,"[157] while Delaware law excludes synergistic effects from the fair value.[158]

In Japanese appraisal cases, the fair value is calculated in two steps. The first step is to calculate the objective value that is not affected by the cash-out transaction. The average market price for the last couple of months is used for the valuation of listed companies' stock. The second step is to add the expected future increase of the market price (premium), which the plaintiff shareholders cannot enjoy.

If the court considers the *ex ante* procedure is not fair, it tends to add a certain percent of the objective value as the premium, while the court tends to admit the part of the TOB price that exceeds the objective value as the reasonable premium, that is, admit the TOB price as the fair value, if the court considers the *ex ante* procedure is fair.

The Supreme Court showed, in the Jupiter Telecom case of 2016,[159] that the TOB price should be respected, if the TOB is made after going through the procedure that is generally considered to be fair, even in cases of conflicts of interest cashout. After the Jupiter Telecom decision, appraisal suits raised by activist shareholders in MBO and going private cases decreased because the plaintiff cannot expect to obtain the premium over the TOB price if the procedure is admitted as fair.[160]

7.5.3 China

7.5.3.1 Boards' Fiduciary Duty in a Friendly Takeover

Chinese law attempts to define the connotation of the fiduciary duties imposed on directors of listed companies through a series of forward and reverse rules.[161] However, the provisions on fiduciary duties in the

156 *See* Transcript *supra* note 5, at 127 (Kenichi Sekiguchi).

157 *See* Companies Act, Art. 469; M&A Guideline section 2.2, footnote 14.

158 Delaware General Corporation Law §262 (h). *See in re* Appraisal of Panera Bread Co., No. 2017-0593, 2020 WL 506684 (Del. Ch. Jan. 31, 2020).

159 *In re* Appraisal of Jupiter Telecom, 70-6 MINSHU 1145 (Sup. Ct. July 1, 2016).

160 Moreover, there are no cases in Japan that decide a lower price than the TOB price as the fair value; the plaintiff shareholders can enjoy 6 percent interest, which far exceeded the market interest rate, until April 2020. Minority shareholders had an incentive to pursue the appraisal remedy even if they were satisfied with the TOB price.

161 Company Law 2018, Arts. 147 and 148; Company Law 2023, Arts. 179 and 180.

Company Law and the Administrative Measures on the Acquisition of Listed Companies are too broad and general.

Article 8 of the Takeover Rules stipulates that "The directors, supervisors, and senior managers of the acquired company owe a duty of loyalty and diligence to the company, and shall treat all acquirers fairly." The Company Law defines fiduciary duty through a series of prohibitive rules, and the Guidelines for the Articles of Association of Listed Companies give suggestions on the definition of the duty of diligence. Although the legal text is broad, these laws and regulations fail to clearly define the connotation of the substance of fiduciary duties and are ambiguous for legal practitioners.[162]

Moreover, directors or senior managers are prohibited from favoring one bidder over another by providing financial assistance.[163] Nor are directors or senior managers allowed to expel one bidder by initiating anti-takeover actions that put the interests of management over those of shareholders. This fiduciary duty rule, however, lacks practicality. For instance, it is unclear how to define and evaluate "equal treatment." The board may have to pick one bidder out of several competitors. In this scenario, the concept of "equal treatment" without clear parameters may not work. The ambiguity of this fiduciary duty rule may unnecessarily invite frivolous litigation.

Article 33 of the Takeover Rules is a loose and incomplete board neutrality rule. Although this clause attempts to clarify the obligations of the board in takeover transactions, the restrictions on the board are general and vague.[164]

[162] The language in Article 8 of the Measures for the Administration of Acquisitions of Listed Companies is general in nature. It stipulates that the board "should treat all acquirers who acquire the company fairly," "protect the interests of the company and its shareholders," and should not "abuse its power to set improper obstacles to a takeover" and should not "damage the legitimate rights and interests of the company and its shareholders."

[163] Article 8 of the Takeover Rules state

> The decisions made and the measures taken by the board of directors of a target company for the takeover shall be good for maintaining the rights of the company and its shareholders, and shall not erect any improper obstacle to the takeover by misusing its authorities, nor may it provide any means of financial aid to the purchaser by making use of the sources of the target company or damage the lawful rights and interests of the target company or its shareholders.

[164] First, the applicable period of Article 33 is "after the acquirer makes an informative announcement to before the completion of the tender offer," which means that this rule

7.5.3.2 Appraisal Rights

Article 74 of the Company Law is a Chinese appraisal rule: "The shareholder who voted against any of the following corporate actions can request the company to purchase back their shares at a reasonable price: . . . (2) a merger, demerger . . . of the company or disposal of the assets of the company."[165] Unfortunately, the statute does not provide any guidance as to what constitutes a "reasonable price." In practice, the parties may have to engage a third-party evaluation firm or an accounting firm to provide a price.

The Chinese courts are not as sophisticated as the Delaware courts in applying the appraisal statute. In practice, the Chinese courts determine the "reasonable price" to be paid for shares of the dissenting shareholders by the target company's net asset value.[166] For a public company, the court will also consider using the market value of the company's shares. However, both the net asset value and the market value are flawed in the methods for determining the "reasonable price" of the target shares.

In a controller freeze-out setting, the market value of the corporation is subject to manipulation – a controller can easily manipulate the market value of the controlled corporation.[167] Using the market value of the corporation creates perverse incentives for the controller – "the greater the misconduct by the majority, the less they need to pay for the minority's shares."[168]

only applies to the behavior of the board after the tender offer has occurred, and does not apply to defensive measures taken against hostile takeovers. Second, ". . .the board must not . . . cause a significant impact on the company's assets, liabilities, equity or operational results," which suggests a narrow scope of application to such defensive measures that may cause significant impact. As long as the defensive measures taken by the board prior to the tender offer or do not have a significant impact on the company's operation, equity, liabilities, and assets, approval from shareholders' meeting is not needed.

165 Company Law 2018, Art. 74; Company Law 2023, Art. 89.

166 *See*, e.g., Chunfen Chen v. Shanghai Guanghua Accounting Firm (The People's Court of Shanghai Huangpu District, May 17, 2014), http://www.hshfy.sh.cn:8081/flws/text.jsp?pa=ad3N4aD0yJnRhaD2jqDIwMTOjqbvGxtbD8bb+KMnMKbP119a12jIyMbrFJnd6PQPdcssPdcssz.

167 The market prices a controlled corporation based on the disclosed plans of its controller. If the market starts to believe that the controller will undermanage the firm, the market price will drop to reflect this belief. If the market value of the corporation were used to value the corporation, the controller would be encouraged to undermanage, since the more he undermanages, the less he would have to pay for the minority interest in a freeze-out merger. Lawrence A. Hammermesh & Michael L. Wachter, *The Fair Value of Cornfields in Delaware Appraisal Law*, 31 Iowa J. Corp. L. 119, 132 (2005).

168 *See* John C. Coffee, Jr., *Transfers of Control and the Quest for Efficiency: Can Delaware Law Encourage Efficient Transactions While Chilling Inefficient Ones?*, 21 Del. J. Corp. L. 359, 407 n. 224 (1996).

Using the liquidation value of the corporation also tends to undervalue the corporation. The liquidation value standard values the corporation as a collection of assets, without regard to the future cash flow generated by these assets and the future growth opportunities of the corporation. Since the price the stockholders paid for their shares in the target company reflects both the company's assets and its future prospects, it will be unfair and to the shareholder's detriment if he is only offered its net asset value back.

Unfortunately, this is currently the case in China. If an acquirer successfully acquires 35 percent of the target company (with no further obligation to purchase the remainder of the shares due to the loophole under Article 56 of the Takeover Rules discussed earlier), the remaining 65 percent of the shares could be cashed out at a price much lower than what is fair. Thus, the threat of an acquirer's exploitation of the target shareholders' collective action problem is more serious in China compared to other jurisdictions with more shareholder-friendly appraisal rules (e.g., the United States).

China is undergoing a major reform of its securities offering and listing processes by relaxing the government's tight control over market access and listing process, which involves arbitrary discretion and favoritism. The ongoing reform is to weaken CSRC's role in the listing process. As a result, the stock exchanges will determine listing applications. These reform measures are meant to create a more efficient market. It is strongly advocated to transplant US regulatory measures into , including but not limited to an extensive infrastructure of broker-dealers, investment advisors, and enforcement tools.[169] Overseas listing is also painted as a governance mechanism for Chinese SOEs and China's financial markets as a whole.[170] These suggest the fancy and popularity of US approaches and experiences in improving China's capital markets. As a matter of fact, bringing China's takeover law more closely into line with its counterparts in more developed economies has always been one of Chinese characteristics the capital markets have possessed despite more systemic hurdles

[169] *See* Stuart R. Cohn &Yinzhi Miao, *The Dragon and the Eagle: Reforming China's Securities IPO Laws in the U.S. Model, Pros and Cons*, 17 WASH. UNIV. GLOB. STUD. L. REV. 327, 328 (2018).

[170] *See* Yinzhi Miao, *The Interplay of the State and the Firms: Overseas Listing as a Governance Institution for Chinese SOEs*, 10 FRONTIERS L. IN CHINA 46, 46 (2015).

in the marketplace, such as investor protection, institutional safety, and systemic stability.[171]

As discussed, the Chinese hybrid model of takeover law (combining various elements from both the US and the UK laws) does not adequately protect the target shareholders. Although the Chinese legislature attempted to transplant the protective devices of both the US and the UK models, such legal transplant has been unsuccessful due to the legislature's lack of understanding of the reasons behind such rules and China's own market conditions.[172] In the market for corporate control, it has been said, a different economic environment could trigger a shift away from the markets.[173] China's economic environment, so different from that in the US and the UK, could easily distort the US or UK rules, which have different underlying logics. Furthermore, due to the under-developed appraisal rules in China, the target shareholders are facing even graver threats from an acquirer who seeks to exploit their collective action problem. Legal transplant may make little sense if the legislature simply plagiarizes foreign laws. Ultimately, a regime of market-oriented corporate governance works in a market economy and vice versa. Similarly, legal transplant is conducive to legal and regulatory reforms only if the transplanted rules are placed in a similar market environment. Otherwise, legal transplant can easily be turned to be meaningless.

[171] *See* Hui Huang, *The New Takeover Regulation in China: Evolution and Enhancement*, 42 INT'L LAW. 153, 174–175 (2008).

[172] *See* Hui Huang, *China's Takeover Law: A Comparative Analysis and Proposals for Reform*, 30 DEL. J. CORP. L. 145, 145 (2005).

[173] *See* Bengt Holmstrom & Steven N. Kaplan, *Corporate Governance and Merger Activity in the United States: Making Sense of the 1980s and 1990s*, 15 J. ECON. PERSP. 121, 140 (2001).

8

Creditors

Although creditors, as monetary capital providers, share the incentive to monitor human capital providers with shareholders, they prefer risk-averse management as fixed claimants.

Creditors are not granted legal corporate governance rights not only because debt claims can be executed by the government, but also because creditors can protect themselves through contractual schemes. Creditors can obtain contractual protections, such as collaterals, guarantees, and covenants, against shareholder–creditor agency problems, such as asset dilution and asset substitution.[1]

Although creditors have no legal corporate governance right, they play a participatory or even supervisory role in the corporate governance of debtor companies, even during their healthy financial stage. Even without active monitoring, creditors control the firm's access to capital because periodic payments withdraw cash from the borrower firm and the priority of debt claim can impede the future ability of the firm to raise capital from outside investors.[2]

Section 8.1 will compare the practices regarding creditors', particularly banks', role in *ex ante* monitoring of solvent firms. Section 8.2 will compare the practices of renegotiation in financially distressed firms. Section 8.3 will compare the legal bankruptcy systems. Section 8.4 will compare the debtor directors' fiduciary duty during the zone of insolvency, as a legal institution for adjusting a discontinuity between corporate law and bankruptcy regimes.

[1] *See* Reinier Kraakman, et al., The Anatomy of Corporate Law: A Comparative and Functional Approach 111–113 (3d ed. 2017).

[2] *See* George Triantis, *The Role of Debt in the Governance of US Business, in* Enterprise Law: Contracts, Markets, and Laws in the US and Japan 125 (Zenichi Shishido ed., 2014).

8.1 *Ex Ante* Monitoring by Debt: The Role of Banks

In many countries, banks watch their debtor companies and try to keep them financially healthy. In the event of default, creditors have a contingent right to remove assets and possibly to force liquidation. Such a contingent "ownership" of creditors will influence the relationship among players in the firm even when it is financially healthy.[3]

In many countries, corporate law provides mandatory disclosure and legal capital to control shareholder–creditor agency problems in solvent firms.[4] The international shift of the way of debt financing from via bank to via markets has increased coordination costs for creditors.[5]

8.1.1 *The United States*

The prevailing view was that creditors, including banks, do not play an active role in corporate governance in the United States, although the existence of debt reduces management waste. However, banks and other institutional investors play an active role in the governance of the firm whose business stumbles, even when the business is far from being insolvent and continues to pay its debts. Once a firm turns out to be no longer able to borrow on an unsecured basis from many banks, it has to hold its debt in a revolving credit facility controlled by a handful of banks, among which the lead bank typically monitors the debtor.[6]

The banks will obtain a security interest in substantially all of the debtor's assets, including its cash flow, which Article 9 of the Uniform Commercial Code, and especially revised Article 9, has made it possible. Modern technology also enables the lender to know precisely how much cash a debtor has at any given time. The ability to cut off a debtor's cash flow is a much more potent threat than the threat to repossess the debtor's equipment.[7]

The loan agreements for the revolving credit facilities set out negative and affirmative covenants, which give the lender substantial veto on any major decision and access to the debtor's books and records. and defines events of default.[8]

[3] *See* Kraakman, et al., *supra* note 1, at 109.
[4] *See id.* at 119–127.
[5] *See id.* at 110.
[6] *See* Douglas G. Baird & Robert K. Rasmussen, *Private Debt and the Missing Lever of Corporate Governance*, 154 U. Pa. L. Rev. 1209, 1216, 1226 (2006).
[7] *See id.* at 1228, 1229.
[8] *See id.* at 1231–1232.

Because human capital becomes increasingly industry-specific, rather than firm-specific, it is possible for the lender to bring in turnaround specialists, so-called Chief Restructuring Officers (CRO) to take over the business, in the event of default under the loan covenants.[9]

Since the 2008 financial crisis, two major developments have occurred in the US capital markets: the rise in private debt and the increased influence of private equity (PE).[10]

A series of regulations after the 2008 Financial Crisis limited the credit supply from the banking sector and left many gaps for a wide variety of non-bank lenders to fill; among them, direct lenders have become major debt providers for middle-caped market PE buyouts.[11]

Direct lenders raise closed-end funds, either private debt funds or business development companies (BDCs), and make loans to corporations without bank syndication. Their general partners (GPs) are compensated in management fees and carried interest, similar to private equity and venture capital funds. Direct lenders mostly lend to PE buyout deals.[12]

While nonbanks in general adopt a more arm's length approach than banks, direct lenders appear to closely monitor their borrowers as banks do.[13]

During the coronavirus disease 2019 (COVID-19) pandemic, direct lenders demonstrated greater flexibility than banks in resolving distressed borrowers through out-of-court renegotiation with a higher likelihood of equity injection by the PE sponsors.[14]

8.1.2 Japan

The so-called main bank had been the major monitor of Japanese companies, but after financial deregulation and the banking crisis in the late

[9] *See id.* at 1233.

[10] The latter phenomenon, which some commentators call turning from the lender-control paradigm to the sponsor-control paradigm, will be articulated in Section 8.2 (*see infra* notes 59–61 and their accompanying text). *See* Vincent S. J. Buccola, *Sponsor Control: A New Paradigm for Corporate Reorganization*, 90 U. Chi. L. Rev. 1, 4 (2023).

[11] *See* Young Soo Jang, *Are Direct Lenders More Like Banks or Arm's-Length Investors?* SSRN, 8–9 (2024), https://ssrn.com/abstract=4529656.

[12] *See id.* at 9–10, 12.

[13] *See id.* at 38. Banks still play an important role of liquidity creation. Banks provide more revolver financing than direct lenders to PE-backed firms. See *id.* at 40–41.

[14] *See id.* at 41.

1990s, the main bank system has grown more heterogeneous. Although main banks became less important to those firms with a bond rating of single A or higher, other firms continue to rely on bank monitoring.[15]

The main bank system has some unique characteristics compared to the normal comparison between public debt (commercial paper or corporate bond) and private debt (bank borrowing) regarding the possibility of renegotiation. The main bank monitoring is stronger than the normal private debt contract, contingent on the financial situation of the client firms, and its way of intervention is systematic.[16]

The main bank monitoring is contingent monitoring. Main banks do not intervene as long as debtor companies are profitable, but once they turn to red ink, main banks exercise their voice. In the close to an insolvent situation, the main banks strongly request management to restructure, including the sale of subsidiaries and laying off employees, which would never be incorporated in the business plan prepared by Japanese management.[17]

Another characteristic of the main bank monitoring is delegated monitoring. The main bank is responsible for monitoring its client debtor companies even when they are profitable. Other banks can rely on the main bank for monitoring their non-main debtor companies. Japanese banks, as a whole, can save on monitoring costs by delegating monitoring to each other.

Because the main bank has daily transactions with the debtor company, it can closely monitor the in-and-out of the bank account and the fluctuation of the balance of the borrowings.[18]

The main bank monitoring looked successful during the Japanese rapid economic growth era in the 1960s and 1970s because banks played the monetary capital allocation role when the monetary capital was scarce resource and banks shared the interest of expanding the debtor companies'

[15] *See* Yasuhiro Arikawa & Hideaki Miyajima, *Relational Banking in Post-Bubble Japan: Co-existence of Soft and Hard-Budget Constraint*, *in* Corporate Governance in Japan: Institutional Change and Organizational Diversity 51, 75 (Masahiko Aoki et al. eds., 2007); Zenichi Shishido, *The Incentive Bargain of the Firm and Enterprise Law: A Nexus of Contracts, Markets, and Laws*, *in* Enterprise Law: Contracts, Markets, and Laws in the US and Japan 1, 19 (Zenichi Shishido ed., 2014).

[16] *See* Bruce E. Aronson et al., *Enterprise Law Conference of 2014: Edited Transcript*, SSRN (2014), https://papers.ssrn.com/sol3/papers.cfm?abstract_id=2501143 [hereinafter Transcript] 138 (Hideaki Miyajima).

[17] *See id.*

[18] *See* Transcript, *supra* note 16, at 140 (Hiroshi Mitoma).

business with all other stakeholders including shareholders when Japanese companies had "frontiers" or new markets to be developed.

Japanese main banks, however, failed to monitor the use of free cash flow, abundant money that cannot be invested by the company, during the economic bubble in the late 1980s, when the growth of the Japanese economy stopped and Japanese companies lost their frontier. After the burst of the bubble, the main bank monitoring did not necessarily maximize the firm's value. A statistical study shows that main bank commitments imposed soft-budget constraints on firms with poor performance.[19]

During the bubble period, in the 1980s and early 1990s, there was a big shift from bank borrowing to corporate bonds, but again the bank debt recovered, and now the dependence on bank loans is almost at the same level as in the 1990s. It may imply that the corporate sector still has a strong demand for renegotiation or insurance.[20]

8.1.3 China

The current Chinese financial system is characterized by the dominance of four state-owned commercial banks and three policy banks. Bank loans make up the major part of the Chinese debt market. All Chinese banks held about 12 trillion RMB (approximately US$1.7 trillion) of corporate bonds on or off their balance sheets.[21] Big Four Banks held about 4.1 trillion renminbi (RMB) (approximately US$580 billion) worth of bonds issued by companies and financial institutions at the end of 2017.

The Chinese government announced a broad set of economic reforms in 2013 to reduce the power of state-owned companies in strategic sectors of the economy. But banks' lending decisions are still heavily influenced by government policies, and both the lenders and borrowers, especially when they are state controlled, expect a government bailout when they face poor economic performance.[22] As a result, Chinese banks

19 *See* Arikawa & Miyajima, *supra* note 15, at 75.

20 *See* Miyajima, *supra* note 16, at 140.

21 Reuters & Bloomberg, *Curbing China's Corporate Debt Could Hit Economic Growth, Reports Warns*, South China Morning Post (June 4, 2018, 12:15 PM), https://www.scmp.com/news/china/economy/article/2149108/curbing-chinas-corporate-debt-could-hit-economic-growth-report.

22 *See* Yiming Hu, Siqi Li, Thomas W. Lin & Shilei Xie, *Large Creditors and Corporate Governance: The Case of Chinese Banks*, 10 Rev. of Acct. & Fin. 332, 337 (2011).

continued to approve loans to highly indebted state-owned firms.[23] The central government continued to encourage local governments to lay out the stimulus spending, which indeed was executed by the state-controlled banks, leading to both wasteful lending by state banks and credit bubbles.

Bank's monitoring role in Chinese companies is a mixed picture. In China, firms with better financial performance generally enjoy lower loan spreads.[24] However, firms that have existing bank loans but perform worse economically in terms of leverage ratio and asset turnover ratio may still have a good chance of getting their bank loans renewed because banks with a higher involvement, and so higher risk of loss, are more willing to help their borrowers.[25] While banks have gained some discretion in determining specific loan terms, such as interest rates based on borrowers' economic fundamentals, the state-owned enterprises (SOEs) have still been supported financially by the government with cheap credit through the state banking system and money creation.[26] Thus, Chinese banks play only a limited role in monitoring and disciplining borrowers, especially when borrowers are SOEs.

8.2 Renegotiation in Financially Distressed Firms and Government Subsidization

Renegotiation is often made between financially distressed firms and banks for the postponement of interest payments, waiving a part of the principal, and infusion of new money, among others. Major creditors, such as main banks, often lead the private reorganization of distressed firms. The government often subsidizes or bails out large distressed firms if their liquidation would cause social disasters. Such examples include the US government's rescue of General Motors (GM) and the Japanese government's rescue of Japan Airlines (JAL).[27]

[23] *See* Hersh Shefrin, *The Lesson from Moody's Overdue Downgrade of China's Debt*, Forbes (May 28, 2017, 6:00 AM), https://www.forbes.com/sites/hershshefrin/2017/05/28/the-lesson-from-moodys-overdue-downgrade-of-chinas-debt/#66606a9465ef.

[24] *See* Hu et al., *supra* note 22, at 362.

[25] *See id.* at 350, 351, 362. This is similar to the main bank rescue phenomenon in Japan.

[26] *See id.* at 337.

[27] As a comparison between GM case and JAL case, *see* Gen Goto, *Reduction of Retirees' Benefits upon the Reorganization of a Company*, *in* Enterprise Law: Contracts, Markets, and Laws in the US and Japan 161 (Zenichi Shishido ed., 2014).

8.2.1 The United States

To avoid the reputational damage and the delay in the bankruptcy procedure, major creditors, shareholders, and management of distressed firms try to go for the out-of-court workout, but it is done on a consent basis. Dispersed creditors increase the difficulty of achieving a private solution. The pre-packaged bankruptcy is a way to combine the advantages of an out-of-court workout, which can reduce reputational damage, and a formal bankruptcy, which can compulsorily cut the claims of disagreeing creditors according to the reorganization plan.[28]

The precise meaning of pre-packaged Chapter 11 is that when the plan of reorganization is agreed upon by the requisite majority of creditors before filing for Chapter 11, the court can approve the plan quickly. This procedure is, however, not used very much because the requirements of the disclosure statement, which should be disclosed to creditors in advance, are very severe. Therefore, instead of pre-packaged Chapter 11, pre-negotiated or pre-arranged Chapter 11 practices are used in the US. Before applying to the formal bankruptcy procedure, most creditors agree on the baseline reorganization plan, then they file for bankruptcy, and they vote for the plan to bind disagreeing creditors.[29]

The US Bankruptcy Law sets forth several mechanisms to protect creditors' interests from debtors' inappropriate or even fraudulent behaviors. Two such mechanisms are preferential transfer and fraudulent transfer.

The trustee can avoid any preferential transfer made to certain creditors right before bankruptcy. A transfer is presumptively a preference if it is made for the benefit of a creditor on account of an antecedent debt, during the ninety days[30] before the bankruptcy petition, and while the debtor is insolvent (Bankruptcy Code §547(f) presumes for the ninety-day period), provided that the transfer leaves that creditor better off than it would have been had the transfer not been made and had the debtor's assets been liquidated (preferential transfer rule).[31]

The trustee can also avoid fraudulent transfers incurred two years[32] before bankruptcy. Fraudulent transfer can be established by the trustee

[28] *See* Transcript, *supra* note 16, at 158 (Gen Goto).

[29] See Transcript, *supra* note 16, at 161 (Shinjiro Takagi).

[30] When the transferee is an insider, the period is extended to one year before the filing of the petition.

[31] Barry E. Adler, Anthony J. Casey & Edward R. Morrison, Baird and Jackson's Bankruptcy: Cases, Problems, and Materials 433 (2020).

[32] §548 of the Bankruptcy Code imposes a two-year lookback period. Some states may have a longer lookback period than two years. For instance, New York has a lookback period of six years.

as both intentional fraud and constructive fraud. As for intentional fraud, which is generally hard to establish, the Uniform Voidable Transactions Act (UVTA) §4 and Bankruptcy Code §548(a)(1)(A) provide that a transfer is voidable if it was made "with actual intent to hinder, delay, or defraud any creditor of the debtor."[33] As for constructive fraud which is often litigated, the UVTA §5 and Bankruptcy Code §548(a)(1)(B) provide that a transfer or obligation incurred for less than "a reasonably equivalent value" is voidable if the debtor "was insolvent at [the time of the transfer or obligation] or became insolvent as a result."[34]

Despite these protections, creditors are facing an increased number of hardball transactions carried out by debtors that harm existing creditors' interests. So-called hardball recapitalizations have emerged in recent years as an important feature in the landscape of corporate financial distress because the foundations of lender control gradually diminished after the 2008 financial crisis.[35] Since 2016, borrowers have sought to incur super-senior debt, priming existing first-lien lenders, on the strength of aggressive though plausible interpretations of their loan contracts.[36] The two common transaction forms of hardball recapitalizations are the "dropdown" and the "uptier" transactions.[37]

In a dropdown transaction, the borrower transfers collateral backing its existing loans to a subsidiary deemed by the credit agreement to be an "unrestricted subsidiary."[38] The borrower carves out unrestricted subsidiaries to attain a bargaining position against debtors and avail the flexibility provided by unrestricted subsidiaries.[39] Because their balance sheets are not consolidated with the borrower's, unrestricted subsidiaries are ideal for housing high-growth add-on business lines.[40] Firms often use unrestricted subsidiaries to finance faster-growing segments of their business.[41]

One famous example of a dropdown transaction is the J. Crew Transaction in 2016, where J. Crew transferred its trademarks to an unrestricted subsidiary.[42] The act of transferring the collateral causes

[33] *Id.* at 364.
[34] *Id.*
[35] Vincent S. J. Buccola & Greg Nini, *The Loan Market Response to Dropdown and Uptier Transactions*, 53 J. L. STUD. 489, 495 (2024).
[36] *Id.* at 490.
[37] *Id.*
[38] *Id.*
[39] *Id.* at 496–497.
[40] *Id.*
[41] *Id.*
[42] *Id.* at 493.

the lender's lien to be released.[43] Because indebtedness and lien covenants do not apply to unrestricted subsidiaries, the borrower can re-pledge the collateral to support new secured debt.[44] The subsidiary immediately leases back the collateral's use, so there is no effect on the borrower's operations.[45] However, the transaction subordinates the pre-existing secured lenders because they are now subordinated to the lenders of newly created debt.[46]

In an uptier transaction, the borrower persuades a majority of lenders to amend the loan contract to allow the issuance of new debt backed by a superior lien.[47] Unlike a typical loan amendment, the borrower does not offer to compensate all consenting lenders on a pro-rata basis.[48] The recent trend that gives rise to an uptier transaction is that some loan contracts have begun to establish exceptions to the general rule prohibiting assignments to the borrower.[49] These exceptions sought to replicate bond issuers' longstanding ability to repurchase debt trading below par.[50] Two common exceptions declare that, notwithstanding a general prohibition on borrower repurchases, the borrower or its affiliates can buy loans through (1) an auction procedure open to all lenders on a pro-rata basis (typically run by the administrative agent) or (2) on a non-pro-rata basis in what is called "open market" repurchases.[51] The contracts that allow repurchase through auction or open market transactions also carve out from the general pro-rata sharing rule the proceeds of such exceptional repurchases.[52]

One example of an uptier transaction is the Serta Simmons Transaction in 2020, where Serta created $1.075 billion of new, super-priority debt, of which $200 million would represent new money for the business, while the remaining $875 million would be used to repurchase consenting lenders' loans.[53] First-lien lenders were not invited to participate and were subordinated to more than a billion dollars of incremental debt.[54]

43 *Id.* at 490.
44 *Id.*
45 *Id.*
46 *Id.*
47 *Id.*
48 *Id.*
49 *Id.* at 501.
50 *Id.*
51 *Id.*
52 *Id.*
53 *Id.* at 502.
54 *Id.*

The reasons for the emergence of hardball recapitalization are twofold. First, the bargaining power held by the debtor increases significantly. Term loans, traditionally held by the banks that provided a borrower's revolving credit, were increasingly sold to non-bank institutions – collateralized loan obligation (CLOs), loan mutual funds, private credit funds, and the like.[55] As lenders became more diffuse and renegotiation therefore became more costly, restrictions on borrower activity loosened.[56] This led to the virtual disappearance of financial maintenance covenants from term loan contracts.[57] Second, the bankruptcy judge tends to view those hardball transactions as a contractual matter. The fact that debtors can exploit the loopholes in the contract is because banks are sophisticated lenders and agree to the loose contractual terms earlier on. Thus, taking advantage of contractual terms is not considered a violation of the "implied covenant of good faith and fair dealing."[58]

Since the global financial crisis of 2008, private equity sponsors, as the owners of large, distressed firms, have increased and now they are predominant.[59] When private equity owns the equity of the firms, the firms act much differently from ordinary publicly traded firms. The managers and members of the board of the portfolio firm are partners of the private equity fund and have skin in the game. The directors strongly favor sponsors' incentives, particularly to avoid bankruptcy.[60]

To secure liquidity without having to resort to Chapter 11, private equity sponsored firms often resort to hardball recapitalization, such as the dropdown and the non-pro rata uptier.[61] Private equity sponsors are sometimes willing to put in new cash, so they may have a stronger bargaining power vis-à-vis senior creditors.

55 *Id.*

56 *Id.*

57 *Id.*

58 For instance, in *in re* Serta Simmons Bedding, LLC, Judge David Jones states that "While the result may seem harsh, there is no equity to achieve in this case. Sophisticated financial titans engaged in a winner-take-all battle. There was a winner and a loser. Such an outcome was not only foreseeable, it is the only correct result. The risk of loss is a check on unrestrained behavior." *In re* Serta Simmons Bedding, LLC, 2023 Bankr. LEXIS 1479, 42 (Bankr. S.D. Tex. June 6, 2023). Since the Credit Agreement between Serta and lenders was the product of negotiations between sophisticated parties, all of whom were fully aware of the terms of the agreement and their implications, the uptier transaction did not violate "implied duty of good faith and fair dealing." *See id.* at 503.

59 *See* Jang, *supra* note 11, at 1.

60 *See id.* at 5, 32.

61 Most hardball recapitalizations are made by PE sponsored firms. *See* Buccola, *supra* note 10, at 34.

8.2.2 *Japan*

Financially distressed firms always try to renegotiate with their creditors for the postponement of payment of interest and principal. Banks and long-term trade creditors, such as suppliers, usually accept renegotiation and wait, but promissory note holders will not.

Settlement of Japanese B2B transactions has been done by promissory notes.[62] Paying by promissory note means sellers will wait for actual payment until the due date, so it is a way of credit granting between business companies. Promissory notes are transferable. Once a promissory note is transferred, the debtor company will be forced to go bankrupt if it fails to meet the due date.

Main banks are expected to rescue their debtor companies if they turn out to be financially distressed, and main banks actually do it if a debtor's failure will have a huge impact on the economy.[63] Main banks try to obtain a compromise with other creditors to avoid legal bankruptcy. Main banks will sit in the driver's seat of private reorganizations. A good example is the main bank role played by Sumitomo Bank in the case of the Mazda turnaround in the middle of the 1970s.[64] In the late 2010s, Mitsubishi Tokyo Bank played a similar role in the case of Kobe Steel turnaround.[65]

However, the main bank rescue of distressed companies has pros and cons. It may keep zombie companies, which should be removed from the market, alive and cause economic inefficiency from a macroeconomic perspective. After the banking crisis of 1997, in order to hide the non-performing loans, the main banks would like to help the client firms survive by giving additional money to these firms.[66] The

[62] Nowadays, however, the use of promissory notes is decreasing and the settlement system is moving toward electric settlement.

[63] Most SMEs, which are forced to consider private workouts, are no longer able to obtain a main bank rescue. Instead, the case of using a quasi-legal workout, such as the Council for the Revitalization of Small and Medium Enterprises (https://www.chusho.meti.go.jp/keiei/saisei/index.html), is increasing.

[64] *See* Richard Pascale & Thomas P. Rohlen, *The Mazda Turnaround*, 9 J. Japanese Stud. 219 (1983).

[65] Falsifications of quality data by Kobe Steel were revealed in 2017 (*see* Nikkei, July 17, 2018), and the company faced financial difficulties. The main bank of Kobe Steel, Mitsubishi Tokyo Bank, rescued Kobe Steel by committing additional loans and sending a special team for reformation, etc., just as Sumitomo Bank rescued Mazda forty years ago.

[66] *See* Miyajima, *supra* note 16, at 139.

Japanese government also contributes to such banks' "ever-greening" loans.[67]

Major government subsidization is made via public credit guarantee for small and medium enterprises (SMEs), which currently covers 80 percent of the total debt. It is criticized for creating a soft-budget problem and decreasing the incentive of banks to monitor debtor companies.

After the Japanese financial crisis of 1997, the government provided major banks with a huge amount of subsidization to strengthen their equity capital.

8.2.3 *China*

China's changing financial market and regulatory landscape in many senses show a strong characteristic of being a regulatory state with a jungle of financial laws, rules, and regulations. This regulatory network, while improving China's banking supervision, also enhances the government's interventionist role in running the banking and financial system. Meanwhile, the market-oriented instruments and tools are not in a decisive position to solve market failures or to improve financial resource redistribution. China's financial system, particularly the banking system, is still a government-controlled sector.[68] In recent years, the Chinese government has been in a continuous effort to lower the leverage ratio of the corporate debt. Recent solutions are twofold.

8.2.3.1 Debt-for-Equity Swap Program

The swap program was not new in China and was used by the government to restructure large SOEs[69] and to spin off non-performing loans from highly distressed banks to asset management corporations (AMC) in the 1990s.[70] SOEs in the 1990s suffered huge deficits at an average deficit ratio of 25–30 percent and the annual loss of the SOEs was

[67] *See* Joe Peek & Eric S. Rosengren, *Unnatural Selection: Perverse Incentive and the Misallocation of Credit in Japan*, 95 Am. Econ. Rev. 1144, 1144 (2005).

[68] *See* Michael F. Martin, *China's Banking System: Issues for Congress*, CRS Rep. (Feb. 20, 2012), https://crsreports.congress.gov/product/pdf/R/R42380/5.

[69] *See* Russell Smyth, Junli Wang & Xin Deng, *Equity-for-Debt Swaps in Chinese Big Business: A Case Study of Restructuring in One Large State-Owned Enterprise*, 10 Globalization & Comp.: Big Bus. in Asia 382, 382 (2004).

[70] *See* Jianbo Lou, *AMCs and Debt-Equity Swaps in China: Can They Really Solve the State Commercial Bank NPL Problem?*, 4 Y.B. Int'l Fin. & Econ. L. 304, 319 (1999).

renminbi 35–48 billion (approximately US$4.9–6.7 billion).[71] Bad loans had a series of impacts on SOEs, banks, and the real economy. The swap program was introduced to bail out distressed SOEs and banks.

Under the swap, a debt holder receives shares in exchange for the cancelation of the debt. The debt-for-equity swaps are put in place to lower corporate leverage ratios and to help struggling borrowers stay in business. In addition, the borrowers can increase their capital. A creditor may convert its rights over the loan into the equity of the debtor, and then realize returns from a future sale of equity, trade sale, or other distributions from the debtor. Creditors may also obtain capital gains and dividends after the borrowers recover from their distress. Turning creditors into shareholders allows lenders to monitor the borrowers more effectively, given their effective participation in corporate governance. The downside of a large-scale debt-for-share swap is the emergence of universal banks and the more distorted role of banks in financial and capital markets.

Different from the 1990s, nowadays the swaps are largely led by the banks, which would set up their own asset management companies (AMCs) to dispose of debts. Bank-run swaps are more effective as banks monitor debtor companies through covenants in the loan agreements to restrain the moral hazard in borrowers' risk-taking activities.

Prior to the swaps, banks possessed some tools, such as foreclosure on collateral, reorganization, or legal actions to monitor, which is important to the bank-dependent firms' corporate governance.[72] After the swaps, banks become controlling shareholders and have a direct involvement in and impact on corporate governance and performance.[73]

While banks are facing both competition pressure from their peers and capital adequacy pressure from banking regulation and internal compliance requirements, their self-interest is to dispose of non-performing loans more effectively compared with state-controlled AMCs, which are furnished with political targets to achieve. Given the fact that the banking sector's current

[71] *See* Zhu Hongjian, *Laizi "Bawu" de Baogao Woguo Gongye Jingji Shili* [Reports from Eight-Five Plan, Enhanced Industrial Capacity of China], Renmin Ribao [People Daily] (Dec. 29, 2000, 05:04 PM), http://www.people.com.cn/GB/channel1/10/20000921/243860.html.

[72] *See* Sungyoon Ahn & Wooseok Choi, *The Role of Bank Monitoring in Corporate Governance: Evidence from Borrowers' Earnings Management Behavior*, 33 J. Banking & Fin. 425 (2009).

[73] *See* Andrei Shleifer & Robert W. Vishny, *Large Investors and Corporate Control*, 94 J. Pol. Econ. 461 (1986); David J. Denis & Jan M. Serrano, *Active Investors and Management Turnover Following Unsuccessful Control Contests*, 40 J. Fin. Econ. 239 (1996).

nonperforming loan ratio is not as high as the one in the 1990s, the swaps should be conducted without excessive government intervention. Banks, as the creditors and collateral assets handy, are in the best position to negotiate and enter into more favorable terms for the swaps.

However, the swaps may not necessarily be safe for banks depending on the corporate's likelihood to recover from its financial distress. Insolvency may turn the lender into a worse scenario, as a shareholder ranks last in the priority order of distribution of outstanding assets. In the case that the borrower does not recover from its distress, banks holding non-performing equities face more risks as stock prices may fluctuate more than debt. Besides, banks and AMCs usually have more appetite for fixed-income debt than equity. If the debt is in good standing and there is no default, investors then have no incentive to forgo stable fixed returns for uncertain equity gains by debt-equity swap.

For the borrower, converting debt into equity on the balance sheet or "financial engineering" does not boost its earnings. Most of the borrowers in the swaps are distressed companies with limited prospects for recovery without simultaneous corporate restructuring aimed at restoring profitability. Structural transformation of these distressed companies is usually time-consuming.

Market-oriented debt-to-equity swaps are mainly concentrated in such industries as steel, coal, chemicals, and equipment manufacturing, and are dominated by SOEs, especially local SOEs. Swaps can also be pursued or encouraged by the government as a window-dressing tool to avoid a large-scale bankruptcy of enterprises.

8.2.3.2 Mixed Share Reform

This is a relatively new scheme aiming to reform the SOE that is in heavy loss through partial privatization of the SOE. It is believed that introducing private capital participation in SOEs will help alleviate financial liability and improve the profitability of SOEs.

In 2015, the Chinese government put forward the so-called mixed-ownership reform[74] to "invigorate torpid SOEs,"[75] which is motivated by

[74] Guidelines of the CCP Central Committee and the PRC State Council to Deepen Reform of the State-owned Enterprises (promulgated on Aug. 24, 2015); Opinions of the State Council on the Development of Mixed-Ownership Reform in SOEs (promulgated on Sept. 23, 2015).

[75] The State Council of the People's Republic of China, *China Issues Guideline to Deepen SOE Reforms* (Sept. 13, 2015, 5:37 PM), http://english.www.gov.cn/policies/latest_releases/2015/09/13/content_281475189210840.htm.

the benefits of improved corporate governance and performance in SOEs through the sharing of control between the controlling state shareholders and non-state shareholders. State ownership leads to political dominance, which makes SOEs less efficient and profitable. Studies show that listed companies with politically connected CEOs actually performed worse than their counterparts.[76] The program encourages POEs to participate in the reform through various means, such as buying stakes and convertible bonds from or conducting share rights swaps with the SOEs. Selling shares to SOEs' own employees is also listed as one of the means.[77]

Given the small portion of shares to be sold to POEs, the scheme does not substantially dilute the state ownership in major SOEs. Also, because of the small portion of shares to be owned by the POEs, POEs are not keen to possess such shares, as the minority shareholder protection scheme is not strong enough to protect their legal interests when they have to be trapped in the dispute with the controlling shareholders, which usually are state-owned or state-connected. This also explains the non-popularity of this scheme when it is put forward to the market. Some SOEs' mixed share schemes did not attract much private capital in the end.

8.3 Legal Bankruptcy as the End Game Norm

Bankruptcy is the endgame of the incentive bargaining among the four players. Bankruptcy is a trigger to terminate their repeated game. From the game-theoretic point of view, the existence of a trigger is indispensable to keep repeated games efficiently made. Before privatization, the "labor-owned" companies in Eastern European countries were not allowed to go bankrupt, and as a result, they were extremely inefficient.

Corporate bankruptcy law not only provides ex-post rule of incentive bargaining in the insolvent firm but also affects incentive bargaining in the solvent firm *ex ante*. An unpaid creditor may seek a court order enforcing its claim against the debtor's assets. When the firm has defaulted generally on its credit obligations, its creditors have the option to become owners of all its assets. Then the creditors will face a coordination problem. Each creditor has the incentive to enforce individually.

[76] *See* Joseph P. H. Fan, T. J. Wong & Tianyu Zhang, *Politically Connected CEOs, Corporate Governance, and Post-IPO Performance*, 84 J. FIN. ECON. 330, 330–357 (2007).

[77] *See id.*

The creditors have the right to trigger bankruptcy proceedings against firms that are insolvent, which transforms creditors' individual entitlements to seize or attach particular assets into entitlements to participate in a collective process.[78]

An important goal of corporate bankruptcy law is the value maximization of assets, for which the automatic stay plays an important role. Another important goal is the preservation of claims that would exist outside of bankruptcy. The basic priority structure is that secured creditors come first up to the value of their collateral, and then unsecured creditors come next, and then shareholders at the bottom. The priority structure prevents asset substitution problems where debtors can exchange safe assets for risky assets and gamble the company, and allows lenders to avoid problems of asymmetric information because they can focus only on the value of their collateral. These two goals can conflict with each other because shareholders have the incentive to delay, and over-secured creditors have the incentive to have a fire sale.[79]

The corporate bankruptcy law provides two measures: the liquidation procedure and the rehabilitation/reorganization procedure. The liquidation is the procedure to sell the debtor's assets and distribute the sales money to the creditors. Secured creditors can exercise their rights because there is no necessity to restrict the execution of the security interest to rehabilitate the debtor's business.[80] The debtor corporation is dissolved, its business no longer exists, and all human capital providers lose their jobs. If the discounted future cash flow value of the debtor corporation overwhelms its liquidation value, taking a rehabilitation procedure is more economically efficient and better for most stakeholders than taking a liquidation procedure. This section will focus on the rehabilitation procedure.

The legal reorganization plan must meet the three principles: liquidation value guarantee; equality among the same rights; and fair and equitable difference among different rights. The third principle is fulfilled along with the absolute priority rule, which requires the cost of valuation of the firm's going concern value. Some measures for decreasing its cost are taken in each jurisdiction.[81]

[78] *See* KRAAKMAN, ET AL., *supra* note 1, at 117.

[79] *See* Transcript, *supra* note 16, at 143 (Kenneth M. Ayotte).

[80] *See* KAZUHIKO YAMAMOTO, TOSAN SHORI HO NYUMON [INTRODUCTION TO INSOLVENCY LAW] 61 (6th ed. 2024).

[81] *See* Wataru Tanaka, *Cramdown versus Extinguishing Security Interests: Secured Claims in Bankruptcy in the United States and Japan*, *in* ENTERPRISE LAW: CONTRACTS, MARKETS, AND LAWS IN THE US AND JAPAN 150 (Zenichi Shishido ed., 2014).

8.3.1 *The United States*

Dispersed creditors increase the difficulty of achieving a private solution, and it becomes increasingly valuable to have the option of a bankruptcy procedure that helps creditors take ownership of a firm that continues to operate.[82]

One characteristic of the US Chapter 11 is its easy access to the legal reorganization procedure. The debtor corporation can file without cause of bankruptcy, such as insolvency. The reorganization procedure starts with the Chapter 11 filing, and at the same time, all debt collections by creditors are suspended due to the automatic stay. Such rules encourage the debtor to file early, and even financially distressed firms in the United States utilize Chapter 11 as a tool of smooth restructuring.[83]

Although most of the management of the debtor keeps management rights as the debtor in possession (DIP), the management must obtain the agreement of the creditors' committee to proceed with the important procedures. The bankruptcy court restricts its role as a neutral arbiter.[84]

At least, in the early days of the current bankruptcy code that came into play in 1978, the dominant view was that Chapter 11 was a manager-friendly or shareholder-friendly system, and excess delay was the problem. One such example is the Eastern Airlines case.[85]

Now, bankruptcy practice has changed a lot, although the bankruptcy code has not changed very much. Creditors have a lot of control over bankruptcy outcomes.[86] When companies file for bankruptcy, in over 90 percent cases, all their assets are pledged as collateral to secured creditors, which makes it hard for the company to borrow from a new lender. Section 364 of the Bankruptcy Code gives the debtor the ability to borrow at a seniority that they would not be able to borrow outside of bankruptcy, which enables the DIP financing and plays an important liquidity-providing role. The DIP loan is the new loan that the company takes on when it files a bankruptcy petition, but the covenants in the DIP

[82] *See* KRAAKMAN, ET AL., *supra* note 1, at 142–143.

[83] *See* YAMAMOTO, *supra* note 80, at 6–7.

[84] *See id.* at 7.

[85] Eastern Airlines used the filing of a relatively minor affiliate to establish venue for the much larger core firm. Eastern Airlines managers headed to New York to take advantage of its manager-friendly posture on issues such as extending the so-called exclusivity period. David A. Skeel Jr., *Bankruptcy Judges and Bankruptcy Venue: Some Thoughts on Delaware*, 1 DEL. L. REV. 17 (1998).

[86] *See* Transcript, *supra* note 16, at 144–145 (Kenneth M. Ayotte).

loan are very stringent, and the DIP creditors substantially control the debtor company.[87]

In the United States, secured creditors can credit bid for an asset sale under § 363,[88] which governs the extraordinary use of property during the administration of a bankruptcy case.[89] Credit bidding enables a secured creditor to bid up to the face value of its loan as consideration for the assets a bankrupt debtor proposes to sell, along with any residual amount in cash.[90]

8.3.2 Japan

Besides the liquidation procedure, Japanese bankruptcy laws provide two rehabilitation/reorganization procedures: the Civil Rehabilitation Act and the Corporate Reorganization Act. The former is for a DIP-led procedure. The latter is for trustee-led procedure and can restrict creditors' rights more powerfully with rigid procedures.[91]

Private workouts are more popular than legal workouts,[92] and play a significant role in the threat of tough bankruptcy proceedings.[93] Management of distressed firms is reluctant to file for legal bankruptcy because of severe punishment of management ex post.[94] Not only main

[87] *See id.* at 145, 147.

[88] Section 363(k) provides:

> At a sale under subsection (b) of this section of property that is subject to a lien that secures an allowed claim, unless the court for cause orders otherwise the holder of such claim may bid at such sale, and, if the holder of such claim purchases such property, such holder may offset such claim against the purchase price of such property.

[89] Vincent S. J. Buccola & Ashley C. Keller, *Credit Bidding and the Design of Bankruptcy Auctions*, 18 Geo. Mason L. Rev. 99, 105 (2010).

[90] *Id.* at 100.

[91] *See* Yamamoto, *supra* note 80, at 249.

[92] Recently, quasi-legal workout procedures have been developed with the involvement of a neutral third-party organization such as the Council for the Revitalization of SMEs, Alternative Dispute Resolution (ADR) for Business Turnaround, Regional Economy Vitalization Corporation of Japan (REVIC), and Guidelines for Business Recovery, etc. of SME. *See* Kazuyoshi Takada, Comparison of Bankruptcy Practices in Japan and the U.S. (Dec. 31, 2023) (unpublished manuscript) (on file with authors).

[93] *See* Kraakman, et al., *supra* note 1, at 143.

[94] Management will be punished both practically and legally if the company goes bankrupt. Practically, CEOs of most non-listed companies are required to personally guarantee bank loans and thus if the company goes bankrupt, CEOs will be forced to become personally bankrupt, too. Legally, creditors of a bankrupt company can pursue directors' personal liability under the Companies Act Article 429 (*see infra* notes 132–134 and their

banks but also most creditors want to avoid legal bankruptcy because its outcome is unpredictable depending on who will be the trustee, and because the main bank, in particular, will get out of the driver's seat and receive dramatically reduced information from the debtor company, once a legal proceeding starts.[95] Main banks are also afraid of damaging the business value of debtor companies by using legal bankruptcy proceedings, which require involving all creditors and are publicly disclosed.[96]

Japanese reorganization and rehabilitation proceedings are not transparent, conducted behind closed doors by the court without the involvement of creditors. Creditors' committees are rarely organized. A creditor is forced to negotiate with trustees one by one, so her bargaining power is limited.[97] The unpredictability is a big problem. The expectation about the legal process works as a threat point of the private workout. If the expectation is unpredictable or not so transparent, it does not work as a good threat point.[98]

8.3.2.1 Comparison with US Bankruptcy Laws and Practices

Compared to the US chapter 11, Japanese rehabilitation/reorganization laws give bankruptcy judges wider discretion and restrict party autonomy. Japanese bankruptcy judges tend to value fairness or justice rather than bargaining between debtors and creditors. Super-priority DIP loans and section 363 sales are not available.

Japanese management's psychological barrier to filing the legal procedure is much higher than that of its US counterpart. The biggest problem of Japanese bankruptcy laws and practices is delayed filing and, as a result, low recovery rate.

8.3.3 China

In 2006, China enacted its first bankruptcy code. Two purposes of the code are to "fairly liquidate credits and debts [and] safeguard the legitimate rights and interests of creditors and debtors."[99]

accompanying texts). Civil Rehabilitation Act Article 143 also provides the procedure for the assessment of directors' liability.

95 Transcript, *supra* note 16, at 141 (Hiroshi Mitoma).

96 *See* Takada, *supra* note 92.

97 *See* Transcript, *supra* note 16, at 151 (Shijiro Takagi).

98 *See* Transcript, *supra* note 16, at 160 (Noriyuki Yanagawa).

99 Law of the People's Republic of China on Enterprise Bankruptcy (2006), Art. 1.

Enterprise Bankruptcy Law exists to compensate creditors. At present, China does not allow for individual bankruptcy. However, the Enterprise Bankruptcy Law allows for a fair distribution of debt. For companies seeking to raise funds, the bankruptcy law is important because it describes the method of payment on debts if the company becomes insolvent. The risk associated with repayment affects the amount and interest rate creditors are willing to accept. Debts are paid in priority, with debts of a higher priority being paid in full before debts of a lower priority. As a result, secured assets are protected from being used to repay other creditors.

8.3.3.1 Bankruptcy Declaration

The liquidation group[100] may submit the case to the court for a bankruptcy declaration after it finds the company insolvent in the course of liquidation.[101] The court may also make a bankruptcy declaration if the company is unable to repay the debts due, and its assets prove insufficient to repay the debts, or it apparently lacks the capacity to settle the debts.[102] While the courts may have more discretion in making bankruptcy declarations, the courts' function in practice is somehow limited due to the restrictive role the judiciary plays in Chinese society. For instance, the courts have to handle bankruptcy cases under the leadership of the local committee of the Communist Party and coordinate with the local government, that is, the local financial supervisory body.[103] The local government, on the other hand, is very unwilling to rely on

[100] The liquidation group of a listed company shall be composed of its directors or the persons decided on by the shareholders' meeting (Company Law 2023, Art. 232). Where a company fails to set up a liquidation team to conduct liquidation at the expiration of the prescribed time limit, its creditors may apply to a people's court for designating relevant persons to form a liquidation team for liquidation (Company Law 2023, Art. 233). The liquidation group plays a similar role as the trustee in the US bankruptcy proceeding. The liquidation group is tasked to check up on the property of the company and draw up a balance sheet and an inventory of its assets separately, notify the creditors by notice or announcement; dispose of and liquidate the company's unfinished business; pay off the tax arrears and the taxes generated in the process of liquidation; clear up claims and debts; dispose of the property remaining after the company pays off its debts; and participate in civil lawsuits on behalf of the company (Company Law 2023, Arts. 233–234).

[101] Company Law 2023, Art. 232.

[102] Enterprise Bankruptcy Law, Arts. 2, 107.

[103] Supreme People's Court's Opinions on Certain Issues Concerning Correctly Handling Enterprises Bankruptcy Cases to Maintain the Market Order with Judicial Protection, issued by the Supreme People's Court on June 12, 2009, section 2.

liquidation procedures as a solution to the debt crisis. Bankrupting firms means more laid-off employees, which would cause social instability. This is the major obstacle for the courts to accept liquidation applications. In addition, the courts need to make use of mediation in the process of handling bankruptcy cases.[104]

8.3.3.2 Creditors' Committee

The creditors' committee has extensive involvement in the bankruptcy case. For instance, the administrator must report to the creditors' committee for any significant asset disposition activities affecting the interests of the creditors. The creditors' committee also supervises the management, disposition, and distribution of the bankruptcy estate. In particular, creditors may ask the court to remove the administrator and review the administrator's compensation, supervise the administrator, determine whether the debtor should remain as a going concern, or adopt the reorganization plan, settlement agreement, or other asset disposition plan.

8.3.3.3 Repayment Queue

Prior to the enactment of the Enterprise Bankruptcy law, workers' compensation claims were often paid ahead of secured claims. The Enterprise Bankruptcy Law reverses the current practice and provides that in a liquidation, secured claims receive distributions to the extent of the value of the collateral, and any deficiency claim is treated as a general unsecured claim.

The unsecured creditors should receive their distribution in the following order: First, post-bankruptcy administrative costs and expenses are entitled to first priority in distribution; Second, post-bankruptcy liabilities for "common benefits" are entitled to second priority in distribution; Third, workers' compensation claims are entitled to third priority in distribution; Fourth, social insurance expenses not included in third priority distribution and tax claims are entitled to fourth priority in payment; and Fifth, general unsecured claims are the last to be paid from the debtor's estate.

8.3.3.4 Reorganization

The Enterprise Bankruptcy Law devotes an entire chapter to reorganization. The Enterprise Bankruptcy Law allows all creditors to vote on a

[104] *Id.* at section 3, Art. 9.

reorganization plan and divides the creditors into four classes for plan voting purposes: secured creditors, workers' compensation claimants, tax claimants, and other general unsecured creditors. In addition, the court may allow the holders of *de minimis* claims to vote on the plan as a separate class.

Under the Enterprise Bankruptcy Law, a creditors' meeting must be held to vote on the reorganization plan. The plan must be approved by an affirmative vote of two-thirds of the total amount of the claims in each class and a majority of the creditors in such class that are present at the creditors' meeting.[105] The plan can be approved only if all four voting classes vote in favor of the plan, although the court may "cram down" a dissenting class if certain conditions are satisfied.[106] In addition, the law allows DIP financing by the DIP or the administrator.[107]

8.3.3.5 Comparison with US Bankruptcy Laws and Practices

Although China's 2006 Enterprise Bankruptcy Law modeled the US bankruptcy law, there are still important differences in the law and practice.[108]

The eligibility standard for bankruptcy is not as clear and easy to meet as the U.S. Bankruptcy Code, which leaves much room for Chinese bankruptcy judges to exercise their discretion on whether to accept a bankruptcy case, and this actually discourages bankruptcy filings.[109]

The automatic stay under the Chinese Enterprise Bankruptcy Law is less effective than that under the U.S. Bankruptcy Code.[110] Besides its coverage being more limited,[111] the fifteen-day time gap between bankruptcy filing and the court's acceptance of the case becomes a de facto

105 This requirement is similar to the U.S. Bankruptcy Code and the exit mechanisms under UK administration such as schemes of arrangement.

106 This is also similar to the cramdown process in the United States and UK. However, it remains to be seen whether cramdown under the new law is a feasible alternative.

107 But Chinese law is silent as to whether the DIP lender can be entitled to super-priority status or a priming lien, as provided under the U.S. Bankruptcy Code.

108 *See* Yan Zhan, Convergence of Bankruptcy Practices in China and the U.S.: A Comparative Study of Chinese and the U.S. Bankruptcy Laws (Dec. 31, 2023) (unpublished manuscript) (on file with authors).

109 *See id.*; Yujia Jiang, *The Curious Case of Inactive Bankruptcy Practice in China: A Comparative Study of US and Chinese Bankruptcy Law*, 34 Nw. J. Int'l L. & Bus. 559, 569 (2013).

110 *See* Zhan, *supra* note 108.

111 Automatic stay under the Chinese Enterprise Bankruptcy Law does not cover administrative proceedings and non-adjudicating proceedings like mediations, while automatic stay under the U.S. Bankruptcy Code does.

public announcement to invite all creditors to collect on their debts, and this also discourages bankruptcy filings.[112] Moreover, switching between liquidation and reorganization is less flexible under the Chinese Enterprise Bankruptcy Law.[113] As a result, about 80 percent of US corporate bankruptcies are Chapter 11 reorganization, while 83 percent of Chinese corporate bankruptcies are liquidation.[114]

In addition, the level of specialization of the bankruptcy court is still much lower in China compared to the United States, though bankruptcy court specialization is gradually developing in China.[115]

8.4 Directors' Fiduciary Duty during the Zone of Insolvency

Theoretically, there is a discontinuity between corporate law and bankruptcy law regimes. The residual claimant of the firm changes from shareholders to creditors in the event of insolvency, and, accordingly, the residual control moves from shareholders to creditors.

Practically, however, it is impossible to identify when the firm turns from solvent to insolvent. We need to suppose the zone of insolvency as if the change is not non-linear but linear. Although, legally, shareholders still have voting right during the zone of insolvency, their residual claim is almost zero, but it will never be negative because of their limited liability. As a result, shareholders will have an incentive to gamble at the cost of creditors.

In the bankruptcy law regime, trustees or DIP managers are requested to run the company in the interest of creditors. The problem is what the duty of directors should be when the company is insolvent or near insolvent, but it is outside of a formal bankruptcy procedure.[116]

Laws in many jurisdictions have mechanisms to discourage controlling shareholders from impairing creditors' interests in the vicinity of insolvency, such as controlling shareholders' liability as de facto or shadow directors, equitable subordination of shareholder loans in bankruptcy, piercing the corporate veil, and fraudulent conveyance laws.[117]

112 *See* Zhan, *supra* note 108; Jiang, *supra* note 109, at 571.
113 *See* Zhan, *supra* note 108; Jiang, *supra* note 109, at 568.
114 *See* Dean Corbae & Pablo D'Erasmo, *Reorganization or Liquidation: Bankruptcy Choice and Firm Dynamics*, 88 Rev. Econ. Stud. 2239, 2243 (2021); Bo Li & Jacopo Ponticelli, *Going Bankrupt in China*, 26 Rev. of Fin. 449, 451 (2022).
115 *See* Zhan, *supra* note 108; Li & Ponticelli, *supra* note 114, at 456–457.
116 *See* Goto, *supra* note 28, at 153.
117 *See* Kraakman & Armour, *supra* note 1, at 114.

8.4.1 The United States

The US case laws on the directors' fiduciary duty in the zone of insolvency have been dramatically changed.

In *Credit Lyonnais*, the Delaware Chancery Court held that the board of a firm "operating in the vicinity of insolvency" owed its fiduciary duty not just to shareholders but also to the corporate enterprise as a whole.[118] After *Credit Lyonnais*, directors could be held liable to creditors as well as shareholders, if the firm was in the zone of insolvency.[119]

Academic commentators increasingly argued against fiduciary duty shifting by *Credit Lyonnais*.[120] In *Gheewalla*,[121] the Delaware Supreme Court reversed *Credit Lyonnais* and rejected the idea of shifting fiduciary duties in the zone of insolvency.[122]

In *Quadrant*, the Delaware Chancery Court held that the directors and officers of insolvent firms did not owe a fiduciary duty to creditors.[123] The court clearly stated that even if the directors took an excessively risky course of decision, the decision would be protected by the business judgment rule.[124]

The US case law looks to preserve the discontinuity between the corporate law regime and bankruptcy law regime and requires the director to consider only the interest of shareholders when the company is outside of the formal bankruptcy procedure.

In the zone of insolvency, nothing changes. Even in insolvency, no clear substantive shift of directors' fiduciary duty to creditors, but creditors could bring a derivative suit to enforce the directors' fiduciary duty toward the corporation.[125]

Before *Gheewalla* and *Quadrant*, when a corporation became insolvent, rather than pursuing high-risk strategies for the benefit of

[118] Credit Lyonnais Bank Nederland, N.V. v. Pathe Commc'ns Corp., No. 12150, 1991 Del. Ch. LEXIS 215, at 34 (Del. Ch. 1991).

[119] *See* Jared A. Ellias & Robert J. Stark, *Bankruptcy Hardball*, 108 CAL. L. REV. 745, 759 (2020).

[120] *See* e.g., Baird & Rasmussen, *supra* note 6, at 1248; *see also* Ellias & Stark, *supra* note 119, at 760.

[121] N. Am. Catholic Educ. Programming Found. v. Gheewalla, 930 A. 2d 92 (Del. 2007).

[122] *See* Ellias & Stark, *supra* note 119, at 760.

[123] Quadrant Structured Prod. Co. v. Vertin, 102 A.3d 155, 176 (Del. Ch. 2014).

[124] *Id.* at 192; *See* Ellias & Stark, *supra* note 119, at 761.

[125] *See* Transcript, *supra* note 16, at 157 (Bruce Aaronson).

shareholders, directors must seek to protect creditors' claims to corporate assets and earnings.[126]

After *Quadrant*, directors can now favor some creditors over others without having to worry about liability as long as the transfer is not subject to the preferential transfer rule.[127] *Quadrant* will protect directors when they adopt a high-risk business strategy that might benefit shareholders when a corporation is insolvent.[128]

Although it is true that, after *Quadrant*, the directors can advance the interest of shareholders at the expense of creditors with the business judgment rule,[129] the directors can also favor the creditors if they choose. If the directors have a minimal stake, as in most widely held public firms, they may care more about preserving their reputation[130] and try to maximize the value of the firm for the benefit of both shareholders and creditors.[131]

8.4.2 *Japan*

Companies Act Article 429 seems to take the way to introduce some continuity by imposing the duty on directors to consider the interest of creditors if the company is insolvent or nearly insolvent.[132]

Article 429 imposes civil liability on directors to a third party. Third parties include creditors. This provision has been used by creditors of

126 *See* J. Douglas Bacon & Jennifer A. Love, *When Good Things Happen to Bad People: Practical Aspect of Holding Directors and Managers of Insolvent Corporations Accountable*, 10 J. Bankr. L. Prac. 185, 186 (2001); Ellias & Stark, *supra* note 119, at 761.

127 *See supra* notes 30–31 and their accompanying texts. *See also* John L. Reed & Henry duPont Ridgely, *Delaware Court of Chancery Issues Significant Ruling on the Ability of Creditors to Assert Fiduciary Duty Claims against Directors: Key Takeaways*, LEXOLOGY (May 14, 2015), https://www.lexology.com/library/detail.aspx?g=f9502050-0946-4636-8f54-f125e8eaba06; Ellias & Stark, *supra* note 119, at 762.

128 *See* Mark S. Chehi, John K. Lyons & Ana Lucia Hartado, *Delaware Court of Chancery Decisions Clarifies Fiduciary Issues of Insolvent Company Context*, Skadden, Arps, Slate, Meagher & Flom LLP (Jan. 2015), https://www.skadden.com/insights/publications/2015/01/delaware-court-of-chancery-decision-clarifies-fidu/ [https://perma.cc/LK5Q-4HW5]; Ellias & Stark, *supra* note 119, at 762.

129 *See*, e.g., the recent phenomena of hardball recapitalizations. *See supra* notes 35–61 and their accompanying texts. *See also* Buccola, *supra* note 10, at 24.

130 *See id.* at 21–22.

131 On this point, I owe a lot to a comment by Douglas Baird (E-mail from Douglas Baird, Professor at University of Chicago, Law School, to Zenichi Shishido, Professor of Law, Musashino University Law Faculty (Jan. 8, 2024)) (on file with authors).

132 *See* Goto, *supra* note 28, at 153.

insolvent companies, mostly SMEs. When these companies become insolvent, creditors tend to use Article 429 to collect from the directors who are often controlling shareholders. One typical situation is when the company purchases materials from its suppliers by promissory notes,[133] although its directors know that it is very unlikely that the company can pay on their due dates. Another typical situation is when a director is running a company recklessly with too little capital. Many Japanese court cases have imposed civil liability on directors in these situations. It can be considered as proof that the Japanese Companies Act takes the position that the directors of insolvent or near-insolvent companies owe some duty to take creditors' interest into consideration.[134]

8.4.3 China

Directors in Chinese companies generally do not bear duties to creditors when insolvency or reorganization takes place.[135] Hence, even when the company is in the zone of insolvency, directors must act primarily in the interest of the shareholders of the company, provided that such activities should not harm the national interest, public interest, and legitimate rights and interests of any other person, including creditors of the company.[136] However, if the directors abuse the independent status of the company and the limited liability of shareholders to escape debts, which "seriously damages the interests of any creditor of the company," the directors should assume joint duties as regards the company's debt to the creditors.[137] When a Chinese company finds itself in the zone of insolvency and undergoes liquidation, or is effectively bankrupt, there would be a shift in focus to the protection of legitimate third-party rights.[138]

133 *See supra* note 62 and its accompanying text.

134 *See* Goto, *supra* note 28, at 153–154.

135 *See* Zhang Xuewen, *Gongsi Pochan Bianyuan Dongshi Budang Jili de Falu Guizhi [Legal Regulation of Improper Incentives for Directors of Companies on the Brink of Corporate Bankruptcy]*, 34 Xiandai Faxue [Modern Law Science] 93, 93, 99 (2012); Allen & Overy, *Directors' Duties and Liabilities in Financial Distress During Covid-19* (July 2020), https://www.allenovery.com/global/-/media/allenovery/2_documents/news_and_insights/campaigns/directors_duties_a_global_perspective/updated_2/peoples_republic_of_china.pdf?rev=3f07fbf641a64b9e97641cfc64d61b47.

136 Company Law 2023, Arts. 1, 23, 180, 181, 232, 262.

137 *Id.* Art. 23.

138 *See* Allen & Overy, *supra* note 135. However, Chinese Company Law and Chinese Enterprise Bankruptcy Law do not explicitly mention that directors owe a duty to creditors in the zone of insolvency. *See* Zhang, *supra* note 135, at 100.

Directors, shareholders, and senior managers of the insolvent company assume civil liability if the company is insolvent due to their failure to act with diligence and honesty.[139] According to the Company Law, they are disqualified from acting as directors, supervisors or senior managers of any company for a period of three years from the end of the insolvency proceedings.[140] Directors are also jointly and severally liable to creditors for losses to the property of the company if their breach of duties makes liquidation unworkable.[141]

Apart from the Company Law, directors of listed companies in China are subject to additional rules in terms of director duties and liabilities promulgated by the China Securities Regulatory Commission (CSRC). Article 83 of the Code of Corporate Governance for Listed Companies states that a listed company should respect the legitimate rights of stakeholders, including banks and other creditors, employees, customers, suppliers, and communities, and maintain effective communication and cooperation with stakeholders to jointly promote the sustainable and healthy development of the company.[142] Moreover, if directors fail to fulfill their fiduciary duties and thus incur any major irregularity, rule-breaking act, or major risk to the company, the CSRC may order the company to remove them from their directors' positions.[143]

The Criminal Law seems harsher on the officers working in SOEs. Officers in direct charge of SOEs are subject to criminal detention or imprisonment for up to three years if they engage in irregular practices for personal interests and cause the company or enterprise's bankruptcy or serious losses.[144]

139 Enterprise Bankruptcy Law, Art. 125.

140 Company Law 2023, Art. 178(3); Enterprise Bankruptcy Law, Art. 125.

141 Wei Shen, Corporate Law in China: Structure, Governance and Regulation 272 (2015).

142 The State Council of the People's Republic of China, *Code of Corporate Governance for Listed Companies* (Sept. 30, 2018), https://www.gov.cn/gongbao/content/2019/content_5363087.htm.

143 Securities Law, Art. 152.

144 Criminal Law, Art. 168.

PART IV

Types of Firms

9

Start-Ups and Venture Capital Markets

Venture capitalists organize a venture capital (VC) fund by raising funds from investors and invest in multiple start-up companies. There are three major players: providers of risk money (investors), entrepreneurs, and a specialized financial intermediary (venture capitalist) who connects the monetary capital providers (MCPs) and the human capital providers (HCPs).

The whole structure of VC investment is two-tiered incentive bargaining between MCPs and HCPs. The first tier is the relationship between investors (MCPs) and venture capitalists (HCPs), and the second tier is the relationship between venture capitalists (MCPs) and entrepreneurs (HCPs). In other words, venture capitalists have double characteristics: HCPs in the relationship with investors and MCPs in the relationship with entrepreneurs.[1]

Section 9.1 describes the incentive bargaining between investors and venture capitalists. Section 9.2 describes the incentive bargaining between venture capitalists and entrepreneurs. Section 9.3 focuses on exits for monetary capital and for human capital. Section 9.4 compares venture habitats and the roles of government in the three countries.

9.1 Venture Capital Funds: Incentive Bargaining between GPs and LPs

VC funds are organized as limited partnerships (LPs), of which general partners (GPs) are venture capitalists and LPs are investors. The availability of the limited partnership that guarantees investors' limited liability, GPs' autonomy to run the fund, and pass-through taxation, is important to stimulate the VC market.[2]

[1] *See* Figure 9.1.

[2] *See* Jack S. Levin & Donald E. Rocap, Structuring Venture Capital, Private Equity, and Entrepreneurial Transaction ch. 10 (1997); Zenichi Shishido &

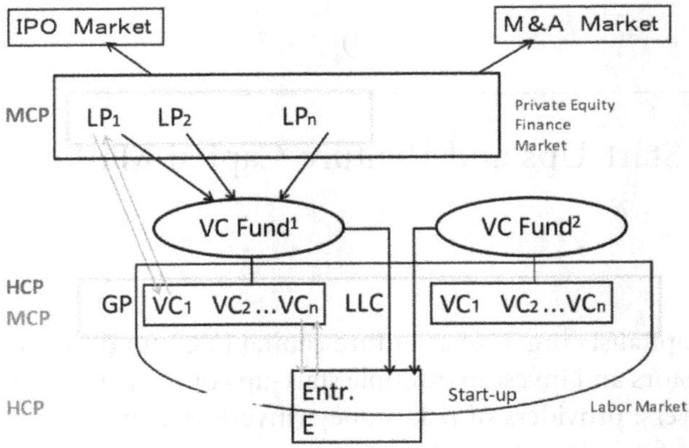

Figure 9.1 Two-tier incentive bargaining of the VC (venture capital) investment. VC fund = venture capital fund; VC = venture capitalist; IPO = initial public offering; M&A = mergers and acquisitions; Entre = entrepreneurs; E = employees; MCP = monetary capital providers; HCP = human capital providers.

LPs (investors), as the MCPs, give GPs (venture capitalists), as the HCPs, huge equity incentives, called carried interest. GPs will usually gain 20 percent profit of the VC fund for their 1 percent monetary investment. GPs also receive a management fee, which is usually around 2 percent of the amount of LPs' investment (2–20 rule).[3]

The duration of VC funds is usually ten years. After ten years, VC funds must be liquidated, and the assets will be distributed among partners according to their shares. LPs have a fixed exit right, and GPs have a time limit to manage the fund. Usually, GPs try to find start-ups to which they invest in the first five years and try to grow these portfolio companies for aiming for an early exit, either by initial public offering (IPO) or by mergers and acquisitions (M&A), in the last five years.[4]

The limited partnership as a vehicle for VC funds was introduced to Japan and China relatively recently. Now, most contractual practices, which have been developed in the United States, are used in both countries.

This section will compare particularly the following points in three countries: percentage of carried interest and management fee in practice and tax treatment; GPs' profile, for example, retired entrepreneurs,

Venture Law Forum (VLF), Bencha Kigyo no Houmu • Zaimu Senryaku [Law and Finance of Venture Companies in Japan] 136 (2010).

3 *See* Levin & Rocap, *supra* note 2; Shishido & VLF, *supra* note 2, at 164–165.

4 *See* Levin & Rocap, *supra* note 2; Shishido & VLF, *supra* note 2, at 62, 144, 412.

finance people; LPs' profile, for example, pension funds, banks, business corporations, wealthy individuals, government; LPs' monitoring right; availability of pass-through taxation.

9.1.1 The United States

VC funds are organized as limited partnerships. A VC as the GP gains equity return from the limited partnership. Typically, the VC invests 1 percent of the total investment and gains 20 percent of the fund's profit. This practice is called "carried interest" and gives the VC a hyper equity incentive. Additionally, the VC charges a management fee, usually between 1.5 and 2.5 percent of the committed capital. The carried interest has not been challenged by the Internal Revenue Service (IRS) so far, although there are some arguments.[5]

Although GPs have strong autonomy to run the VC fund, GPs give LPs certain monitoring devices, such as the investment guideline, observing the investment committee, keyman clause, disclosure of accounting books, auditing, and exercising a voice in the management of the fund.

Limited partnership agreements also include the provisions regarding GPs' expected conflicts of interest, such as self-dealing, sharing investment opportunities and exit opportunities among multiple funds that the same GPs manage, GPs' investments by their own accounts, and compensation for hands-on support for the portfolio companies.

Both GPs and LPs enjoy the benefit of pass-through taxation by organizing their VC fund as a limited partnership. The limited partnership is not a taxed entity, and each partner will be taxed on their own payoff. Partners can avoid double taxation, which is inevitable if they organize their VC fund as a corporation, and also can use the capital loss, if they suffer, to decrease their own tax.

Not only the VC fund is organized as a pass-through entity, that is, a limited partnership, but also the VC (GP) is organized as a pass-through entity, that is, limited liability company, and venture capitalists can personally enjoy pass-through taxation.

Most venture capitalists in Silicon Valley have entrepreneurial experience, while most venture capitalists outside of Silicon Valley have a financial

[5] *See* Victor Fleischer, *Two and Twenty: Taxing Partnership Profits in Private Equity Funds*, 83 N.Y.U. L. Rev. 1 (2008); Adam Lawton, *Taxing Private Equity Carried Interest Using an Incentive Stock Option Analogy*, 121 Harv. L. Rev. 846 (2008); William G. Cochran, *Searching for Diamond in the Two-and-Twenty Rough: The Taxation of Carried Interests*, 66 Stan. L. Rev. 953 (2014).

background. Such a difference among venture capitalists reflects the difference in VC investment practice in Silicon Valley and outside of Silicon Valley.

Most LPs of VC funds are institutional investors, such as pension funds and university endowments. The reformation of the Employee Retirement Income Security Act (ERISA) of 1979 and relaxation of investment regulation expanded pension funds' investment to VC funds.[6] Fund managers of institutional investors have their own track record and have a strong incentive to monitor the GP seriously.

9.1.2 Japan

The LPs, as a vehicle for venture capitalists and investors to raise funds,[7] was not available until 1998 in Japan.[8] Now, most VC funds are organized as the limited partnership sharing basic agreements between the GPs and the LPs as US counterparts.

Most Japanese VC funds adopt GP management fees and GP compensation structures that are in line with the 2–20 rule. The Japanese IRS has not challenged the practice of carried interest.

The incentive mechanism and corporate governance of many Japanese VC funds are problematic. First, most venture capitalists have no equity incentive. They are "salarymen" who are seconded to VC companies, GPs of VC funds, from their parent financial institutions. They have no incentive to take risks but have an incentive to make safe portfolio investments. LPs are either their parent financial institutions or their cross-shareholding partner companies. The share of capital being invested by institutional investors, such as pension funds, is negligible, although there is no legal restriction for pension funds to invest in VC funds. Most LPs have a weak incentive to monitor venture capitalists from the point of financial return of the funds. As a result, low IRR funds can survive.[9]

Recently, independent VC funds, which take the US-style incentive mechanism, have increased in number, and their venture capitalists personally gain carried interest by taking advantage of pass-through taxation.

[6] *See* Chapter 2, nn.14–19 and their accompanying texts.

[7] The three elements are necessary for the vehicle: LPs' limited liability, autonomy of the GP, and pass-through taxation.

[8] Before that, Japanese VC funds were forced to use either the general partnership that cannot guarantee limited liability for investors, or the Delaware limited partnership.

[9] *See* Zenichi Shishido, *Does Law Matter to Financial Capitalism? The Case of Japanese Entrepreneurs*, 37 FORDHAM INT'L L. J. 1087, 1119–1120 (2014).

The limited partnership is required to be registered. Until recently, pass-through entities, such as the limited liability partnership (LLP),[10] cannot be registered as a GP. If venture capitalists would like to enjoy pass-through taxation, they need to register themselves as GPs and accept the risk of unlimited liability. In 2023, the Ministry of Justice permitted LLPs to be registered as GPs of limited partnership,[11] then now individual venture capitalists can enjoy both pass-through taxation and limited liability as their US counterparts.

Corporate VCs have also increased, both in numbers and investment amount, because large corporations have finally recognized the importance of start-ups as their alliance partners.

9.1.3 China

The limited partnership was adopted in 2006 as a vehicle for venture capitalists and investors to raise funds.[12] Most VC funds in China are organized as limited partnerships sharing basic agreements between the GPs and the LPs as US counterparts, although Chinese limited partnerships differ in several aspects from the Delaware limited partnerships.[13]

While most Chinese VC funds follow the 2–20 rule for GP management fees and GP compensation structures, there is some variance.[14]

Many local venture capitalists have a financial background, particularly as investment bankers, without a market track record.[15] Venture capitalists are employees of VC firms, and their compensations consist of a base salary and performance-related bonuses, which include annual bonuses, project-based bonuses, project-based carried interests, co-investment returns, and employee benefits. Base salary and bonuses constitute the largest part, project-based carried interests, and employee co-investment returns occupy a relatively small portion.[16]

One unique trend of Chinese VC development is that more and more Chinese VC funds start to adopt a dual GP structure where two GPs take on management roles. This reflects the conflicts between the high market

[10] In Japan, the LLC is not a pass-through entity.

[11] Ministry of Just., Notification by Director General of the Civil Affairs Bureau (June 12, 2023).

[12] *See* Lin Lin, Venture Capital Law in China 20 (2021).

[13] *See id.* at 47–58.

[14] *See id.* at 83–86.

[15] *See id.* at 10, 65–66.

[16] *See id.* at 89.

demand for fundraising and the excessive regulation of fundraising in China, which made it extremely difficult for VC firms to get licenses, prompting these firms to appoint registered GPs as fund managers.[17]

Regarding LPs, individuals and families are the major investors in VC fundraising, partially because institutional investors have long been prohibited from making equity investments.[18] Since 2008, regulators in China have begun to relax restrictions barring institutional investors from making equity investments, and the number of institutional investors has increased.[19] Listed companies also invest in VC to acquire needed technologies to achieve strategic development.[20]

A unique characteristic of Chinese practice in VC funds is LP activism. Compared to the United States, Chinese LPs are more active and eager to participate in management, including in key decisions on the selection of portfolio companies, particularly via investment strategic committees.[21] However, recent reforms are likely to limit LP activism, such as limiting the LPs to an advisory role in an advisory committee and limiting LPs' interference with the investment decisions of the GPs.[22]

Government Guidance Funds (GGFs) have played an important role in the Chinese VC market at both the central and local levels since 2002. However, these GGFs can cause problems of excessive government intervention and flawed selection of fund managers.[23] Moreover, managers working at the GGF-backed VC firms generally earned less compared to managers at private VC firms.[24]

Although the Chinese government attempts to invite foreign investment in VC funds, its regulation of foreign funds is not aligned with the incentives of foreign investors.[25]

9.2 Start-Ups: Incentive Bargaining between Entrepreneurs and Venture Capitalists

In the second-tier incentive bargaining, venture capitalists are MCPs, and entrepreneurs are HCPs. Entrepreneurs found start-ups as stock

[17] *See id.* at 80–83.
[18] *See id.* at 21.
[19] *See id.* at 67.
[20] *See id.* at 74.
[21] *See id.* at 77.
[22] *See id.* at 80.
[23] *See id.* at 92–104.
[24] *See id.*
[25] *See id.* at 104–110.

corporations and obtained equity finance from VC funds. VC funds invest in the stock, the convertible preferred stock if it is available, of start-up companies. Venture capitalists, as GPs of VC funds, select the start-up companies they invest in and monitor the management of the start-up companies (entrepreneurs) for accelerating the growth of the companies (hands-on investment).[26]

In jurisdictions where the convertible preferred stock is not available as a legal system, such as Japan before 2000 and China, several contractual schemes are used to fix the incentive bargaining between venture capitalists and entrepreneurs without using the convertible preferred stock.[27]

Points of comparison in this section are divided into three areas: first, incentive bargaining on sharing cash flow such as stock-option, sweat equity, and liquidation preference; second, incentive bargaining on sharing control such as, how long founders keep the stock majority, how founders and venture capitalists share the board seats, veto rights, how staged financing is used; and third, contractual schemes without using the convertible preferred stock, for example, put option and VAM.[28]

9.2.1 The United States

In the second-tier incentive bargaining, venture capitalists as MCPs give entrepreneurs as HCPs huge equity incentive, so called sweat equity, while entrepreneurs give venture capitalists substantial monitoring power. This scheme is used for solving the double-moral hazard, or the two-sided agency problem, which occurs when both players expect the risk of opportunistic behavior by the opposite party, and as a result, both players hesitate to provide their own monetary or human capital.[29] We can observe the combination of incentive bargaining on sharing cash flow and incentive bargaining on sharing control between entrepreneurs and venture capitalists.[30]

[26] *See* Bernard S. Black & Ronald J. Gilson, *Venture Capital and the Structure of Capital Markets: Banks versus Stock Markets*, 47 J. FIN. ECON. 243, 252–254 (1998). Empirical studies on the relationship between VC hands-on investment and start-ups' performance show varied results. Some studies report no relationship. *See* I. C. MacMillan, D. M. Kulow & R. Kyoylian, *Venture Capitalists' Involvement in Their Investments: Extent and Performance*, 4 J. BUS. VENTURING 21 (1988). Some studies report a positive relationship. *See* H. Sapienza, *When Do Venture Capitalist Add Value?*, 7 J. BUS. VENTURING 9 (1992).

[27] *See infra* notes 44, 65 and their accompanying texts.

[28] *See infra* notes 66–69 and their accompanying texts.

[29] *See* Shishido, *supra* note 9, at 1089, 1102.

[30] *See* Steven N. Kaplan & Per Stromberg, *Financial Contracting Theory Meets the Real World: An Empirical Analysis of Venture Capital Contracts*, 70 REV. ECON. STUD. 281 (2003).

The convertible preferred stock, to which VC funds invest, plays an important role in this second-tier incentive bargaining. The convertible preferred stock can make it easier to differentiate its issuing price from that of common stock, give VC funds liquidation preference and contractual controlling rights, such as board seats and veto rights. The convertible preferred stock will be automatically converted to common stock in a qualified IPO, then venture capitalists make an exit in the stock market, and entrepreneurs realize their sweat equity and regain control from venture capitalists.[31] Several VC funds invest in the same convertible preferred stock (same series) as a syndicate investment.

By using the convertible preferred stock, the founders and VCs make incentive bargaining separately on cash flow rights and control rights. VCs organize a syndicate in each financing round and share the same interest as the same preferred stockholders. The lead VC, as the representative of investors to the same financing round, bargains with the founder.[32]

As the result of incentive bargaining on sharing cash flow, the preferred stockholders (VCs) obtain liquidation preference not only in real liquidations but also in M&A exits (deemed liquidation) and the common stockholders (the founders) obtain sweat equity, which allows the founders to keep more equity relative to their amount of investment, by differentiate the issuing price of common stock and that of preferred stock.[33] VCs also allow the founders a stock option pool for giving equity incentives to employees and newly hired persons.[34]

Regarding the difference between the issuing price of common stock and that of preferred stock, less than ten times used to be considered as the safe harbor (the 10-to-1 rule).[35] However, under the regulations IRC

[31] *See* Black & Gilson, *supra* note 26, at 243.

[32] *See* Olav Sorenson & Toby Stuart, *Syndication Networks and the Spatial Distribution of Venture Capital Investments*, 106 Am. J. Socio. 1546 (2001); Xuan Tian, *The Role of Venture Capital Syndication in Value Creation for Entrepreneurial Firms*, 16 Rev. Fin. 245 (2012); Ramana Nanda & Matthew Rhodes-Kropf, *Coordination Frictions in Venture Capital Syndicates*, *in* The Oxford Handbook of Entrepreneurship and Collaboration 352 (Jeffrey J. Reuter, Sharon Matusik & Jessica F. Jones eds., 2019).

[33] An example of sweat equity, *see* Michael J. Halloran, Robert V. Gunderson, Jr., Jorge del Calvo, Thomas W. Kintner & Julie M. Robinson, Venture Capital and Public Offering Negotiation 6–11 (3d ed. 2000).

[34] *See* Scott Kupor, *The Lack of Options for (Startup Employees') Options*, Andreessen Horowitz (June 23, 2016), https://a16z.com/the-lack-of-options-for-startup-employees-options/.

[35] *See* Ronald J. Gilson & David Schizer, *Understanding Venture Capital Structure: A Tax Explanation for Convertible Preferred Stock*, 116 Harv. L. Rev. 874, 889 (2003).

§409A of 2009, the standard for fair market value became stricter, and now the safe harbor is considered either 5-to-1 or 3-to-1.[36]

As a result of incentive bargaining on sharing control, VCs obtain contractual controlling rights while they are minority shareholders. VCs in each financing round usually obtain one board seat by using the class voting of preferred stock and veto rights on several important issues.[37] Another important mechanism for VCs to obtain actual control is staged financing.[38] The founders will have an incentive to follow VCs' advice and increase the firm's value for making the next round of financing.

On the voting right, the founders usually lose their majority voting right in early rounds and almost never keep majority voting right at the time of IPO.[39]

As a result, the founders abandon their control to VCs in the early stage for obtaining sweat equity; in other words, the founders can keep more equity than otherwise.[40] VCs are active monitors and change the CEO from the founder to a professional manager when the start-up grows to be a large organization.[41]

Although this is the classic Silicon Valley model, such a practice looks to have been changing during the last decade. A declining emphasis on active monitoring by VCs can be observed, because the flood of money into the VC industry strengthens the bargaining power of entrepreneurs, and VCs take the strategy to encourage entrepreneurs to take high risks. Broughman and Wansley call the classic Silicon Valley model the "monitor model" and call the current practice the "risk-seeking model."[42]

9.2.2 *Japan*

Start-ups in Japan have been rapidly changing since around 2010. Before that, VCs mostly invested in common stock, although Silicon Valley type

[36] Interviews by one of the authors with anonymous lawyers in Silicon Valley, Cal. (2015–2023) (on file with one of the authors).

[37] *See* Kaplan & Stromberg, *supra* note 30, at 281; *see* Shishido, *supra* note 9, at 1091.

[38] *See* Black & Gilson, *supra* note 26, at 253; PAOL GOMPERS & JOSH LERNER, THE VENTURE CAPITAL CYCLE 139 (1999); Shishido, *supra* note 9, at 1091.

[39] *See* Kaplan & Stromberg, *supra* note 30, at 310; *see* Shishido, *supra* note 9, at 1091.

[40] *See* Thomas Hellmann, *The Allocation of Control Rights in Venture Capital Contracts*, 29 RAND J. ECON. 57 (1998).

[41] *See* T. Hellmann & Manju Puri, *Venture Capital and the Professionalization of Start-up Firms: Empirical Evidence*, 57 J. FIN. 169 (2002).

[42] Brian J. Broughman & Matthew T. Wansley, *Risk-Seeking Governance*, 76 VAND. L. REV. 1299 (2023).

convertible preferred stock can be used since corporate law reformations of 2000 and 2001.[43]

Start-ups and VCs were under the shadow of the main bank system. Start-ups substantially relied on bank loans for financing risk money. Most equity finance was provided by bank subsidiary VCs. VCs required the founder's duty to stock buy-back, which resembles the president's personal guarantee in Japanese bank loan practice.[44]

Equity incentive was not widely used both for VCs and for founders. Major VCs were bank subsidiary companies, and venture capitalists were salarymen who obtained a fixed salary. Founders did not obtain sweat equity, which was considered to possibly be taxed as gift by Japanese IRS.[45]

The illiquid external labor market made entrepreneur candidates hesitate to spin off from big companies and made founders stick to the majority ownership of their companies because there were limited job opportunities outside of their companies.[46]

The illiquid M&A market made VCs risk-averse and lead them to small amount investments to later-stage companies, just as the portfolio investment, because their exit opportunities were limited to either IPOs or repurchase by the founder.[47]

Before 2010, start-ups were not recognized as an important part of the Japanese business system.

Since around 2010, however, Japanese start-ups have rapidly changed toward the Silicon Valley model.

After around 2020, most new VC investments are made to convertible preferred stock, although it is used mostly for VCs to obtain the liquidation preference, and its enforcement mechanisms, such as class voting and veto rights, are not widely used.[48]

Equity incentive is gradually accepted. Silicon Valley type independent VCs are increasing, and their venture capitalists personally gain carried

[43] *See* Shishido, *supra* note 9, at 1095.
[44] *Id.* at 1092.
[45] *Id.* at 1112; *see* SHISHIDO & VLF, *supra* note 2, at 366–375.
[46] *See* ZENICHI SHISHIDO & VENTURE LAW FORUM (VLF), SUTA-TOAPPU TOSHI KEIYAKU: MODERU KEIYAKU TO KAISETSU [JAPANESE START-UP FINANCING DOCUMENTS: ANNOTATED MODEL CONTRACTS] 5 (2020). *See also* Augustin Landier, *Start-up Financing: From Banks to Venture Capital* (U. CHI. SCH. OF BUS., Working Paper, 2003).
[47] *See* SHISHIDO & VLF, *supra* note 46, at 5.
[48] *Id.* at 13, 16.

interest by taking advantage of pass-through taxation.[49] The practice of sweat equity has been rapidly widespread since the Japanese IRS recognized the different values of common stock and preferred stock.[50]

The mentality of young elites has changed. The percentage of new graduates of elite universities who take the choice of being entrepreneurs or working at start-ups into consideration seriously is increasing.[51]

The M&A market has been gradually developing. Founders who are not sticking to IPO as an exit but consider M&A exit seriously are increasing.[52] Large companies have finally recognized that alliances with start-ups are indispensable for disruptive innovations and now consider purchasing start-ups as an important business tactic.[53] Corporate VCs are also increasing both in numbers and amount of investment.[54]

The reputational market and venture ecosystem have been developing and make incentive bargaining between founders and VCs smoother.[55] However, the practice of stock buyback duty and founders' stickiness to majority shareholding have not yet changed.[56]

9.2.3 China

Prior to 2005, convertible preferred stock was not allowed in China.[57] In December 2005, the China Securities Regulatory Commission (CSRC) enacted the Measures for the Administration of Equity Incentives of Listed Companies (effective in January 2006), which explicitly encourages the usage of stock options.[58] Under the Company Law 2018 (effective until July 1, 2024), the legality of convertible preferred stock options is still

49 *Id.* at 7.
50 *Id.*
51 *Id.* at 6.
52 *Id.*
53 *Id.*
54 *Id.* at 6–7.
55 *Id.* at 7.
56 *Id.* 13–14.
57 Before 2005, companies were prohibited from granting stock options under the Chinese law. *See* Lei Luo, *Determinants of Stock Option Use by Chinese Companies*, 31 J. Applied Bus. Rsch. 1355, 1356 (2015).
58 Measures for the Administration of Equity Incentive Plans of Listed Companies (for Trial Implementation) (promulgated by China Securities Regulatory Commission on Dec. 31, 2005, effective Jan. 1, 2006), Lawinfochina, https://www.lawinfochina.com/display.aspx?id=29161&lib=law.

undetermined. While various Chinese government agencies[59] jointly promulgated the Interim Measures for the Administration of Start-Up Investment Enterprises (effective in March 2006), which explicitly encouraged the use of convertible preferred stocks for start-ups in November 2005,[60] the Chinese Company Law still does not endorse the use of convertible preferred stocks.[61] Due to the ambiguity in the legality of the convertible preferred stock, VC practitioners in China often include contractual preference rights and convertible rights for the investors in the investment agreement, which are only protected by contract law but not Chinese Company Law.[62]

Without using the convertible preferred stock, VCs, start-up companies, and founder–shareholders agree on major items widely used in VC investment contracts in the United States, such as liquidation preferences, preemptive rights, right of first refusal, tag-along rights, drag-along rights, and veto rights, by implementing them in charters, shareholder agreements or both, although their legal enforceability is uncertain.[63] Such a situation of practices is similar to the situation in the pre-convertible preferred stock era in Japan.[64]

In addition to these US-style financial agreements, another contractual agreement, so-called Value Adjustment Mechanism (VAM), is widely used as an enforcement mechanism. A VAM is a contractual agreement

[59] These agencies include the State Development & Reform Commission, Ministry of Science & Technology, Ministry of Finance, Ministry of Commerce, People's Bank of China, State Administration of Taxation, State Administration for Industry and Commerce, China Banking Regulatory Commission, China Securities Regulatory Commission, and State Administration for Foreign Exchange.

[60] Interim Measures for the Administration of Start-Up Investment Enterprises (promulgated by State Development & Reform Commission, Ministry of Science & Technology, Ministry of Finance, etc. on Nov. 11, 2005, effective Mar. 1, 2006), LAWINFOCHINA, http://www.lawinfochina.com/display.aspx?lib=law&id=4738&CGid=.

[61] In fact, the Chinese Company Law does not explicitly allow a company to issue convertible preferred stock under the "one share one vote principle." The interim measure authorizing issuance of convertible preferred stock ranks lower in terms of legal hierarchy than the Chinese Company Law, which is made by the National People's Congress. Company Law 2018, Arts. 103, 125, and 126.

[62] *See* LIN, *supra* note 12, at 178, 210. Some scholars also argue that preferred stock in China did not function well because China lacks stringent securities regulations and a stock market-centered economy market to facilitate the effective usage of convertible preferred stock provisions. *See* Olivia-Nathale Adamski, Convertible Preferred Stock: Testing the Legal Framework of the US Venture Capital Model in China (LL.M. thesis, University of British Columbia, 2015) (on file with University of British Columbia Library).

[63] *See* LIN, *supra* note 12, at 148–177.

[64] *See* SHISHIDO & VLF, *supra* note 2, at 231–260.

between the VC fund and its portfolio company's shareholders (often the largest shareholder, controller, or the founder). The VC fund can adjust the valuation of the company without incurring additional costs, for example, by receiving cash compensation paid jointly and severally by the company and its founders or shareholders if the agreed conditions (listing or financial performance) are not met.[65]

Although Professor Lin observes VAMs are only prevalent in the Chinese market,[66] the stock buyback duty of the founder–shareholder, which was widely used in the pre-convertible preferred stock era and is still retained to be used in Japan, is very similar to the Chinese VAM. Both were invented as an investor's self-help contractual mechanism in the absence of sufficient legal institutions, particularly the convertible preferred stock, and have problematic effects on the relationship between VCs and founders.

However, the laws regarding the legality of preferred stocks are changing. The new Chinese Company Law of 2023 (effective July 1, 2024) explicitly allows the issuance of different classes of stocks[67] which could include preferred stocks,[68] stocks with voting rights different from those of ordinary stocks,[69] or restricted stocks.[70] Although the preferred stock, including class voting and veto rights, is permitted, whether the convertible stock is permitted or not is still ambiguous.

9.3 Exits

Availability of exits for human capital and monetary capital influences the ways of incentive bargaining between HCPs and MCPs.

The existence of a liquid external labor market decreases the risk of entrepreneurs because it makes it easier for them to find jobs even if they fail their enterprises and enables them to cede control to venture capitalists more easily.[71] By obtaining control of portfolio companies, venture capitalists can decrease their risk of investment in private equity and can leave entrepreneurs with a larger equity share.[72]

65 *See* LIN, *supra* note 12, at 177–179.
66 *Id.* at 146, 178.
67 Company Law 2023, Art. 144.
68 *Id.*, Art. 144(1).
69 *Id.*, Art. 144(2).
70 *Id.*, Art. 144(3).
71 *See* Landier, *supra* note 46.
72 *See* Hellmann & Puri, *supra* note 41.

The degree of availability of exit by IPO and M&A affects the strategy of venture capitalists on how to incentivize entrepreneurs and to decrease their risk. Particularly, the existence of a liquid M&A market decreases the risk for venture capitalists and enables them to give entrepreneurs more equity share. The illiquid M&A market incentivizes venture capitalists to seek alternative exits, such as a put option.[73]

This section will compare exit options for monetary capital: IPO, M&A, secondary market, and put option; and exits for human capital, that is, liquidity of the external labor market.

9.3.1 The United States

The United States has a liquid external labor market for HCPs, both founders and employees, to exit from a start-up company. Particularly, in Silicon Valley, changing companies frequently is the norm.[74] California Business and Professions Code §16600 that prohibits covenants not to compete is considered to contribute to an increase in the liquidity of the external labor market and venture spin-offs in Silicon Valley.[75] The experience of failure from taking a risk to start a business is appreciated.[76] It is easy for failed entrepreneurs to find a next job that pays more than their previous jobs.[77] Such a liquid external labor market encourages the entrepreneur candidates to take a risk of quitting a current job and start a new business.

Regarding exits for MCPs, besides National Association of Securities Dealers Automated Quotations (NASDAQ), the top IPO market in the world, the M&A market is very liquid in the United States. While the number of exits by M&As is significantly higher than those by IPOs, the total cash proceeds raised by M&A exits are only slightly more compared to IPO exits.[78] Large companies are eager to purchase start-ups with new

[73] *See* Shishido & VLF, *supra* note 46, at 5.

[74] *See* Annalee Saxenian, Regional Advantage: Culture and Competition in Silicon Valley and Rout 128 (1994).

[75] *See* Ronald J. Gilson, *The Legal Infrastructure of High Technology Industrial Districts, Silicon Valley, Route 128, and Covenants Not to Compete*, 74 N.Y.U. L. Rev. 575 (1999).

[76] *See* Saxenian, *supra* note 74.

[77] *See* Landier, *supra* note 46.

[78] In the fourth quarter of 2019, there were 20 IPO exits and 153 M&A exits. In the first quarter of 2020, there were 15 IPO exits and 154 M&A exits. CBINSIGHTS, *Q1'20 M&A And IPO Trends in the US* (May 7, 2020), https://www.cbinsights.com/research/mergers-acquisitions-ipos-us-startups/. Regarding the total cash proceeds, M&A exit size was about 150 billion in 2020 while IPO exit size was about 117 billion in 2020. Kevin Dowd & Peter Walker, *State of Private Markets: Q1 2023*, Carta (May 1, 2023),

technology, rather than to develop new technologies in-house. It is often better for founders, too, to expand their business under the umbrella of a big company more quickly.[79]

M&As are usually made in the form of a reverse triangular merger, by which the acquired company turns into a wholly owned subsidiary of the acquiring company. The shareholders of the acquired company, that is, the founder, employees, VCs, obtain the stock of the acquiring company, which does not need to use cash.[80]

Secondary markets, which provide founders and employees with liquidity of their stocks before IPO, are also being developed. Secondary sales of founder equity have become increasingly common and are recognized as schemes of providing founders with an environment to take risks.[81]

9.3.2 Japan

The Japanese external labor market has been illiquid because of the lifetime employment system and the company community norm. Once an employee of a large company quit his job to start his company, he not only could not go back to his previous company but also could not find another job with equivalent pay as his previous company, if his company fails. There are fewer spin-off cases compared in the United States.[82] Such an illiquid external labor market makes not only entrepreneur candidates risk-averse but also founders stick to keeping control of their companies.[83]

Although the liquidity of the Japanese external labor market is gradually increasing, it is still not as liquid as that in the United States.

https://carta.com/blog/state-of-private-markets-q1-2023/; James Thorne, *Silicon Valley's Banner Year on Wall Street Reshapes IPO Landscape*, PitchBook (Dec. 9, 2020), https://pitchbook.com/news/articles/silicon-valleys-banner-year-on-wall-street-reshapes-ipo-landscape.

79 As a good example, Cisco Systems acquired many start-ups, which have technologies fitting to a part of Cisco's router network. For instance, in 2023, Cisco acquired Code BGP, which allows Cisco ThousandEyes to expand its BGP monitoring capabilities. Cisco also acquired Valtix to incorporate its cloud network security technology into Cisco's Security Cloud portfolio. CISCO, *Acquisitions by Year*, https://www.cisco.com/c/en/us/about/corporate-strategy-office/acquisitions/acquisitions-list-years.html.

80 *See* Shishido & VLF, *supra* note 46, at 295–297.

81 *See* Broughman & Wansley, *supra* note 42, at 6.

82 *See* Alan Hyde, Working in Silicon Valley: Economic and Legal Analysis of a High-Velocity Labor Market (2003).

83 *See* Shishido & VLF, *supra* note 46, at 5.

Japanese IPO markets have rapidly developed since the launch of the Mothers Market (now Growth Market) in the Tokyo Stock Exchange in 1999. The Mothers Market is one of the easiest IPO markets in the world, with its low requirements for listing. Although the Mothers Market has contributed a lot to the development of the Japanese start-up industry, its low requirements for listing[84] encourage founders to make immature IPOs, and are criticized as the major cause of too many small-cap listed companies and just a few unicorns.

The biggest problem of the exit for MCPs in Japan is its small M&A market. Under the shadow of the company community norm,[85] founders dislike to sell their companies and large companies seek to in-house development of new technology without acquiring high-tech start-ups.[86]

Such an illiquid M&A market makes VCs risk-averse and gives them an incentive to make small investments in many later-stage companies because their investments are inevitably very risky all-or-nothing ones.[87]

Although the Japanese M&A market is gradually developing, it is still not as liquid as the US counterpart.

Also, secondary markets have not yet been developed.

9.3.3 *China*

Traditionally, China's stock markets do not provide enough exit channels for VC investors since the two Main Boards set stringent listing requirements for start-ups.[88] The Small and Medium Enterprise (SME) Board was established in 2004, and a new NASDAQ-like secondary board, ChiNext, was launched in 2009.[89] Since 2013, the National Equities Exchange and Quotation System (NEEQ), known as the New Third Board, has become an important exit channel for VC-backed start-up companies.[90] In July 2019, the Shanghai Stock Exchange established the Science and Technology Innovation Board ("STAR Board"), the

84 The listing requirement to the Growth Market is more than 500 million yen ($3.3 million) circulating stock.

85 Regarding the company community, *see* Chapter 2, n.124; Zenichi Shishido, *Japanese Corporate Governance: The Hidden Problems of Corporate Law and Their Solutions*, 25 DEL. J. CORP L. 185, 201–205 (2000).

86 *See* SHISHIDO & VLF, *supra* note 46, at 5–6.

87 *Id.* at 5.

88 *See* LIN, *supra* note 12, at 12.

89 *Id.* at 19–20.

90 *Id.* at 21.

NASDAQ-equivalent public board, for start-ups to raise capital.[91] The STAR Market is the first Chinese stock market to allow companies with dual-class share structures to get listed.[92] Companies have begun to take advantage of this opportunity, with UCloud Technology Ltd. being the first company to list on the new board with a dual-class share structure in April 2019.[93] Nowadays, the STAR Board and the ChiNext Board are the most popular IPO venues for start-ups. Among the 534 IPO exits in 2020, 145 (28 percent) IPOs are from the STAR Board, and 107 (20 percent) IPOs are from the ChiNext Board.[94]

M&A is considered to be a less feasible exit option compared to IPO in China for three reasons. First, local governments can use their administrative powers to delay or obstruct M&A activities, especially those related to SOEs.[95] In addition, foreign M&A activities face tight scrutiny. Under the Provisions on Foreign Investors' Merger and Acquisition of Domestic Enterprises, any M&A activity by foreign-invested enterprises requires approval from the Ministry of Commerce (MOFCOM) or a provincial department in charge of commerce.[96] Second, the Chinese government has exerted stringent control over debt financing, which makes it difficult to finance M&A deals with debt. According to Article 20(3) of the General Rules for Loans issued by the People's Bank of China in 1996, bank loans cannot be used to fund equity investments.[97] Thus, this is an enormous obstacle for VC firms seeking debt financing in M&A activities. Third, leveraged buyouts (LBOs) by foreign funds also attract MOFCOM's scrutiny, as evident by the failed LBO of state-owned construction company Xugong by Carlyle.[98] The deal raised political concerns that the Chinese government was selling state assets to foreigners too cheaply.[99] Even though Carlyle reduced its offer from 85 to 45 percent of the equity, the MOFCOM still did not grant approval for the LBO.[100]

91 *See* Gary Hui, *China Venture Capital Market and Exit Environment*, WILSHIRE (2021), https://assets-global.website-files.com/60f8038183eb84c40e8c14e9/61aea87ee9d5fad821f7295f_China-Venture-Capital-Market-and-Exit-Environment.pdf.

92 *See* LIN, *supra* note 12, at 247.

93 *Id.*

94 *See* Hui, *supra* note 91, at ex. 7.

95 *See* LIN, *supra* note 12, at 281.

96 *Id.*

97 *Id.* at 282.

98 *Id.* at 284.

99 *Id.*

100 *Id.*

Nonetheless, the number of M&A exits in the VC industry has been increasing in recent years, especially when the stock market is not performing well.[101] The number of M&A exits has increased significantly from 462 in 2014–to 1,823 in 2020, while the number of IPO exits in 2020 is only 992.[102] Furthermore, on March 7, 2014, the State Council issued a new Opinion on Further Optimizing the Market Environment for the Merger and Restructuring of Enterprises (Opinion) that aimed at reducing the scope of projects subject to government approval and removing the pre-examination procedure for takeover reports of listed companies.[103] In addition, a mandatory 75 percent loan-to-deposit ratio was removed under the 2015 amendments to the Law of the People's Republic of China on Commercial Banks, which may lead Chinese banks to lend more.[104] Overall, M&A as an exit option is gaining popularity among VC investors.[105]

9.4 Venture Ecosystem and the Role of Government

There are several geographic areas in the world where entrepreneurs, venture capitalists, and other important players in supporting start-ups gather. At the same time, abundant risk money is provided to those areas. All these factors are organically bonded, and we will call these areas "venture ecosystems" that provide start-ups with a good environment to grow fast.[106]

No venture ecosystem arises spontaneously except in Silicon Valley. There are very few areas in the world where all three indispensable factors for VC markets: risk money, entrepreneurs, and venture capitalists, exist from the beginning. Therefore, governments need to play some role in growing VC markets in their countries.[107] Many governments in the world have made trials and errors in the history of VC markets.

[101] *See* Qu Yunxu & Denise Jia, *Private Equity in China Heads for Exits amid Three-Year Stock Slump*, NIKKEI (Feb. 6, 2024), https://asia.nikkei.com/Spotlight/Caixin/Private-equity-in-China-heads-for-exits-amid-three-year-stock-slump.

[102] *See* Hui, *supra* note 91.

[103] *See* LIN, *supra* note 12, at 287.

[104] *Id.* at 288.

[105] *See* Hui, *supra* note 91, at ex. 5.

[106] *See* SHISHIDO & VLF, *supra* note 2, at 104–126.

[107] *See* Ronald J. Gilson, *Engineering a Venture Capital Market: Lessons from American Experience*, 55 STAN. L. REV. 1067 (2003).

Professor Ronald Gilson provides a useful prescription regarding how governments should engineer a VC market. There are two things for governments to do: inducing the development of the necessary specialized financial intermediaries (venture capitalists) and providing risk money. Then, entrepreneurs will reveal themselves. At the same time, Professor Gilson gives governments a warning not to make direct funding by themselves, but to let VCs choose portfolio companies and maintain the pattern of intense incentives coupled with intense monitoring.[108]

Governments also play an important role in growing venture ecosystems by providing legal infrastructure, IPO markets, and physical infrastructures, such as incubation facilities.

Points of comparative study in this section include: current situation of venture ecosystems; legal infrastructure, for example, availability of limited partnership, availability of convertible preferred stock, tax treatment of carried interest and sweat equity; IPO markets; physical infrastructures, for example, incubating facilities, start-up campuses, cluster towns; government subsidies; and role of universities as incubators of deep tech start-ups.

9.4.1 The United States

Silicon Valley is the most successful venture ecosystem in the world. All indispensable players for the start-up and VC industry gather in a relatively narrow geographic area. Huge amount of money flooded into the area. All these factors are organically bonded, and the incentive bargaining among the players is made economically efficient. Much research on this ecosystem has been published[109] and not only other states in the United States but also other countries in the world have tried to learn from the Silicon Valley success and implement the system in their own states and countries.

Contrary to the general impression, the US federal government has played an important role in stimulating the VC industry and nurturing start-up companies.

During the Cold War, governmental projects for defense and aerospace purposes supported technology developments and innovations in

[108] *Id.*

[109] *See, e.g.*, SAXENIAN, *supra* note 74; *see* GOMPERS & LEARNER, *supra* note 38; CHONG-MOON LEE, WILLIAM F. MILLER, MARGUERITE GONG HANCOCK & HENRY S. ROWEN, THE SILICON VALLEY EDGE: A HABITAT FOR INNOVATION AND ENTREPRENEURSHIP (2000); HYDE, *supra* note 82.

the fields of aviation, space, nuclear power, electronics, computing, and the Internet, for which start-ups played important roles.[110]

The Small Business Innovation Research (SBIR) program, which started in 1982, and the Small Business Technology Transfer (STTR) program, which started in 1992, award over $3 billion to small businesses annually.[111]

The Amendment of the ERISA in 1979 deregulated the "prudent man" rule governing pension fund investments and significantly increased funds flowing into the VC industry.[112]

The Bayh–Dole Act of 1980 stimulated the commercialization of the research results originating from universities and supported start-up companies springing out of university research, particularly in biotech.[113]

The Creating Helpful Incentives to Produce Semiconductors and Science Act of 2022 (CHIPS Act) provides significant support to start-up companies in semiconductor research and development (R&D).[114]

A lot of local governments have also tried to stimulate venture habitats and create venture ecosystems like Silicon Valley. A successful case is the Massachusetts Life Sciences Center, whose project started in 2008 and successfully transformed the life science cluster in Boston into a venture ecosystem.

9.4.2 Japan

Since the 1980s, the Japanese government, particularly the Ministry of International Trade and Industry (MITI, now the Ministry of Economic, Trade, and Industries [Japan] [METI]), has tried to stimulate start-ups and the VC industry with governmental funds, tax incentives, and the improvement of legal systems. Those policies, however, did not have a significant impact, probably because start-ups had not been recognized as key players in the Japanese business system, and most governmental policies did not sufficiently take incentive points into consideration.

Although the Japanese start-up and VC industry finally took off in the 2010s and large companies recognized the importance of start-ups as their alliance partners, their growth was much slower than not only the

[110] *See* Chapter 2, nn.7–10 and their accompanying texts.
[111] *See* Chapter 2, nn.12–13 and their accompanying texts.
[112] *See* Chapter 2, nn.14–19 and their accompanying texts.
[113] *See* Chapter 2, nn.20–21 and their accompanying texts.
[114] *See* Chapter 2, nn.22–25 and their accompanying texts.

United States, but also Germany, France, England, Singapore, and Korea. The Japanese government felt a sense of danger and prioritized the start-up and VC industry in its industrial policy. The Kishida Administration started the Five-year Program of Promoting Start-Ups in 2023, which tries to improve the institutional infrastructure of start-ups and VC investments, including a one trillion yen (approximately, $67 billion) budget for subsidizing the VC industry.[115] Local governments are also competing to create venture ecosystems.[116]

Venture habitat has gradually matured. The number of serial entrepreneurs is increasing, and they are beginning to play an important role as angel investors and mentors. Start-up-related events, such as pitches and networking parties, are held almost every day somewhere in Tokyo and other cities. The human network has been rapidly expanded, and the reputational market has been created.[117]

9.4.3 *China*

In the 1980s, the Chinese government sought to replicate the US success in developing an effective VC market. Several government-backed VC firms were set up to provide financing to high-tech start-ups.[118]

One special type of government involvement in China's VC market is the GGF set up by either the central or local governments.[119] GGFs include the government-oriented industry guidance fund, the State VC Investment Guidance Fund, and the SME Technology Innovation Fund.[120] Local governments tend to set up a management or investment committee to be the highest decision maker of the fund, headed by senior officers of the local government.[121] GGFs generally will establish a separate management office to manage the daily operation of the fund.[122] Alternatively, GGF can delegate the management of the fund to

115 *See* Shishido & VLF, *supra* note 46, at 8.

116 For example, Tokyo Metropolitan announced to develop huge start-up incubation facility in Tokyo. Nikkei, *Tokyo Formulates Startup Strategy, Establishes Support Bases, etc.* (Nov. 24, 2022), https://www.nikkei.com/article/DGXZQOCC245W50U2A121C200000/0.

117 *See* Shishido & VLF, *supra* note 46, at 7–8.

118 *See* Lin, *supra* note 12, at 16–17.

119 *See id.* at 92.

120 *See id.*

121 *See id.*

122 *See id.*

professional financial institutions.[123] The number of GGFs has increased rapidly due to a surge in demand for capital. In 2016 alone, 547 new GGFs were established, and the total fund size exceeded 3.5 trillion renminbi (RMB) (about USD 486 billion).[124]

The Chinese central government has gradually moved toward a "Government Led plus Market Operation" model in providing public funding starting in 2014.[125] Instead of directing the operations of the government-backed funds, the central government starts to position itself as a limited participant by only providing funding.[126]

The rapid development of the VC industry in China demonstrates that governments can facilitate the creation of a VC market via appropriately calibrated governmental interventions.[127] Importantly, the government should limit its role to providing funding while leaving fund management to private financial professionals who possess the right incentives.[128]

Moreover, the Chinese government also provides support for VC companies in particular industries. For instance, to mobilize resources into high-tech industries, the Chinese government launched the 2006 Medium and Long-Term Plan for Science and Technology and created the National IC Fund of 2014.[129] The Chinese new wave of regional policies aims to create urban high-tech clusters that seek to connect multiple medium-large cities instead of allowing a single, huge, core city to develop.[130]

From 1980 to 2018, total donations to Chinese universities reached 32 billion RMB (USD 4.5 billion).[131] Compared to the United States, the size of university endowment funds in China is much smaller, and as a result, the universities' participation in the VC market is more limited. One example of such participation is the Tsinghua University Education Foundation's VC investments in Qidi VC (now THG Ventures).[132]

123 *See id.* at 93.
124 *See id.* at 94.
125 *See id.* at 22.
126 *See id.*
127 *See id.* at 43.
128 *See id.*
129 *See* Chapter 2, nn.77–83 and their accompanying texts.
130 *See* Chapter 2, nn.96–98 and their accompanying texts.
131 *See* Lin, *supra* note 12, at 73.
132 *See id.* at 74.

10

Listed Family Firms

When we talk about listed companies, we usually imagine the Berle and Means type of dispersed ownership company, but it is not necessarily the typical listed company in the real world. Actually, the prevalence of family firms among listed companies is a worldwide phenomenon, not only in emerging countries but also in developed countries.[1]

Characteristics of listed family firms vary depending on the country, although there is some diversification in a country. Many regional studies and comparative studies on listed family firms have been made in many different countries.[2]

Interestingly, the typical characteristic of listed family firms in a certain country is a mirror reflecting its corporate governance practice, markets, social norms, and law.[3]

In this chapter, we will compare listed family firms in the three major economies, focusing on the relationship between their stock ownership structure and their management, their performance compared to listed non-family firms, and their implication for corporate governance practice in each country.

[1] *See* Stijn Claessens, Simeon Djankov & Larry H. P. Lang, *The Separation of Ownership and Control in East Asian Corporations*, 58 J. Fin. Econ. 81 (2000); Mara Faccio & Larry H. P. Lang, *The Ultimate Ownership of Western European Corporations*, 65 J. Fin. Econ. 365 (2002); Ronald C. Anderson & David M. Reeb, *Founding Family Ownership and Performance: Evidence from the S&P 500*, 58 J. Fin. 1301 (2003); Takuji Saito, *Family Firms and Firm Performance: Evidence from Japan*, 22 J. Japanese & Int'l. Econ. 620 (2008); Hokuto Dazai, Takuji Saito, Zenichi Shishido & Noriyuki Yanagawa, *Corporate Governance and Firm Performance: An Implication from Japanese Listed Family Firms*, 16 Asian J. L. & Econ. (forthcoming 2025).

[2] *See, e.g.*, Vipin Gupta, Nancy Levenburg, Lynda Moore, Jaideep Motwani & Thomas Schwarz, *Anglo vs. Asian Family Business: A Cultural Comparison and Analysis*, 3(2) J. Asia Bus. Stud. 46 (2009); Nugroho Sukamdani, *Family Business Dynamics in Southeast Asia: A Comparative Study of Indonesia, Malaysia, Singapore, and Thailand*, 11 J. Asean Stud. 197 (2023).

[3] *See* Dazai et al., *supra* note 1, at ch. 5, ch. 7.

Section 10.1 introduces typical types of listed family firms in the three countries, particularly from the perspective of the relationship between stock ownership structure and management. Section 10.2 compares the economic performance of listed family firms, particularly non-founder firms, and that of listed non-family firms in the three countries. Section 10.3 considers implications of the typical type of listed non-founder firms and their relative performance to that of listed non-family firms to the corporate governance in general of each country.

10.1 Types of Listed Family Firms: Relationship between Stock Ownership Structure and Management

In most listed family firm studies, the listed family firm is defined as a listed company in which the founder or the founder's heir is a senior manager (president or chair) and/or the founding family is a large shareholder.[4] The cut-off line of stock ownership of listed family firm studies is different, reflecting the stock ownership structure in each region.[5] Studies on Europe and Asia mostly use 20 percent,[6] and studies on the United States and Canada mostly use 5 percent.[7] Studies on Japan mostly use more relaxed cut-off lines than other regions, such as among the top ten largest shareholders, because the stock ownership structure of Japanese listed family firms is the most dispersed in the world.[8]

Listed family firms can be categorized into founder firms, in which the founder is a senior manager, and non-founder firms, in which the founding family keeps influence over management by substantial ownership and/or heir manager after the founder retires. Non-founder firms can be further

4 *See, e.g.*, Mengyuan Chen, Jason Zezhong Xiao & Yang Zhao, *Confucianism, Successor Choice, and Firm Performance in Family Firms: Evidence from China*, 69 J. Corp. Fin. 1 (2021); Wangfeng Zhang & Lihong Cao, *Family Involvement, Internal Control and Agency Costs – Evidences from China's Listed Family Firms*, 7 Persp. in Sci. 45 (2016); Salvatore Sciascia, Pietro Mazzola, Joseph H. Astrachan & Torsten Pieper, *Family Involvement in the Board of Directors: Effects on Sales Internationalization*, 51 J. Small Bus. Mgmt. 83 (2013).

5 Listed firms with more than 20% family ownership are 26% of the total listed in Continental Europe, 23% in North America, 45% in East Asia, and only 5% in Japan. Rafael La Porta, Florencio Lopez-de-Silanes & Andrei Shleifer, *Corporate Ownership around the World*, 54 J. Fin. 471 (1999).

6 *Id.*

7 *See* Anderson & Reeb, *supra* note 1; Belen Villalonga & Raphael Amit, *How Do Family Ownership, Control and Management Affect Firm Value?*, 80 J. Fin. Econ. 385 (2006).

8 *See* Dazai et al., *supra* note 1, at ch. 3, sec. 2.

categorized into three types:[9] firms with family ownership and family management, firms with family ownership without family management, and firms with family management without family ownership.

The typical type of family firms is a firm with family ownership and family management. The possible benefit of such a firm is to minimize the owner–manager agency problem, while the possible cost is that of the large shareholders–small shareholders agency problem.[10] The large shareholders may pursue action for private benefits at the expense of other shareholders and firm performance.[11]

10.1.1 The United States

Family firms[12] constitute over 35 percent of the Standard and Poor's 500 (S&P 500) companies and, on average, families own nearly 18 percent of their firms' outstanding equity.[13] Family control and influence in the S&P 500 can be even more extensive than these ownership levels suggest.[14] For example, in firms where the family does not have outright majority ownership, their control of board seats is 2.75 times greater than their equity stake would indicate.[15] A full one-third of all Fortune 500 companies are family-controlled, and about 60 percent of publicly traded firms remain under family influence.[16]

Among the family firms within the S&P 500, 45.0% of the chief executive officers (CEOs) are family members and 55.0% are professional

9 Parissa Haghirian, Routledge Handbook of Japanese Business and Management 50 (2016).

10 *See* Rafael La Porta, Florencio Lopez-de-Silanes, Andrei Shleifer & Robert W. Vishny, *Investor Protection and Corporate Valuation*, 57 J. Fin. 1147 (2002); Stijn Claessens, Simeon Djankov, Joseph P. H. Fan & Larry H. P. Lang, *Disentangling the Incentive and Entrenchment Effects of Large Shareholdings*, 57 J. Fin. 2741 (2002); Benjamin Maury, *Family Ownership and Firm Performance: Empirical Evidence from Western European Corporations*, 12 J. Corp. Fin. 321 (2006); Dazai et al., *supra* note 1, at ch. 2.

11 *See* Andrei Shleifer & Robert W. Vishny, *A Survey of Corporate Governance*, 52 J. Fin. 737 (1997); Hokuto Dazai, Takuji Saito, Zenichi Shishido & Noriyuki Yanagawa, *Family Firms and the Professional Manager Market*, SSRN (2016), https://papers.ssrn.com/sol3/papers.cfm?abstract_id=2811057.

12 A notable 90% of businesses in the United States are family businesses (approximately 17 million), employing 59% of the workforce and accounting for 49% of the country's gross domestic product. Ernesto J. Poza, Family Business 1, 28 (2013).

13 *See* Anderson & Reeb, *supra* note 1.

14 *See Id.*

15 *Id.*

16 Poza, *supra* note 12.

managers.[17] Of the 45.0% family CEOs, 14.5% are founders and 30.4% are founders' heirs.[18] Family firms, on average, are smaller than non-family firms.[19]

When the founders retire, they tend to hire a professional manager and sell out their shares.[20] Therefore, the prevalence of family firms in the United States is relatively low compared to other countries. Still, 47 percent of listed companies are family firms. Professional managers manage the majority of non-founder family firms.[21] Heir-managing family firms often use dual-class stock to keep control.[22]

10.1.2 Japan

According to a study of Japanese listed family firms[23] which covers firms listed on the first and the second section of the Tokyo Stock Exchange during the period from 1991 to 2020, non-family firms and family firms were almost 50 percent each, on a cumulative total number of firm-year basis. Its definition of the listed family firm is the listed firm in which the founding-family member is the senior manager, either president or chairman, and/or the founding family is within the top ten largest shareholders.[24] The study categorizes listed family firms into three types: founder firm, in which the founder is alive;[25] heir-managing firm, in which a family member is the senior manager; and non-heir-managing firm, in which the founding family is among the top ten shareholders but non-family members are the senior managers. Among listed family firms,

17 Anderson & Reeb, *supra* note 1, at 1314.

18 *Id.*

19 *Id.*

20 *See* Dazai et al., *supra* note 11.

21 *See* Ronald C. Anderson, Augustine Duru & David M. Reeb, *Founders, Heirs, and Corporate Opacity in the United States*, 92 J. Fin. Econ. 205–222 (2009).

22 *See* Belen Villalonga & Raphael H. Amit, *How Are U.S. Family Firms Controlled?*, 22 Rev. Fin. Stud. 3047 (2009).

23 *See* Dazai et al., *supra* note 1.

24 On average, family ownership of heir-managing firms is 13.052 percent. Most heir-managing firms (82.7%) have less than 20% family ownership, and a significant number (37.0%) have less than 5% family ownership. The less than 5 percent group includes companies with negligible or unknown family ownership, that is, founding families are not within the top ten largest shareholders. The average ratio of the tenth largest shareholder is 1.639 percent. *Id.* at ch. 3.

25 The study takes the wider definition of "founder firm" than most family-firm studies to exclude the indirect influence of the founder, which may distort the result of the performance analysis of heir-managing firms. *Id.*

founder firms were 41%; heir-managing firms were 46%; non-heir-managing firms were 13%.[26]

There are many listed family firms, in which founding families have no substantial voting rights but keep senior management positions. Dual-class voting stock and pyramidal ownership structure are not available in Japan.[27] Therefore, once the founding family decreases its ownership share, mostly because of either large equity financing or a high inheritance tax rate, it loses control by voting rights. The question of why founding families can keep senior manager positions even after losing substantial ownership in Japan is often raised.[28]

Also, the family members often participate directly in management rather than supervising outside management as major shareholders after the founder's death. This is another peculiar trend for Japanese family firms that differs from the global trend.[29]

10.1.3 China

Regarding the definition of family firms, among the literature on listed family firms in China, a widely used definition of a family firm is a private enterprise whose ultimate owner is either an individual or a family and holds the largest ownership stake.[30] The family's ultimate ownership should be over 20 percent.[31]

Unlike other economies, family business is relatively new in China since China just began its transformation from a planned to a market-oriented economy in 1978. In 1981, China's communist party clearly stated, for the first time, that some private enterprises were necessary complement to the public (state) ownership economy, and since then, the private sector has grown rapidly and has played an increasingly important role in maintaining China's rapid economic development.[32]

[26] *Id.*

[27] *See* Morten Bennedsen, Vikas Mehrotra, Jungwook Shim & Yupana Wiwattanakantang, *Dynastic Control without Ownership: Evidence from Post-War Japan*, 142 J. Fin. Econ. 831 (2021).

[28] *Id.*

[29] *See* Mike Burkart, Fausto Panunzi & Andrei Shleifer, *Family Firms*, 58 J. Fin. 2167 (2003).

[30] *See* Chen et al., *supra* note 4, at 6.

[31] *See* Zhang & Cao, *supra* note 4, at 47.

[32] *See* Di Cai, Jin-hui Luo & Di-fang Wan, *Family CEOs: Do They Benefit Firm Performance in China?*, 29 Asia Pac. J. Mgmt. 926 (2012).

Chinese family firms are going through rapid growth both in quantity and in firm size. The number of Chinese listed family firms was 2,327 in 2018, accounting for 64.5 percent of total listed firms.[33] Most listed family firms in China are controlled through pyramids.[34] Family owners usually have less than full ownership of the intermediate firms along the pyramids, so they hold excessive control over ownership, causing family ownership and family control to diverge.[35] In the face of weak shareholder protection afforded by formal institutions in China, Chinese family owners usually prefer to appoint family members as CEOs to guarantee control and protect their interests.[36] From 2004 to 2007, 90.5 percent of listed family firms in China were controlled through pyramids, and 54.4 percent were managed by family CEOs.[37] On average, family owners hold 25.6 percent ownership, as measured by cash-flow rights, but 36.4% control, as measured by control rights.[38] Approximately 52.7 percent of family firms have a non-family large shareholder with at least 10 percent ownership.[39] That is, 52.7 percent of firms have multiple-large shareholder structures.[40] These non-family large shareholders tend to be state-owned and institutionally held shareholders.[41] Non-family shareholders generally favor multiple-large shareholder structures because they can more effectively balance family owners' power compared to the situation where the family has the sole dominant ownership.[42]

[33] Kefan Lu, Non-Family CEO Compensation and Firm Performance: Evidence from Chinese Listed Family Firms 1 (M.S. dissertation, Cornell University, 2020) (on file with Cornell University Library eCommons).

[34] *See* Cai et al., *supra* note 32, at 926.

[35] *See id.*

[36] *See id.* at 926–927.

[37] *Id.* at 927.

[38] *Id.*

[39] *Id.* at 927–928.

[40] *Id.* at 928. Another study also shows that multiple-large shareholders (MLS) in Chinese family firms are common. In Chinese family firms, the average ratio of shares held by the controlling shareholder is about 32.14%, and 11.96% and 5.13% are held by the second and the third largest shareholders, respectively. Gongmeng Chen, Michael Firth & Liping Xu, *Does the Type of Ownership Control Matter? Evidence from China's Listed Companies*, 33 J. Banking & Fin. 171 (2009).

[41] Institutionally held shareholders include institutional investors and the holders of foreign individual shares and foreign corporate shares. Huaili Lv & Wanli Li, *Collusions in Chinese Family Firms: An Informal Institution-Based View of Multiple Large Shareholders*, 31 J. Applied Bus. Rsch. 1531, 1537 (2015).

[42] *See* Cai et al., *supra* note 32, at 928.

10.2 Listed Family Firms Performance

Empirical studies on listed family firms' performance, relative to listed non-family firms, have been made in many countries.[43] Generally speaking, founder firms' performance is significantly better than that of non-family firms.[44] It is not surprising because the founders of listed companies must be good managers by definition. Therefore, current academic interest is on the relative performance of non-founder firms, which varies by country.

10.2.1 The United States

Empirical research tends to show that listed family firms in the United States enjoy stronger firm performance than non-family firms.[45] More specifically, Tobin's q in family firms is 10 percent higher than in non-family firms.[46] This relationship is little affected by the consideration of other blockholders or by the discrepancy between the family's ownership and control rights.[47] The relation between founding-family holdings and firm performance is nonmonotonic; performance first increases as family ownership increases, but then decreases with increasing family ownership.[48]

Research also shows that the performance of the US-listed family firms varies based on CEO status.[49] Founders are associated with greater firm values.[50] Professional managers also exhibit a significant and positive association with Tobin's q. However, heir CEO are unrelated to market performance, suggesting that market participants view founder heirs as similar to CEOs in non-family firms.[51] Some empirical studies even show

[43] *See, e.g.*, Villalonga & Amit, *supra* note 7; Francisco Pérez-González, *Inherited Control and Firm Performance*, 96 Am. Econ. Rev. 1559 (2006); *see* Saito, *supra* note 1; Vikas Mehrotra, Randall Morck, Jungwook Shim & Yupana Wiwattanakantang, *Adoptive Expectations: Rising Son in Japanese Family Firms*. 108 J. Fin. Econ. 840 (2013).

[44] *See* Hokuto Dazai, Takuji Saito, Zenichi Shishido & Noriyuki Yanagawa, *The Rising Son under the Shadow of Company Communities: Do Japanese Family Firms Really Excel?* SSRN (2015), https://papers.ssrn.com/sol3/papers.cfm?abstract_id=2648590.

[45] *See* Anderson & Reeb, *supra* note 1, at 1303.

[46] *Id.* at 1321.

[47] *See id.* at 1303.

[48] *See id.*

[49] *See id.*

[50] *See id.* at 1321.

[51] *See id.*

that Tobin's q of the heir CEO firms is lower than that of non-family firms.[52]

Some studies show that firms that appoint family CEOs significantly underperform relative to firms that promote professional managers: operating return on assets (ROA) is 14 percent lower within three years of a transition.[53] Firms with a family CEO who did not attend a prestigious college underperform relative to firms that promote professional managers.[54] These differences in performance are not observed in firms with family CEOs who attended prestigious colleges.[55] Additionally, the college attended by non-family managers does not predict subsequent declines in firm performance, as expected if non-family CEOs had to demonstrate their competence before getting the top job.[56]

The most valuable listed family firms in the United States tend to be those in which independent directors balance family board representation.[57] In contrast, in firms with continued founding-family ownership and relatively few independent directors, firm performance is significantly worse than in non-family firms.[58] A moderate family board presence provides substantial benefits to the firm.[59] Moreover, Tobin's q is positively related to officer and director ownership (less family holdings).[60]

Family ownership tends to generate value when it is combined with certain forms of family control and management.[61] Family control in excess of ownership is often manifested in the form of multiple share classes, pyramids, cross-shareholdings, or voting agreements.[62] These mechanisms reduce shareholder value, with the reduction in value being proportional to the excess of voting over cash flow rights.[63] Family management adds value when the founder serves as the CEO of the

52 *See* Villalonga & Amit, *supra* note 7.
53 Pérez-González, *supra* note 43, at 1560.
54 *See id.* at 1561.
55 *See id.*
56 *See id.*
57 *See* Ronald C. Anderson & David M. Reeb, *Board Composition: Balancing Family Influence in S&P 500 Firms*, 49 ADMIN. SCI. Q. 209, 209 (2004).
58 *See id.*
59 *See id.*
60 *See* Anderson & Reeb, *supra* note 1, at 1321.
61 *See* Villalonga & Amit, *supra* note 7, at 414.
62 *See id.*
63 *See id.*

family firm or as its Chairman with a non-family CEO, but destroys value when the heir serves as Chairman or CEO.[64]

In heir-CEO firms, control-enhancing mechanisms have a mildly positive impact on value.[65] This positive impact suggests that the mechanisms play a different role in these firms or at least send a weaker signal to the market: If control-enhancing mechanisms are put in place by heirs, it may be perceived as a defensive move to counter the dilution of their ownership stake that would come with firm or family growth.[66] If it is the founder who sets up such mechanisms, it may be seen as a more proactive move to appropriate private benefits of control.[67] Nevertheless, non-family shareholders in heir-CEO firms are worse off than they would have been in a non-family firm.[68]

10.2.2 Japan

According to Mehrotra et al.'s data, heir-managing firms outperformed not only non-family firms but also family firms run by salaryman CEOs, as measured by both ROA and Tobin's q (all listed firms from 1962 to 2000).[69] Dazai et al.'s data show some of the same results reached by Mehrotra et al., but some different results as well. It is true that family firms (excluding founder firms) outperform non-family firms in ROA for the same period (1962–2000) and for the same samples (all listed companies) as Mehrotra et al.'s data. Tobin's q is, however, worse in family firms than in non-family firms.[70]

The relative performance of heir-managing firms to non-family firms varied across three eras: high economic growth era (from 1962 to 1985); bubble economy era (from 1986 to 1992); and after the bubble low growth era (from 1993 to 2000). Although heir-managing firms performed better during the bubble economy era and the low-growth era in terms of ROA, there was no statistically significant difference between non-family firms and heir-managing firms in the high economic growth era.[71]

64 *See id.*
65 *See id.*
66 *See id.*
67 *See id.*
68 *See id.*
69 *See* Mehrotra et al., *supra* note 43.
70 *See* Dazai et al., *supra* note 44. *See also* Saito, *supra* note 1.
71 *See* Dazai et al., *supra* note 11.

Dazai et al. 2025, by using pooled Ordinary Least Squares (OLS) regressions, show that the ROA of heir-managing firms is about 0.2 percent higher than that of non-family firms and the ROE of heir-managing firms is about 0.9 percent higher than that of non-family firms (listed firms on the first and the second sections of Tokyo Stock Exchange from 1991 to 2010).[72]

10.2.3 China

Confucianism contributes some unique characteristics to Chinese family firms. Confucianism promotes filial piety, submission, and obedience of subordinates toward superiors, which are likely to induce steward-like behavior of family managers and contribute to the solution of agency problems.[73]

However, Confucian values prevalent in Chinese family firms may also exert negative effects on agency problems since recruitment and promotion of key positions are often made based on the family superior's personal preference, instead of formal and transparent selection procedures.[74] It may easily lead to the entry of unqualified family members into the business.[75] In addition, Confucianism stresses strict ethics and hierarchical order, which easily induces the paternalism of the family superior.[76] Due to the lack of scientific decision-making procedures in many of China's family firms, irrational strategies and inefficient investment decisions are often made by family superiors based on individual experiences or judgments, thus exacerbating the agency problems.[77]

Empirical studies suggest that in China, family involvement in management does not relate to firm performance.[78] This may be due to the country's growing shift to market capitalism, under which the fulfillment of self-interests and personal economic advancement are increasingly gaining in importance. This change toward a market ethic may have actually changed family managers' value orientations and offset the influence of traditional Confucian values and norms, resulting in neither

[72] *See* Dazai et al., *supra* note 1, at ch. 3 sec. 4.
[73] *See* Zhang & Cao, *supra* note 4, at 46.
[74] *See id.*
[75] *See id.*
[76] *See id.*
[77] *See id.*
[78] The measures for firm performance in this study include both financial and non-financial measures. They are return on investment (ROI), sales growth, market share, product/service quality, and operational efficiency. *See* Youngok Kim & Fei Yi Gao, *Does Family Involvement Increase Business Performance? Family-Longevity Goals' Moderating Role in Chinese Family Firms*, 66 J. Bus. Rsch. 265, 269 (2013).

steward- nor agent-like behavior of family managers.[79] The impacts of family firms on performance are contingent on several factors.

First, the effect of family involvement in management on performance depends on the extent to which a firm supports family-longevity goals. The greater the support for family-longevity goals, the greater the positive relationship between family involvement in management and performance.[80] Family managers tend to display more steward-like behavior when their organization strongly supports family interests, and a firm's family goals can enable family managers to channel firm resources to support family-longevity goals, which will improve the firm's business performance.[81]

Furthermore, studies also suggest that in China, the firm performance impacts of family firms depend on their chosen corporate governance mechanism. For instance, when the founder remains as CEO, the use of control-enhancing mechanisms by the family with relatively dominant ownership rights will encourage the collusion of family members, which will hurt the interests of minority shareholders.[82] Family firms will, in turn, be penalized with a significant loss in firm performance measured by returns on assets (ROA).[83]

When family firms are managed by the founder, concentrated ownership by the family with the involvement of family management alleviates the owner–manager conflict and improves performance.[84] Better performance in family firms mainly originates from the founder occupying the positions of Chairman of the Board and CEO or remaining as Chairman with a relative CEO.[85] When a relative acts as Chairman, a relative CEO's impact on firm performance is indistinguishable from that of a professional.[86] The total absence of the family from monitoring and management tends to result in a significant loss in performance.[87] However, a controlling family using control-enhancing mechanisms such as pyramids will hurt firm performance and firm

79 *See id.* at 271.
80 The measures for firm performance are ROI, sales growth, market share, product/service quality, and operational efficiency. *Id.* at 269.
81 *See id.* at 271.
82 *See* Jing Zhou, On Kit Tam & Ping Yu, *An Investigation of the Role of Family Ownership, Control and Management in Listed Chinese Family Firms*, 12 ASIAN BUS. & MGMT. 197, 199 (2013).
83 *See id.*
84 Performance benefits here refer to the improvement of ROA. *See id.* at 204.
85 *See id.* at 199.
86 *See id.*
87 *See id.*

performance declines proportionately to the excess of family control over ownership rights.[88]

In general, firm performance[89] rises with increasing family shareholdings to a threshold and then decreases.[90] The preservation of management in the family will alleviate the owner–manager agency problem, thereby benefiting firm performance.[91] However, if the founder's control is greatest, as reflected in overwhelming ownership rights with the use of control-enhancing mechanisms, family managers are more likely to facilitate these mechanisms to expropriate minority shareholders, and family firms will, in turn, be penalized by performance losses.[92]

In terms of the age of family firms, listed family firms in China are much younger compared to those in the United States and Japan. Most Chinese listed firms are still managed by the first generation, that is, the founder.[93] As a result, the performance data for heir-run family firms in China are limited.

10.3 Implications to the Corporate Governance in General

The typical type of listed non-founder firms and their performance, relative to that of listed non-family firms, have a lot of implications for the corporate governance in general of each country because the characteristics of listed non-founder firms often reflect markets, social norms, and laws of each country.[94]

Prevalent types of listed family firms vary by country, probably because of its minority shareholder protection law[95] and the size of the manager market.[96]

The relative performance of listed non-founder firms can be explained by several reasons: the founding family's monitoring effect as a large shareholder, firm-specific ability of heir managers, the incentive of heir

[88] *See id.* at 217–218.
[89] Performance measured by ROA. *Id.* at 204.
[90] *See id.* at 218.
[91] *See id.*
[92] *See id.*
[93] *See* Nianhang Xu, Qingbo Yuan, Xuanyu Jiang & Kam C. Chan, *Founder's Political Connections, Second Generation Involvement, and Family Firm Performance: Evidence from China*, 33 J. Corp. Fin. 243, 245 (2015).
[94] *See* Dazai et al., *supra* note 1, at ch. 5, ch. 7.
[95] *See* Burkart et al., *supra* note 29, at 2167.
[96] *See* Dazai et al., *supra* note 11.

managers, the owner–manager agency problem, the large shareholders–small shareholders agency problem, etc.

10.3.1 The United States

In the United States, the minority shareholder protection law is highly developed, and the size of the manager market is large. Therefore, the founder can easily choose an able professional manager from the external manager market as their successor CEO and does not need to worry about the risk of being squeezed out even after the founding family turns into a minority shareholder.[97]

Generally speaking, heir-managing firms perform worse than professional-managing firms, of which professional managers are more able than heir managers in most cases and could have enough equity incentive through equity compensation in the US practice.[98]

Based on the result of comparative performance of heir-managing firms and non-family firms, the separation of ownership and management seems to work in the United States, where the liquid external manager market provides able CEO candidates, the well-developed stock market efficiently monitors management, and equity biased managerial compensation package gives professional managers substantial equity incentive that mitigates shareholder–manager agency problem.[99]

Outside directors are more prevalent in non-family firms than in family firms.[100] Unaffiliated large shareholders (independent entities holding 5% or more of the firm's shares) also significantly differ between family firms (8.35 percent) and non-family firms (11.84 percent).[101] CEOs in family firms earn nearly 10.0 percent less of their total pay in equity-based forms compared to CEOs in non-family firms.[102]

Family CEOs are, on average, eight years younger than professional managers at the time of their appointment.[103]

97 *See id.* at 1–2, 6–8; *see* Burkart et al., *supra* note 29, at 2167.

98 *See* Pérez-González, *supra* note 43, at 1559–1588; *see* Villalonga & Amit, *supra* note 7, at 385–417; *see* Dazai et al., *supra* note 11, at 1, 4.

99 *See* Brian J. Hall & Jeffrey B. Liebman, *Are CEOS Really Paid Like Bureaucrats?*, 113 Q. J. ECON. 653 (1998). *See also* Dazai et al., *supra* note 1, at ch. 5.

100 *See* Anderson & Reeb, *supra* note 1, at 1314.

101 *Id.*

102 *Id.*

103 Pérez-González, *supra* note 43, at 1560 (investigating the impact of inherited CEO positions on the performance of publicly traded US corporations). It uses data from

In the United States, founders often hire professional managers early on.[104] By the time a founder retires, their family retains only marginal ownership.[105] The efficiency of handing over control to professional managers in the United States has been well established.[106] The family firm life-cycle hypothesis suggests that family firms will evolve toward being widely held firms where there is an active market for corporate control since the market provides greater opportunity for a family to sell its controlling stakes at a premium.[107] Publicly listed family firms will tend to be short-lived in the United States because there are both incentives and mechanisms to enable their transition to widely held corporate ownership and professional management.[108] Although the management is extensively professionalized, US publicly listed firms retain family involvement through board participation or controlling equity interests that are often exercised through the agency of the trustee.[109]

10.3.2 Japan

In Japan, the minority shareholder protection law is highly developed[110] and the size of the manager market is small.[111] The founder cannot easily choose able professional managers from the external manager market as their successor CEO[112] and does not need to worry about the risk of being squeezed out even after the founding family turns into a minority

335 management transitions in firms with concentrated ownership or founding family involvement. In this sample, 122 successions (36.4 percent) are classified as involving a "family" CEO when the incoming chief executive was related by blood or marriage to the departing CEO, to the founder, or to the largest shareholder of the corporation. The remaining 213 observations are classified as "unrelated" successions.

104 *See* Burkart et al., *supra* note 29, at 2168.

105 *See id.*

106 *See* Michael Carney, Eric Gedajlovic & Vanessa M. Strike, *Dead Money: Inheritance Law and the Longevity of Family Firms*, 38 Entrepreneurship Theory & Prac. 1261, 1273 (2014).

107 *See id.*

108 *See id.*

109 *See id.*

110 *See* Dazai et al., *supra* note 11, at 8–9; Simone Djankov, Rafael La Porta, Florencio Lopez-de-Silanes & Andrei Shleifer, *The Law and Economics of Self-Dealing*, 88 J. Fin. Econ. 430–465 (2008).

111 *See* Dazai et al., *supra* note 11, at 5–8.

112 *See infra* note 119 and its accompanying text. Mehrotra et al. raise a hypothesis that the adopted son-in-law practice in Japan enables the founder to choose able managers from outside of the company community. *See infra* note 117 and its accompanying text.

shareholder.[113] Therefore, the typical type of non-founder firm is the firm with family management without family ownership.[114]

The question would be raised as to why founding families can keep sending senior managers without voting control.[115] The answer is probably because heir-managing firms generally perform better than non-family firms managed by salaryman managers.[116] Moreover, non-family shareholders, including not only inside shareholders, such as banks, but also outside shareholders, such as institutional investors, have no strong incentive to vote against family managers.

There are possible explanations for the relatively better performance of heir-managing firms. Mehrotra et al. raise a hypothesis that the adopted son-in-law practice in Japan enables the founder to choose able managers from outside of the company community, and the possibility of succession of the CEO position by an adopted son-in-law works as a substitute for the hostile takeover, that is, the threat to real sons.[117] Dazai et al. suggest that relatively high managerial ownership of heir managers, which is hard to realize in non-family firms in Japan, works as equity incentive.[118]

Based on the result of the comparative performance of heir-managing firms and non-family firms, the Japanese case provides the example that the separation of ownership and management does not always work. In Japan, the illiquid external manager market cannot provide able CEO candidates, CEO candidates other than heirs are practically limited to salaryman managers in a company community.[119] Company communities pursue their private benefit and the insider-dominated stock market cannot monitor company communities. The company community norm does not allow salaryman managers to obtain substantial equity compensation. Only heir managers can obtain substantial equity incentives in Japanese listed companies.[120]

113 *See* Carney et al., *supra* note 106.

114 *See* Dazai et al., *supra* note 1, at ch. 3 sec. 2.

115 *See* Morten Bennedsen, Kasper Meisner Nielsen, Francisco Pérez-González & Daniel Wolfenzon, *Inside the Family Firm: The Role of Families in Succession Decisions and Performance*, 122 Q. J. Econ. 647 (2007).

116 *See supra* note 72 and its accompanying text.

117 *See* Mehrotra et al., *supra* note 43.

118 *See* Dazai et al., *supra* note 1, at ch. 3 sec. 4.

119 *See* Zenichi Shishido, *Japanese Corporate Governance: The Hidden Problems of Corporate Law and Their Solutions*, 25 Del. J. Corp. L. 189 (2000); *see* Dazai et al., *supra* note 11, at 5–8.

120 *See* Dazai et al., *supra* note 1, at ch. 5.

Relative performance between heir-managing firms and non-family firms in high-growth era and low-growth era, including both the economic bubble era and after the bubble era, suggests that the traditional Japanese model does not work during the low-growth era, although it worked during the high-growth era.[121]

While keeping the core element of the traditional Japanese corporate governance,[122] Japanese heir-managing firms also incorporate three elements of the Anglo-American style top managers' incentive mechanism, heir manager's substantive equity incentive;[123] fast track carrier path;[124] and longer tenure.[125]

Dazai et al. conclude,

> These characteristics of top managers are extraordinal in Japanese listed non-family firms, which were bounded by egalitarian stakeholder model that used to give incentives to work hard to company community members or full-time regular employees during the high economic growth era, but turned out to be an anchor to change during the lost decades. Only listed family firms were free from the constraints of the egalitarian seniority system in Japan.[126]

10.3.3 China

10.3.3.1 Family Office Succession

Compared to Japanese and American family firms, most listed family firms in China are still at an early stage. According to a survey conducted

[121] *See* Hokuto Dazai, Takuji Saito, Zenichi Shishido & Noriyuki Yanagawa, *Japanese Corporate Governance from the Perspective of Family Firms*, SSRN, 11–12 (2016), https://papers.ssrn.com/sol3/papers.cfm?abstract_id=2811069.

[122] In particular, shareholder monitoring is weak in Japanese non-family firms. *See* Chapter 2, Figure 2.2; *see* Dazai et al., *supra* note 1, at ch. 7.

[123] Management ownership of Japanese heir-managing family firms (4.4 percent on average) is not higher than the largest listed companies in the United States (2.2 percent on average in 1994). *See* Hall & Liebman, *supra* note 99, at 659–661. It is, however, extremely higher than management ownership of non-family firms in Japan (0.22 percent on average). *See* Dazai et al., *supra* note 1, at 15.

[124] Heir managers' career path is much faster than that of salaryman managers. On average, heir managers are appointed as directors around thirty-five-year old and become presidents in their late forties while salaryman managers are appointed as directors in their early fifties and become presidents around sixty-year old. *See* Dazai et al., *supra* note 1, at ch. 5.

[125] Heir managers' tenure as president is much longer than that of salaryman managers. On average, the former is approximately fifteen years and the latter is approximately five-and-a-half years. *Id.*

[126] *Id.*

by PwC, most of the family firms in China are quite young: 75 percent are still under the control of the first-generation founders. As to the handover of family firms, only 21 percent of family owners have established a succession plan, and only 41 percent of them intend to hand over the power (either ownership or management power, or both) to the next generation.[127]

For those family firms with initial founders approaching retirement, to guarantee families' control over the business, most founders choose their children or other blood-related heirs as top managers after they retire.[128] Due to the weak investor protection regime and relationship culture in China, some specialized assets, such as trust from other family members and connections with other stakeholders, are crucial to the profitability of family firms.[129] However, it is hard for founders to completely transfer these specialized assets to their heirs.[130] Moreover, the one-child policy imposes human capital constraints for within-family succession. Taken together, the lack of specialized assets and capabilities presents difficulties for successors when inheriting their family business.[131]

In order to help their heirs establish a reputation for competency, Chinese family firm founders sacrifice their reputation and firms' financial performance by managing earnings downward before intra-family successions in the hope of improving future earnings when their heirs take the family business.[132] The result is more significant for firms with founders having poverty experiences and political connections.[133] Firms' institutional investors and the legal environment inhibit founders' earnings management behavior, but independent directors do not have any significant impact on the association between succession and earnings management.[134] Empirical results suggest that strategic downward earnings management avoids the large decline of stock prices around the within-family successions in the short term but is detrimental to firms' long-term financial performance.[135]

127 *See* Lu, *supra* note 33, at 1.
128 *See* Chan Guo, *Sustainable Development of Chinese Family Firms: A Perspective from Downward Earnings Management before Successions*, 14 Sustainability 9344, 9345 (2022).
129 *See id.*
130 *See id.*
131 *See id.* at 9345–9346.
132 *See id.* at 9345.
133 *See id.*
134 *See id.* at 9346.
135 *See id.* at 9361.

10.3.3.2 Family Firms and Innovation

Families may be involved in approving and monitoring strategic choices as board directors, as well as in formulating and implementing these choices as executives. According to empirical research on the listed family firms in China, family involvement in board decisions tends to strengthen the positive relationship between research and development (R&D) investment and innovation performance, whereas family involvement in the management team tends to weaken this positive relationship.[136]

In China, while family involvement in the board can play a positive role in approving innovation strategies and monitoring the innovation process, the presence of outside directors is also important for ensuring the company's access to external resources.[137] This governance mechanism of having both family members and non-family members on the board enhances the effectiveness of R&D investment, and a higher ratio of family members in boards may imply greater innovation efficiency.[138]

On the other hand, family involvement in management teams reduces access to the professional labor market.[139] As entrepreneurial family firms expand, employing non-family managers becomes necessary because of limitations in the number of able and willing family members. Gradually, the competitive advantage of family firms will depend more on the innovative and up-to-date knowledge of non-family members and the ability to filter out outdated knowledge possessed by family members.[140] Meanwhile, the innovation performance generated by R&D investment is mainly dependent on the knowledge creation process, which relies on efficient knowledge sharing, absorption, and combination.[141] Family involvement in management teams, which reduces access to the external labor market, is definitely detrimental to the combination of diverse knowledge.[142]

Furthermore, family involvement in management teams may not solve agency problems efficiently because owner–managers of family firms are less subject to external constraints relating to accountability, disclosure,

[136] *See* Qiang Liang, Xinchun Li, Xueru Yang, Danming Lin & Danhui Zheng, *How Does Family Involvement Affect Innovation in China?*, 30 Asia Pac. J. Mgmt. 677, 682 (2013).
[137] *See id.*
[138] *See id.*
[139] *See id.*
[140] *See id.*
[141] *See id.*
[142] *See* Michael Carney, *Corporate Governance and Competitive Advantage in Family-Controlled Firms*, 29 Entrepreneurship Theory & Prac. 249, 255 (2005).

and transparency, in part because concentrated ownership allows owners to exempt themselves from external monitoring.[143] Too much family involvement in management undermines the recombination of dispersed knowledge possessed by non-family members and reduces the implementation efficiency of innovation strategies. Consequently, in China, stronger family involvement in management teams results in less R&D investment effectiveness.[144]

10.3.3.3 Family Firms and Risk-Taking

According to a study of more than 1,500 Chinese listed firms over four years of observation (2015–2018), Chinese family firms are generally more risk-averse than Chinese non-family firms because family firms tend to reject projects that are likely to threaten social, emotional, and affective endowment,[145] even if such projects could improve their long-term performance.[146]

Among Chinese family firms, family firms' risk-taking varies with their board diversity.[147] Those with fewer non-family members on the board generally take more risks because concentrated family ownership enables family managers to take more risks in pursuing their private benefits as they face little external monitoring by other shareholders.[148] This shows that having non-family members on the board would limit the risk-taking of family firms.[149]

10.3.3.4 Family Firms and Investment Behavior

Family firms in China are subject to the underinvestment problem rather than the overinvestment problem, which is manifested in the dependence

143 *See id.*

144 *See* Liang et al., *supra* note 136, at 682.

145 Such endowments include the opportunity to pass the firm on to future generations, reputational advantages from being associated with the firm, and the preservation of benevolent ties among family members and with other stakeholders. *See* Cheng Zhang & Le Luo, *Board Diversity and Risk-Taking of Family Firms: Evidence from China*, 17 Intl' Entrepreneurship & Mgmt. J. 1569, 1570 (2021).

146 The level of risk-taking is measured by their Z-scores and innovation intensity. The Z-score was calculated as a firm's return on assets (ROA) plus its capital asset ratio (CAR) divided by the annual standard deviation of its asset returns (ROA). The Z-score measured the distance from the bankruptcy of each firm in a particular year. *Id.* at 1569, 1570, 1576, 1585.

147 *See id.* at 1571.

148 *See id.* at 1585.

149 *See id.*

of corporate investments on internally generated cash flows.[150] However, family firms' political ties with the government can encourage the firm to make riskier investments, especially for financially constrained family firms because political connection can enable family firms to obtain external capital such as bank loans more cheaply.[151]

[150] *See* Nianhang Xu, Xinzhong Xu & Qingbo Yuan, *Political Connections, Financing Friction, and Corporate Investment: Evidence from Chinese Listed Family Firms*, 19 Eur. Fin. Mgmt. 675, 697 (2013).

[151] *See id.* at 693, 697.

PART V

Legislative Policies

11

Law-Making and Incentive Bargaining

So far, we have examined how enterprise law, as a given infrastructure, affects incentive bargaining among the four players in the three economies. In the real world, however, enterprise law is not static but dynamic. Enterprise law itself is changing as a result of incentive bargaining among the four players and lawmakers. In this chapter, we will examine how enterprise law is changing from the law-making participants' incentive point of view.

Although enterprise law consists of several areas of law, such as corporate law, securities regulation, employment law, bankruptcy law, tax law, intellectual property law, and antitrust law and each area of law has its unique law-making procedure and law-making participants, in this chapter, we will focus on the law-making of corporate law and securities regulation as a starting point of analyzing law-making of enterprise law because these are the two major "listed companies' laws."

In Section 11.1, we will categorize corporate law into statutory law, case law, and soft law, and compare their law-making procedures in the three economies. In Section 11.2, we will compare ways of incentive bargaining in law-making in the three economies.

11.1 Categories of Source of Law and Their Law-Making Procedures

Corporate law consists not only of statutory law but also of case law and soft laws. In this section, we will compare the law-making procedure of each source of law category in the three countries.

11.1.1 The United States

The United States is a common-law country, and case law plays a more important role than statutory law. Soft laws, such as governmental guidance and best practice codes, are not as important as they are in Japan.

A distinctive characteristic of the US corporate law is the existence of competition among different states and between state laws and federal laws. Each state has its own corporate law independently, as long as it is not in conflict with the federal securities law. Although a general understanding is that states govern internal corporate affairs and the federal government governs the external trading of the firm's securities, the demarcation is uncertain, and Congress could intervene in the traditional state corporate law area. Sarbanes–Oxley Act (SOX), which regulates corporate governance matters, such as the power of the audit committee and internal control systems, is a typical example.[1]

Each company can choose its franchise state corporate law, notwithstanding the major geographic area of its business. Historically, various states like Delaware and New Jersey compete with each other to attract corporate managers to incorporate in their states.[2] Now the state of Delaware has won the race, and the vast majority of listed companies are Delaware corporations.[3] This subsection will focus on corporate law-making in the state of Delaware.

The most noteworthy trait of Delaware's corporate law is that the most important and controversial legal rules are promulgated by the judiciary, rather than enacted by the legislature.[4]

The Delaware judiciary consists of eight courts.[5] Delaware has a specialized judiciary for corporate law cases on both the trial and appeals court levels.[6] The Delaware Court of Chancery is a specialized corporate trial court that decides cases without juries and appeal is directly to the Delaware Supreme Court.[7] Many supreme court justices also come from the chancery court.[8]

[1] Mark J. Roe, *Delaware Competition*, 117 HARV. L. REV. 588, 592, 596, 645 (2003).

[2] Under the Delaware corporate law (Del. Code. Ann. Tit. 8, §§ 241, 251), shareholders cannot reincorporate the firm by themselves, unless the board, actually managers, recommends reincorporation. *See id.* at 595.

[3] Whether the state competition for corporate charters is a race to the bottom or a race to the top is an enduring issue in the US corporate law. *See id.* at 591, 593–596.

[4] Marcel Kahan & Edward B. Rock, *Symbiotic Federalism and the Structure of Corporate Law*, 58 VAND. L. REV. 1573, 1591 (2005).

[5] Curtis Alva, *Delaware and the Market for Corporate Charters: History and Agency*, 15 DEL. J. CORP. L. 885, 902 (1990).

[6] Kahan & Rock, *supra* note 4, at 1602.

[7] *Id.*

[8] *Id.*

Delaware courts continue the historic division between law and equity, and the Court of Chancery is a court of equity.[9] The Court of Chancery consists of one chancellor and six vice-chancellors, and they are nominated by the Governor and must be confirmed by the Senate for twelve-year terms.

Delaware judges enjoy a significant degree of political independence because both Chancery and Supreme Court judges are appointed on merit rather than elected.[10] The Delaware Constitution requires a balance between the Democratic Party and the Republican Party in the appointment of Delaware judges.[11]

Another unique characteristic of Delaware case law is its limited stare decisis effect.[12] The decision of one chancery court does not have strong binding power, and the Delaware Supreme Court often overturned chancery court decisions even when the chancery court opinions seemed to have developed predictable legal standards.[13]

Furthermore, Delaware's corporate law issues are addressed exclusively through private lawsuits.[14] Delaware has no regulatory agency that enforces its corporate law, either through fines, injunctions, cease-and-desist orders, or criminal proceedings.[15]

Although Delaware's elected representatives are formally lawmakers in Delaware, they play an insignificant role in designing Delaware's statutory corporate law.[16] It is the Council of the Corporation Law Section of the Delaware Bar Association, rather than a legislative committee, that drafts the proposed amendments to the General Corporation Law.[17]

11.1.2 Japan

Although Japan is a civil law country and its legal system is based on statutory law, case law remains an important source of law in Japan, and Supreme Court decisions have binding power. Various types of soft laws,

[9] Alva, *supra* note 5, at 903.

[10] Jill E. Fisch, *The Peculiar Role of the Delaware Courts in the Competition for Corporate Charters*, 68 U. Cin. L. Rev. 1061, 1094 (1999).

[11] *Id.*

[12] *Id.* at 1078.

[13] *Id.*

[14] Kahan & Rock, *supra* note 4, at 1604.

[15] *Id.*

[16] *See* Kahan & Rock, *supra* note 4, at 1600. *But see* Roberta Romano, *The States as a Laboratory: Legal Innovation and State Competition for Corporate Charters*, 23 Yale J. Reg. 209, 225, footnote 42 (2006).

[17] Romano, *supra* note 16.

such as governmental guidance and best practice codes, play an important role as well.

Statutory laws in the area of corporate law are mostly proposed by the Ministry of Justice (MOJ), which is the ministry in charge of corporate law planning. The Ministry of Economy, Trade, and Industries (METI), which is in charge of industry policy planning, and the Financial Service Agency (FSA), which is in charge of securities market law planning, are also involved in the making of corporate law and sometimes initiating corporate law reforms.[18]

Statutory corporate laws used to be proposed to the Diet as cabinet-proposed bills without exception. After making inquiries to industries, the first draft is prepared by bureaucrats, including judges, prosecutors, and legal experts dispatched from METI and large law firms. The draft is then discussed by the Committee of Legal Reform (*Hosei Shingikai*), which consists of representatives of interest groups and neutral experts who are mostly corporate law academics. After gathering public comments, the final draft is submitted to the Diet. Sometimes, provisions regarding politically salient issues are modified at the Diet.[19]

A big change in the legislation channel occurred in 1997. A bill of reformation of corporate law regarding stock options was proposed by Diet members for the first time in the history of corporate law reformations. Since then, the legislation channel has been pluralized, and the ways of lobbying by stakeholders have been diversified.[20]

Securities regulation is one of the important laws governing listed companies. Japanese securities regulation consists of both the statutory law (the Financial Instruments and Exchange Act) and the Tokyo Stock Exchange Rules.

Reformations of the Financial Instruments and Exchange Act are initiated by the FSA and discussed in the Committee of Financial Law (*Kinyu Shingikai*), which consists of representatives of interest groups, such as securities firms, listed companies, consumers, and neutral

[18] *See* MASAFUMI NAKAHIGASHI & HIDEMASA MATSUI, KAISHAHO NO SENTAKU – ATARASHII SHAKAI NO KAISHAHO WO MOTOMETE [CORPORATE LAW'S CHOICE – SEARCHING FOR THE CORPORATE LAW IN MODERN SOCIETY] 37 (2010).

[19] *See* ZENICHI SHISHIDO, SADAKAZU OSAKI, NOBUYUKI KINOSHITA, HIROHIKO NAKAHARA, YUICHIRO MIZUMACHI & TETSUYA WATANAB, INSENTHIBU BAGENINGU TO KIGYO HO: KIGYO NO ISSHO PUROJEKUTO [INCENTIVE BARGAINING AND ENTERPRISE LAW: THE LIFE OF AN ENTERPRISE] 974 (2025).

[20] *See* NAKAHIGASHI & MATSUI, *supra* note 18, at 40.

experts. Political conflicts do not exist in most cases, and politicians are rarely involved.[21]

A big difference between Japanese securities regulation and the US securities regulation lies in their enforcement schemes. While both public enforcement by the Securities and Exchange Commission (SEC) and private enforcement play an important role in the United States,[22] Japanese enforcement of securities regulation heavily relies on public enforcement by the Securities and Exchange Surveillance Commission in the form of criminal sanctions and the administrative monetary penalty, and private enforcement plays a limited role.[23]

In Japan, case laws play an important role in the corporate law area. Japanese judges are career civil servants and are considered to be economically and politically neutral.[24] They are bound by precedents and influenced by academic theses, case critiques, and the media.

The 8th Division of Tokyo District Court plays an important role as the corporate law specialized court. The specialization of judges is progressing, as in intellectual property law, and contributes to the increase in predictability of corporate law cases. Most corporate law judges have studied in the US law schools, and Delaware case laws influence Japanese case laws a lot.[25]

Recently, soft laws have become frequently used and very influential in business practices. Soft laws are convenient tools for the government to launch policy push reforms.[26] The statutory law reformation takes too long a time and incurs too much cost to obtain a consensus among all interest groups. Successful examples are METI & MOJ's Takeover Guidelines of 2005, METI's management buyout (MBO) Guidelines of 2007, METI's mergers and acquisitions (M&A) Guidelines of 2019, and

[21] *See* SHISHIDO ET AL., *supra* note 19, at 961.

[22] *See* Howell E. Jackson & Mark J. Roe, *Public and Private Enforcement of Securities Laws: Resource-Based Evidence*, 93 J. FIN. ECON. 207–238 (2009).

[23] *See* SHISHIDO ET AL., *supra* note 19, at 966.

[24] *See id. But see* J. Mark Ramseyer & Eric B. Rasmusen, *The Case for Managed Judges: Learning from Japan after the Political Upheaval of 1993*, 154 U. PA. L. REV. 1879 (2006).

[25] *See* Curtis J. Milhaupt & Zenichi Shishido, *The Enduring Relevance of the Poison Pill: A U.S.-Japan Comparative Analysis*, 28 STAN. J.L. BUS. & FIN. 336, 344–345 (2023). For example, in the Nippon Broadcasting case (*see* Chapter 7, nn.16–18 and their accompanying texts), the expert opinion of Prof. John Coffee, Jr., regarding the Unocal rule and the Revlon rule contributed to the raider-plaintiff's win of the suit. Livedoor v. Nippon Broadcasting, Tokyo High Ct. Mar. 23, 2005, 1899 HANJI 56 (John Coffee, Jr., expert opinion).

[26] *See infra* note 128 and its accompanying text.

METI's Guidelines for Corporate Takeovers of 2023.[27] They affect the practices in the areas, including conflicts of interest, by offering safe harbors.

Best practice codes, such as the stewardship code and the corporate governance code, are not legally binding and merely recommend best practices based on the comply-or-explain rule. These codes, however, have substantial binding power on most Japanese companies because they want to avoid the cost of explaining. A good example is introducing independent directors. The Japanese traditional board is a managing board, and because of the company community norm, there were no independent directors in most listed companies until around 2000.[28] Although MOJ had tried to reform corporate laws to require listed companies to have at least one independent director, it had not been successful until the reformation of 2019 because of the strong resistance by the Japanese Business Round Table (*Keidanren*). Since the Japanese Corporate Governance Code of 2015 required listed companies to explain the reason for not having an independent director, the adoption of independent directors has rapidly increased.[29] Voluntary restraints by stock exchanges and securities industry associations, which are a kind of soft law, have played an important role in securities regulation.[30]

Tokyo Stock Exchange rules are formulated by the board of Tokyo Stock Exchange, Inc., which is a private stock corporation. Therefore, they are formally soft laws but substantively hard laws for the listed companies. The exchange rules include not only the listed–delisted

[27] In 2023, the electric motor giant, Nippon Densan Corporation (NIDEC), acquired a machine tool company, Takisawa, by hostile takeover. Shigenobu Nagamori, chief executive officer (CEO) of NIDEC, told the newspaper reporter that the acquisition was based on the METI's Guidelines for Corporate Takeovers, which clearly indicate that the board of the target company should take the acquisition proposal into consideration seriously, even it is an unsolicited one. M&A News, *NIDEK's Nagamori: "Acquisitions without Consent Are a Model Case for M&A,"* NIKKEI (Sept. 14, 2023), https://www.nikkei.com/article/DGXZQOUC144SK0U3A910C2000000/.

[28] *See* Zenichi Shishido, *The Monitoring Board Revisited, in* CORPORATE LAW AND ECONOMICS 36, 41 (Adam B. Badawi ed., 2023).

[29] *See id.* at 44–45. In addition to the Corporate Governance Code, the 2014 Amendments of the Companies Act, which clearly favored "comply" over "explain" why it would be inappropriate for listed large companies with a board of *kansayaku* to appoint any outside director (Art. 327-2), contributed to an increase in outside directors. Regarding the political analysis of the process of the 2014 Amendment of the Companies Act, *see* Manabu Matsunaka, *Politics of Japanese Corporate Governance Reform: Politicians do Matter*, 15 BERKELEY BUS. L. J. 154 (2018).

[30] *See* SHISHIDO ET AL., *supra* note 19, , at 962-963.

criteria, but also the regulations of listed companies' issuance of preferred stock, issuance of new stock without shareholders' preemptive right, and independent directors. The draft rules are discussed in several working groups before being decided by the board of directors and authorized by the FSA.[31]

11.1.3 China

11.1.3.1 Legislative Process in China

In China, the National People's Congress (NPC) is the supreme legislative body, the State Council, which supervises the executive branches is the administrative organ, the Supreme People's Court (SPC) and local courts constitute the judicial branch, and the Supreme People's Procuratorate implements the right of prosecution.[32] The NPC supervises legislative, administrative, and judicial organs. The relationship among them is the making of decisions and the implementation of those decisions.[33]

The NPC has the power to enact and amend the basic laws, including criminal law and civil law.[34] The NPC also has the power to amend the Constitution, although the procedure is different from the ordinary law-making procedure (requiring a two-thirds majority).[35] The NPC Standing Committee also has the power to interpret the Constitution and laws.[36]

The NPC is the supreme but not the only legislative body in China.[37] The 1982 Constitution of the People's Republic of China articulates the major organs that can enact laws or normative documents having legal effect.[38] These organs are the National People's Congress; the NPC Standing Committee; the State Council; the people's congresses at the provincial level; and the people's congresses of national autonomous regions, special economic zones, and special administrative regions.[39]

31 *See id.*
32 Susan Xue, *China's Legislative System and Information: An Overview*, 22 Gov't. Info. Q. 322, 323 (2005).
33 *Id.*
34 *Id.* at 324.
35 *Id.*
36 *Id.*
37 *Id.* at 323.
38 *Id.*
39 *Id.*

11.1.3.2 Sources of Corporate Laws in China

1. *Laws Made by the NPC and its Standing Committee*: As a matter of legislative principle, only the laws enacted by the NPC or its Standing Committee can formally be designated as "laws" (falü), and "laws" must be made to govern the country's basic civil and economic systems.[40]

2. *Administrative Regulations Made by the State Council*: An enactment of the State Council may be titled "regulations," "provisions," or "measures," depending on the scope of the subject matter. When the State Council exercises the delegated law-making power, its enactment will be called a "provisional" one.[41]

3. *Departmental Rules Made by the Ministries under the State Council:* The various ministries, commissions, bureaus, and the People's Bank of China (China's central bank) are allowed to enact departmental rules within the bounds of their respective power.[42] For instance, the State Administration for Industry and Commerce (SAIC), which is in charge of the registration of enterprises, makes rules in this area. The China Securities Regulatory Commission (CSRC), which is the State regulator of China's securities markets, issues the largest amount of corporate and securities rules, covering corporate articles of association, corporate governance, corporate finance, information disclosure, M&A, shares transfer, listing, and delisting of companies. The Ministry of Commerce (MOFCOM) also makes rules in relation to foreign participation in China-incorporated companies. The Ministry of Finance makes rules relating to companies' accounting practices and connected transactions. The State-owned Assets Supervision and Administration Commission (SASAC) enacts rules related to the administration of State assets in enterprises. The National Development and Reform Commission (NDRC), which is in charge of formulating the country's macroeconomic development policies and strategies, occasionally makes rules concerning the regulation and operation of companies.[43]

[40] Examples include: Company Law of the PRC, Securities Law of the PRC, Sino-Foreign Equity Joint Venture Law of the PRC, Sino-Foreign Co-operative Joint Venture Law, Wholly Foreign-owned Enterprise (WFOEs) Law of the PRC, Partnership Enterprise Law of the PRC, Wholly Individually-owned Enterprises Law of the People's Republic of China. *See* Jiangyu Wang, Company Law in China (2014).

[41] Examples include: Administrative Regulations of the PRC on Company Registration, Provisional Regulations on the Administration of the Issuing and Trading of Shares, Implementing Rules of the Sino-Foreign Equity Joint Venture Law. *Id.* at 11–12.

[42] *Id.* at 12–13.

[43] Examples include: Measures on the Registration of Registered Capital of Companies (Promulgated by the State Administration of Industry and Commerce); Opinions on

4. *Local Enactments*: Governments at the provincial level and in large cities are also granted law-making power.[44] In the area of corporate law, local regulations, especially those made by governments in Shenzhen and Shanghai, preceded national legislation. For example, even before the 1993 Company Law, the Shenzhen municipality had already enacted rules to regulate the restructuring of its state-owned enterprises (SOEs).[45] Local law could also play an important role in creating innovative legal institutions and filling the gaps left by national law.

5. *Judicial Interpretation, Case Law Equivalent*: The SPC makes law by issuing a variety of interpretations, regulations, notices, replies, opinions, and policy statements (collectively, "interpretations"). Most interpretations are binding upon the courts; others are highly persuasive and likely to be followed by the courts. Sometimes the interpretations issued by SPC are rather general.[46] While these judicial decisions are not a formal source of law in China, some decisions do create legal norms and are persuasive or even binding in practice.[47] The most noticed cases are those judgments or summaries of judgments selected and published by

Several Issues concerning Law Application in the Examination and Approval, and Registration of Companies with Foreign (Promulgated by the State Administration of Industry and Commerce, MOFCOM, General Administration of Customs, and State Administration of Foreign Exchange); Guidelines on Articles of Association for Listed Companies (Promulgated by the China Securities Regulatory Commission); Guidelines for Introducing Independent Directors to the Board of Directors of Listed Companies (Promulgated by the China Securities Regulatory Commission); Code of Corporate Governance for Listed Companies (Promulgated by the China Securities Regulatory Commission); Rules on the General Shareholders' Meeting of Listed Companies (Promulgated by the China Securities Regulatory Commission); Measures for the Administration of Initial Public Offering and Listing of Shares (Promulgated by the China Securities Regulatory Commission); Measures on Information Disclosure by Listed Companies (Promulgated by the China Securities Regulatory Commission); Measures on Administration of Takeover of Listed Companies (Promulgated by the China Securities Regulatory Commission); Measures Governing the Acquisition of Domestic Enterprises by Foreign Investors (Promulgated on Aug. 8, 2006 by the MOFCOM, SASAC, State Tax Administration, China Securities Regulatory Commission, and State Administration of Foreign Exchange). *Id.*

44 *See id.* at 13–14.

45 *Id.*

46 Examples include: Provisions on Several Issues Concerning the Application of the PRC Company Law (1) (Promulgated by the SPC on Apr. 28, 2006, effective as of May 9, 2006), Provisions on Several Issues Concerning Trial of Civil Disputes Related to the Restructuring of Enterprises (Promulgated by the SPC on Jan. 3, 2003, effective as of Feb. 1, 2003), Several Provisions on Trial of Civil Damage Cases Arising from False Representation in the Securities Market (Promulgated by the SPC on Jan. 9, 2003, effective as of Feb. 1, 2003). *Id.* at 14–16.

47 *See id.* at 16.

the SPC in the Gazette of the Supreme People's Court, which are considered "authoritative and an important means through which the SPC provides guidance to lower courts with regard to their adjudicative work."[48]

6. *Rules Made by Self-Regulatory Organizations*: The Securities Association of China (SAC) and the two securities exchanges, namely the Shanghai Stock Exchange (SSE) and the Shenzhen Stock Exchange, are officially considered "self-regulatory organizations" in China's securities markets.[49] They are empowered to make self-regulatory rules.[50] In the Chinese context, those rules should have a much larger binding force on the operation of companies simply because the so-called Self-Regulatory Organizations (SROs) are under tight governmental control, whose enactments are in fact heavily endorsed by the State.[51]

The two securities exchanges have promulgated numerous sets of rules to govern listing, trading, information disclosure, corporate finance, corporate governance, M&A, and corporate social responsibility. For the listed companies, securities firms, and investors, complying with the trading and listing rules of the securities exchanges can be just as important as meeting the requirements of laws and regulations.[52]

11.1.3.3 NPC Legislative Process

The NPC and its Standing Committee are the leading lawmakers in China.[53] The NPC is composed of delegates elected from all the provinces, autonomous regions, and municipalities directly under the central government, and delegates elected by the military.[54] The NPC delegates are elected for a five-year term and they meet in session once a year.[55] One session normally lasts one-to-two weeks to enact and amend the most important laws in China.[56]

Since the NPC only meets once a year for a short time, the country can't wait that long to conduct law-making activities.[57] As a result, the

[48] *Id.*
[49] *See id.*
[50] *See id.*
[51] *See id.* at 17
[52] *See id.* at 18.
[53] *See* Xue, *supra* note 32, at 326.
[54] *Id.*
[55] *Id.*
[56] *Id.*
[57] *Id.*

Constitution entrusts the national legislative power to the NPC Standing Committee when the NPC is not in session.[58] The NPC Standing Committee is the permanent arm of the NPC and is composed of the chair, vice chairs, secretary general, and members.[59] The heads of the NPC Standing Committee are normally former state leaders, for example, Li Peng, a former premier; Wan Li, a former vice premier; and Wu Bangguo, another former vice-premier of the State Council.[60] Members of the Standing Committee are elected by the NPC plenary session for a five-year term (157 members in the 10th NPC Standing Committee).[61] Although the most fundamental legislation is reserved for the NPC alone, its Standing Committee may conduct much of the routine business.[62] When the NPC is not in session, the Standing Committee enacts supplements and amendments to NPC statutes as long as these do not contradict the basic principles embodied in the statutes.[63] Consequently, except for revisions to the Constitution and basic laws, which are reserved to the NPC, the NPC Standing Committee undertakes a large amount of legislative work.[64] The NPC Standing Committee undertakes routine legislation activities and co-exercises national legislative powers with the NPC.[65]

Since 1983, special committees and agencies have been set up within the NPC.[66] Currently, the NPC has nine special committees, which consist of influential politicians and legal professionals, to help it discharge its legal responsibilities.[67] These special committees, especially the Law Committee, have been playing a significant role in the process of drafting bills, reviewing and revising bills, and collecting and digesting suggestions and proposals from NPC delegates and the general public.[68] They are very influential in investigating and deliberating draft legislation and bringing ministries, specialists, scientific research, and educational units into the legislative process.[69]

58 *See id.*
59 *Id.*
60 *Id.*
61 *Id.*
62 *Id.*
63 *Id.*
64 *Id.*
65 *See id.*
66 *Id.* at 327.
67 *Id.*
68 *Id.*
69 *Id.*

In practice, the NPC Standing Committee and the State Council, particularly the latter, introduce most bills.[70] The State Council has been responsible for many important legislative initiatives, and its bills are normally drafted by the relevant ministries and commissions of the State Council with the assistance of its Legislative Affairs Bureau.[71] In the period 1979–1988, 70 percent of the legislation enacted by the NPC and its Standing Committee resulted from the State Council's bills.[72] Since their establishment in the 1980s and 1990s, the Constitution and Law Committee[73] and other special committees of the NPC have gradually taken over a share of law drafting.[74]

In terms of law-making procedure, the first step is often that a bill sponsor needs to introduce the bill either to the NPC or its Standing Committee, and deliberation includes a background of the bill and legislative intent.[75] The NPC needs one or two rounds of discussion before voting.[76] Second, the legislative power began taking into consideration the interests of relevant ministries, organizations, and suggestions from experts.[77] With the approval of the Chairman of the NPC, some major bills may be open to the general public for suggestions and comments.[78]

11.1.3.4 PRC Enterprise Bankruptcy Law as an Example

The general view is that the lack of an adequate bankruptcy regime in China has been a serious issue in the enforcement of contracts and debt recovery. Consequently, various reform proposals have been made to tackle these weaknesses in the bankruptcy regime, such as alleviating the negative impact of dominant state ownership on market discipline and on the regulatory capacity of the state, building an institutional investor base, and strengthening the role of banks in corporate governance.[79]

70 *See id.* at 329.
71 *Id.*
72 *Id.*
73 The Constitution and Law Committee is one of the ten special committees of the current NPC. It is responsible for reviewing and proposing amendments to the current law and interpreting the Constitution. *See* Baojun Wang, *The Chinese Characteristics of the Constitutional Review System: Looking Back, Examining and Forward-looking*, 4 ACAD. J. OF MGMT. & SOC. SCI. 33, 34 (2023).
74 Xue, *supra* note 32, at 329.
75 *Id.*
76 *Id.*
77 *Id.*
78 *Id.*
79 *See* World Bank Group [WBG], *China's Management of Enterprise Assets: The State as a Shareholder*, WBG WDS/1998-1 (June 5, 1997); World Bank Group [WBG], *Bankruptcy*

Before the promulgation of the People's Republic of China (PRC) Enterprise Bankruptcy Law, an insolvency law regime concerning SOEs was adopted in the Enterprise Bankruptcy Law of the People's Republic of China in 1986,[80] while the insolvency of non-SOEs was subject to a separate regime framed in chapter 19 of the PRC Civil Procedure Law,[81] which introduced rudimentary provisions for the bankruptcy of legal persons in general. Insolvencies concerning foreign-invested enterprises (FIEs) were primarily regulated under the Civil Procedure Law.[82] The Supreme People's Court's Opinions on the Civil Procedure Law, issued on July 14, 1992, clarified that the court could refer to the 1986 Bankruptcy Law in addition to the Civil Procedure Law.[83]

This bifurcated insolvency system was overhauled recently. Chapter 19 was deleted from the Civil Procedure Law, and later, the Bankruptcy Law was repealed by the Enterprise Bankruptcy Law,[84] which attempts to unify two separate regimes previously applicable to SOEs and non-SOEs, respectively.

When the Bankruptcy Law was first referred to the NPC in the spring of 1986, it had won widespread leadership and organizational support, and many objections of key constituencies had been met through careful amendment. Nevertheless, the widely circulated and harsh criticisms raised by many NPC delegates eventually made the broad implementation of the law politically untenable when it came into effect two years later.[85]

of State Owned Enterprises in China: A Case and Agenda for Reforming the Insolvency Problem, WBG (Sept. 20, 2000).

80 Enterprise Bankruptcy Law of the People's Republic of China (promulgated by the Standing Committee of the National People's Congress on Dec. 2, 1986, effective Nov. 1, 1988), LAWINFOCHINA, https://www.lawinfochina.com/display.aspx?lib=law&id=1170.

81 First adopted on April 9, 1991, by the NPC and latest amended with effect from April 1, 2008.

82 This was clarified by Article 206 of the PRC Civil Procedure Law (1991), which stated that the 1986 Bankruptcy Law (trial) applied to procedures for debt repayment by insolvent SOEs and the provisions of chapter 19 of the PRC Civil Procedure Law did not apply to non-legal person enterprises, sole proprietorships and partnerships of natural persons.

83 Civil Procedure Law, Art. 253.

84 The Bankruptcy Law of the People's Republic of China (Promulgated at the 23rd session of the Standing Committee of the 10th National People's Congress on Aug. 27, 2006, and effective from July 1, 2007). Enterprise Bankruptcy Law, Art. 136.

85 *See* Murray Scot Tanner, *How a Bill Becomes a Law in China: Stages and Processes in Lawmaking*, 141 THE CHINA Q. 39, 59 (1995).

11.2 Incentive Bargaining with Lawmakers: Ways of Incentive Bargaining

Statutory laws are legislated by politicians according to the parliament system of each country and the legislators in a narrow sense are politicians who are elected by voters.[86] In this section, lawmakers of statutory laws include not only politicians but also bureaucrats who initiate and draft the proposed bill. Lawmakers of case laws are judges, and lawmakers of soft laws regarding corporate and securities regulation areas are bureaucrats of the ministry in charge of either the stock exchange or industries.

Corporate law reforms can be categorized according to who initiated the reform. The legal reforms, which are initiated by the lawmakers to change the practice, can be called the "policy push" reform. The legal reforms, which are initiated by the stakeholders (in most cases, the management) to enable practices that could not be done within the existing legal system, can be called the "demand pull" reform.[87] The demand-pull reforms usually have an immediate influence on practice. The influential policy push reforms either have the power of direct regulation or successfully stimulate the practical demands.[88]

Salience plays an important role as a trigger of the corporate law reforms.[89] Politicians play an important role in legal reform in case big scandals of large corporations are revealed because the general public demands new regulations on large corporations. In other words, in the areas where voters and politicians have no interest, such as corporate law and securities regulations, actors other than politicians play a major role in the legal reforms.[90]

86 In China, about 20–50 percent NPC members are nominated by the Communist Party. Susan V. Lawrence & Michael F. Martin, *Understanding China's Political System* (CONG. RSCH. SERV., R41007, 2013).

87 Zenichi Shishido, *Reform in Japanese Corporate Law and Corporate Governance: Current Changes in Historical Perspective*, 49 AM. J. COMP. L. 653, 656 (2001).

88 *Id.* at 676.

89 *See* PEPPER D. CULPEPPER, QUIET POLITICS AND BUSINESS POWER: CORPORATE CONTROL IN EUROPE AND JAPAN (2011).

90 *See* Manabu Matsunaka, *Koporeto Gabanansu to Seiji Katei* (*Corporate Governance and Political Process*), *in* KOPORETO GABANANSU KAIKAKU NO TEIGEN – KIGYO KACHI KOJO • KEIZAI KASSEIKA HENO MICHISUJI [REFORMING CORPORATE GOVERNANCE: THE ROAD TO IMPROVING FIRM VALUE AND STIMULATING THE ECONOMY] 429, 453 (Zenichi Shishido & Gen Goto eds., 2016). *But see infra* note 129 and its accompanying text; Matsunaka, *supra* note 29, at 175.

11.2.1 The United States

In Delaware's corporate law jurisprudence, partisan conflicts and monetary contributions played a limited role.[91] Proposed laws are adopted without amendment or debate by the Delaware legislature, and the usual party politics either do not exist or at least play an insignificant role.[92]

Lobbying often takes the form of technical legal briefs[93] within the Corporation Law Section of the Delaware Bar.[94] All amending, redrafting, or debating that affects proposed legislation occur within the Corporate Law Section.[95] The parties who lobby for specific reforms in the Delaware General Corporation Law, including Delaware and out-of-state attorneys, in-house corporate counsel, corporate managers, and corporation service companies, all provide their opinions to the Corporate Law Section instead of the General Assembly.[96]

For instance, the top three corporation service companies each have a representative in the Corporate Law Section of the Delaware Bar Association.[97] Although the corporation service companies do not lobby the General Assembly directly,[98] they meet regularly with the Secretary of State, the Assistant Secretary of State, and the Director of the Division of Corporation Administration and Policy to discuss potential legislative reform.[99] They also meet with the Corporate Law Section of the Delaware Bar Association every year to present their legislative recommendations.[100]

The most famous and significant legislative overturning of judge-made law is Delaware General Corporation Law section 102(b)(7) after the *Smith v. Van Gorkom* case. The Delaware Supreme Court in *Smith v. Van Gorkom* greatly increased the exposure of directors' liabilities for breaching the duty of care.[101] The decision, described by many commentators as "one of the worst decisions in the history of corporate law," triggered the enactment of section 102(b)(7),[102] which enables companies to opt

[91] *See* Kahan & Rock, *supra* note 4, at 1612.
[92] *Id.* at 1614.
[93] *See id.* at 1612.
[94] *Id.* at 1614.
[95] Alva, *supra* note 5, at 900.
[96] *Id.* at 901.
[97] *Id.* at 902.
[98] *See id.*
[99] *Id.*
[100] *Id.*
[101] Smith v. Van Gorkom, 488 A.2d 858 (Del. 1985).
[102] Kahan & Rock, *supra* note 4, at 1596.

out of personal liability for good-faith breaches of the duty of care.[103] The legislation of section 102(b)(7) after the *Van Gorkom* decision reflects a typical demand-pull legislation. Directors of Delaware corporations worried about the increased risk of being held liable and lobbied through the Corporate Law Section of the Delaware Bar Association. Major players of corporate law-making in Delaware, such as the Delaware and out-of-state attorneys, in-house corporate counsel, corporate managers, and corporation service companies,[104] share the same interest in keeping Delaware as the dominant franchise of the US corporations and have demanded such legislation.[105]

Although the general perception is that the legislative overturning of judge-made corporate law rarely took place in Delaware.[106] Twenty-nine cases were the subject of legislative amendments from 1967 to 2005 that either reversed or clarified the decisions. Eleven of the twenty-nine amendments were explicit reversals of cases, and another eleven amendments were clarifications or resolutions of issues that were ambiguous, confusing, or unanswered in the judicial opinions.[107]

Major lawmakers of the US securities regulation, or federal corporate law, are Congress, the SEC, the federal courts, and the New York Stock Exchange.[108] Legislative lobbying also took place at the Congressional level. One significant example is the Bankruptcy Abuse Prevention and Consumer Protection Act (BAPCPA) of 2005, which is sometimes regarded as the "significant change in United States' bankruptcy legislation since 1978."[109] BAPCPA makes it more difficult for middle-income families to file for Chapter 7 bankruptcy because of the introduction of the "means test."[110]

103 *Id.*

104 In addition to these major players who care about the rules' content, the average citizen in Delaware also has an incentive to improve their welfare by increasing the revenues from the corporate franchise tax. Moreover, local interest group pressure on corporate law from labor unions and local companies are weaker than they are in other larger states. *See* Roe, *supra* note 1, at 594.

105 Although the proposal initially caused much controversy within the Delaware Bar Association, and a local attorney firmly opposed the proposal, the attorney was finally convinced, and the bill was approved unanimously. *See* Alva, *supra* note 5, at 914–915.

106 See Kahan & Rock, *supra* note 4, at 1596.

107 Romano, *supra* note 16, at 225, n. 42.

108 *See* Roe, *supra* note 1, at 598–600.

109 Robert H. Scott, *Bankruptcy Abuse Prevention and Consumer Protection Act of 2005: How the Credit Card Industry's Perseverance Paid Off*, 41 J. ECON. ISSUES 943, 943 (2007).

110 Under BAPCPA, debtors must pass a new "means test" to file under Chapter 7. Only debtors whose monthly family income averaged over the six months prior to filing is less than the median monthly family income level in their state can pass the means test.

Prior to BAPCPA, Chapter 7 accounts for 70 percent of personal bankruptcy because it eliminated most non-secured debt such as credit card debt.[111] After BAPCPA, the percentage of Chapter 7 filings fell below 30 percent.[112] One of the main drivers for the Senate to pass BAPCPA (Senate Bill 256) on March 11, 2005, is the continuous lobbying effort by the credit card companies. Until 2005, credit card companies were losing $4 billion annually due to bankruptcy filings.[113] Between 1999 and 2005, credit card companies spent around $25 million on lobbying to reform personal bankruptcy legislation.[114] After BAPCPA, credit card companies are estimated to recoup $4 billion a year (a 7.5 percent increase in revenue).[115]

SOX, which was adopted by Congress as a reformation of the Securities Exchange Act just after the Enron and WorldCom fraudulent disclosure scandals, is a good example of salience law[116] and a policy push legislation. At the same time, SOX is always referred to as an example of a federal invasion of the state's corporate law area.[117]

While federal agencies like the SEC have the power to enact regulations on securities and accounting standards, their legislative power is still limited by incentive bargaining between the industry and Congress. For example, in 2000, Arthur Levitt, then chairman of the SEC, wanted to address the conflict of interest issue in the accounting industry by proposing an SEC rule that bars accountants from acting as consultants.[118] The accounting industry lobbied forty-six members of Congress to call or write personal letters to Levitt questioning the proposed rule, and some lawmakers threatened to withdraw funding from the SEC.[119] Eventually, the SEC rejected Levitt's proposal due to the pressure.[120]

Thus, BAPCPA prevents middle- or high-income debtors from taking advantage of Chapter 7. *See* Michelle J. White, *Bankruptcy Reform and Credit Cards*, 21 J. ECON. PERSP. 175, 185–186 (2007).

111 Scott, *supra* note 109, at 944.

112 *Id.*

113 *Id.* at 943.

114 In particular, MBNA, one of the largest issuers of credit cards in the United States at that time, spent more than $17 million lobbying Congress from January 1999 to June 2004. *See* Scott, *supra* note 109, at 945.

115 *Id.*

116 *See* Roberta Romano, *The Sarbanes-Oxley Act and the Making of Quack Corporate Governance*, 114 YALE L. J. 1521 (2005).

117 *See* Roe, *supra* note 1, at 645.

118 *See* Catherine E. Vance & Paige Barr, *The Facts & Fiction of Bankruptcy Reform*, 1 DEPAUL BUS. & COMM. L. J. 361, 366, n.19 (2003).

119 *See id.*

120 *See id.*

11.2.2 Japan

In the corporate law area, it is rare for a specific statutory law reformation to be an issue in an election campaign because of its low salience. The major place of incentive bargaining takes place in the Committee of Legal Reform, which consists of the representatives of interest groups and neutral academics. Because of its consensus-based decision-making process, each member has a quasi-veto and, as a result, drafted new laws tend to be made under the Pareto efficiency rule. In other words, it is hard to change the status quo if any interested groups will be worse off.[121]

The year 1997 is the turnaround year in two ways. First, the traditional Japanese corporate governance started to change, and the shareholders' voice was strengthened after the financial crisis of 1997. Second, the legislation channel was pluralized after the first reformation of corporate law proposed by Diet members was made in 1997.[122]

Before the turnaround of 1997, stakeholders other than the management, i.e., shareholders, creditors, and employees, did not use their voice in the corporate law legislation. Most shareholders were inside shareholders, and their major interest is to keep long-term transactions with the issuing companies rather than to maximize investment return. Institutional investors who have the incentive to reflect their interest as genuine shareholders in corporate law legislation did not appear in the Japanese corporate governance scene. Banks can protect their interest by themselves. Trading partners have no incentive to insist on their interests as creditors because they are debtors at the same time. Japanese labor unions are not industry unions but company unions, and they "ride on the same boat" with the management. Employees share the same interest with management under the company

[121] For example, Companies Act Article 440 I and II, which require all corporations, including small corporations, to publicly disclose the summary of their balance sheets, are mostly ignored. Although drafters of the Ministry of Justice and academic committee members have tried to make the statutes more effective several times, the representatives of small and medium corporations strongly opposed them, and the attempts of reformation failed. *See* SHISHIDO ET AL., *supra* note 19, at 971-972.

[122] *See supra* note 20 and its accompanying text. *See also* Matsunaka, *supra* note 29, at 178–179. At the same time, METI's influence on corporate law reformations, which had been substantially dominated by the Ministry of Justice, has rapidly increased, probably because the need to stimulate the economy became consensus among Japanese citizens during the economic downturn. Young bureaucrats of METI proposed many reformations. They had incentives to stimulate Japanese economy by using their new ideas.

community norm[123] and they do not have their own interests reflected in corporate law legislation.[124]

During the era when the Committee of Legal Reform was the only channel of corporate law legislation, the committee member corporate law scholars played the role of the guardian of minority shareholders and creditors based on the consensus that their protection is a legal issue.[125]

After the bubble burst of 1990, institutional shareholders, who used to be hidden from the Japanese corporate governance scene, became more active in using their direct monitoring power either by exit or by voice. At the same time, the mandatory nature of Japanese corporate law was partly changed by the demand-pull reforms. Mandatory laws prohibiting demanded practices have been individually changed into enabling laws in the 1990s.[126]

After the turnaround of 1997, in addition to the pluralizing legislation channel, corporate law legislation turned out to be a tool for achieving the objectives of economic policy, and the pressure of stakeholders' demands strengthened.[127] Politicians started to play an important role in corporate law legislation. The strong policy of "deregulation" under the Koizumi administration from 2001 accelerated demand-pull reforms. The "burden of proof" of the necessity of deregulation changed from management to lawmakers.[128] Finally, in 2005, the basic characteristic of corporate law changed from a mandatory law nature to an enabling law nature.

Although politicians increased their influence in corporate law legislation, until the 2005 reform, it was the era of demand-pull reforms, in other words, politicians led manager-friendly reforms. In the 2014 reform, politicians, the second Abe administration, and the Liberal Democratic Party (LDP) party, engaged in a management-unfriendly reform, that is, a strong policy push reform to require large listed companies to appoint at least an outside director, without salience, probably driven by the incentive to conquer long-standing stagnation.[129]

123 Regarding the company community, *see* Chapter 2, n.124; Zenichi Shishido, *Japanese Corporate Governance: The Hidden Problems of Corporate Law and Their Solutions*, 25 DEL. J. CORP. L. 189, 201–205 (2000).

124 *See* NAKAHIGASHI & MATSUI, *supra* note 18, at 76–79.

125 *See id.* at 237. *See also* SHISHIDO ET AL., *supra* note 19, at 972.

126 *See* Shishido, *supra* note 87, at 671–673.

127 *See* NAKAHIGASHI & MATSUI, *supra* note 18, at 40.

128 *Id.* at 237–238.

129 *See* Matsunaka, *supra* note 29, at 168–170, 175–184.

Recently, US-style lobbying by large start-up companies to avoid regulations against their new business started to emerge in Japan. Mid-carrier civil servants of the ministry in charge, METI in particular, are head-hunted by such companies.

The short history of rulemaking regarding anti-hostile takeover defenses is a good example of incentive bargaining in law-making. Japanese defense rules have been made both by court cases and by soft law, such as governmental guidelines.[130] Different interests were reflected in the defense rule by the latter informal rulemaking process.[131]

A fundamental question can be raised about Japan's gravitation toward a modified version of the Delaware-style poison pill: Why Delaware? Even if Japanese policymakers sought to adopt a "global standard" in the development of defensive measures, another "global" standard evident in the UK Takeover Code was also available.[132]

The UK Takeover Code has many supporters in Japan because of its clear rules and strong minority protection, which is a much-favored narrative in Japan.[133] However, its clear rule does not give discretion to the board to block bids that are not acceptable to the "company community."[134] Besides such practical barriers to implementing the UK law, the intellectual attraction of Delaware law could draw a parallel to the adoption of the French Civil Code in the Meiji period.[135] After the war, the vast majority of young judges and civil servants who turned out to be influential for law-making in their later careers studied in the United States and learned Delaware corporate law at US law schools. It is natural for lawmakers in that era, in the wake of hostile acquisitions, to introduce Delaware law, which they are most familiar with.[136]

130 *See supra* note 27 and its accompanying text.

131 *See* Matsunaka, *supra* note 90, at 456.

132 *See* Milhaupt & Shishido, *supra* note 25, at 349.

133 Regarding "narrative," *see* Mark J. Roe & Roy Shapira, *The Power of the Narrative in Corporate Lawmaking*, 11 Harv. Bus. L. Rev. 233 (2021).

134 Regarding the company community, *see* Chapter 2, n.124; Shishido, *supra* note 123, at 201–205.

135 The role of familiarity and intellectual attraction to legal transplantation has played out in earlier periods of Japanese legal reform. Following the Meiji Restoration (1868), the Japanese government sent scholars to England, France, and Germany to study their legal systems. The scholar sent to France ultimately proved to be the most influential upon his return. As a result, Japan adopted a code-based system heavily influenced by the French Civil Code, with some additional influences of German and English law. *See* Milhaupt & Shishido, *supra* note 132, at 345.

136 *See* Milhaupt & Shishido, *supra* note 132, at 345.

Reformations of Japanese securities regulation include both demand-pull legislation initiated by listed companies that are very important stakeholders and policy push legislation initiated by the FSA that watches the international trend. Their demarcation is blurred.[137]

Japan's Sarbanes–Oxley Act (J-SOX), which was enacted as a part of the Financial Instruments and Exchange Act of 2006, just after the fraudulent disclosure scandals of Seibu and Kanebo in 2004, is a good example of salience law and policy push legislation, just as the SOX in the United States.[138] It was, however, not initiated by politicians, but by the FSA, which had been observing what was going on in the US. Therefore, both the existence of scandals and the "globalization" narrative[139] motivated the FSA to enact J-SOX.[140]

11.2.3 China

11.2.3.1 Stages of Chinese Law-Making and Incentive Bargaining

The Chinese law-making process may be divided into five major stages.[141]

The first stage is agenda-setting, which entails getting a particular draft law on the agenda of major state law-making agencies.[142] Often, an organizational sponsor for the law is required to proceed further.[143]

The second stage is inter-agency review, which involves consensus-building about the draft law among major state agencies. As a draft law receives attention from higher levels of the legislative system, the politics of the process gradually shift toward the more closed and bureaucracy-dominated politics of the inter-agency review process.[144] The dominant

137 *See* SHISHIDO ET AL., *supra* note 19, at 967-968.

138 *See* Zenichi Shishido & Sadakazu Osaki, *Reverse Engineering SOX versus J-SOX: A Lesson in Legislative Policy, in* ENTERPRISE LAW: CONTRACTS, MARKETS, AND LAWS IN THE US AND JAPAN 349, 351 (Zenichi Shishido ed., 2014).

139 *See* Roe & Shapira, *supra* note 133.

140 Enactment of the fair disclosure rule in 2017 is a similar case. The fair disclosure rule was enacted in the United States in 2000. After revealing several unfair disclosure cases, the FSA introduced the US-type fair disclosure rule. *See* SHISHIDO ET AL., *supra* note 19, at 969.

141 Tanner, *supra* note 85, at 45.

142 Major state law-making agencies include the State Council and its ministries, as well as the NPC (including its Standing Committee).

143 Tanner, *supra* note 85, at 52.

144 *Id.* at 53.

arena is often the State Council, and Central ministries become the key actors, and the process shifts from swift competitive entrepreneurship to slow bargaining and consensus building.[145] Due to the extended period of negotiation, the drafts that emerge from inter-agency review tend to have significant bureaucratic weight, and much fewer changes are made in the later, more open phase of opinion solicitation.[146]

The third stage is top leadership approval of a draft "in principle," and drafted laws at this stage tend to have an identified, dedicated, and politically weighty patron, either a central leader or a major central-level organization.[147]

The fourth stage is the Standing Committee of the National People's Congress (NPC) review, debate, and passage of the law. The NPC review stage begins when the Committee Chairmen's Group refers the draft to one or more of the Standing Committee's Special Committees. Established in 1983 and greatly expanded after 1987, these issue-based committees are staffed primarily with former high-ranking party and state officials who have recently retired from the key ministries, departments, mass organs, and localities concerned with the issues under each particular committee's provenance; thus, they provide the NPC with much policy expertise and the bureaucratic connections necessary for it to review meaningfully and amend draft legislation.[148]

Official special committee recommendations for revising draft legislation, published in the NPC Bulletin, routinely suggest major revisions that represent setbacks for the drafting ministries.[149] Upon recommendation of the appropriate special committees, the Standing Committee Party Group determines when to list the draft for debate by either the Standing Committee or the full NPC.[150] If a draft faces serious opposition in the NPC, the strong preference of NPC leaders is to avoid the embarrassment of a significant public display of "no" votes.[151] In such cases, the NPC often withholds the law from a vote while insisting on significant revisions.[152]

The fifth stage is the implementation of the Law passed by the NPC.

145 *Id.*
146 *Id.* at 54.
147 *Id.* at 53.
148 *Id.* at 58.
149 *Id.*
150 *Id.*
151 *Id.*
152 *Id.*

11.2.3.2 Chinese Corporate Law and Incentive Bargaining

Due to the efforts of the reformists[153] in the political party, Chinese corporate law is moving toward liberalizing the economy and increasing the enforcement power of the corporate law. The first Company Law in China came into force on July 1, 1994. This law was further amended on October 27, 2005. The amended Company Law of 2005 expanded the previous one with the addition of two new chapters, reduced the original 230 clauses to 219 clauses, amended 91 clauses, added 44 new clauses, and deleted 13 clauses.[154]

Unlike the Company Law of 1994, which leaves little room for judicial involvement, the amended Company Law of 2005 increased the availability of judicial review.[155] This seemingly dramatic change enhanced the ability of parties to litigate corporate statutes,[156] thereby making corporate rules more "enabling" than before. Moreover, the PRC economy had become increasingly open and market-oriented. Hence, a reshuffle in China's corporate law was required to boost the operational efficiency and productivity of Chinese companies and to serve the structural needs of China's capital market. Although this was an appropriate time for a change, the Chinese government did not undertake a wholesale reform of the existing Company Law. Rather, in recognition of the need for a more business-friendly corporate law, China has adopted a piecemeal or step-by-step approach by, *inter alia*, easing certain restrictions on capital rules, enhancing existing corporate governance and introducing more shareholder protection provisions.[157] The amended Company Law, therefore, represents a staging post or stepping stone when China is moving toward an eventual consolidation of one corporate regime, applicable to domestic entities, as well as FIEs.[158]

153 One example of such reformists is Premier Li Keqiang, who pushed the amendment of the Chinese Company Law in 2013.

154 Wei Shen, *Fading Registered Capital Rules under the Amended Chinese Company Law: Sweeping Changes in Uncertain Contexts*, 8 Int'l Co. & Com. L. Rev. 270 (2014).

155 *Id.* The Company Law 2005 promoted capacity building of the People's Courts, particularly in the application of mechanisms transplanted from foreign jurisdictions, such as lifting the corporate veil and the statutory derivative action to adapt to China's specific legal environment. *See* Xianchu Zhang, *Company Law Reform in China*, *in* Law & Policy for China's Market Socialism 39, 46 (John Garrick ed., 2012).

156 *See* Shen, *supra* note 154.

157 *See* Zhang, *supra* note 155, at 42.

158 The Amended Company Law of 2005 represents a trend toward market-friendly regulations. The amended company law removed some privileges previously held exclusively by SOEs. The amended company law also transplanted Western corporate law concepts,

In December 2013, the Company Law was amended again by the NPC at its sixth meeting and the amendments came into effect on March 1, 2014. This new round of amendments reflects the instructions given by Premier Li Keqiang in a State Council executive meeting[159] held on October 25, 2013. In that meeting, Li Keqiang proposed to reform the existing registered capital filing system to promote entrepreneurship and commercial freedom. The amendments made to the Company Law of 2013 mainly focus on corporate finance rules, which abolished the paid-in capital, minimum registered capital, instalment of registered capital contribution, restriction on the percentage of contribution in cash, and capital verification. The newly amended Company Law reformed the company incorporation system to streamline the registration formalities and relax the threshold for setting up a company in China. These changes facilitate and simplify the procedure of incorporating companies in China, thereby encouraging innovation and entrepreneurship.

Apart from reform-minded political leaders, another supporting group for the reformation of the corporate law is the NPC delegates from coastal, wealthy provinces; however, their proposal may counter opposition from groups that are disadvantaged by liberalization, such as traditional SOEs.

For instance, at the 2004 annual meetings of the NPC, thirty-six NPC delegates from Zhejiang Province, thirty-two delegates from Fujian Province, thirty-one delegates from Shanghai Province proposed to introduce the common law's veil-piercing doctrine to the new company law and this proposal gained support from various interest groups including the SAIC, MOFCOM, local lawyers' associations, local judges, arbitrators, and academics.[160] However, one part of the proposal, Article 19(2),[161] received strong opposition from the SASAC, a very powerful State Council agency.

such as lifting the corporate veil, cumulative voting power in management elections, and fiduciary duties of directors, supervisors, and senior officers, further bridging the gap between Chinese company law and US company law. *See id.* at 42–43.

159 The purpose of the State Council's Executive Meeting was to reform the registered capital system.

160 *See* Chao Xi, *Who Writes Corporate Law Rules? The Making of the "Piercing the Corporate Veil Rule" as a Case Study*, *in* THE DEVELOPMENT OF THE CHINESE LEGAL SYSTEM: CHANGE AND CHALLENGES 169 (Guanghua Yu ed., 2011).

161 Article 19(2) of the proposal states that "the controlling shareholder of the company shall remain independent from the company in respect of personnel, finance and business. Where personnel, finance, and business of the controlling shareholder

SASAC resisted Article 19(2) to protect the interests of SOEs under its supervision because the line between the SOEs and their subsidiaries often blurred, and Article 19(2) would increase SOEs' exposure to liability of its subsidiaries.[162] As a result of SASAC's resistance, Article 19(2) was removed in its entirety from the Amendment Bill submitted for review.[163]

This suggests that although the Chinese party-state is powerful, Chinese corporate law is not a product of bargaining just among government agencies and the judicial courts, but a product of bargaining among various interest groups.[164]

Foreign pressure also facilitates the reformation of the FIE Laws[165] because Chinese Company Law alone cannot adequately deal with various cross-border issues resulting from China's rapidly developing economy. Disputes involving foreign investors and FIEs are increasing with the surge of foreign investment in China.[166]

The SPC reported that the proportion of disputes involving FIEs accounts for 20 percent of foreign-related civil and commercial cases. In response to the inadequacy, the SPC tried to facilitate the resolution of FIE-related disputes by issuing the Provisions on Several Issues Concerning the Trial of Disputes Involving FIEs I on August 16, 2010. Provisions I came into effect on August 16, 2010. Although the Provisions are not as comprehensive and full-fledged as expected, they offer an adequate clarification of the FIE Laws and have had a significant impact on both judicial practices and business behaviours in foreign investment activities. The SPC is taking a pragmatic approach to FIE

commingle with those of the company, the controlling shareholder shall be jointly liable for the debts of the company." *Id.* at 170.

162 *See id.* at 170–171.

163 *See id.* at 171.

164 These interest groups include both state and non-state actors, such as individual NPC delegates (and groups of NPC delegates), members of the National Committee of the Chinese People's Political Consultative Conference (CPPCC), All-China Federation of Trade Unions, localities, industry associations, lawyers' associations, large SOEs, academics, and the SPC. *See id.* at 160, 168.

165 "FIE Laws" refers to FIE-related laws and regulations governing FIEs such as Equity Joint Ventures (EJVs), Contractual Joint Ventures (CJVs), and Wholly Foreign-owned Enterprises (WFOEs).

166 *See* Kwok-Chiu Fung, Hitomi Iizaka, & Sarah Y. Tong, *Foreign Direct Investment in China: Policy, Recent Trend and Impact*, 33 GLOB. ECON. REV. 99, 99 (2004); Shen, *supra* note 154, at 275.

investment disputes, which is consistent with the market-oriented judicial trend in other jurisdictions.[167]

Given the existence of two parallel corporate law regimes (Company Law for domestic companies and FIE Laws for foreign companies), many benefits of the amended Company Law may not flow through to the FIEs and foreign investors.[168] The Chinese legislature has now moved toward harmonizing these two parallel corporate law regimes. Taking advantage of the ongoing US-China trade war, the Chinese government sped up the legislative process by passing the new Foreign Investment Law of 2019, which substantively abolished three FIE Laws. As a result, the Company Law would be uniformly applied to both domestic and FIEs thereafter. This suggests that foreign pressure is also a strong factor in shaping China's corporate law.[169]

167 *See id.* at 275, n.33.

168 FIE Laws are "special laws" outlining different corporate structure and governance rules with respect to FIEs. Therefore, the relationship between FIE Laws and the Company Law is *per generalia specialibus non derogant*; i.e., the general does not detract from the specific and in practice, the FIE Laws may take precedence over the Company Law largely because the approval authority, the Ministry of Commerce(MOFCOM) of the People's Republic of China and its local branches, are used to apply more specific FIE Laws (including various implementing rules respectively applicable to EJVs, CJVs, and WFOEs) and may continue to apply their own conventional practices to FIEs. *See* Shen, *supra* note 154, at 275.

169 *See* May Tan-Mullins & Peter S. Hofman, *The Shaping of Chinese Corporate Social Responsibility*, 43 J. CURRENT CHINESE AFF. 3, 3 (2014) (Observing that international pressure is one of the main drivers for emerging corporate social responsibility issues in China). *See also* David Gerber, *Economics, Law & Institutions: The Shaping of Chinese Competition Law*, 26 WASH. U. J.L. & POL'Y 271, 281 (2008) (Observing that foreign pressure has provided "an impetus" for the enactment of Chinese competition law).

REFERENCES

Acharya, Viral V., Stewart C. Myers & Raghuram G. Rajan, *The Internal Governance of Firms*, 66 J. FIN. 689 (2011).

Adamski, Olivia-Nathale, *Convertible Preferred Stock: Testing the Legal Framework of the US Venture Capital Model in China* (LL.M. thesis, University of British Columbia, 2015).

ADLER, BARRY E., ANTHONY J. CASEY & EDWARD R. MORRISON, BAIRD AND JACKSON'S BANKRUPTCY: CASES, PROBLEMS, AND MATERIALS (2020).

Aggarwal, Dhruv, Ofer Eldar, Yael Hochberg & Lubomir P. Litov, *The Rise of Dual-Class Stock IPOs* (NAT'L BUREAU OF ECON. RSCH., Working Paper No. 28609, 2021).

Aguiar, Marcos et al., *SASAC: China's Megashareholder*, BCG PERSP. (Dec. 1, 2007), http://www.bcgperspectives.com/content/articles/globalization_strategy_sasac_chinas_megashareholder.

Ahn, Sungyoon & Wooseok Choi, *The Role of Bank Monitoring in Corporate Governance: Evidence from Borrowers' Earnings Management Behavior*, 33 J. BANKING & FIN. 425 (2009).

Allen, Franklin, Elena Carletti & Robert Marquez, *Stakeholder Governance, Competition, and Firm Value*, 19 REV. FIN. 1315 (2015).

ALLEN, WILLIAM T., REINIER KRAAKMAN & VIKRAMADITYA S. KHANNA, COMMENTARIES AND CASES ON THE LAW OF BUSINESS ORGANIZATION (2021).

Alva, Curtis, *Delaware and the Market for Corporate Charters: History and Agency*, 15 DEL. J. CORP. L. 885 (1990).

Amaya, Naohiro, *The Ethics of Harmony and the Logic of the Antimonopoly Law*, *in* JAPANESE LAW IN CONTEXT: READING IN SOCIETY, THE ECONOMY, AND POLITICS 597 (Curtis J. Milhaupt et al. eds., 2001).

Anderson, Ronald C. & David M. Reeb, *Founding Family Ownership and Performance: Evidence from the S&P 500*, 58 J. FIN. 1301 (2003).

Board Composition: Balancing Family Influence in S&P 500 Firms, 49 ADMIN. SCI. Q. 209 (2004).

Anderson, Ronald C., Augustine Duru & David M. Reeb, *Founders, Heirs, and Corporate Opacity in the United States*, 92 J. Fin. Econ. 205 (2009).

Anslinger, Patricia, Dennis Carey, Kristin Fink & Chris Gagnon, *Equity Carve-outs: A New Spin on the Corporate Structure*, 33 McKinsey Q. 165 (1997).

Aoki, Masahiko & Hue Patrick, eds., The Japanese Main Bank System: Its Relevance for Developing and Transforming Economies (1995).

Aoki, Masahiko, Hugh Patrick & Paul Sheard, *The Japanese Main Bank System: An Introductory Overview, in* The Japanese Main Bank System: Its Relevance for Developing and Transforming Economies (Masahiko Aoki & Hugh Patrick eds., 1995).

Appel, Ian, *Governance by Litigation*, SSRN (2019), https://ssrn.com/abstract=2532278.

Arikawa, Yasuhiro & Hideaki Miyajima, *Relational Banking in Post-Bubble Japan: Co-existence of Soft and Hard-Budget Constraint, in* Corporate Governance in Japan: Institutional Change and Organizational Diversity 51 (Masahiko Aoki et al. eds., 2007).

Armour, John, Bernard Black, Brian R. Cheffins & Richard Nolan, *Private Enforcement of Corporate Law: An Empirical Comparison of the United Kingdom and the United States*, 6 J. Empirical Legal Stud. 687 (2009).

Armour, John, Jack B. Jacobs & Curtis J. Milhaupt, *The Evolution of Hostile Takeover Regimes in Developed and Emerging Markets: An Analytical Framework*, 52 Harv Int'l L. J. 219 (2011).

Aronson, Bruce E., *Japanese Corporate Governance Reform: A Comparative Perspective*, 11 Hastings. Bus. L.J. 85 (2015).

et al., *Enterprise Law Conference of 2014: Edited Transcript*, SSRN (2014), https://papers.ssrn.com/sol3/papers.cfm?abstract_id=2501143.

Bacon, J. Douglas & Jennifer A. Love, *When Good Things Happen to Bad People: Practical Aspect of Holding Directors and Managers of Insolvent Corporations Accountable*, 10 J. Bankr. L. Prac. 185 (2001).

Badlam, Justin, Stephen Clark, Suhrid Gajendragadkar, Adi Kumar, Sara O'Rourke & Dale Swartz, *The CHIPS and Science Act: Here's What's in It*, McKinsey & Co. (Oct. 4, 2022), https://www.mckinsey.com/industries/public-sector/our-insights/the-chips-and-science-act-heres-whats-in-it.

Bai, Chong-En, Qiao Liu, Joe Zhou Lu, Frank M. Song & Junxi Zhang, *Corporate Governance and Firm Valuations in China*, SSRN (2002) http://ssrn.com/abstract=361660.

Bai, Yanjie, *Social Capital of the Firm and Its Impact on Performance: A Social Network Analysis, in* The Management of Enterprises in the People's Republic of China 275 (Anne S. Tsui & Chung-Ming Lau eds., 2002).

Bainbridge, Stephen M., *Preserving Director Primacy by Managing Shareholder Interventions*, *in* RESEARCH HANDBOOK ON SHAREHOLDER POWER 231 (Jennifer G. Hill & Randall S. Thomas eds., 2015).

The Board of Directors, *in* THE OXFORD HANDBOOK OF CORPORATE LAW AND GOVERNANCE 275 (Jeffery N. Gordon & Wolf-Georg Ringe eds., 2018).

Baird, Douglas G. & Robert K. Rasmussen, *Private Debt and the Missing Lever of Corporate Governance*, 154 U. PA. L. REV. 1209 (2006).

Bebchuk, Lucian A., *The Case against Board Veto in Corporate Takeovers*, 69 U. CHI. L. REV. 973 (2002).

Bebchuk, Lucian A., Alma Cohen & Charles C. Y. Wang, *Golden Parachutes and the Wealth of Shareholders*, 25 J. CORP. FIN. 140 (2014).

BEBCHUK, LUCIAN A. & JESSE M. FRIED, PAY WITHOUT PERFORMANCE: THE UNFULFILLED PROMISE OF EXECUTIVE COMPENSATION (2004).

Bebchuk, Lucian A. & Robert Jackson Jr., *The Law and Economics of Blockholder Disclosure*, 2 HARV. BUS. L. REV. 39 (2012).

Bebchuk, Lucian A. & Roberto Tallarita, *The Illusory Promise of Stakeholder Governance*, 106 CORNELL L. REV. 91 (2020).

Beck, Kasper Ingeman & Kjeld Erik Brødsgaard, *Corporate Governance with Chinese Characteristics: Party Organization in State-Owned Enterprises*, 250 CHINA Q. 486 (2022).

Bennedsen, Morten, Vikas Mehrotra, Jungwook Shim & Yupana Wiwattanakantanget, *Dynastic Control without Ownership: Evidence from Post-War Japan*, 142 J. FIN. ECON. 831 (2021).

Bennedsen, Morten, Kasper Meisner Nielsen, Francisco Perez-Gonzalez & Daniel Wolfenzon, *Inside the Family Firm: The Role of Families in Succession Decisions and Performance*, 122 Q. J. ECON. 647 (2007).

BERLE, ADOLF A. & GARDINER C. MEANS, THE MODERN CORPORATION AND PRIVATE PROPERTY (1932).

Bhabra, Harjeet S. & Tiemei Li, *Independent Directors and Corporate Performance: Evidence from Listed Firms in China*, 8 CORP. OWNERSHIP & CONTROL 145 (2011).

Black, Bernard S., *Shareholder Passivity Reexamined*, 89 MICH. L. REV. 520 (1990).

Black, Bernard S. & Ronald J. Gilson, *Venture Capital and the Structure of Capital Markets: Banks versus Stock Markets*, 47 J. FIN. ECON. 243 (1998).

Black, Bernard S. & Reinier Kraakman, *A Self-enforcing Model of Corporate Law*, 109 HAR. L. REV. 1911 (1996).

Bonvillian, William B., *Emerging Industrial Policy Approaches in the United States*, INFO. TECH. & INNOVATION FOUND. (Oct. 4, 2021), https://itif.org/publications/2021/10/04/emerging-industrial-policy-approaches-united-states/.

Bourveau, Thomas, Yun Lou & Rencheng Wang, *Shareholder Litigation and Corporate Disclosure: Evidence from Derivative Lawsuits*, 56 J. Acct. Rsch. 797 (2018).

Bowie, Carol, *ISS 2016 Board Practices Study*, Harv. L. Sch. F. Corp. Governance (June 1, 2016), https://corpgov.law.harvard.edu/2016/06/01/iss-2016-board-practices-study.

Brandi, Tim Oliver, *The Strike Suit: A Common Problem of the Derivative Suit and the Shareholder Class Action*, 98 Dick. L. Rev. 355 (1993).

Briggs, Thomas W., *Corporate Governance and the New Hedge Fund Activism: An Empirical Analysis*, 32 J. Corp. L. 681. (2007).

Broughman, Brian J. & Matthew T. Wansley, *Risk-Seeking Governance*, 76 Vand. L. Rev. 1299 (2023).

Bu, Yuanshi, Chinese Business Law (2010).

Buccola, Vincent S. J., *Sponsor Control: A New Paradigm for Corporate Reorganization*, 90 U. Chi. L. Rev. 1 (2023).

Buccola, Vincent S. J. & Ashley C. Keller, *Credit Bidding and the Design of Bankruptcy Auctions*, 18 Geo. Mason L. Rev. 99 (2010).

Buccola, Vincent S. J. & Greg Nini, *The Loan Market Response to Dropdown and Uptier Transactions*, 53 J. L. Stud. 489 (2024).

Buchanan, John, Dominic Heesang Chai & Simon Deakin, *Agency Theory in Practice: A Quantitative Study of Hedge Fund Activism in Japan*, 22 Corp. Gov.: Int'l Rev. 296 (2014).

Burkart, Mike, Fausto Panunzi & Andrei Shleifer, *Family Firms*, 58 J. Fin. 2167 (2003).

Cai, Di, Jin-hui Luo & Di-fang Wan, *Family CEOs: Do They Benefit Firm Performance in China?*, 29 Asia Pac. J. Mgmt. 926 (2012).

Cai, Hongbin, Hanming Fang & Lixin Colin Xu, *Eat, Drink, Government: An Investigation of Corruption from Entertainment and Travel Costs of Chinese Firms* (Nat'l Bureau of Econ. Rsch., Working Paper No. 11592, 2005), https://www.nber.org/papers/w11592.

Calhoun, George, *The Sad End of Jack Ma Inc.*, Forbes (June 7, 2021), https://www.forbes.com/sites/georgecalhoun/2021/06/07/the-sad-end-of-jack-ma-inc/?sh=5928988b123a.

Campbell, Dennis, International Employment Law (2012).

Carney, Michael, *Corporate Governance and Competitive Advantage in Family-Controlled Firms*, 29 Entrepreneurship Theory & Prac. 249 (2005).

Carney, Michael, Eric Gedajlovic & Vanessa M. Strike, *Dead Money: Inheritance Law and the Longevity of Family Firms*, 38 Entrepreneurship Theory & Prac. 1261 (2014).

Chang, Xuemei & Hongyi Cheng, *What Is the Resilience of the Chinese Communist Party*, People (July 3, 2017), http://theory.people.com.cn/n1/2017/0703/c40531-29377703.html.

Chao, Xi, *In Search of an Effective Monitoring Board Model: Board Reforms and the Political Economy of Corporate Law in China*, 22 Conn. J. Int'l Law 1 (2006).

Chapman, Tom, *Why Is CEO Turnover in the US So High?*, Business Chief (Nov. 10, 2023), https://businesschief.com/leadership-and-strategy/why-is-us-ceo-turnover-so-high.

Chehi, Mark S., John K. Lyons & Ana Lucia Hartado, *Delaware Court of Chancery Decisions Clarifies Fiduciary Issues of Insolvent Company Context*, Skadden, Arps, Slate, Meagher & Flom LLP (Jan. 2015), https://www.skadden.com/insights/publications/2015/01/delaware-court-of-chancery-decision-clarifies-fidu/.

Chen, Feng, *Individual Rights and Collective Rights: Labor's Predicament in China*, 40 Communist & Post-Communist Stud. 59 (2007).

Chen, Feng, Qingyuan Li & Li Xu, *Universal Demand Laws and the Monitoring Demand for Accounting Conservatism*, 48 J. Bus. Fin. & Acct. 1246 (2020).

Chen, Gongmeng, Michael Firth & Liping Xu, *Does the Type of Ownership Control Matter? Evidence from China's Listed Companies*, 33 J. Banking & Fin. 171 (2009).

Chen, Mengyuan, Jason Zezhong Xiao & Yang Zhao, *Confucianism, Successor Choice, and Firm Performance in Family Firms: Evidence from China*, 69 J. Corp. Fin. 1 (2021).

Chen, Weitseng, *Arbitrage for Property Rights: How Foreign Investors Create Substitutes for Property Institutions in China*, 24 Wash. Int'l L. J. 47 (2015).

Choi, Heejung, Ju Hyun Kim, Jungwon Suh & Shuilian Yu, *Ownership Concentration and Financial Policy of China's Listed Firms*, 79 China Econ. Rev. 1 (2023).

Choi, Stephen Jung & Adam C. Pritchard, Securities Regulation: Cases and Analysis (2019).

Chun, Benjamin, *A Brief Comparison of the Chinese and United States Securities Regulations Governing Corporate Takeovers*, 12 Colum. J. Asian L. 99 (1998).

Claessens, Stijn, Simeon Djankov, Joseph P. H. Fan & Larry H. P. Lang, *Disentangling the Incentive and Entrenchment Effects of Large Shareholdings*, 57 J. Fin. 2741 (2002).

Claessens, Stijn, Simeon Djankov & Larry H. P. Lang, *The Separation of Ownership and Control in East Asian Corporations*, 58 J. Fin. Econ. 81 (2000).

Clarke, Donald C., *The Independent Director in Chinese Corporate Governance* 31 Del. J. Corp. L. 125 (2005).

Cochran, William G., *Searching for Diamond in the Two-and-Twenty Rough: The Taxation of Carried Interests*, 66 Stan. L. Rev. 953 (2014).

Coffee, John C. Jr., *Transfers of Control and the Quest for Efficiency: Can Delaware Law Encourage Efficient Transactions while Chilling Inefficient Ones?*, 21 DEL. J. CORP. L. 359 (1996).

Expert Opinion for Livedoor v. Nippon Broadcasting, 289 BESSATSU SHOJI HOMU 409 (2005).

Cohn, Stuart R. & Yinzhi Miao, *The Dragon and the Eagle: Reforming China's Securities IPO Laws in the U.S. Model, Pros and Cons*, 17 WASH. UNIV. GLOB. STUD. L. REV. 327 (2018).

Combs, Robert, *ANALYSIS: Unions, on a Roll, Are Reeling in the Workers*, BLOOMBERG NEWS (Aug. 21, 2023), https://news.bloomberglaw.com/bloomberg-law-analysis/analysis-unions-on-a-roll-are-reeling-in-the-workers.

Cooter, Robert D. & Thomas S. Ulen, *An Economic Case for Comparative Negligence*, 61 N.Y.U. L. REV. 1067 (1986).

Corbae, Dean & Pablo D'Erasmo, *Reorganization or Liquidation: Bankruptcy Choice and Firm Dynamics*, 88 REV. ECON. STUD. 2239 (2021).

COX, JAMES D., THOMAS HAZEN & F. HODGE O'NEAL, CORPORATIONS (1997).

Cui, Wei, *Administrative Decentralization and Tax Compliance: A Transactional Cost Perspective*, 65 UNIV. OF TORONTO L. J. 187 (2015).

CULPEPPER, PEPPER D., QUIET POLITICS AND BUSINESS POWER: CORPORATE CONTROL IN EUROPE AND JAPAN (2011).

Dau-Schmidt, Kenneth G., *Labor Law and Industrial Peace: A Comparative Analysis of the United States, the United Kingdom, Germany and Japan under the Bargaining Model*, 8 TULANE J. INT'L & COMP. L. 117 (2000).

Promoting Employee Voice in the American Economy: A Call for Comprehensive Reform, 94 MARQUETTE L. REV. 765 (2011).

DAU-SCHMIDT, KENNETH G., ROBERTO L. CORRADA, CHRISTOPHER DAVID RUIZ CAMERON, CÉSAR F. ROSADO MARZÁN, MICHAEL M. OSWALT & RAFAEL GELY, LABOR LAW IN THE CONTEMPORARY WORKPLACE (4th ed. 2024).

DAU-SCHMIDT, KENNETH G., MATTHEW W. FINKIN, RUBEN J. GARCIA & JASON R. BENT, LEGAL PROTECTION FOR THE INDIVIDUAL EMPLOYEE (6th ed. 2021).

Dau-Schmidt, Kenneth G. & Michael D. Ray, *The Definition of "Employee" in American Labor and Employment Law*, 53 BULL. COMP. LAB. REL. 59 (2004).

Dazai, Hokuto, Takuji Saito, Zenichi Shishido & Noriyuki Yanagawa, *The Rising Son under the Shadow of Company Communities: Do Japanese Family Firms Really Excel?* SSRN (2015), https://papers.ssrn.com/sol3/papers.cfm?abstract_id=2648590.

Family Firms and the Professional Manager Market, SSRN (2016), https://papers.ssrn.com/sol3/papers.cfm?abstract_id=2811057.

Japanese Corporate Governance from the Perspective of Family Firms, SSRN (2016), https://papers.ssrn.com/sol3/papers.cfm?abstract_id=2811069.

Corporate Governance and Firm Performance: An Implication from Japanese Listed Family Firms, 16 ASIAN J. L. & ECON. (forthcoming 2025).

Denis, David J. & Jan M. Serrano, *Active Investors and Management Turnover Following Unsuccessful Control Contests*, 40 J. FIN. ECON. 239 (1996).

Djankov, Simeon, Rafael LaPorta, Florencio Lopez-de-Silanes & Andrei Shleifer, *The Law and Economics of Self-Dealing*, 88 J. FIN. ECON. 430 (2008).

Dobbin, Frank R., *The Social Construction of the Great Depression: Industrial Policy During the 1930s in the United States, Britain, and France*, 22 THEORY & SOC'Y 1 (1993).

Dowd, Kevin & Peter Walker, *State of Private Markets: Q1 2023*, CARTA (May 1, 2023), https://carta.com/blog/state-of-private-markets-q1-2023/.

Easterbrook, Frank H. & Daniel R. Fischel, *The Proper Role of a Target's Management in Response to a Tender Offer*, 94 HARV. L. REV. 1161 (1981).

Egashira, Kenjiro, *Nihon no Kigyoshihai [Corporate Control in Japan]*, 7 KIHON HOGAKU: KIGYO [BASIC LEGAL THEORY: ENTERPRISE] 73 (1983).

EGASHIRA, KENJIRO, KABUSHIKI KAISHA HO [LAWS OF STOCK CORPORATIONS] (9th ed. 2024).

Eguchi, Takaaki & Zenichi Shishido, *The Future of Japanese Corporate Governance: Japan's Internal Governance and Development of Japanese-Style External Governance through Engagement*, *in* RESEARCH HANDBOOK OF SHAREHOLDER POWER 552 (Jennifer G. Hill & Randall S. Thomas eds., 2015).

EISENBERG, MELVIN A., THE STRUCTURE OF THE CORPORATION (1974).

Eldar, Ofer, Tanja Kirmse, & Michael D. Wittry, *The Rise of Anti-Activist Poison Pills* (EUR. CORP. GOVERNANCE INST., Working Paper No. 689, 2023), https://perma.cc/S6PC-WLMT.

Ellias, Jared A. & Robert J. Stark, *Bankruptcy Hardball*, 108 CAL. L. REV. 745 (2020).

Faccio, Mara & Larry H. P. Lang, *The Ultimate Ownership of Western European Corporations*, 65 J. FIN. ECON. 365 (2002).

Fan, Dennis K. K., Chung-Ming Lau & Shukun Wu, *Corporate Governance Mechanisms*, *in* THE MANAGEMENT OF ENTERPRISES IN THE PEOPLE'S REPUBLIC OF CHINA 211 (Anne S. Tsui & Chung-Ming Lau eds., 2002).

Fan, Dongfang, *Labor Contract Law Strengthens Chinese Union*, 8 CHINA BRIEF (Feb. 4, 2008 03:04 PM), https://jamestown.org/program/labor-contract-law-strengthens-chinese-union/.

Fan, Joseph P. H., T. J. Wong & Tianyu Zhan, *Politically Connected CEOs, Corporate Governance, and Post-IPO Performance*, 84 J. FIN. ECON. 330 (2007).

Fan, Joseph P. H., T. J. Wong, & Tianyu Zhang, *Institutions and Organizational Structure: The Case of State-owned Corporate Pyramids*, 29 J.L. Econ. & Org. 1217 (2012).

Feinerman, James V., *New Hope for Corporate Governance in China?*, 191 China Q. 590 (2007).

Feng, Gordon (Minghao) & Peter (Yi) Zhu, *Employee Share Plans in China: Regulatory Overview*, Thomson Reuters Prac. L. (2025), https://uk.practicallaw.thomsonreuters.com/9-507-4557?transitionType=Default&contextData=(sc.Default)&firstPage=true.

Fisch, Jill E., *The Peculiar Role of the Delaware Courts in the Competition for Corporate Charters*, 68 U. Cin. L. Rev. 1061 (1999).

Fisch, Jill E., Sean J. Griffith & Steven D. Solomon, *Confronting the Peppercorn Settlement in Merger Litigation: An Empirical Analysis and a Proposal for Reform*, 93 Tex. L. Rev. 557 (2015).

Fleischer, Victor, *Two and Twenty: Taxing Partnership Profits in Private Equity Funds*, 83 N.Y.U. L. Rev. 1 (2008).

Flynn, Jack, 30 *Average Bonus Statistics [2023]: What Is the Average Bonus Percentage*, Zippia (Oct. 18, 2022), https://www.zippia.com/advice/average-bonus-statistics/.

Fox, Merritt B., *Civil Liability and Mandatory Disclosure*, 109 Colum. L. Rev. 237 (2009).

Frater, Patrick, *Alibaba Completes $4 Billion Takeover of Youku Tudou*, VARIETY (Apr. 5, 2016), https://variety.com/2016/biz/asia/alibaba-completes-youku-tudou-takeover-1201746908/.

Frye, Timothy & Andrei Hand, *The Invisible Hand and the Grabbing Hand*, 87 Am. Econ. Rev. 354 (1997).

Fung, Kwok-Chiu, Hitomi Iizaka & Sarah Y. Tong, *Foreign Direct Investment in China: Policy, Recent Trend and Impact*, 33 Glob. Econ. Rev. 99 (2004).

Gallagher, Mary, John Giles, Albert Park & Meiyan Wang, *China's 2008 Labor Contract Law: Implementation and Implications for China's Workers*, 68 Human Rels. 197 (2015).

Gerber, David, *Economics, Law & Institutions: The Shaping of Chinese Competition Law*, 26 Wash. U. J. L. & Pol'y. 271 (2008).

Gilson, Ronald J., *Reflections in a Distant Mirror: Japanese Corporate Governance through American Eyes*, 1998 Colum. Bus. L. Rev. 203 (1998).

The Legal Infrastructure of High Technology Industrial Districts, Silicon Valley, Rout 128, and Covenants Not to Compete, 74 N.Y.U. L. Rev. 575 (1999).

Engineering a Venture Capital Market: Lessons from American Experience, 55 Stan. L. Rev. 1067 (2003).

Gilson, Ronald J. & Jeffery N. Gordon, *The Agency Costs of Agency Capitalism: Activist Investors and the Revaluation of Governance Rights*, 113 Colum. L. Rev. 863 (2013).

Board 3.0: What the Private-Equity Governance Model Can Offer to Public Companies, 32 J. APPLIED CORP. FIN. 1 (2020).

Gilson, Ronald J. & Curtis J. Milhaupt, *Economically Benevolent Dictators: Lessons for Developing Democracies*, 59 AM. J. COMP. L. 227, 265–268 (2011).

Gilson, Ronald J. & Mark J. Roe, *Lifetime Employment: Labor Peace and the Evolution of Japanese Corporate Governance*, 99 COLUM. L. REV. 508 (1999).

Gilson, Ronald J. & David Schizer, *Understanding Venture Capital Structure: A Tax Explanation for Convertible Preferred Stock*, 116 HARV. L. REV. 874 (2003).

GOMPERS, PAOL & JOSH LERNER, THE VENTURE CAPITAL CYCLE (1999).

GOO, S. H., ANNE CARVER & JOHN WHITMAN, CORPORATE GOVERNANCE: THE HONG KONG DEBATE (2003).

Goranova, Maria & Lori Verstegen Ryan, *Shareholder Activism: A Multidisciplinary Review*, 40 J. MGMT. 1230 (2014).

Gordon, Jeffrey N., *Institutions as Relational Investors: A New Look at Cumulative Voting*, 94 COLUM. L. REV. 124 (1994).

The Rise of Independent Directors in the United States, 1950–2005: Of Shareholder Value and Stock Market Price, 59 STAN. L. REV. 1465 (2007).

Shareholder Activism, the Short-Termist Red-Herring, and the Need for Corporate Governance Reform, CLS BLUE SKY BLOG (Mar. 28, 2016), https://clsbluesky.law.columbia.edu/2016/03/28/shareholder-activism-the-short-termist-red-herring-and-the-need-for-corporate-governance-reform/.

The Rejected Threat of Corporate Vote Suppression: The Rise and Fall of the Anti-Activist Pill, 2022 COLUM. BUS. L. REV. 206 (2022).

et al., *Shareholder Activism and the Role of Independent Directors in Japan, Edited Transcript* SSRN (2020), https://papers.ssrn.com/sol3/papers.cfm?abstract_id=3752246.

Goshen, Zohar & Assaf Hamdani, *Corporate Control and Idiosyncratic Vision*, 125 YALE L. J. 560 (2016).

Goshen, Zohar & Saron Hannes, *The Death of Corporate Law*, 94 N.Y.U. L. REV. 263 (2019).

Goshen, Zohar & Richard Squire, *Principal Costs: A New Theory for Corporate Law and Governance*, 117 COLUM. L. REV. 767 (2017).

Goshen, Zohar & Reilly S. Steel, *Barbarians Inside the Gates: Raiders, Activists, and the Risk of Mistargeting*, 132 YALE L. J. 411 (2022).

Goto, Gen, *Reduction of Retirees' Benefits upon the Reorganization of a Company*, *in* ENTERPRISE LAW: CONTRACTS, MARKETS, AND LAWS IN THE US AND JAPAN 161 (Zenichi Shishido ed., 2014).

GOUREVITCH, PETER A. & JAMES SHINN, POLITICAL POWER AND CORPORATE CONTROL: THE NEW GLOBAL POLITICS OF CORPORATE GOVERNANCE (2005).

Gregory, Holly J., Rebecca Grapsas & Clair Holland, *The Latest on Proxy Access*, HARV. L. SCH. F. CORP. GOVERNANCE (Feb. 1, 2019), https://corpgov.law.harvard.edu/2019/02/01/the-latest-on-proxy-access/.

Grossman, Sanford J. & Oliver D. Hart, *The Cost and Benefit of Ownership: A Theory of Vertical and Lateral Integration*, 94 J. POL. ECON. 691 (1986).

Guo, Chan, *Sustainable Development of Chinese Family Firms: A Perspective from Downward Earnings Management before Successions*, 14 SUSTAINABILITY 9344 (2022).

Gupta, Vipin, Nancy Levenburg, Lynda Moore, Jaideep Motwani & Thomas Schwarz, *Anglo vs. Asian Family Business: A Cultural Comparison and Analysis*, 3(2) J. ASIA BUS. STUD. 46 (2009).

Gutiérrez, María & Maribel Sáez, *Deconstructing Independent Directors*, 13 J. CORP. L. STUD. 63 (2013).

Hadzismajlovic, Zack, *FIRRMA Becomes Law, Reforming CFIUS, Export Controls, and Forever Changing Diligence in Foreign Direct Investment and Structuring of Public and Private Equity Deals*, 30 INTELL. PROP. & TECH. L. J. (2018), file:///C:/Users/81803/Downloads/FIRRMA%20Becomes%20Law,%20Reforming%20CFIUS,%20Export%20Controls,%20and%20Forever%20Changing%20Diligence%20in%20Foreign%20Direct%20Investment%20and%20Structuring%20of%20Public%20and%20Private%20Equity%20Deals.pdf.

HAGHIRIAN, PARISSA, ROUTLEDGE HANDBOOK OF JAPANESE BUSINESS AND MANAGEMENT (2016).

Hall, Brian J. & Jeffrey B. Liebman, *Are CEOs Really Paid Like Bureaucrats?*, 113 Q. J. ECON. 653 (1998).

Halloran, Michael J., Robert V. Gunderson, Jr., Jorge del Calvo, Thomas W. Kintner, & Julie M. Robinson, VENTURE CAPITAL AND PUBLIC OFFERING NEGOTIATION (3d ed. 2000).

Hammermesh, Lawrence A. & Michael L. Wachter, *The Fair Value of Cornfields in Delaware Appraisal Law*, 31 IOWA J. CORP. L. 119 (2005).

Harvey, Philip, *Learning from the New Deal*, 39 REV. BLACK POL. ECON. 87 (2012).

Heilmann, Sebastian & Lea Shih, *The Rise of Industrial Policy in China, 1978–2012*, 17 HARVARD-YENCHING INST. WORKING PAPER SER. 1 (2013).

Hellmann, Thomas, *The Allocation of Control Rights in Venture Capital Contracts*, 29 RAND J. ECON. 57 (1998).

Hellmann, Thomas & Manju Puri, *Venture Capital and the Professionalization of Start-up Firms: Empirical Evidence*, 57 J. FIN. 169 (2002).

Herbst-Bayliss, Svea, *Cutera Fires CEO, Stock Tumbles and Large Investor Speaks Out*, REUTERS (Apr. 12, 2023 04:24 PM), https://www.reuters.com/business/cutera-fires-ceo-exec-chairman-after-their-push-board-shakeup-2023-04-12/.

Hermalin, Benjamin E., *Trends in Corporate Governance*, 60 J. FIN. 231 (2005).

Transparency and Corporate Governance, *in* ENTERPRISE LAW: CONTRACTS, MARKETS, AND LAWS IN THE US AND JAPAN 342 (Zenichi Shishido ed., 2014).

Hermalin, Benjamin E. & Michael S. Weisbach, *Information Disclosure and Corporate Governance*, 67 J. FIN. 195 (2012).

Understanding Corporate Governance through Learning Models of Managerial Competence, 48 ASIAN-PACIFIC J. FIN. STUD. 7 (2019).

Herszenhorn, David M. & David E. Sanger, *Bush Approves $17.4 Billion Auto Bailout*, N.Y. TIMES (Dec. 19, 2008), https://www.nytimes.com/2008/12/19/business/worldbusiness/19iht-20autoB.18826530.html.

HILL, CLAIRE A., BRIAN JOSE MIGUEL QUINN & STEVEN DAVIDOFF SOLOMON, MERGERS AND ACQUISITIONS: LAW, THEORY, AND PRACTICE (2019).

Ho, Virginia Harper, *Corporate Social Responsibility in China: Law & the Business Case for Strategic CSR*, 12 S.C. J. INT'L L. & BUS. 1 (2015).

Hohaus, Bolko, *Share Buybacks and Employee Stock Options*, 16 CESIFO FORUM 79 (2015).

Holmstrom, Bengt & Steven N. Kaplan, *Corporate Governance and Merger Activity in the United States: Making Sense of the 1980s and 1990s*, 15 J. ECON. PERSP. 121 (2001).

Howard, Phoebe Wall, Eric D. Lawrence & Jamie L. LaReau, *UAW President Shawn Fain: We've Reached a Tentative Deal with Ford after 41 Days on Strike*, DETROIT FREE PRESS (Oct. 25, 2023, 7:31 PM), https://www.freep.com/story/money/cars/ford/2023/10/25/uaw-strike-ford-reaches-tentative-deal-with-union-sources-say/71318908007/.

Hu, Grace Jinying & Marc Goergen, *A Study of Ownership Concentration, Control and Evolution of Chinese IPO Companies*, SSRN (2001), https://papers.ssrn.com/sol3/papers.cfm?abstract_id=286612.

Hu, Yiming, Siqi Li, Thomas W. Lin, & Shilei Xie, *Large Creditors and Corporate Governance: The Case of Chinese Banks*, 10 REV. OF ACCT. & FIN. 332 (2011).

Huaili, Lv & Wanli Li, *Collusions in Chinese Family Firms: An Informal Institution-Based View of Multiple Large Shareholders*, 31 J. APPLIED BUS. RSCH. 1531 (2015).

Huang, Grace & Kanoko Matsuyama, *Activist Fund Executives on Board Bolstered Olympus, CEO Says*, JAPAN TIMES (Mar. 28, 2022), https://www.japantimes.co.jp/news/2022/03/28/business/corporate-business/activist-fund-executives-bolstered-olympus/.

Huang, Hui, *China's Takeover Law: A Comparative Analysis and Proposals for Reform*, 30 DEL. J. CORP. L. 145 (2005).

The New Takeover Regulation in China: Evolution and Enhancement, 42 INT'L LAW. 153 (2008).

Huang, Tianlei & Nicolas Véron, *The Private Sector's Share of China's Largest Listed Companies Continued to Decline to 43 Percent in the Second Half of 2022*, PIIE (Feb. 2, 2023), https://www.piie.com/blogs/realtime-economics/2023/private-sectors-share-chinas-largest-listed-companies-continued.

Huang, Zhangkai, Lixing Li, Guangrong Ma & Lixin Colin Xu, *Hayek, Local Information, and the Decentralization of State-owned Enterprises in China* (WBG Dev. Rsch. Grp. Fin. & Priv. Sector Dev. Team, Policy Research Working Paper No. 7321, 2015).

Hui, Gary, *China Venture Capital Market and Exit Environment*, Wilshire (2021), https://assets-global.website-files.com/60f8038183eb84c40e8c14e9/61aea87ee9d5fad821f7295f_China-Venture-Capital-Market-and-Exit-Envir on ment.pdf.

Hutchens, Walter, *Private Securities Litigation in China: Material Disclosure about China's Legal System?*, 24 U. Pa. J. Int'l Econ. L. 599 (2003).

Hyde, Alan, Working in Silicon Valley: Economic and Legal Analysis of a High-Velocity Labor Market (2003).

Iida, Hidefusa, Kinyu Shohin Torihiki Ho [Financial Instruments and Exchange Law] (2023).

Iwakura, Masakazu, *Kyogoteki Kokaikaitsuke Jokyo niaru Taisho Jojokigyo no Torishimariyaku no Kodojunsoku – Kihan to [Code of Conduct, Norms, Duties, Etc. of Directors of Listed Company Targets in Competitive Tender Offers]*, 20 Hitotsubashi Hogaku 11 (2021).

Jackson, Howell E. & Mark J. Roe, *Public and Private Enforcement of Securities Laws: Resource-Based Evidence*, 93 J. Fin. Econ. 207 (2009).

Jacoby, Sanford M., The Embedded Corporation: Corporate Governance and Employment Relations in Japan and the United States (2005).

Convergence by Design: The Case of CalPERS in Japan, 55 Am. J. Comp. L. 239 (2007).

Janeway, William H., Ramana Nanda & Matthew Rhodes-Kropf, *Venture Capital Booms and Start-Up Financing*, 13 Ann. Rev. Fin. Econ. 111 (2021).

Jang, Young Soo, *Are Direct Lenders More Like Banks or Arm's-Length Investors?*, SSRN (2024), https://papers.ssrn.com/sol3/papers.cfm?abstract_id=4529656.

Jensen, Michael C., *Agency Cost of Free Cash Flow, Corporate Finance, and Takeovers*, 76 Am. Econ. Rev. 323 (1986).

Takeovers: Their Causes and Consequences, 2 J. Econ. Persp. 21 (1988).

Jiang, Fuxiu & Kenneth A. Kim, *Corporate Governance in China: A Survey*, 24 Rev. Fin. 733 (2020).

Jiang, Wei, Tao Li & Randall Thomas, *The Long Rise and Quick Fall of Appraisal Arbitrage*, 100 Boston Univ. L. Rev. 2133 (2020).

Jiang, Yujia, *The Curious Case of Inactive Bankruptcy Practice in China: A Comparative Study of US and Chinese Bankruptcy Law*, 34 Nw. J. Int'l L. & Bus. 559 (2013).

JOHNSON, CHALMERS, MITI AND THE JAPANESE MIRACLE: THE GROWTH OF INDUSTRY POLICY, 1925–1975 (1986).

Kahan, Marcel & Edward B. Rock, *How I Learned to Stop Worrying and Love the Pill: Adaptive Responses to Takeover Law*, 69 U. CHI. L. REV. 871 (2002).

Symbiotic Federalism and the Structure of Corporate Law, 58 VAND. L. REV. 1573 (2005).

Kang, Sang Yop, *The Vanke-Baoneng Case and Beyond: Hostile Takeover and Corporate Governance in China* (PEKING UNIV. SCH. TRANSNAT'L. L. RSCH. PAPER, 2018).

Unravelling China's Hostile Takeover Landscape: The Reduced Significance of Corporate Governance (PEKING UNIV. SCH. TRANSNAT'L. L. Rsch. Paper, 2024).

Kang, Yong, Lu Shi, & Elizabeth D. Brown, *Chinese Corporate Governance – History and Institutional Framework*, RAND CORP. (2008), https://www.rand.org/pubs/technical_reports/TR618.html.

Kaplan, Steven N. & Per Stromberg, *Financial Contracting Theory Meets the Real World: An Empirical Analysis of Venture Capital Contracts*, 70 REV. ECON. STUD. 281 (2003).

Kim, Hwa-Jin, Haruka Okihara & Stephen Woodcock, *Importing Hazardous Substances from the United States: The Poison Pill in Japan and Korea*, 10 J. KOREAN L. 1 (2010).

Kim, Youngok & Fei Yi Gao, *Does Family Involvement Increase Business Performance? Family-Longevity Goals' Moderating Role in Chinese Family Firms*, 66 J. BUS. RSCH. 265 (2013).

Kitagawa, Toru, *Complementarity among the Abusive Dismissal Rule, Company Community Norms, and Illiquid External Labor Market: Transformation of Directors' Fiduciary Duty under Japanese Corporate Law*, *in* ENTERPRISE LAW: CONTRACTS, MARKETS, AND LAWS IN THE US AND JAPAN 70 (Zenichi Shishido ed., 2014).

KLEIN, WILLIAM A. & JOHN C. COFFEE, JR., BUSINESS ORGANIZATION AND FINANCE: LEGAL AND ECONOMIC PRINCIPLES (10th ed. 2007).

Koh, Alan K., Masafumi Nakahigashi & Dan W. Puchniak, *Land of the Falling "Poison Pill": Understanding Defensive Measures in Japan on their Own Terms*, 41 U. PA. J. INT'L L. 687 (2020).

Kolesar, Andrew L., *Can State and Local Tax Incentives and Other Contributions Stimulate Economic Development*, 44 TAX LAW. 285 (1990).

Kortum, Samuel & Josh Lerner, *Assessing the Contribution of Venture Capital to Innovation*, 31 RAND J. ECON. 674 (2000).

KRAAKMAN, REINIER, ET AL., THE ANATOMY OF CORPORATE LAW: A COMPARATIVE AND FUNCTIONAL APPROACH (3d ed. 2017).

Kupor, Scott, *The Lack of Options for (Startup Employees') Options*, ANDREESSEN HOROWITZ (June 23, 2016), https://a16z.com/the-lack-of-options-for-startup-employees-options/.

Kushige, Takaaki, Yuki Sato, Johnathon Brown & Keiko Kanda, *Executive Pay in Japan Seeks to Improve Corporate Value*, WTW (Jan. 18, 2024), https://www.wtwco.com/en-hk/insights/2024/01/executive-pay-in-japan-seeks-to-improve-corporate-value#about-the-study.

Kwan, Chi Hung, *Can China Reform State-Owned Enterprises without Privatization? – Creation of a Fair and Competitive Market Environment as the Second-Best Option*, RIETI (2020), https://www.rieti.go.jp/en/china/19041101.html.

Landier, Augustin, *Start-up Financing: From Banks to Venture Capital* (U. Chi. Sch. of Bus., Working Paper, 2003).

La Porta, Rafael, Florencio Lopez-de-Silanes & Andrei Shleifer, *Corporate Ownership around the World*, 54 J. Fin. 471 (1999).

La Porta, Rafael, Florencio Lopez-de-Silanes, Andrei Shleifer & Robert W. Vishny, *Investor Protection and Corporate Valuation*, 57 J. Fin. 1147 (2002).

Lau, Kun Luen Alex & Angus Young, *Why China Shall Not Completely Transit from a Relation Based to a Rule Based Governance Regime: A Chinese Perspective*, 21 Corp. Gov.: Int'l Rev. 577 (2013).

Lawrence, Susan V., *Shareholder Lawsuits: Ally of the People*, 165 Far E. Econ. Rev. 26 (2002).

Lawrence, Susan V. & Michael F. Martin, *Understanding China's Political System*, Cong. Rsch. Serv. R41007 (2013), https://www.congress.gov/crs-product/R41007.

Lawton, Adam, *Taxing Private Equity Carried Interest Using an Incentive Stock Option Analogy*, 121 Harv. L. Rev. 846 (2008).

Lee, Chong-Moon, William F. Miller, Marguerite Gong Hancock & Henry S. Rowen, The Silicon Valley Edge: A Habitat for Innovation and Entrepreneurship (2000).

Lee, Thomas W., *The Management of People in Chinese Enterprises*, *in* The Management of Enterprises in the People's Republic of China 51 (Anne S. Tsui & Chung-Ming Lau eds., 2002).

Leng, Yu, *Wuxi IC Industry Development Has Won 20 Billion "Big Red Envelopes"*, Wuxi Daily (Jan. 25, 2017), http://www.wxrb.com/news/wxxw/201701/t20170125_1264722.shtml.

Levin, Jack S. & Donald E. Rocap, Structuring Venture Capital, Private Equity, and Entrepreneurial Transaction (1997).

Li, Bo & Jacopo Ponticelli, *Going Bankrupt in China*, 26 Rev. Fin. 449 (2022).

Li, Cindy & Paul Tierno, *The Role of Debt and Shadow Banking in China's Economy*, Fed. Rsrv. Bank of S.F. (Jan.14, 2019), https://www.frbsf.org/banking/asia-program/pacific-exchanges-podcast/role-of-debt-and-shadow-banking-in-chinas-economy/.

Li, Dongming & Deng Shiqiang, *An Empirical Study on the Structure and Power of Board of Directors in Listed Companies*, 10 Sec. Mkt. Report 25 (1999).

Li, Jie & Cheng Qian, *Zhengfu Chuangye Touzi Yindao Zijin de Zinfazhan Yu Wenti Fenxi – Yi Jiangssheng Weili [New Development and Problem Analysis of Government Venture Capital Guiding Fund – Taking Jiangsu Province as an Example]*, 6 JINGJI YANJIU DAOKAN 80 (2016), https://tinyurl.com/nhk2z5kk.

Li, Mao-Chang, *Legal Aspects of Labor Relations in China: Critical Issues for International Investors*, 33 COLUM. J. TRANSNAT'L L. 521 (1995).

LI, SHAOMIN, MANAGING INTERNATIONAL BUSINESS IN RELATION-BASED VERSUS RULE-BASED COUNTRIES (2009).

Liang, Qiang, Xinchun Li, Xueru Yang, Danming Lin & Danhui Zheng, *How Does Family Involvement Affect Innovation in China?*, 30 ASIA PAC. J. MGMT. 677 (2013).

Licht, Amir N., *State Intervention in Corporate Governance: National Interest and Board Composition*, 13 THEORETICAL INQUIRIES L. 597 (2012).

Lin, Lauren Yu-Hsin & Curtis J. Milhaupt, *Party Building or Noisy Signaling? The Contours of Political Conformity in Chinese Corporate Governance*, 50 J. LEGAL STUD. 187 (2021).

LIN, LIN, VENTURE CAPITAL LAW IN CHINA (2021).

Lin, Lin-Wen & Curtis J. Milhaupt, *We Are the (National) Champions: Understanding the Mechanism of State Capitalism in China*, 65 STAN. L. REV. 697 (2013).

Lin, Shaowei & David Cabrelli, *Legal Protection for Minority Shareholders in China*, 8 FRONTIERS L. CHINA 266 (2013).

Lin, Yifu, *New Structural Economics: A Framework for Rethinking Development*, WORLD BANK OPEN KNOWLEDGE REPOSITORY (2010), https://openknowledge.worldbank.org/bitstream/handle/10986/19919/WPS5197.pdf?sequence=1&isAllowed=y.

Lin, Yu-Hsin & Yun-chien Chang, *Do State-Owned Enterprises Have Worse Corporate Governance? – An Empirical Study of Corporate Practices in China*, 23 EUR. BUS. ORG. L. REV. 711 (2021).

Lipton, Martin, *Pills, Polls, and Professors Redux*, 69 U. CHI. L. REV. 1037 (2002).

It's Time to Adopt the New Paradigm, HARV. L. SCH. F. CORP. GOVERNANCE (Feb. 11, 2019), https://corpgov.law.harvard.edu/2019/02/11/its-time-to-adopt-the-new-paradigm/.

Liu, Hong & Ting-Yan Wang, *The Institutionalization and Effectiveness of Transnational Policy Transfer: The China–Singapore Suzhou Industrial Park as a Case Study*, 41 PUBLIC ADMIN. & DEV. 103 (2021).

Lou, Jianbo, *AMCs and Debt-Equity Swaps in China: Can They Really Solve the State Commercial Bank NPL Problem?*', 4 Y.B. INT'L FIN. & ECON. L. 304 (1999).

Lu, Haitian, Hongbo Pan & Chenying Zhang, *Political Connectedness and Court Outcomes: Evidence from Chinese Corporate Lawsuits*, 58 J. LAW & ECON. 829 (2015).

Lu, Kefan, *Non-Family CEO Compensation and Firm Performance: Evidence from Chinese Listed Family Firms* (M.S. dissertation, Cornell University, 2020).

Lu, Tong, *Development of System of Independent Directors and the Chinese Experience* (Inst. of World Econ. & Pol., 2003), Ctr. for Int'l Priv. Enter. http://www.cipe.org/china/development.htm.

Luo, Lei, *Determinants of Stock Option Use by Chinese Companies*, 31 J. Applied Bus. Rsch. 1355 (2015).

MacMillan, Ian C., David M. Kulow & Roubina Kyoylian, *Venture Capitalists' Involvement in Their Investments: Extent and Performance*, 4 J. Bus. Venturing 21 (1988).

Martin, Michael F., *China's Banking System: Issues for Congress*, CRS Rep. (Feb. 20, 2012), https://crsreports.congress.gov/product/pdf/R/R42380/5.

Maskin, Eric & Jean Tirole, *The Remarks in the Property Rights Literature*, 66 Rev. Econ. Stud. 139 (1999).

Matsunaka, Manabu, *Koporeto Gabanansu to Seiji Katei* [*Corporate Governance and Political Process*], *in* Koporeto Gabanansu Kaikaku no Teigen: Kigyo Kachi Kojo Keizai Kasseika heno Michisuji [Reforming Corporate Governance: The Road to Improving Firm Value and Stimulating the Economy] 429 (Zenichi Shishido & Gen Goto eds., 2016).

Politics of Japanese Corporate Governance Reform: Politicians Do Matter, 15 Berkeley Bus. L. J. 154 (2018).

Matsushita, Mitsuo, *The Antimonopoly Law of Japan*, *in* Global Competition Policy 151 (Edward Montgomery Graham & J. David Richardson eds., 1997).

Maury, Benjamin, *Family Ownership and Firm Performance: Empirical Evidence from Western European Corporations*, 12 J. Corp. Fin. 321 (2006).

McMurray, Marcia M., *An Historical Perspective on the Duty of Care, the Duty of Loyalty, and the Business Judgment Rule*, 40 Vand. L. Rev. 605 (1987).

Mehrotra, Vikas, Randall Morck, Jungwook Shim & Yupana Wiwattanakantang, *Adoptive Expectations: Rising Sons in Japanese Family Firms*, 108 J. Fin. Econ. 840 (2013).

Miao, Yinzhi, *The Interplay of the State and the Firms: Overseas Listing as a Governance Institution for Chinese SOEs*, 10 Frontiers L. China 46 (2015).

Milhaupt, Curtis J., *In the Shadow of Delaware: The Rise of Hostile Takeovers in Japan*, 105 Colum. L. Rev. 2171 (2005).

Bull-Dog Sauce for the Japanese Soul-Courts, Corporations and Communities – A Comment on Haley's View of Japanese Law, 8 Wash. U. Global Stud. L. Rev. 345 (2009).

Takeover Law and Managerial Incentives in the United States and Japan, *in* Enterprise Law: Contracts, Markets, and Laws in the US and Japan 177 (Zenichi Shishido ed., 2014).

The State as Owner – China's Experience, 36 OXFORD REV. ECON. POL'Y. 362 (2020).

Milhaupt, Curtis J. & Zenichi Shishido, *The Enduring Relevance of the Poison Pill: A U.S.–Japan Comparative Study*, 28 STAN. J. L. BUS. & FIN. 336 (2023).

Milhaupt, Curtis J. & Wentong Zheng, *Beyond Ownership: State Capitalism and the Chinese Firm*, 103 GEO. L. J. 665 (2015).

Miller, Stephen, *Companies Ramp Up Stock Compensation to Compete for Talent*, SHRM (Mar. 1, 2022), https://www.shrm.org/resourcesandtools/hr-topics/compensation/pages/companies-ramp-up-stock-compensation-to-compete-for-talent.aspx.

Min, Geeyoung, *Shareholder Voice in Corporate Charter Amendments*, 43 J. CORP. L. 289 (2017).

Mitchell, Tom, *China: Strike Force*, FIN. TIMES (June 10, 2010), https://www.ft.com/content/a6aca74e-74c5-11df-aed7-00144feabdc0.

Mitoma, Hiroshi, *Jojo Kigyo niokeru Teijikabunusisokai Unei no Jittai to Minaoshi no Hokosei [The Practice of Operating Annual Shareholders' Meetings of Listed Companies and a Suggested Revision]*, *in* KOPORETO GABANANSU KAIKAKU NO TEIGEN: KIGYO KACHI KOJO KEIZAI KASSEIKA HENO MICHISUJI [REFORMING CORPORATE GOVERNANCE: THE ROAD TO IMPROVING FIRM VALUE AND STIMULATING THE ECONOMY] 135 (Zenichi Shishido & Gen Goto eds., 2016).

MIYAJIMA, HIDEAKI, SANGYO SEISAKU TO KIGYO TOCH NO KEIZAISHI [ECONOMIC HISTORY ON INDUSTRIAL POLICY AND CORPORATE GOVERNANCE] (2004).

Miyajima, Hideaki, *The Diversification of Corporate Governance Arrangements: Ownership Structure and the Board of Directors*, *in* ENTERPRISE LAW: CONTRACTS, MARKETS, AND LAWS IN THE US AND JAPAN 267 (Zenichi Shishido ed., 2014).

Corporate Governance Reform, and Ownership, and Control: Perspective from Japan, 30 ASIAN J. POL. SCI. 260 (2023), http://doi/org/10.1080/02185377.2022.2159177.

Miyajima, Hideakai & Fumiaki Kuroki, *The Unwinding of Cross-Shareholding in Japan: Causes, Effects, and Implications*, *in* CORPORATE GOVERNANCE IN JAPAN: INSTITUTIONAL CHANGE AND ORGANIZATIONAL DIVERSITY 79 (Masahiko Aoki et al. eds., 2007).

Miyajima, Hideaki & Ryo Ogawa, *Convergence or Emerging Diversity?: Understanding the Impact of Foreign Investors on Corporate Governance in Japan*, RIETI Discussion Paper (2016), https://www.rieti.go.jp/jp/publications/dp/16e053.pdf.

MIZUMACHI, YUICHIRO, RODO-HO NYUMON [INTRODUCTORY LABOR LAW] (2d ed. 2020).

SHOKAI RODO-HO [DETAILED GUIDE TO LABOR LAW] (3d ed. 2023).

Morita, Hatsuru, *Wagakuni ni Keiei Handan Gensoku ha Sonzai Shiteitanoka [Has the Business Judgement Rule Existed in Japan?]* 1858 SHOJI HOMU 4 (2006).

Morita, Sumio, Naoto Ogawa, Yuki Sato & Johnathon Brown, *CEO Pay Landscape in Japan, the U.S. and Europe – 2020 Analysis*, WTW (Dec. 9, 2020), https://www.wtwco.com/en-in/insights/2020/12/ceo-pay-landscape-in-japan-the-us-and-europe-2020-analysis.

Mundy, Simon, *Samsung Reveals Chinese Labor Breaches*, FIN. TIMES (Nov. 26, 2012), http://www.ft.com/intl/cms/s/0/60bde16c-37a0-11e2-8edf-00144feabdc0.html#axzz3A3LjqVjY.

Muvunza, Taurai & Terrill L. Frantz, *Disturbing the Peace: Anatomy of the Hostile Takeover of China Vanke Co.*, SSRN (2020) https://papers.ssrn.com/sol3/papers.cfm?abstract_id=3547244.

Myerson, Allen R., *O Governor, Won't You Buy Me a Mercedes Plant?*, N.Y. TIMES (Sept. 1, 1996), https://www.nytimes.com/1996/09/01/business/o-governor-won-t-you-buy-me-a-mercedes-plant.html.

Nagata, Kazuaki, *TSE Finally Ramps Up Market Reform One Year after Questionable Restructuring*, JAPAN TIMES (Apr. 18, 2023), https://www.japantimes.co.jp/news/2023/04/18/business/tse-market-reform-ramp-up/.

Nakagawa, Takehisa, *Administrative Informality in Japan: Governmental Activities Outside Statutory Authorization*, 52 ADMIN. L. REV. 175 (2000).

NAKAHIGASHI, MASAFUMI & HIDEMASA MATSUI, KAISHAHO NO SENTAKU – ATARASHII SHAKAI NO KAISHAHO WO MOTOMETE [CORPORATE LAW'S CHOICE – SEARCHING FOR THE CORPORATE LAW IN MODERN SOCIETY] (2010).

Nakazato, Minoru, J. Mark Ramseyer & Eric Rasmusen, *Executive Compensation in Japan: Estimating Levels and Determinants from Tax Records*, 20 J. ECON. & MGMT. STRATEGY 843 (2011).

Nanda, Ramana & Matthew Rhodes-Kropf, *Coordination Frictions in Venture Capital Syndicates*, *in* THE OXFORD HANDBOOK OF ENTREPRENEURSHIP AND COLLABORATION 352 (Jeffrey J. Reuter, Sharon Matusik & Jessica F. Jones eds., 2019).

Naughton, Barry, *Chinese Industrial Policy and the Digital Silk Road*, 15 ASIA POL'Y 23 (2020).

Nishiyama, Kengo, *Kabushiki Hoyukozo no Henka ga Unagasu "Kigyo to Kabunushi • Toshika tono Atarashii Kankei" Kochiku* [*Change of Stock Ownership Structure Urges to Build the "New Relationship between Companies and Shareholders/ Investors"*], NOMURA SUSTAINABILITY Q. (2022) Autumn, 179.

Oyako-Jojo no Jyokyo (2022 Nendomatsu) [*The Current Situation of Parent-Subsidiary Double-Listing at the End of March 2023*], NOMURA INST. CAP. MKT. RSCH. (2023) AUTUMN, 112, http://www.nicmr.com/nicmr/report/repo/2023_stn/2023sum11.html.

ODAKA, KONOSUKE, TSUSHO SANGYO SEISAKUSHI 1980–2000 SORON [POLITICAL HISTORY OF THE INDUSTRIAL POLICY 1980–2000 GENERAL REMARKS] (2013).

Ohira, Yuji, *NIDEC to Buy Japan's Takisawa, Will Launch Tender Bid Thursday*, NIKKEI ASIA (Sept. 13, 2023), https://asia.nikkei.com/Business/Business-deals/Nidec-to-buy-Japan-s-Takisawa-will-launch-tender-bid-Thursday.

OKAZAKI, TETSUJI, KEIZAISHI KARA KANGAERU HATTEN TO TEITAI NO RONNRI [CONSIDERING THE LOGIC OF DEVELOPMENT AND STAGNATION FROM THE PERSPECTIVE OF ECONOMIC HISTORY] (2017).

Osaki, Sadakazu, *Regulation of Japan's Capital Markets and the Battle for Control of Nippon Broadcasting System*, 18 NOMURA CAP. MKT. REV. 25 (2005).

Pack, Howard & Kamal Saggi, *The Case for Industrial Policy: A Critical Survey* (Policy Research Working Paper Series 3839, THE WORLD BANK, 2006), https://siteresources.worldbank.org/INTRANETTRADE/Resources/Internal-Training/HowardPack_KamalSaggiPaper.pdf.

Pagano, Marco & Paolo Volpin, *Managers, Workers, and Corporate Control*, 60 J. FIN. 841 (2005).

Pascale, Richard & Thomas P. Rohlen, *The Mazda Turnaround*, 9 J. JAPANESE STUD. 219 (1983).

Peek, Joe & Eric S. Rosengren, *Unnatural Selection: Perverse Incentive and the Misallocation of Credit in Japan*, 95 AM. ECON. REV. 1144 (2005).

Peij, Stefan C., Pieter-Jan Bezemer & Gregory F. Maassen, *The Effectiveness of Supervisory Boards: An Exploratory Study of Challenges in Dutch Boardrooms*, 7 INT'L J. BUS. GOVERNANCE & ETHICS 191 (2012).

Pérez-González, Francisco, *Inherited Control and Firm Performance*, 96 AM. ECON. REV. 1559 (2006).

Petrucci, Caley & Guhan Subramanian, *Pills in a World of Activism and ESG*, 1 CHI. BUS. L. REV. 417 (2022).

PEZaoCan, *Analysis of Government Industrial Fund Policy and Practice Operation (Part II)*, SINAFINANCE (Oct. 27, 2017), https://cj.sina.com.cn/article/detail/6390473642/454172?column=fund&ch=9

Pollman, Elizabeth, *The Making and Meaning of ESG*, 14 HARV. BUS. L. REV. 403 (2024).

Powell, Benjamin C., *Equity Carve-Outs as a Technology Commercialization Strategy: An Exploratory Case Study of Thermo Electron's Strategy*, 30 TECHNOVATION 37 (2010).

Powers, Sara, *UAW Strike 2023: Biden Joins UAW Picket Line, Trump Heads to Michigan*, CBS NEWS (Sept. 27, 2023), https://www.cbsnews.com/detroit/news/uaw-strike-2023-heres-what-to-know-as-biden-lands-in-michigan-heads-to-the-picket-line/.

POZA, ERNESTO J., FAMILY BUSINESS (2013).

Preen, Mark, *The Yangtze River Delta Integration Plan*, CHINA BRIEFING (June 6, 2018), https://www.china-briefing.com/news/yangtze-river-delta-integration-plan/.

Puchniak, Dan W. & Luh Luh Lan, *Independent Directors in Singapore: Puzzling Compliance Requiring Explanation*, 65 AM. J. COMP. L. 265 (2017).

Puchniak, Dan W. & Masafumi Nakahigashi, *Japan's Love for Derivative Actions*, 45 VAND. L. REV. 1 (2021).

Puchniak, Dan W., Zhang Wei & Zhou Chun, *China's Rules-Based, Free Market, for Shareholder Activism: Overlooked Reality or Empirical Mirage?*, ECGI (Apr. 5, 2024), https://www.ecgi.global/content/china%E2%80%99s-rules-based-free-market-shareholder-activism-empirical-mirage-or-overlooked-reality.

Qu, Yunxu & Denise Jia, *Private Equity in China Heads for Exits amid Three-Year Stock Slump*, NIKKEI (Feb. 6, 2024), https://asia.nikkei.com/Spotlight/Caixin/Private-equity-in-China-heads-for-exits-amid-three-year-stock-slump.

Quan, Xiaofeng, Cheng Xiang & Ru Gao, *Reputation Is Golden: Superstar CEOs and Trade Credit*, 51 J. BUS. FIN. & ACCT. 631 (2024).

Ramirez, Juan Luis Jay, Anwar Y. Salimi & Hassan Hefzi, *The Impact of Tax Incentives on the Location of Manufacturing Facilities*, 5 J. BUS. & ACCT. 76 (2012).

Ramseyer, J. Mark & Eric B. Rasmusen, *The Case for Managed Judges: Learning from Japan after the Political Upheaval of 1993*, 154 U. PA. L. REV. 1879 (2006).

Ran, Guanggui, Qiaoling Fang, Shuai Luo & Kam C. Chan, *Supervisory Board Characteristics and Accounting Information Quality: Evidence from China*, 37 INT'L REV. OF ECON. & FIN. 18 (2015).

Rapp, Robert N., *The Proper Role of Securities Act Section 12 (2) as an Aftermarket Remedy for Disclosure Violations*, 47 BUS. LAW. 711 (1992).

Reed, John L. & Henry DuPont Ridgely, *Delaware Court of Chancery Issues Significant Ruling on the Ability of Creditors to Assert Fiduciary Duty Claims against Directors: Key Takeaways*, LEXOLOGY (May 14, 2015), https://www.lexology.com/library/detail.aspx?g=f9502050-0946-4636-8f54-f125e8eaba06".

Reed, John L. & Matt Neiderman, *Good Faith and the Ability of Directors to Assert 102 (b)(7) of the Delaware General Corporation Law as a Defense to Claims Alleging Abdication, Lack of Oversight, and Similar Breaches of Fiduciary Duty*, 29 DEL. J. CORP. L. 111 (2004).

Reuters & Bloomberg, *Curbing China's Corporate Debt Could Hit Economic Growth, Reports Warns*, SOUTH CHINA MORNING POST (June 4, 2018, 12:15 PM), https://www.scmp.com/news/china/economy/article/2149108/curbing-chinas-corporate-debt-could-hit-economic-growth-report.

Rock, Edward, *For Whom Is the Corporation Managed in 2020?: The Debate Over Corporate Purpose*, 76 Bus. L. 363 (2021).

Roe, Mark J., Strong Managers, Weak Owners: The Political Roots of American Corporate Finance (1994).

Roe, Mark J., *Delaware Competition*, 117 Harv. L. Rev. 588 (2003).

Roe, Mark J. & Roy Shapira, *The Power of the Narrative in Corporate Lawmaking*, 11 Harv. Bus. L. Rev. 233 (2021).

Romano, Roberta, *The Sarbanes–Oxley Act and the Making of Quack Corporate Governance*, 114 Yale L. J. 1521 (2005).

The States as a Laboratory: Legal Innovation and State Competition for Corporate Charters, 23 Yale J. Reg. 209 (2006).

Rubery, Jill & Damian Grimshaw, The Organization of Employment: An International Perspective 192 (2003).

Saito, Takuji, *Family Firms and Firm Performance: Evidence from Japan*, 22 J. Japanese & Int'l Econ 620 (2008).

Sandler, Erick M., Jeffrey P. Mueller & Palak Sharma, *The Delaware Supreme Court Adopts a Universal Demand-Futility Test in Facebook Investors' Derivative Suit*, Day Pitney (Sept. 27, 2021), https://www.daypitney.com/insights/publications/2021/09/27-the-delware-supreme-court-adopts/.

Sapienza, Harry J., *When Do Venture Capitalist Add Value?*, 7 J. Bus. Venturing 9 (1992).

Saxenian, Annalee, Regional Advantage: Culture and Competition in Silicon Valley and Rout 128 (1994).

Schipani, Cindy A. & Junhai Liu, *Corporate Governance in China: Then and Now*, *in* Corporate Governance: Values, Ethics and Leadership 491 (Lawrence E. Mitchell ed., 2009).

Schweizer, Denis, Thomas Walker & Aoran Zhang, *Cross-Border Acquisitions by Chinese Enterprises: The Benefits and Disadvantages of Political Connections*, 57 J. Corp. Fin. 63 (2019).

Sciascia, Salvatore, Pietro Mazzola, Joseph H. Astrachan & Torsten Pieper, *Family Involvement in the Board of Directors: Effects on Sales Internationalization*, 51 J. Small Bus. Mgmt. 83 (2013).

Scott, Robert H., *Bankruptcy Abuse Prevention and Consumer Protection Act of 2005: How the Credit Card Industry's Perseverance Paid Off*, 41 J. Econ. Issues 943 (2007).

Scott, W. Richard, *The Changing World of Chinese Enterprises: An Institutional Perspective*, *in* The Management of Enterprises in the People's Republic of China 65 (Anne S. Tsui & Chung-Ming Lau eds., 2002).

Seki, Takaya, *Legal Reform and Shareholder Activism by Institutional Investors in Japan*, 13 Corp. Governance 377 (2005).

Shefrin, Hersh, *The Lesson from Moody's Overdue Downgrade of China's Debt*, Forbes (May 28, 2017), https://www.forbes.com/sites/hershshefrin/2017/

05/28/the-lesson-from-moodys-overdue-downgrade-of-chinas-debt/#66606a9465ef.

Shen, Wei, *Fading Registered Capital Rules under the Amended Chinese Company Law: Sweeping Changes in Uncertain Contexts*, 8 INT'L CO. & COM. L. REV. 270 (2014).

CORPORATE LAW IN CHINA: STRUCTURE, GOVERNANCE AND REGULATION (2015).

Shen, Wei & Rohan Price, *Confucianism, the Rise of Worker Activism and Labor Law in China*, 12 CHINA: AN INT'L J. 115 (2014).

Shen, Wei & Colin Mengshan Xu, *Collective Action Problems in Chinese Takeover Rules: Deficiency and Difficulty in Protecting Target Shareholders in a Hybrid Regime*, 32 EUR. BUS. L. REV. 905 (2021).

Shepardson, David & Joseph White, *UAW Reaches Deal with GM, Ending Strike against Detroit Automakers*, REUTERS (Oct. 30, 2023), https://www.reuters.com/business/autos-transportation/gm-reaches-tentative-deal-with-uaw-source-says-2023-10-30/.

Shishido, Zenichi, *A Texan Raid on a Japanese Company*, 16 JAPAN ECHO 61 (1989).

Japanese Corporate Governance: The Hidden Problems of Corporate Law and Their Solutions, 25 DEL. J. CORP. L. 189 (2000).

Reform in Japanese Corporate Law and Corporate Governance: Current Changes in Historical Perspective, 49 AM. J. COMP. L. 653 (2001).

DOKIZUKE NO SHIKUMI TOSHITENO KIGYO: INSENTHIBU SHISUTEMU NO HOSEIDORON [THE FIRM AS AN INCENTIVE MECHANISM: THE ROLE OF LEGAL INSTITUTIONS] (2006).

The Turnaround of 1997: Changes in Japanese Corporate Law and Governance, *in* CORPORATE GOVERNANCE IN JAPAN: INSTITUTIONAL CHANGE AND ORGANIZATIONAL DIVERSITY 310 (Masahiko Aoki et al. eds., 2007).

Does Law Matter to Financial Capitalism? The Case of Japanese Entrepreneurs, 37 FORDHAM INT'L L. J. 1087 (2014).

The Incentive Bargain of the Firm and Enterprise Law: A Nexus of Contracts, Markets, and Laws, *in* ENTERPRISE LAW: CONTRACTS, MARKETS, AND LAWS IN THE US AND JAPAN 1 (Zenichi Shishido ed., 2014).

The Monitoring Board Revisited, *in* CORPORATE LAW AND ECONOMICS 36 (Adam B. Badawi ed., 2023).

Specificity, Enforceability, and Stickiness of Contracts, 57 INT'L LAW. 475 (2024).

SHISHIDO, ZENICHI, MUNETAKA FUKUDA & MASATO UMETANI, JOINT VENTURE STRATEGIES: DESIGN, BARGAINING, AND THE LAW (2015).

Shishido, Zenichi & Sadakazu Osaki, *Reverse Engineering SOX versus J-SOX: A Lesson in Legislative Policy*, *in* ENTERPRISE LAW: CONTRACTS, MARKETS, AND LAWS IN THE US AND JAPAN 349 (Zenichi Shishido ed., 2014).

JOJO KAISHA HO [LAWS OF LISTED COMPANIES] (2023).

SHISHIDO, ZENICHI & VENTURE LAW FORUM (VLF), BENCHA KIGYO NO HOUMU ZAIMU SENRYAKU [LAW AND FINANCE OF VENTURE COMPANIES IN JAPAN] (2010).

& VENTURE LAW FORUM (VLF), SUTA-TOAPPU TOSHI KEIYAKU: MODERU KEIYAKU TO KAISETSU [JAPANESE START-UP FINANCING DOCUMENTS: ANNOTATED MODEL CONTRACTS] (2020).

Shishido, Zenichi, Sadakazu Osaki, Nobuyuki Kinoshita, Hirohiko Nakahara, Yuichiro Mizumachi & Tetsuya Watanabe, *Zadankai: Kigyo no Issho Purojekuto* [*Discussion: The Life of An Enterprise Project*], ser. 1131 NBL 19 (2018)–1237 NBL 66 (2023).

INSENTHIBU BAGENINGU TO KIGYO HO: KIGYO NO ISSHO PUROJEKUTO [INCENTIVE BARGAINING AND ENTERPRISE LAW: THE LIFE OF AN ENTERPRISE] (2025).

Shleifer, Andrei & Robert W. Vishny, *A Survey of Corporate Governance*, 52 J. FIN. 737 (1997).

Large Investors and Corporate Control, 94 J. POL. ECON. 461 (1986).

Silver, Hilary, *Is Industrial Policy Possible in the United States? The Defeat of Rhode Island's Greenhouse Compact*, 15 POL. & SOC'Y 333 (1987).

Skeel Jr., David A., *Bankruptcy Judges and Bankruptcy Venue: Some Thoughts on Delaware*, 1 DEL. L. REV. 17 (1998).

Skocpol, Theda & Kenneth Finegold, *State Capacity and Economic Intervention in the Early New Deal*, 97 POL. SCI. Q. 255 (1982).

Smyth, Russell, Junli Wang & Xin Deng, *Equity-for-Debt Swaps in Chinese Big Business: A Case Study of Restructuring in One Large State-Owned Enterprise*, 10 GLOBALIZATION & COMP.: BIG BUS. IN ASIA 382 (2004).

Sonnenfeld, Jeffrey, *Another Suicidal Board?: How DuPont's Directors Failed Ellen Kullman*, FORTUNE (Oct. 13, 2015), https://fortune.com/2015/10/13/dupont-board-ellen-kullman/.

Sorenson, Olav & Toby Stuart, *Syndication Networks and the Spatial Distribution of Venture Capital Investments*, 106 AM. J. SOCIO. 1546 (2001).

Succar, Patricia, *The Need for Industrial Policy in LDC's – A Re-statement of the Infant Industry Argument*, 28 INT. ECON. R. 521 (1987).

Sukamdani, Nugroho, *Family Business Dynamics in Southeast Asia: A Comparative Study of Indonesia, Malaysia, Singapore, and Thailand*, 11 J. ASEAN STUD. 197 (2023).

Sun, Qian, Wilson H. S. Tong & Jing Tong, *How Does Government Ownership Affect Firm Performance? Evidence from China's Privatization Experience*, 29 J BUS. FIN. ACCT. 1 (2002).

Sun, Wei, *Zhengfu he Shichang Guanxi Shijiao xia de Zhengfu Yindao Jijin Guifan Fazhan Yanjiu [Research on Normative Development of Government*

Guiding Funds from the Perspective of Government and Market Relationship], 21 JINGJI YANJIU CANKAO 72 (2018).

Takahashi, Hiroaki & Koji Kawamura, *Foreign Direct Investment Regimes Japan 2024*, ICLG.COM (Nov. 16, 2023), https://iclg.com/practice-areas/foreign-direct-investment-regimes-laws-and-regulations/japan.

Tam, On Kit, *Ethical Issues in Evolution on Corporate Governance in China*, 37 J. BUS. ETHICS 303 (2002).

Tan, Justin, *Innovation and Risk-Taking in a Transitional Economy: A Comparative Study of Chinese Managers and Entrepreneurs*, 16 J. BUS. VENTURING 359 (2001).

Tanaka, Wataru, *Cramdown versus Extinguishing Security Interests: Secured Claims in Bankruptcy in the United States and Japan*, *in* ENTERPRISE LAW: CONTRACTS, MARKETS, AND LAWS IN THE US AND JAPAN 150 (Zenichi Shishido ed., 2014).

Tanaka, Wataru & Gen Goto, *Nihon ni okeru Akuthibizumu no Chokiteki Eikyo* [*The Long-term Effect of Hedge Fund Activism in Japan*] *in* JSDA Capital Market Forum (Dai-2-ki) Kenkyu Ronbunsyu [The 2nd JSDA Capital Market Forum Research Papers] (Nihon Shokengyo Kyokai, 2020) 115, https://www.jsda.or.jp/about/kaigi/chousa/JCMF/gototanakaronbun2.pdf.

Tan-Mullins, May & Peter S. Hofman, *The Shaping of Chinese Corporate Social Responsibility*, 43 J. CURRENT CHINESE AFFS. 3 (2014).

Tanner, Murray Scot, *How a Bill Becomes a Law in China: Stages and Processes in Lawmaking*, 141 THE CHINA Q. 39 (1995).

TENEV, STOYAN, CHUNLIN ZHANG & LOUP BREFORT, CORPORATE GOVERNANCE AND ENTERPRISE REFORM IN CHINA – BUILDING THE INSTITUTIONS OF MODERN MARKETS (2002).

Thorne, James, *Silicon Valley's Banner Year on Wall Street Reshapes IPO Landscape*, PITCHBOOK (Dec. 9, 2020), https://pitchbook.com/news/articles/silicon-valleys-banner-year-on-wall-street-reshapes-ipo-landscape.

Tian, Xiangang, *Analysis of the Functions of Supervisory Board System in Modern Chinese Companies*, 51 INT'L J. L. & MGMT. 153 (2009).

Tian, Xuan, *The Role of Venture Capital Syndication in Value Creation for Entrepreneurial Firms*, 16 REV. FIN. 245 (2012).

TIROLE, JEAN, THE THEORY OF CORPORATE FINANCE (2006).

Triantis, George, *The Role of Debt in the Governance of US Business*, *in* ENTERPRISE LAW: CONTRACTS, MARKETS, AND LAWS IN THE US AND JAPAN 125 (Zenichi Shishido ed., 2014).

Vance, Catherine E. & Paige Barr, *The Facts & Fiction of Bankruptcy Reform*, 1 DEPAUL BUS. & COMM. L. J. 361 (2002).

Varottil, Umakanth, *Minority Shareholders Rights, Powers and Duties: The Market for Corporate Influence*, *in* COMPARATIVE CORPORATE GOVERNANCE 346 (Afra Afsharipour & Martin Gelter eds., 2021).

Verkerke, J. H., *What We Know (and Don't Know) about How Employment Protection Law Affects Employment*, *in* ENTERPRISE LAW: CONTRACTS, MARKETS, AND LAWS IN THE US AND JAPAN 53 (Zenichi Shishido ed., 2014).
VerWey, John, *Chinese Semiconductor Industrial Policy: Past and Present*, 2019 J. INT'L COM. & ECON. 1 (2019).
Villalonga, Belén & Raphael Amit, *How Do Family Ownership, Control and Management Affect Firm Value?*, 80 J. FIN. ECON. 385 (2006).
How Are U.S. Family Firms Controlled?, 22 REV. FIN. STUD. 3047 (2009).
VOGEL, EZRA F., JAPAN AS NUMBER ONE: LESSONS FOR AMERICA (1979).
Waldenberger, Franz, *Management in Germany – Control and Incentive Mechanism* (German Institute for Japanese Studies Working Paper, 2017).
Waldmeir, Patti, *China Workers Get to Grips with Rights*, FIN. TIMES (June 13, 2010), https://www.ft.com/content/eb955a12-770a-11df-ba79-00144feabdc0.
Walton, Nina, *Crowding Theory and Executive Compensation*, 13 THEORETICAL INQUIRIES L. 429–455 (2012).
Wang, Baojun, *The Chinese Characteristics of the Constitutional Review System: Looking Back, Examining and Forward-looking*, 4 ACAD. J. OF MGMT. & SOC. SCI. 33 (2023).
Wang, Haiyan, Richard P. Appelbaum, Francesca Degiuli & Nelson Lichtenstein, *China's New Labor Contract Law: Is China Moving towards Increased Power for Workers*, 30 THIRD WORLD Q. 485 (2009).
WANG, JIANGYU, COMPANY LAW IN CHINA (2014).
Wang, Wenge, *Ownership Concentration and Corporate Control in Chinese Listed Companies*, 11 US-CHINA L. REV. 57 (2014).
WANG, YONGQIN, DEMYSTIFYING THE CHINESE MIRACLE: THE RISE AND FUTURE OF RELATIONAL CAPITALISM (2013).
Wang, Zhaofeng, *Corporate Governance under State Control: The Chinese Experience*, 13 THEORETICAL INQUIRIES L. 487 (2012).
Watanabe, Tetsuya, *Income and Incentives for Corporate Transactions: A Japanese Perspective*, *in* ENTERPRISE LAW: CONTRACTS, MARKETS, AND LAWS IN THE US AND JAPAN 150 (Zenichi Shishido ed., 2014).
Weiler, Paul, *Striking a New Balance: Freedom of Contract and the Prospects for Union Representation*, 98 HARV. L. REV. 351 (1984).
Weiner, Michael, *Can the NLRB Deter Unfair Labor Practices? Reassessing the Punitive-Remedial Distinction in Labor Law Enforcement*, 52 UCLA L. REV. 1579 (2005).
Weinstein, Olivier, *The Shareholder Model of the Corporation, between Mythology and Reality*, 3 ACCT., ECON. & L. 43 (2013).
Weiss, Elliott J. & Lawrence J. White, *File Early, then Free Ride: How Delaware Law (Mis) Shapes Shareholder Class Actions*, 57 VAND. L. REV. 1797 (2004).

Weng, Charlie Xiao-Chuan, *Lifting the Veil of Words: An Analysis of the Efficacy of Chinese Takeover Laws and the Road to a Harmonious Society*, 25 COLUM. J. ASIAN L. 180 (2012).

West, Mark D., *Why Shareholders Sue: The Evidence from Japan*, 30 J. LEGAL STUD. 351 (2001).

White, Michelle J., *Bankruptcy Reform and Credit Cards*, 21 J. ECON. PERSP. 175 (2007).

Widen, R. Scott, *Delaware Law, Financial Theory and Investment Banking Valuation Practice*, 4 N.Y.U. J. L. & BUS. 579 (2008).

Xi, Chao, *Who Writes Corporate Law Rules? The Making of the "Piercing the Corporate Veil Rule" as a Case Study*, *in* THE DEVELOPMENT OF THE CHINESE LEGAL SYSTEM: CHANGE AND CHALLENGES 169 (Guanghue Yu, ed., 2011).

Xin, Qingquan, Anze Bao & Fang Hu, *West Meets East: Understanding Managerial Incentives in Chinese SOEs*, 12 CHINA J. ACCT. RSCH. 177 (2019).

Xu, Guangdong, Tianshu Zhou, Bin Zeng & Jin Shi, *Directors' Duties in China*, 14 EUR. BUS. ORG. L. REV. 57, 60 (2013).

Xu, Nianhang, Qingbo Yuan, Xuanyu Jiang & Kam C. Chan, *Founder's Political Connections, Second Generation Involvement, and Family Firm Performance: Evidence from China*, 33 J. CORP. FIN. 243 (2015).

Xu, Nianhang, Xinzhong Xu & Qingbo Yuan, *Political Connections, Financing Friction, and Corporate Investment: Evidence from Chinese Listed Family Firms*, 19 EUR. FIN. MGMT. 675 (2013).

Xu, Peng & Wataru Tanaka, *Baishu Boeisaku in za Shado obu Kabushiki Mochiai – Jirei Kenkyu [Anti-Takeover Measures in the Shadow of Cross-Shareholding: A Case Study]*, 1885 SHOJIHOMU 4 (2009).

Xue, Susan, *China's Legislative System and Information: An Overview*, 22 GOV'T. INFO. Q. 322 (2005).

YAMAMOTO, KAZUHIKO, TOSAN SHORI HO NYUMON [INTRODUCTION TO INSOLVENCY LAW] (6th ed. 2024).

Yashiro, Atsushi, *Selection and Promotion of Managers in Japanese Companies: Present and Future Perspectives*, 10 JAPAN LAB. REV. 25 (2013).

Yoshimori, Masaru, *Whose Company Is It? The Concept of the Corporation in Japan and the West*, 28 LONG RANGE PLAN. 33 (1995).

Yu, Weiping & Hao Hu, *Corporate Social Responsibility in Shaping Corporate Image: An Empirical Study of State-owned Enterprises in China*, *in* CORPORATE SOCIAL RESPONSIBILITY IN ASIA: PRACTICE AND EXPERIENCE 3 (Kim Cheng Patrick Low et al. eds., 2013).

Zhang, Cheng & Le Luo, *Board Diversity and Risk-Taking of Family Firms: Evidence from China*, 17 INTL' ENTREPRENEURSHIP & MGMT. J. 1569 (2021).

Zhang, Jianwei, *Shareholder Activism in China*, N.Y. STATE BAR ASS'N (2019), nysba.org/Sections/International/Seasonal_Meetings/Tokyo_2019/Coursebook/Panel_14_-_Zhang_-_China_-_Shareholder_Activism.html.

Zhang, Wangfeng & Lihong Cao, *Family Involvement, Internal Control and Agency Costs – Evidences from China's Listed Family Firms*, 7 PERSP. IN SCI. 45 (2016).

Zhang, Wei, *Learning from Your Rival? A Surprising Convergence of Chinese and American Corporate and Securities Laws*, 9 U.C. IRVINE J. INT'L, TRANSNAT'L, & COMPAR. L. 77 (2024).

Zhang, Xianchu, *Company Law Reform in China, in* LAW AND POLICY FOR CHINA'S MARKETT SOCIALISM 39 (John Garrick ed., 2012).

Zhang, Xuewen, *Gongsi Pochan Bianyuan Dongshi Budang Jili de Falu Guizhi [Legal Regulation of Improper Incentives for Directors of Companies on the Brink of Corporate Bankruptcy]*, 34 XIANDAI FAXUE [MODERN LAW SCIENCE] 93 (2012).

Zheng, Yongnian, *China's de Facto Federalism, in* FEDERALISM IN ASIA 213 (Baogang He, et al., eds., 2007).

Zhou, Jing, On Kit Tam & Ping Yu, *An Investigation of the Role of Family Ownership, Control and Management in Listed Chinese Family Firms*, 12 ASIAN BUS. & MGMT. 197 (2013).

Zhou, Lei, Feng Wei & Yu Kong, *Do Employee Stock Ownership Plans Affect Corporate Social Responsibility? Evidence from China*, 19 INT'L J. ENV'T RSCH & PUB. HEALTH 1055 (2022).

Zhu, Hongjian, *Laizi "Bawu" de Baogao Woguo Gongye Jingji Shili* [Reports from Eight-Five Plan, Enhanced Industrial Capacity of China], RENMIN RIBAO [People Daily] (Dec. 29, 2000, 05:04 PM), http://www.people.com.cn/GB/channel1/10/20000921/243860.html.

INDEX

Printed by Integrated Books International,
United States of America